The Ecological Context of Children's Play

edited by

Marianne N. Bloch and Anthony D. Pellegrini

ABLEX PUBLISHING CORPORATION
NORWOOD, NEW JERSEY

Library of Congress Cataloging-in-Publication Data

The Ecological context of children's play / edited by Marianne N. Bloch
  and Anthony Pellegrini.
    p. cm.
  Bibliography: p.
  Includes index.
  ISBN 0-89391-520-3
    1. Play—United States. 2. Play—Environmental aspects—United States. 3.
Child development—United States. I. Bloch, Marianne N. II. Pellegrini,
Anthony D.
HQ782.E26 1988
155.4'18—dc19
                                                        88-26756
                                                            CIP

Ablex Publishing Corporation
355 Chestnut Street
Norwood, New Jersey 07648

Table of Contents

Acknowledgments

The idea for this volume was initially developed by Anthony Pellegrini and James Johnson. The original plan was stymied, but was resurrected during informal conversations at a conference by the current co-editors. Some of the original ideas for contributors and the outline of the book were taken, with permission, from the outline drafted by Tony Pellegrini and Jim Johnson. We thank Jim Johnson for his assistance and his authorization to continue with the volume, even though he was unable to remain as a co-editor. We hope he is as pleased with its final publication as we are.

We would also like to thank the contributors to the volume for their patience and hard work in seeing this volume to its completion. While all edited volumes have a time dynamic quite different from that which was originally predicted, the authors awaiting the publication of their excellent contributions in this volume have been unusually tolerant. Again, we hope the final effort warrants their kind patience.

The final development of the ideas for this volume was achieved while the first editor, Marianne Bloch, was a visiting researcher at the Kamehameha Center for Early Education in Honolulu, Hawaii. The cultural–ecological context of Hawaii and the KEEP culture and learning research program, chaired by Cathy Jordan, supported our notions of the importance of the ecological context of play and the importance of cultural and social class considerations in thinking of the ecology of play. It is important to acknowledge the support of Cathy Jordan and Roland Tharp of the KEEP program for the time, space, material, and encouragement for intermixing play with thinking that they provided during this period.

We wish to thank Barbara Bernstein, our editor at Ablex, for her enthusiasm and support for this volume, and hope she is pleased with it. We also acknowledge the important assistance of Carol Davidson who supervised all of the copyediting and production of the volume in its final stages.

This book is dedicated to our parents, Caroline Kalin Nieman and

L. William Nieman and Anne Pellegrini and Antoniio Pellegrini as well as to our children, Ben and Emilie Bloch, and Anna and Adam Pellegrini. Our parents continue to provide us with a life-long context of support for exploration, play, and learning. Our children provide us with continuous reinforcement of the value of play to all aspects of their and our own development.

Finally, we thank Peter C. Bloch and Lee Galda for their continuous help. Both will be happy to see this project come to an end.

1
Ways of Looking At Children, Context, and Play

MARIANNE N. BLOCH
Department of Curriculum and Instruction University of Wisconsin-Madison

ANTHONY D. PELLEGRINI
Institute for Behavioral Research and Early Childhood Education
University of Georgia

INTRODUCTION

This volume was developed to illustrate the fairly wide range of theoretical frameworks, methodologies, and research directions that are current in studies of the ecology of children's play. The authors represent a range of disciplines and disciplinary methods; these include ecological psychology, ethology, cross-cultural psychology and anthropology, education, and architecture. All of the contributors have education and child development as primary concerns; all authors have focused on children's play as an important activity that contributes to child development and education.

As a collection, the chapters illustrate a variety of general and specific points about children's play. Descriptions of children's play across the age span continue to reinforce the idea that the types and forms of children's play in different contexts interact with age (in this volume, individual contributors address the infant-toddler, preschool, and middle childhood age groups). Not surprisingly, the chapters also illustrate that children's play varies depending upon ecological characteristics of the play settings; different chapters focus on the play of children at home and in community settings, play in school, and in the playground. Several contributions emphasize the relationship between home and school contexts and the effect of children's cultural background on their behavior with peers in school, playground, and community settings. All contributors focus on the need to continue to see development and education as a complex process that takes place both within and across contexts. Most authors recognize the important role culture, broadly defined, plays in limiting, defining, or giving meaning to the kinds of contexts children encounter, and construct the experiences they have, within these different contexts.

A CULTURAL-ECOLOGICAL FRAMEWORK

Cultural-ecological theories, most recently described by Bronfenbrenner (1979, 1983), Ogbu (1981), and the Whitings (Whiting, 1980; Whiting & Whiting, 1975), provide a frame for this volume. Each of the cultural ecological models emphasizes the critical role of larger cultural norms, values, beliefs, and a culture's social and economic patterns on the definition of contexts children directly encounter, the experiences they have within these contexts, and on their development. While none of these theories focuses specifically on play, each emphasizes the importance of children's typical activities for development, and the relationship between activities, children's most common social and physical settings, culture and child development. Within this perspective, play, as a dominant activity of children in all cultures, is seen as an activity that both affects and is affected by cultural influences. Play is also seen as an expression of culture (e.g., Whiting & Whiting, 1975), as an important context in which interaction and learning crucial to child development occurs, and as an indicator and expression of child development (see Schwartzman, 1978 for an excellent discussion of the implications of differences in these emphases on how one studies and interprets play).

There are important similarities and differences in current ecological models, many of which are discussed in greater detail in this volume by Garbarino, Gump, Smith, and Bloch. All ecological approaches emphasize the study of behavior in the natural context of everyday life and activities. All seem to have been influenced by Lewinian field theory (e.g., Lewin, 1935) that emphasized the study of the "life space", "psychological field", and, most importantly, behavior as a function of person and environment $B=f(PE)$ (e.g., see Bronfenbrenner, 1979, p. 23; Whiting, 1980, p. 98). Cultural-ecological models are distinguished from other ecological research on children by the importance that is attached to the broader, cultural level influences that affect and constrain the types of immediate contexts children experience.

Within cultural-ecological frameworks, there are also many important differences. In Bronfenbrenner's (1979) theory, described in greater detail in Garbarino's chapter in this volume, the ecological context of development is seen as a set of nested interacting systems, "like a set of Russian dolls"; at the inner-most level is the child's immediate micro-setting, while at the outer-most level, the "macrosystem", cultural ideologies, norms, values, institutional policies, national economic and social patterns define influences of importance. Bronfenbrenner suggests that child development occurs as an interaction among the child, his construction of the environment, and the complex of interacting environmental systems surrounding the child. In contrast to other cultural-ecological theories, Bronfenbrenner's model places more explicit emphasis on the bidirectional influence of children and environment, and the dynamic, and interactive effects of different ecological systems on each other. Bronfenbrenner's model also highlights the importance of studying children's construction of environmental events in different ways than the Whiting or Ogbu models do. In Bronfenbrenner's approach, the child is seen as an individual who is actively constructing knowledge, and perceptions of environmental influences. In the Whitings' model, emphasis is placed on culturally determined interpretations of behavior, activities, events, or pressures; while these interpretations are gained through the insights of individuals, the emphasis is on cultural or group meanings that affect the development of knowledge and behavior. Ogbu's model emphasizes cultural, subcultural ("native") theories of success and child-rearing that are affected by the larger cultural-ecological environment, and that, in turn, affect childrearing techniques, child activities and development.

The cultural-ecological models proposed by Beatrice and John Whiting (Whiting & Whiting, 1975, see Figure 1, p. 1; Whiting, 1980), and John Ogbu (Ogbu, 1981, see Figure 1, p. 422) suggest that children's immediate settings are determined, in part, by the physical, social, and economic norms, requirements, and ideologies of the larger society. In the Whitings' model, for example, a culture's history, its climactic characteristics, and its geographical features, determine the types of "maintenance systems" that prevail within a culture. Maintenance systems consist of subsistence economic patterns, the means of production, settlement patterns, social structure, systems of defense, law and social control, and the division of labor within a culture or society. According to the Whitings, and to Ogbu, differences in maintenance system features, especially subsistence requirements, determine the types of immediate settings adults assign children to (Whiting, 1980; Whiting & Edwards, in press) as well as the competencies they believe children need to acquire for success within a cultural or sub-cultural setting (Ogbu, 1981). Differences in subsistence patterns, social and physical residence patterns, etc. also affect the activities they see and participate in, the caretakers children experience, and the play and work that they do or need to do within their settings. While the Whiting model (Whiting & Whiting, 1975) has been criticized as being overly deterministic, recent modifications emphasize the influence of biological and developmental factors on the experiences children have within different settings and the fact that children affect and are affected by their environment (Konner, 1981; Weisner, 1984; Whiting & Edwards, in press).

From a cultural-ecological perspective, therefore, the environment of influence is defined more widely, perhaps, than in other ecological perspectives. The cultural-ecological environment or context of play includes physical and social aspects of children's immediate settings, such as home, school, neighborhood, or playground. Cultural-ecological contexts, however, also include levels of influence beyond the settings children directly encounter. These broader influences include historical influences that affect the way in which, for example, play is perceived in a given period—its value and its place. The broader influences include cultural and ideological beliefs that affect where play occurs and with whom, or, for example, the meaning that is attached to certain types of play within a cultural or subcultural group. The broader influences also include social and economic policies or practices that alter the types of work parents do, the pressure they feel, and the environments they and their children experience on a daily basis. The critical importance attached to the influence of these broader, indirect features of the ecological context of play are the distinguishing characteristics of cultural-ecological models. They were also an important influence on us as we organized this volume.

These three cultural-ecological models are reflected directly in two of the volume's chapters (Bronfenbrenner's model is described in Garbarino; Whiting's (1980) model is described in Bloch). Features of Ogbu's (1981) approach are described in D'Amato's chapter. In addition, Lewinian field theory (see Lewin, 1935), an important influence on Bronfenbrenner's model as well as in the Whitings' formulation of theory and method (Whiting & Whiting, 1975) is represented in Gump's chapter in this volume.

The volume is also organized to reflect examples of recent research on children's play within the ecological settings of home, school, playground, and neighborhood (in Bronfenbrenner's (1979) theory, the settings defined at the microsystem level of influence). Second, several chapters situate children's play within larger contexts of influence; the volume highlights the importance of other aspects of the larger cultural environment on the nature of the physical and social experiences children experience within their directly experienced settings. Chapters describe the interacting influences of parents and teachers (Swadener & Johnson; Perlmutter & Pellegrini), home and school (D'Amato), the influence of parent work and stress on the environments children experience (Garbarino; Bloch), and historical and cultural influences on children's environments and their play (Garbarino; Slaughter & Dombrowski).

Finally, seven of the thirteen chapters directly focus on issues concerned with the play of children from at-risk, low-income urban, multicultural or cross-cultural backgrounds (Garbarino; Stevenson; Bloch; Moore; Swadener & Johnson; D'Amato; Slaughter & Dombrowski, in order of appearance in the volume); these chapters emphasize the influence biological and psychological factors have on play as well as the critical influence of historical and cultural ideologies on the context of the play opportunities children have. They also illustrate the need for more studies to include culture as an important contextual variable in research definition, sample selection, and interpretative discussion.

DEFINITION OF CONTEXT: THEORETICAL AND METHODOLOGICAL QUESTIONS

A number of the chapters implicitly or explicitly reflect important aspects of the theories and methods we use in studying the ecology of children's play. As a collection, the chapters raise important issues about the uniformity and clarity of our definitions of ecological context, setting, environment, culture, and play (for example, see questions raised in the Gump, Boulton & Smith, Slaughter & Dombrowski chapters). As a collection, they show that there are multiple ways to study the interaction between play and context, and the play of individuals within context. While these statements should be of no surprise to students of the ecology of child development, the chapters push all of us to look and think harder about what we mean and what we do; important differences in research approaches have important implications for the study of the relationships between context and play.

The place of individuals' perceptions. One of the more important definitional dimensions of context involves the place of individuals in the study of the ecological environment or in the definition and measurement of context. Lewin (1935) represented the influence of the individual and his perception of events as *P* in his original B=f(PE) equation; he also clearly separated E (environment) from P. In his contribution to this volume, Gump represents the influence of a person's perception or construction of events, and a person's influence as the "psychological environment", and suggests that ecological environments or settings surround the individual, but do not include a person's psychological perception or construction of the environment. The methods used by other contributors explicitly or implicitly ignore the subjective interpretation of environmental events in their studies of ecological effects. In contrast, the chapters by Moore, D'Amato, and Slaughter and Dombrowski incorporate the view that a person's perception is an integral part of the study of the context, and cannot be artificially separated from definitions and analyses of context.

Determining the influence of individuals versus the environment. In addition to this issue, various contributors wrestle with the ways one can determine the relative influence of the context or situation versus a person on behavior? For instance, what effect does the individual have on the selection or rejection of environments and experiences he or she encounters, and how can one determine this? Boulton and Smith illustrate the utility of sequential behavioral data analysis in this area with their study of preschool children's rough-and-tumble play. Stevenson emphasizes her own and others' recent research with infants and toddlers that also uses sequential analyses of adult–infant interaction to study bidirectionality of influence in home and laboratory contexts. Huston and Carpenter (1985), and Carpenter et al. in this volume display experimental and statistical strategies, respectively, for assessing the influence of individuals and individual characteristics versus the environment on behavior. Moore describes the way in which children's ideas were included in and influenced environmental planning of an outdoor playyard, though he also suggests this is an infrequent way in which children have influence on environments. Through ethnographic analysis of children's gang play on a playground, D'Amato describes children's resistance to adult norms and values within school settings; he also shows the importance, but complicated nature, of describing contexts and subcontexts of importance in studies of children's play (also see Corsaro, 1985; King, 1985 on this point).

How do we evaluate and assess the interactive effects of individuals and their environment, when environments consist of larger and smaller settings or contexts, each theoretically having interactive effects on each other (for example, the effect of micro-systems on meso-, exo-, and macro-systems)? Do economic and cultural systems determine which contexts children encounter completely; to what extent does child and adult behavior determine culture? While these are issues that some are exploring (e.g., Cochran & Henderson, 1984; Garbarino & Associates, 1982), we are far from the stage of easy or complete answers to these questions.

Cross-setting generalizability. Cross-setting specificity or generality of environmental influence is also an important issue. While some imply that behavior learned in one setting will be generalized to other similar settings, others test this idea, or at least recognize the need to test this idea more explicitly. In Whiting's cultural-ecological model, the ease of generalizing behavior from one setting to another is conditioned on the similarity of settings. The determination of "similarity" of settings, however, is still a thorny issue (see Gump's chapter for one approach to this problem). While many assume similarity and dissimilarity of settings can, eventually, be identified by the objective features of environments (e.g., the number of people present; toys, etc.), children's perception of similarity across settings may also be a crucial variable to evaluate. Cross-cultural and anthropological work also questions whether there is cross-setting or cross-sample generalizability; many ethnographic studies assume that cultural contexts are unique and that there is little important generalizable behavior from setting to setting.

Definitions of important within-setting variables to study. Many ecological researchers assume that one can identify important elements of settings that affect behavior, but the way in which people define important variables or elements of settings, or whether they believe they should define such variables depends upon theoretical frameworks, and researchers' definitions of context or setting. For example, Bronfenbrenner's model (Bronfenbrenner, 1979, p. 22), identifies the micro-, meso-, exo-, and macrosystems, and defines aspects of them that, theoretically, should be studied to understand the effect of the ecological context on behavior and development. In contrast, the Ogbu (1981) and Whiting (1981) models do not define different systems or levels of settings; they define, through theory and through research, specific historical, geographical, economic, political, and socio-cultural factors that influence the immediate settings children encounter, and what they can do and learn in them.

The variables that are important in the immediate settings children spend time in are also different across models and across research studies. In Bronfenbrenner's framework, for example, the microsystem is a "pattern of activities, roles, and interpersonal relationships experienced by the developing person in a given setting with particular physical and material characteristics". The "setting" is a "place where people can readily engage in face-to-face interaction—home, day-care center, playground, and so on". For Whiting (1980), on the other hand, intra-cultural settings are defined by the people children encounter, the activities people are doing in a setting, and the interaction that occurs in the setting. Gump (this volume) uses Barker's definition (Barker 1968)—the "setting has a physical locus, is bounded in space and time, and operates according to a program of actions or a standing pattern of behavior, which is congruent with and enclosed by its physical milieu". While there are obvious similarities between these definitions, and the identification of important variables, differences and disagreements about which are the most influential variables or factors, and how to study them remain. The difficulty of defining which variables are most crucial is an issue with which many of the contributors in this volume are still struggling.

Should we examine the effect of settings as "entities" or should we focus on the effect of particular aspects of settings on behavior? As suggested above, in most theoretical and methodological approaches, the effect of particular setting "variables" on behavior is studied; for example, the number of male and female adults or children in a setting is related to child behavior in both Bloch's and in Carpenter, Huston, and Spera's contributions. From this research perspective, the questions are clear: Which variables are theoretically important to study? Which variables are significant influences on behavior and development?

Some anthropological and ecological researchers approach this problem quite differently. Gump (this volume) and Barker (e.g., Barker & Wright, 1951; Barker, 1968) suggest settings should not be divided into discrete physical and social variables but should be viewed as "entities" with distinguishable "programs of action". In Gump's chapter, he describes current efforts to define and differentiate different types of child settings, and to determine which types of settings are most influential on behavior.

Some anthropological and interpretative theories also contest the validity of research that breaks "context" into discrete, hypothetically independent, measures of the environment (e.g., Erickson, 1986; Jacobs, 1987). This perspective is consistent with several other viewpoints mentioned in other sections above: that environments are unique; that environmental effects do not generalize from one setting to another; and that the individual, his perceptions and constructions of events, cannot be separated from the study of the effect of "context".

The questions raised above are reflected in each of the chapters in this volume, through explicit discussion of theory and method (e.g., Garbarino, Gump, Smith, Slaughter, & Dombrowski), or through authors' choices of approaches and methods. Issues seem to revolve around how one can determine behavior-setting influence in the most *reliable, valid, generalizable* and *useful* way? At this point in the study of the ecology of children's play, there appears to be no "one right way". Answers vary according to the disciplinary background of the researcher, and his or her implicit or explicit theories and definitions of how to study the relationship between children's activities and their development within different contexts. We urge readers and researchers to be more critical evaluators of the research assumptions and methods we all use (in this volume and elsewhere) by making these issues and debates more explicit here.

DIFFERENT CONCEPTIONS OF WHAT PLAY IS

It is obvious that the study of the ecological context of play depends on how one thinks about context; it is equally obvious that theories and definitions of play vary, and that these differences are critical to the study of the ecology of children's play. Because there are some excellent discussions of theoretical and methodological issues related to play definition, only a few points highlighted by the contributions in this volume will be highlighted here (for more detailed discussion, see Rubin, Fein, & Vandenberg, 1983; Schwartzman, 1978, particularly 302–324; Smith, this volume; Smith & Vollstedt, 1985 for discussion of debates on the definition of play).

In many of the chapters in this volume, different types of play are defined explicitly, usually in a form that facilitates comparison across research studies. While some authors speak of play more generally (e.g., Garbarino), most use terms and methods that draw on researcher-defined play categories. Many have chosen to use categories that emanate primarily from psychological or developmental theory (e.g., Piaget); others have adopted category systems that have evolved through an interplay of theory and observational research (e.g., the Parten-Smilansky category system). Ethological methods are represented particularly by the Boulton and Smith chapter, where they describe the complex process of determining which behavior patterns are present in what others more generally refer to as "rough and tumble" play. Several of the authors describe children's activities over time, and use the frequency of occurrence of different activities to develop categories of "play" (e.g., Carpenter, Huston, & Spera; Gump to some extent). Bloch's chapter uses this latter method in her study of two cultural groups from the United States and West Africa; this increases the likelihood that different play types are included, and that different images of play might be included in play category definitions.

While each of these approaches has merit, none of them draw on the definitions of children, or adults within a culture or setting. This definitional approach was modeled in Lancy's work (Lancy, 1976) and in King's work with American kindergarten children (e.g., King, 1986). In this volume, it is best reflected in the discussions of Slaughter and Dombrowski.

WHAT ARE IMPORTANT ISSUES TO STUDY? AN OVERVIEW OF THE VOLUME

The volume obviously reflects theoretical and methodological issues. Indeed, the first three chapters, by Garbarino (Chapter 2), Gump (Chapter 3), Boulton and Smith (Chapter 4) are particularly pointed toward theory and method. The remaining chapters of the volume address specific issues or situations of children's play within and across different contexts. Collectively, the authors highlight important issues that they are addressing through their study of children's play within different ecological contexts.

In addition to the theoretical descriptions offered in Garbarino's chapter, Garbarino provides us with an historical perspective on the changing context of American children's play. He addresses one current question in the light of historical changes in American children's environments. Garbarino asks, "Is play a luxury for American children?"; he discusses increasing statistics reflecting the incidence of child abuse, the loss of time and space for play at home and in school settings, and the spectre of the American child as a "hurried child" (Elkind, 1981).

In two chapters, Paul Gump (Chapter 3) and Michael Boulton and Peter K. Smith (Chapter 4) highlight recent theoretical as well as methodological advances in ecological psychological approaches to the study of children's play in different ecological contexts (Gump: home, community, playground, and camp settings; Boulton & Smith: school playground settings). Gump describes definitions of context and behavior setting that clarify notions of context and behavior setting as they are used across disciplines, and, critiques current "loose" definitions and methods claiming to study the context of child development. He also describes current efforts to deal with one important, but thorny problem in ecological research, the determination of cross-setting similarity and difference. Boulton and Smith (Chapter 4) use observations and sequential statistics of children's rough and tumble play to highlight better ways of defining play types, and of analyzing aspects of environments that have effects on play.

The next section of the volume is organized to represent examples of current research on children at different ages and in different settings. The volume is organized developmentally—from infancy to preschool to middle-childhood; while we believe that adolescents and adults also "play" and that their contexts are also important, there are no separate chapters illustrating these points in this volume.

In addition to the developmental organization, the chapters are also organized to highlight play at home and in the community, as well as play in laboratory and school settings. Stevenson's chapter (Chapter 5) describes research that she and others have done on infants and toddlers in home and laboratory settings. She reviews recent literature on parent, sibling, and nonparental caretaker play interaction with infants and toddlers, highlighting the importance of parent responsivity to infant-toddler signals during play. Stevenson's chapter suggests that parent characteristics, such as age or gender, have little influence on parental sensitivity to infant signals, although they do influence other aspects of play behavior. Parent sensitivity to infants and toddlers appears to be influenced by the cultural context of childrearing, parental psychopathology, infant risk status, and infant responsiveness to parent.

Howe and Ungar's chapter (Chapter 6) describes their research on toddler interaction within daycare settings. Using a Vygotskian framework, they analyze features of the cultural-ecological context of child care that facilitate collaborative social interaction between children and other adults; Howe and Ungar then relate these features to the development of toddler social pretend play. Their review of literature highlights the effect of physical space and materials, peer familiarity, and caretaker behavior in the development of social pretend play within the context of daycare centers.

In Chapter 7, Bloch describes the Whiting (1980) cultural-ecological model, and illustrates the importance of using such a framework to analyze the ecology of children's play. Bloch illustrates this by describing her research on American and Senegalese (West African) preschool-age children's play at home and in their community. Aspects of both the physical and social contexts of preschool-age children's play in both cultures are described, and, within each culture, features such as location, play with father, mother, siblings, and peers are related to the type of play children do. The results from the two culture study show that ecological variables that are important within one cultural setting are different from ecological variables of importance in the other; in other words, there were few variables that had similar or consistent relationships with children's play across the two cultures. Despite this general finding, two important similarities—that sibling and peer play predominated in both cultures and that parent–child play was rare—were found; these are discussed in light of recent research that highlights the importance of parent–child play for children's development.

Perlmutter and Pellegrini (Chapter 8) examine the effects of parental (mother and father) and child (age and gender) status variables on the teaching strategies used by parents in a fantasy play situation and assess the relations of parental strategies to children's fantasy play. The linguistic strategies used by 20 parent–child groupings in a fantasy play situation were analyzed. Parents' strategies were coded according to cognitive demand, positive support, and directiveness. Results indicated that strategies did not vary as a function of children's age or gender or parental status. Higher levels of cognitive demands, positive support and directiveness were positively and significantly correlated with children's fantasy play. In contrast, medium levels of cognitive demands were negatively and significantly correlated with children's fantasy play. Results are discussed in terms of Sigel's distancing model.

Carpenter, Huston, & Spera (Chapter 9) present results from a study of 7–11 year old children's time-use in their home and neighborhood settings. They explored specific gender-related hypotheses related to the amount of time and type of activities children did within an ecological context in which adults were present, and ecological contexts in which only children were present. Based on prior studies they hypothesized that girls would spend more time in adult-structured activities that would give them practice in compliance, verbal, and other intellectual skills, while boys would spend more time in peer-only activities which would be related to the development of independence and leadership. In general, their results supported their hypotheses. The results also showed that both family and child characteristics differentiated child time use patterns, and that more time in adult-structured activities was related to measures of child school performance.

In Chapter 10, Robin Moore describes the planning and design process used by an "interdisciplinary" group of children, teachers, community members, and landscape architectural researchers interested in creating a unique outdoor school playground environment for elementary school children in Berkeley, California. He highlights the process of design and the process of ethnographic interviews that were used to incorporate children's own ideas in the design and evaluation of their own playyard. By highlighting children's own comments about their concrete playyard before it was developed into the Washington Environmental Yard, and children's comments after the yard was in use for several years, he emphasizes children's need for and right to better outdoor play spaces. Moore concludes his chapter by calling attention to the lack of attention schools, parents, or society in general pay to this "right" of children for developmentally appropriate spaces for play.

In Chapter 11, Swadener and Johnson highlight current research on the play of children in multicultural and mainstreamed early childhood settings. Their chapter provides one example of cultural-ecological research on children's play that reflects "mesosystem" (Bronfenbrenner, 1979) influences on play. Swadener and Johnson review research on parent–teacher relationships, attitudes, and behavior as these relate to children's play and play environments. These influences include whether children from different backgrounds play alone or together as well as how and where they play. Swadener describes her own ethnographic research on children's play in two multicultural and mainstreamed day care centers to illustrate the individual child characteristics, as well as teacher and parent behavior that influences children's play.

D'Amato's (Chapter 12) provides an ethnographic account of Hawaiian-American boys' rivalry in games played on their elementary school playground. Through intensive observation and interviews, D'Amato traces the interactions and rivalry of boys within and across two gangs, during their second and third grade years at the laboratory school of the Kamehemaha Early Education Project (KEEP) in Honolulu. Through rich portrayals of children's game playing and attempts to maintain friendships and show power and rivalry on the playground, D'Amato illustrates the influence of peer culture and peer-defined social structure on play. In the final section of his chapter, D'Amato links Hawaiian-American home culture orientation, peer reliance and peer culture to the children's reliance on their peers at school. D'Amato also illustrates the utility of a broad based cultural-ecological perspective by relating John Ogbu's theory concerned with minority group school failure (Ogbu, 1981, 1982) to his peer rivalry findings. He suggests that low-income, minority Hawaiian-American children's rivalrous play is a complex response to their perception that they have little possibility for real success through school; with little reason to compete for school success, D'Amato contends that the boys try to succeed in peer-based groups, one against another, on the playground.

In the final chapter of the volume (Chapter 13), Diana Slaughter & Joseph Dombrowski review recent psychological and anthropological literature on children's social pretend play. Slaughter and Dombrowski provide a broad-based review of cross-cultural social pretend play literature that has been done since Schwartzman's (1978) comprehensive review on this topic. They review different theoretical perspectives concerned with the relationship between culture and play, and critically analyze recent research that has focused on what they term "culturally continuous" and "discontinuous" populations. They suggest that most studies have stressed play in culturally continuous populations, where a child's family has lived in its current broad ecological context for at least two generations, and, where the researcher assumes at least, there is little cultural discontinuity between the child's home culture and the dominant cultural context. Studies of culturally discontinuous populations, which include studies of children from newly immigrant families or studies of children's play where the discontinuity between children's home culture and that of the dominant culture are recognized, have been rarer. Their review highlights methodological issues concerned with defining culture and play, and the need for more research on children undergoing culture change, and the need to adapt to multiple cultures.

REFERENCES

Barker, R.G. (1968). *Ecological psychology: Concepts and methods for studying the environment of human behavior.* Stanford, CA: Stanford University Press.

Barker, R.G., & Wright, H.F. (1951). *One boy's day.* New York: Harper and Row.

Bronfenbrenner, U. (1979). *The ecology of human development.* Cambridge, MA: Harvard University Press.

Bronfenbrenner, U., & Crouter, A.C. (1983). The evolution of environmental models in developmental research. In P.H. Mussen (Ed.), *Handbook of child psychology* (Fourth Ed., vol. 1). New York: Wiley.

Cochran, M. (1984, April). *Parental empowerment, social supports, and the influence of social networks on parents' perceptions of children.* Paper presented at the annual meeting of the American Educational Research Association, New Orleans.

Corsaro, W.A. (1985). *Friendship and peer culture in the early years.* Norwood, NJ: Ablex Publishing Co.

Elkind, D. (1981). *The hurried child.* Reading, MA: Addison-Wesley.

Erickson, F. (1986). Qualitative methods in research on teaching. In M. Wittrock (Ed.), *Encyclopedia of educational research* (Third Ed.).

Garbarino, J., & Associates. (1982). *Children and families in the social environment.* San Francisco: Jossey-Bass.

Huston, A.C., & Carpenter, C.J. (1985). The effects of sex-typed activity choices. In L.C. Wilkinson & C.B. Marrett (Eds.), *Gender influences in the classroom.* New York: Academic Press.

Jacobs, E. (1987). Qualitative research traditions: A review. *Review of Educational Research. 57*(1), 1–50.

King, N. (1986). Play in the workplace. In L. Weiss & M. Apple (Eds.), *Ideology and practice.* London: Routledge, Kegan, Paul.

Konner, M.J. (1981). Evolution of human behavior development. In R.H. Munroe, R.L. Munroe, & B.B. Whiting (Eds.), *Handbook of cross-cultural human development* (pp. 3–51). New York: Garland Press.

Lewin, K. (1935). *A Dynamic Theory of Personality.* New York: McGraw-Hill.

Ogbu, J.U. (1981). Origins of human competence: A cultural-ecological perspective. *Child Development, 52,* 413–429.

Rubin, K.H., Fein, G.G., & Vandenburg, B. (1983). Play. In P. Mussen (Ed.), *Handbook of child psychology.* (Fourth Ed., Vol. 4, pp. 693–774). New York: Wiley.

Schwartzman, H. (1978). *Transformations: The anthropology of children's play.* New York: Plenum Press.

Smith, P.K., & Vollstedt, R. (1985). On defining play: An empirical study of the relationship between play and various play criteria. *Child Development, 56,* 1042–1050.

Weisner, T.S. (1984). The social ecology of childhood: A cross-cultural view. In M. Lewis (Ed.), *Beyond the dyad. Genesis of behavior: Volume 4* (pp. 43–58). New York: Plenum Press.

Whiting, B.B. (1980). Culture and social behavior. *Ethos, 2,* 95–116.

Whiting, B.B., & Edwards, C. P. (in press). *The company they keep: The effect of age, gender, and culture on social behavior of children aged two to ten.* Cambridge, MA: Harvard University Press.

Whiting, B.B., & Whiting, J.M.W. (1975). *Children of six cultures.* Cambridge, MA: Harvard University Press.

2

An Ecological Perspective on the Role of Play in Child Development

JAMES GARBARINO
Erikson Institute for Advanced Study in Child Development

AN INTRODUCTION TO CHILDHOOD

In the modern sense of the term in societies developing along Western-style individualized models, to be a child is to be shielded from the direct demands of economic, political, and sexual forces (Garbarino, 1988). In the modern sense of the term, childhood is a protected niche in the human ecology, a special time when we have a special claim upon those who bear us: We have a right to receive support from our families and our communities, regardless of our economic value. Children need not pay their own way and earn their keep. Typically, families want to provide this support, and as a rule they will do so if possible. But when families cannot provide for their children, society recognizes some responsibility to pick up the tab. This deeply held principle gives moral force to ongoing efforts to eliminate poverty from the lives of children (Nelson & Skidmore, 1983), and it gives clear moral significance to data documenting a recent trend toward increased poverty among children (Bronfenbrenner, 1986). The idea of childhood as a niche also implies that children are not direct participants in the cash economy. Work, if they do it, is to be guided, under the protection of their parents, except in the smallest transactions. Consumer purchases are likewise to be kept small and sheltered from commercial advertising that exploits the cognitive, emotional, and social limitations of children. The fact that children are often *not* so shielded is a matter for concern.

Similarly, children are not fair game for political activity. They cannot vote, are not legally responsible, and are not expected to be used by competing political forces in society. More broadly, children

16

are expected to relate to adults on a person-to-person basis, not in the organized bureaucratic way that characterizes adult interaction. Getzels (1974) has referred to this difference as a "particularistic" versus a "universalistic" principle, an emphasis upon *who* one is rather than *what* one does. Childhood is a time to maximize the particularistic and minimize the universalistic, a prescription that should be heeded by educators, politicians, and parents alike.

Finally, children are not supposed to be sex objects. In their behavior, their interests, their attitudes, and their bodies, children are to be protected from overt sexual experiences. As Elkind (1981) points out, in modern Western societies this principle used to be reinforced by the distinctly different clothing worn by children, clothing differentiating them from adults and symbolizing their being off limits sexually (which is not to say that this principle was not violated). To be sure, children are physical, even sensual creatures, but it is the overall character of childhood to be apart from overt sexuality of the kind experienced by adults, or even adolescents (as Sigmund Freud recognized in identifying the "latency period"). As Finkelhor (1979, 1984) makes clear, children are not in a position, developmentally or socially, to give informed consent for sexual involvements. They lack the cognitive and emotional equipment, as well as the independent status necessary to meet the criteria implicit in a liaison between "consenting adults."

If the child is shielded from economic, political, and sexual forces, what is childhood all about then? It is about creating a social space in which to lay the foundation for optimal human development. It is to provide a context in which to bear the fruits of human evolution, and the basic activity of childhood is play. The child is given license to play, and in so doing to explore the world. This play is distinguished from adult work in that it doesn't have production as its goal, although work can be an important activity for children. Child's play is distinguished from adult games, in that it isn't a basis for courtship. Child's play is geared to fantasy as a vehicle for processing experience, testing hypotheses about the self and the world, and having fun. It also provides a domain in which adults and children can communicate in a developmentally facilitating manner, if adults accept the child's definition of the play's reality (Paley, 1983).

Children are shielded so that they can play, and this play is quintessentially human, as Jacob Bronowski (1973) so correctly recognized when he spoke of the human being's "long childhood" as a key to the ascent of our species. As he saw it, childhood is both the cause and effect of cultural evolution. And, we also have evolved culturally because of our playfulness (and all that it produces in the way of intelligence and creativity). We have made a social space for play because our culture can subsidize childhood as a time for "free play."

The second fundamental concern for children is the development of basic competence. Children must become adept at the basic skills of the human community, in language, body control, morality, reasoning, and interpersonal relations. Unless children become competent in these areas they are a problem—for their family, for their society, and for themselves. Childhood is thus also a period of socialization, of adult investment in the creation of socially relevant skills and beliefs, and motives.

Play and developing competence go together, of course, and for the child, are at the top of life's agenda (White, 1959). For the family, they are the goal of socialization. For the community, protecting children is an important part of the social contract. This is childhood in the modern sense of the term, and it is a very worthwhile cultural innovation, one that has emerged over several centuries of cultural evolution. Johansson (1984) has reviewed the history of neglect, abuse, and avoidable death among children in Western societies from medieval to modern times. She documents the demographic emergence of childhood as infant mortality rates were reduced from hundreds per thousand to tens per thousand, and the proportions of children dying before age 5 dropped from roughly 50% to about 10% in industrialized societies. She also adds to the cultural story of how childhood established itself in Western consciousness as a valuable period in the life course (Aries, 1962; DeMeuse, 1974). To bring the concept of childhood to fruition required dramatic decreases in infant mortality, a heated debate about human nature, and a knowledge base about normal child development. The modern concept of childhood, with "free play" as its cornerstone, is a hard-won cultural achievement. It is the rationale for a critique of any social changes (intended or incidental) that encroach upon the lives of children.

Is the protected social space of childhood under attack? Is free play at risk? These questions resonate with an emerging body of social criticism alleging that children are being "hurried" (Elkind, 1981), that children are growing up "without childhood" (Winn, 1983) and that there is occurring an "erosion of childhood" (Suransky, 1983). This line of social criticism may be addressed within the framework established in the question, "can American families afford the luxury of childhood?"

This question correctly pinpoints the fact that childhood involves heavy subsidy by the adult world, particularly parents. It represents a substantial financial and psychic investment. In one sense, of course, children experience childhood by definition, by being young organisms. However, the degree to which they are granted childhood as a protected social space in which to play is another matter. Once we recognize it as a cultural and historical phenomenon we are drawn to an analytical perspective on child development that permits us to assess the interacting forces at work to erode, sustain, or enlarge that protected social space that is childhood. This is a precondition for developing a full view of the human ecology of play.

AN ECOLOGICAL PERSPECTIVE ON HUMAN DEVELOPMENT

In seeking to understand play we move most easily among psychological theories of child development. We are most comfortable approaching children's play from the perspective of emerging cognitive sophistication (particularly social cognition) or reinforced patterns of behavior (particularly as they reflect social learning). These approaches tell us a great deal about the form and function of play. If, however, our goal is to position ourselves to evaluate the *quality* of children's lives with respect to play we need a more avowedly social perspective on development. For this we turn to Urie Bronfenbrenner's rendering of the ecology of child development.

Bronfenbrenner (1979) defines development in decidedly social terms when he writes: "The developmental status of the individual is reflected in the substantive variety and structural complexity of the . . . activities which he initiates and maintains in the absence of instigation or direction of others" (1979, p. 55). Thus development is the drawing of a social map, a map brought to life in behavior as it arises and is understood by the individual. The individual proceeds with the drawing of this map in counterpoint to social experience that arises from the nested social systems of family, school, neighborhood, church, community, society, and culture.

Our task is to understand the forces of the social environment as they impinge upon the child's play. To accomplish this we must first review the concept of "environmental press" and its systematic translation into an ecological model of development.

Environmental press is a term used by ecological psychologists in referring to the combined influence of forces working in a setting to shape the behavior and development of people in that setting. Environmental press arises from the circumstances confronting and surrounding an individual that generate psychosocial momentum tending to guide that individual in a particular direction. As we shall see, the child's environment is multifaceted and multileveled—a complex network of forces.

As in all fields using an ecological framework, ecological psychology looks beyond the individual organism to the organism's environment for questions and explanations about the organism's behavior and development. A set of researchers in this area observed that, "behavior settings are coercive of behavior. People who enter settings are pressed to help enact its program (while at the same time using the setting for their own purposes)" (Gump & Adelberg, 1978, p. 174). Over time, individual behavior tends to become congruent with the situational demands of the environment. Patterns of behavior (such as free play) are reinforced or extinguished depending upon what the environment demands, punishes, or tolerates. This "principle of progressive conformity" is implemented by environmental press (Moos, 1976).

Environmental press is not a single or unitary force, but the resultant influence of all forces interacting within an environment. Various elements of a setting generate behavior-modifying forces that contribute to environmental press. Physical characteristics, for instance, may facilitate or impede access to desired destinations or alternate uses of existing space. Social patterns also may encourage one action or discourage another, or reward one value or attitude and punish another. Further, these influences interact with, and modify, each other, so that physical attributes affect social variables and vice versa.

The presence, strength, and dynamic balance among environmental forces is different, of course, in different settings. Contrasting environments therefore press toward different forms of behavior or directions for development. For example, small social environments (towns, groups, institutions) are associated with patterns of behavior different from large ones (Barker & Gump, 1964). Large secondary schools tend to discourage participation by students while small schools tend to encourage it (Barker & Gump, 1964; Garbarino & Asp, 1981). Environments in which residential concentrations of children are separated from recreational settings by busy streets lined on both sides by parked cars have been found to press toward both injuries to children and pressure on parents to provide regulation (Aldrich 1979; Michelson & Roberts, 1979). All can affect the quality and quantity of play.

Within an ecological framework, the balance of environmental forces is not the sole determinant of outcomes for an organism. The individual organism also figures significantly, of course. Those who study people from an ecological perspective view individuals and their environments as mutually shaping systems, each changing over time, each adapting over time in response to changes in the other. For ecological psychologists, therefore, while environmental press is the environment's contribution to individual–environment transactions, the individual brings to the situation a unique arrangement of personal resources, a particular level of development, and other attributes. Different people thus may react differently to the same environment. The big school–little school findings cited above, for instance (Barker & Gump, 1964; Garbarino & Asp, 1981), applied most significantly to academically marginal students. Further, the same environment may interact differently with the same person at different times. For example, the same busy street that can be life threatening to a child of 4 may be a developmentally appropriate challenge for a 9-year-old, and a mild inconvenience for a teen-ager.

Interindividual differences and intraindividual change require that we consider individual characteristics if attempts are made to predict outcomes of individual–environment interactions. In all environments, there are weaknesses and strengths, sources of sociocultural risk and opportunity (Garbarino & Associates, 1982). These forces may work for or against assurance of the child's basic survival needs; for or against provision of emotional nurturance and continuity; for or against developmentally appropriate attempts at self-determination— in short, for or against the creation of a positive environment for the growth and development of children. They similarly work for or against free play. Forces that support children represent opportunities for adequate, or even enhanced, developmental experiences, while the absence of such characteristics or the presence of threatening forces presents environmental risks to the developing child. For the present purpose, our main interest is in those forces that enhance free play versus those that undermine it.

Ecological psychologists typically focus on the "behavior settings" immediately surrounding and directly affecting the individual (e.g., the home, the neighborhood, the classroom). Clearly these settings are important. However, knowing as we do that the social influences on play extend outward from the most micro to the most macro (culture) it is necessary to move well beyond the child's proximate environment to consider the broader social, economic, and political forces that affect children and those responsible for their care. Such forces are the social, political, and economic engines that drive the behavioral settings in which children play.

Bronfenbrenner's framework guides our attention to the central role of families in the child's social ecology. The family is the exclusive early environment for some children and the primary environment for nearly all. As such, it is a major source of environmental press.

We know also that children function not so much as individuals but as members of families when it comes to entering and being affected by environments beyond their immediate settings (Burgess, Garbarino, & Gilstrap, 1983). The developing needs of families across *their* life course (cf. Aldous & Hill, 1969) are thus essential considerations in an ecological analysis.

To study the ecology of child development is to undertake the scientific study of how the child develops interactively with the immediate social and physical environment, and how aspects of the larger social context affect what goes on in the child's immediate settings. Within this framework the child is viewed as a developing person who plays an active role in an ever-widening world (Garbarino & Associates, 1982). The newborn shapes the feeding behavior of its mother but is confined largely to a crib or a lap and has limited means of communicating its needs and wants. The 10-year-old, on the other hand, influences many adults and other children located in many different settings, and has many ways of communicating. The world of adolescents is still larger and more diverse, as is their ability to influence it. The child and the environment negotiate their relationship over time through a process of reciprocity. Neither is constant; each depends on the other. One cannot predict the future of either without knowing something about the other. Does a handicapped child stand a greater risk of being abused? It depends. Some environments are "vulnerable" to the stresses of caring for such a child, while others are not. Does economic deprivation harm development? It depends on how old one is when it hits, what sex one is, what the future brings in the way of vocational opportunity, what the quality of family life was in the past, what one's economic expectations and assumptions are, and whether one looks at the short term or the long run (cf. Elder, 1974). In short—it depends.

In addition to recognizing the interactive nature of development, an ecological framework also considers the multiple levels at which environmental influences originate. Bronfenbrenner has described the individual's environment as "a set of nested structures, each inside the next, like a set of Russian dolls" (Bronfenbrenner 1979, p. 22). As we ask and answer questions about development at one level, this ecological framework reminds us to look at the next levels beyond and within the immediate setting to find the questions to ask and answer. For example, if we see children and their parents in conflict over time for play we need to look outward to the economy that creates economic demands and opportunities, and to the culture that defines a person's personal worth in monetary terms and thus causes parents to consider the costs of time "spent" on play. In addition, we must look inward to the parent–child relationships that are affected by the changing roles and status of the parents and to temperamental characteristics of the individuals involved (cf. Elder, 1974). Further, we must look "across" to see how systems beyond the family adjust to new conditions over time. For example, if economic pressures increase the need for child care, and schools respond by extending their institutional coverage to younger (formerly "*pre-school*") children, the net result may be to displace developmentally enhancing free play, in favor of more narrowly academic activities (Zigler, 1986). For example, after observing the new state-funded program for 4-year-olds in his school, one elementary school principal remarked, "but all they do is play and eat!" This skepticism regarding the function of play in early childhood is precisely the danger that concerns critics of school-oriented early childhood programs. It reflects contrasting ideologies at work as systems collide. These swirling social forces and interlocking social systems are the stuff on which ecological analyses are made.

Bronfenbrenner's framework posits four general types of environmental systems, categorized by the proximity to and immediacy of its effect on children. Most immediate to the developing child are *microsystems.* These are the joint product of physical settings and behavioral interactions in which individuals experience and create day-to-day reality. Microsystems for children are the places they inhabit, the people who are there with them, and the things they do together. At first, most children experience only one, quite small microsystem—the home—involving interaction with one person at a time in relatively simple activities, such as feeding, bathing, and cuddling. As the child develops, complexity normally increases; the child does more, with more people, in more places. Play assumes an ever-larger role.

We know that the management of "survival needs" (eating, eliminating, etc.) is a critical task for the developing child's microsystem. Play also figures prominently in the process of the microsystem from the early months of life, and eventually is joined by work. Playing, working, and loving—what Freud called the essence of normal human existence—are the principal classes of activities that characterize the child's microsystem. However, the extent to which these activities take place, their quality, and their level of complexity are variables. An environmental microsystem presents a developmental risk to the child if it is characterized by a narrowly restricted range and level of activities; impoverished experience in playing, working, and loving; or stunted reciprocity where genuine *inter*action is lacking and either party seeks to avoid or be impervious to the other. Such neglect and rejection are developmentally dangerous (Garbarino, Guttmann, & Seeley, 1986; Rohner, 1975). At the microsystem level, environmental opportunities for a child are provided by enduring, reciprocal, multi-facted relationships that emphasize meeting survival needs, as well as offering encouragement for playing, practice in loving, and *eventually* a sound introduction to working.

Mesosystems are the relationships between contexts, or microsystems, in which the developing person experiences reality. Important mesosystems for children include relationships between home and school, home and neighborhood, and school and neighborhood. The richness of mesosystems for the child is measured by the number of links, the degree of value consensus, and the level of diversity between microsystems.

The school-home mesosystem is of great developmental significance for the child. In general, we would expect enhanced development where this mesosystem was "characterized by more frequent interaction between parents and school personnel, a greater number of persons known in common by members of the two settings, and more frequent communications between home and school, more information in each setting about the other" (Bronfenbrenner, 1979, p. 218). However, we must add the proviso "that such interconnections not undermine the motivation and capacity of those persons who deal directly with the child to act on his behalf. This qualification gives negative weight to actions by school personnel that degrade parents or to parental demands that undermine the professional morale or effectiveness of the teacher" (Bronfenbrenner, 1979, p. 218). Those familiar with contemporary schooling know that both of these often are problems. For the present purpose, our major concern is the extent to which mesosystems protect and nurture play. Where they undermine play it is likely to be by downgrading the role of "free player" in favor of more directly and immediately "productive" activities. For the affluent child these social forces are likely to favor the child's role as academic learner; for the poor child these are likely to favor the child's role as worker (particularly child care provider, for siblings or self).

The stronger, more positive, and more diverse the links between settings, the more powerful and beneficial the resulting mesosystem will be as an influence on the child's development. A rich range of mesosystems is a developmental opportunity, a poor set of mesosystems produces impaired development, particularly when home and school are involved. The quality of the child's mesosystems often is determined by events in systems where the child herself does not participate but where things happen that have a direct impact on

her parents and other adults who do interact with her. Bronfenbrenner calls these settings "exosystems."

Exosystems are situations having a bearing on a child's development
but in which the developing child does not actually play a direct
role. The child's exosystems are those settings that have power over
his or her life, yet in which the child does not participate. They
include the workplaces of parents (since most children do not have
direct contact with them), and those centers of power, such as school
boards and planning commissions, that make decisions affecting the
child's day-to-day life. These exosystems enhance development when
they make life easier for parents and undermine development when
they make life harder for parents. Thus, exosystem opportunity lies
in situations when they are forces at work outside the family on
behalf of children and their parents. When child rearing "has friends
in high places" the opportunities for child development increase.
The initiative taken by the politically powerful Kennedy family in
advocating in the federal government on behalf of retarded children
is an example, although institutions in the exosystem are generally
of greater importance.

One very important exosystem for urban children is the planning
board. This group can play a large role in determining how well the
interests of children are incorporated into decisions about land use.
Given that a physical environment attractive to children may be
unattractive by adult standards, this is vital (Michelson & Roberts,
1979). For example, children may thrive on "empty lots," (which they
fill with games, i.e., with free play) but which adults see as economically disadvantageous.

In exosystem terms, environmental risk comes about in two ways.
The first is when parents or other significant adults in a child's life
are affected in a way that impoverishes their behavior in the child's
microsystem. For example, Kohn (1977) found that when parents
work in settings that demand conformity rather than self-direction,
they reflect this orientation in their child rearing, thus stifling important aspects of the child's development, with its most likely target
being free play. Other examples include elements of a parent's
working experience that result in an impoverishment of family life,
such as long or inflexible hours, traveling, or stress. The second way
risk flows from the exosystem is when decisions are made in those
settings that adversely affect children or treat them unfairly. For
example, when the school board mandates early schooling employing
narrowly academic curricula that supplant free play or when the
planning commission runs a highway through the child's free play
areas, they jeopardize the child's development.

Thus, exosystem risk comes when the child lacks effective advocates in decision-making bodies. Albee (1980) has gone so far as to identify powerlessness as *the* primary factor leading to impaired development and psychopathology. It certainly plays a large role in determining the fate of groups of children, and may even be very important when considering individual cases, such as whether or not parents are under pressure from their peers to involve children in formal activities at the expense of free play, or when parents are forced to place their children in substandard childcare because the community does not ensure that good care is available. Risk at the exosystem level is often a political matter.

Meso- and exosystems are embedded in the broad ideological and institutional patterns of a particular culture or subculture. This is how the ecological pieces fit together. These patterns are the macrosystem—the "blueprints" for that culture's ecology of human development. These blueprints reflect a people's shared assumption about "how things should be done." A macrosystem is the norms about how development proceeds and the appropriate nature and structure of micro-, meso-, and exosystems. Conventional cultural and ethnic labels (e.g., Anglo, Italian, Indian) suggest unique clusters of ideological and behavioral patterns. Beyond these labels, however, these ideologies and behaviors need to be operationalized and their implications for child development examined. In terms of their consequences for parents and children, we need to know, for example, how similar are the processes of play in two "different" cultures? How does the school-home mesosystem work in two "different" ethnic groups? Simply having different labels does not mean that we necessarily have different macrosystems. One implication of the concept of macrosystem is that we treat cultural and societal factors as continuous rather than dichotomous variables (i.e., on the dimensions of valuing childhood as a protected life space, in legitimizing violence, in validating individualism).

Environmental opportunity in macrosystem terms is a prochild ideology. For example, a society's assumption that families stricken by economic or medical tragedy have a right to public support represents macrosystem opportunity. A strong political base of support for child services is another manifestation of macrosystem opportunity. A third is strong commitment to free play as the foundation for childhood development.

What is environmental risk when it comes to macrosystems? It is an ideology or cultural alignment that threatens to impoverish children's microsystems and mesosystems, and sets exosystems against them. It can be a national economic policy that tolerates or even increases the chances of economic dislocations and poverty for families with young children. It can be institutionalized support for high levels of geographical mobility that disrupts neighborhood and school connections and the social network of parents. It can be a pattern of nonsupport for parents that tolerates or even aggravates intense conflicts between the roles of worker and parent. It can be patterns of racist, sexist, or other values that demean large numbers of parents, thereby undermining the psychological security of their children and threatening each child's self-esteem. In general, macrosystem risk is any social pattern or societal event that impoverishes the ability and willingness of adults to care for children, children to learn from adults, and play to flourish.

To recapitulate, environmental influences on the child's development originate from systems at all four levels in the human ecology of the child. Systems at each level have distinctive characteristics that are relevant to a child's development, and therefore different criteria are appropriate for assessing the impacts of each level on the child. Further, these effects may be either positive or negative—either opportunities or risks.

And, while the family microsystem is usually the most important system for a young child, the overall impact of the environment emerges from the dynamic balance among all influences over time. The importance of and interactions among the various environmental systems is expressed well be deLeone:

> To the large developmental contexts of class and caste one must add more intimate ones of which school, neighborhood, and family are clearly among the most important. For young children, especially, it is through these intimate contexts that contact with the broader dimensions of class, race, and the social and economic order is made. . . . The nature of a society at a given time shapes the structure of social classes; social class influences the nature of family life and experience; racial membership influences likely occupation; through income, occupation helps determine neighborhood. Neighborhood determines where one goes to school, and not only is family background associated with how a child does in school, but it may influence how the school treats a child and the ability of the child and family to manipulate the institutional ropes of a school. Schooling in turn influences subsequent social class standing, and to some extent the skills that the population as a whole develops influence the contours of economic activity, and so on in a series of permutations, combinations, and feedback loops. In the midst of this complex, breathing organism called social structure is the child. (1979, pp. 158–159)

COMMENTARY: CURRENT ISSUES IN THE ECOLOGY OF PLAY

Our ecological perspective is intrinsically historical. As social systems adapt to internal changes and to changes in each other some issues move to the forefront of concern while others recede. The ecology of play reflects this same ebb and flow. What are the current issues of special concern. We may consider two: (1) the transformation of "free" play into "leisure" and "productive activity," and (2) the shifting of supervision of young children from adults to siblings and self. The first issue is evident in the trend toward formalizing childhood activities (through lessons, institutionalized competition, and expensive forms of recreation). The second issue is evident in the "latchkey child phenomenon" (also referred to as "children in self-care").

ARE AMERICAN CHILDREN BEING HURRIED?

Among the affluent, some observers see greater and greater pressure on children to yield dividends. The result is stress and hurrying. Many families are spending unprecedented amounts of money on their children, and they want to see a return on their investment. One writer (Stout, 1983) opened an article on "Bringing Up Better Babies" as follows: "With computers and violins, in swimming pools and gyms, today's baby-boom parents are determined to help their children be the best they can be." For example, lessons and equipment (including computers) are major items in many family budgets. Reppucci (1983) reports that the massive proliferation of organized sports and recreation for children has not been matched by research to determine what, if any, effect they have on speeding up the process of growing up or in altering the experience of play.

Some who have observed the process at work believe, however, that this drive to greater and ever-earlier payoffs increases the pressure on children to perform, to mature, and to succeed in ways that lend prestige to parents (Elkind, 1981). For example, success in school is of unprecedented importance (Garbarino & Asp, 1981), and parents and educators have raised their academic expectations for young children. Many teachers and parents expect children to be reading as they enter first grade (and often express the concern that children who are not reading fluently by Christmas) are delayed and perhaps even possessed of a learning disability. Secondary school graduation has come to be defined as almost a prerequisite for full personhood in American society; for the affluent, a college education is imperative.

All this means that children are under greater pressure to pay off in academic skills than ever before. In this climate free play may seem a luxury children cannot afford.

The competition among affluent families for that success often appears to have the intensity observed among elite Japanese families (Arthur, 1983), who use the term *Mama-gom* (monster mother) to describe this pressure cooker environment. Many affluent parents appear to have concluded that free play is a luxury that their children can ill afford if they are to be successful. This is not totally new, of course. Survey evidence from an affluent suburban community collected by CBS News in the mid-1960s and presented in a film report entitled "16 in Webster Groves" revealed a high level of academic competition and stress among college-bound secondary students. What is new, it seems, is the widespread lowering of the age for this pressure and its spread to more and more families.

These demands for maturity are evident across the board, from the academic to the social, and in varying degrees across the socioeconomic spectrum. Divorce and dating or remarriage by parents, for example, demand interpersonal sophistication on the part of children at an early age, as they must come to terms with their parent(s) being involved in courtship. Most divorced women who are mothers of young children remarry, so most children of divorce experience parental courtship. The glorification of the "sophisticated" life-style in the mass media goes hand in hand with greater demands for children to act "mature."

The net result of these trends appears to be that children have a greater sense of appreciation for the contingent nature of parental involvement. Are children hearing the message, "Hurry up and grow up, I'm busy!"? One is tempted to conclude that many are, particularly in light of the 50-year follow-up to the classic Middletown study. Bahr's analysis (1978) repeated the questions posed to teen-agers about their parents. In 1924, 63% of the female adolescents and 62% of the males reported that the most desirable attribute of a father is the fact that he spends time with his children. By 1977, the figures were 71% and 64%. In 1924, only 35% of the males and 41% of the females placed a premium on mothers who spent time with their children. By 1977, these figures were 58% and 66%. These data suggest that maternal involvement has become more valued, but it also suggests that children recognize that they can't count on their mothers to be available to them any more than they can their fathers. It's nice for both parents to be valued, but is it better for children? What impact does it have on children's play? To understand this we must address our second issue, the pressure on children to replace adult supervision with self-supervision.

ARE CHILDREN CAUGHT BETWEEN THE CHANGING ROLE OF WOMEN AND THE UNCHANGING ROLE OF MEN?

In 1970, 53% of the women polled by a *New York Times* survey named "being a mother and raising a family" and 43% named "being a homemaker," as one of the two or three "most enjoyable things about being a women today." The comparable figures for 1983 were 26% and 8%. "Career, jobs, pay" and "general rights and freedoms" increased from 9% to 28% and from 14% to 32%, respectively. Families need income-generating mothers, whether it be for affluence (two middle-class workers), protection from low income (two blue collar workers), or sheer survival (a single parent). Two income families lift middle-class families into the affluent range, and prevent low-income families from slipping into poverty (Garbarino, 1984). The demand for full utilization of parental income generation leads to a situation in which parents are likely to believe that young children are capable of assuming early responsibility for self-care and that early demands for maturity are in the child's best interest (and by implication there is something wrong with children if they cannot meet those demands). Observers such as Elkind would reply that this is akin to "blaming the victim" (Ryan, 1976) because it inappropriately shifts the responsibility for the situation. In any case, it seems that many adults are taking the position that their families cannot afford to subsidize the child's experience of childhood as it has evolved in Western culture as a desirable stage in life.

Many parents believe they have few alternatives. Women need to work in the cash economy. Despite evidence of some shift in traditional orientations to role division, few men are ready, willing, and able to alter traditional patterns that define child care as the mother's responsibility regardless of her labor force participation (Cherlin, 1984). Indeed, castigating mothers for the risks involved in self-care is also akin to blaming the victim. Clearly, men (or at least forms of sexism) are at the root of the problem in many cases. They are so as separated fathers who fail to provide child support payments (and thus force mothers between an economic rock and a hard place). They are so as fathers who live with their children but don't assume full responsibility for day-to-day care. They are so as unaccommodating workplace managers or as unsympathetic policy makers (a significant problem particularly during a conservative administration).

As Cherlin (1984, p. 435) concludes: "Thus, the destabilizing burden on employed wives seems to be rooted in an ideology of male and female roles that is resistant to change."

This appears to be one reason why some observers feel concerned about infants and preschool children who are in full-time day care. Their parents do not have, or at least do not believe they can afford, the luxury of giving the child and themselves the choice of being at home where developmentally enhancing free play *can* flourish. They need the child to enter the most inexpensive care where regimentation and group needs may suppress developmentally enhancing free play, particularly in profit-oriented centers (Suransky, 1983). They need the child to manage well in care. They need the child to attend school or be in the day-care setting as much as possible. Children may feel or be pressured to keep attending after they become sick, or start attending again before they are well, to make things work better for their parents.

Beverly Cleary, a popular writer for young people, developed a set of characters in her books who exemplify the desirable essence of childhood, but who in recent years have come to speak for and about the dynamics of contemporary demands for maturity. Her Huggins and Quimby families are archetypical middle-class American families, and it is thus significant that in her 1981 book, *Ramona Quimby, Age 8,* the child, Ramona, is besieged by worry that if she becomes sick at school it will interfere with her mother's work schedule. In her 1984 book, *Ramona Forever,* Ramona becomes a latchkey child. Truly, Ramona has entered the 1980s.

This adult need for the child to perform a responsible role may conflict with the idea of childhood as directed by the child's need and timetable. As more and more of daily life becomes incorporated into the cash economy, as maternal employment outside the home reaches ever-higher levels, and as a conservative reaction reinforces traditional role models for men and women that fly in the face of the facts of day-to-day life, what will happen to the quality of life for America's children? Presumably, one thing that will happen is that children will spend ever more time in institutional care and in self-care. In the former, organized activities are the dominant script (Zigler, 1986). In the latter the child may be afraid, may be prohibited from going outside to join in free play with peers, may have a regimen of responsibilities (e.g., child care, cooking, homework) or leisure diversions (mostly television) (Coolsen, Seligson, & Garbarino, 1986). Where is developmentally enhancing free play in this environment?

CONCLUSION

Even this brief review should be enough to demonstrate that an ecological perspective on play can be fruitful in generating a social analysis of play. It directs our attention to issues, issues that are historically oriented and that translate into questions for both research and social policy.

To understand the ecology of play we must understand the human ecology of childhood. We must recognize that every level of human experience, from organismic development to macrosystem change, influences the social space for play and what exactly occurs within that social space. Child development progresses through the interactions of children as biosocial creatures and childhood as cultural invention. This overarching observation should be ever in the forefront of our consciousness as we examine the dynamics and consequences of play in the lives of children.

REFERENCES

Albee, G. (1980). Politics, power, prevention and social change. In G. Gerbner, C. Ross, & E. Zigler (Eds.). *Child abuse: An agenda for action.* New York: Oxford University Press.

Aldous, J., & Hill, R. (1969). Breaking the poverty cycle: Strategies points for intervention. *Social Work, 14,* 3–12.

Aldrich, R. (1979). The influences of man-built environment on children and youth. In W. Michelson, S. Levine, & E. Michelson (Eds.), *The child in the city.* Toronto, University of Chicago Press.

Aries, P. (1962). *Centuries of childhood: A social history of family life.* New York: Knopf.

Arthur, H. (1983). The Japan gap. *American Educator, 10,* 38–44.

Bahr, H. (1978, August). *Change in family life in Middletown: 1924–1977.* Paper presented at the annual meeting of the American Sociological Association, Chicago.

Barker, R., & Gump, P. (1964). *Big school, small school.* Stanford, CA: Stanford University Press.

Bronfenbrenner, U. (1979). *The ecology of human development,* Cambridge, MA: Harvard University Press.

Bronfenbrenner, U. (1986). Ecology of the family as context for human development. *Development Psychology, 22,* 723–742.

Bronowski, J. (1973). *The ascent of man.* Boston, MA: Little, Brown.

Burgess, R., Garbarino, J., & Gilstrap, B. (1983). Violence to the family. In E. Callahen & K. McCluskey (Eds.), *Life-span development psychology.* New York: Academic Press.

Cherlin, A. (1984). Family policy. *Journal of Family Issues, 4,* 427–438.

Cleary, B. (1981). *Ramona Quimby, age 8.* New York, New York: Dell.

Cleary, B. (1984). *Ramona forever.* New York: Dell.

Coolsen, P., Seligson, M., & Garbarino, J. (1986). *When school's out and nobody's home.* Chicago: National Committee for Prevention of Child Abuse.

deLeone, R. (1979). *Small futures.* New York: Harcourt, Brace, Jovanovich.

DeMeuse, L. (1974). *The history of childhood.* New York: Harper Torch Books.

Elder, G. (1974). *Children of the great depression.* Chicago: University of Chicago Press.

Elkind, D. (1981). *The hurried child.* Reading, MA: Addison–Wesley.

Finkelhor, D. (1979). *Sexually victimized children.* New York: Free Press.

Finkelhor, D. (1984). *Child sexual abuse.* New York: Free Press.

Garbarino, J. (1978, January). The impact of social change on children and youth, *Vital Issues, 27.*

Garbarino, J. (1980). Some thoughts on school size and its relation to adolescent development. *Journal of Youth Adolescence, 9,* 169–182.

Garbarino, J. (1984). Child welfare and the economic crisis. *Child Welfare, 53,* 1–15.

Garbarino, J. (1988). *The future as if it really mattered.* Denver: Bookmaker's Guild.

Garbarino, J., & Asp, E. (1981). *Successful school and competent students.* Lexington, MA: Lexington Books.

Garbarino, J., & Associates, (1982). *Children and families in the social environment.* New York: Aldine.

Garbarino, J., Guttmann, E., & Seeley, J. (1986). *The psychologically battered child.* San Francisco: Jossey Bass.

Getzels, J.W. (1974). Socialization and education: A note on discontinuities. *Teacher's College Record, 76,* 218–225.

Gump, P., & Adelberg, B. (1978). Urbanism from the perspective of ecological psychologies. *Environment & Behavior, 10,* 171–191.

Johansson, S.R. (1984, May). *Neglect, abuse, and avoidable death.* Paper presented to a conference on "Child Abuse: A Bio-Social Perspective," convened by the Social Science Research Council, New York.

Kohn, M. (1977). *Class and conformity.* (2nd ed.). Chicago: University of Chicago Press.

Michelson, W., & Roberts, E. (1979). Children and the urban physical environment. In W. Michelson, S. Levine, & A. Spira (Eds.), *The child in the city.* Toronto: University of Toronto Press.

Moos, R. (1976). Evaluating and changing community settings. *American Journal of Community Psychology, 4,* 313–326.

Nelson, R., & Skidmore, F. (1983). *American families and the economy,* Washington, DC: National Academy Press.

New York Times. (1983, December 7). Many Women in Poll Equate Values of Job and Family Life, pp. 1ff.

Paley, V. (1983). *Boys and girls: Superheroes in the dollcorner.* Chicago: University of Chicago Press.

Presser, H. (1984, April). *Work and family.* Colloquium presentation. Pennsylvania State University.

Reppucc, D. (1983, August). *Emerging issues in the ecology of children and families.* Invited address to the annual meeting of the American Psychological Association, Anaheim, CA.

Rohner, R. (1975). *They love me, they love me not.* New Haven, CT: Human Relations Area Files Press.

Ryan, W. (1976). *Blaming the victim.* New York: Vintage.

Stout, K. (1983, October). "Bringing up better babies," *Mainliner Magazine,* pg. 132.

Suransky, R. (1983). *The erosion of childhood.* Chicago: University of Chicago Press.

Winn, M. (1983). *Children without childhood.* New York: Pantheon, 1983.

White, R. (1959). Motivation reconsidered: The concept of competence. *Psychological Review, 66,* 297–333.

Zigler, E. (1986). *Formal schooling for 4 year olds?* Unpublished paper, Yale University, New Haven, CT.

3
Ecological Psychology and Issues of Play

PAUL V. GUMP
University of Kansas

Over the span of 40 years, ecological psychologists have recorded and analyzed children's behavior in their natural habitats. A number of specimen records are available, which show what children actually do in their many settings: children from 2 to 10 in a small Kansas town; elementary schoolchildren at home and in school in a small city in Oregon; urban, suburban, and rural 3-year-olds in Tennessee; one 9-year-old boy at home and at camp in Michigan. These represent some of the subjects' records which have been analyzed and are available at the Spencer Archives, University of Kansas. While most of these investigations did not focus upon play, they did record behaviors that involved play. Some of the findings and concepts from specimen record research have relevance to the struggle to define, describe, and analyze issues in play research.

Most of the records involved child behavior across a number of settings. Observation of the impressive changes in behavior that resulted as subjects crossed setting boundaries led to a basic respect for setting coercivity. Along a number of behavioral dimensions it was manifestly easier to predict a particular children's behavior by asking *where* they were, as opposed to *who* they were. The ecological context of behavior became a research object in its own right and much of the research effort of ecological psychology became, not subject-centered, but setting-centered. The context of play is certainly an issue in much play research, but how the context is to be identified and described is subject to highly varied interpretations (Cheska, 1981). Much conceptual and empirical effort has been invested by ecological psychologists in one kind of context: the behavior setting. Students of play and context might find useful material in ecological research.

This chapter will first present some of the major specimen record research as it can be related to play; then it will describe some of the conceptual and empirical work with settings in which play occurs. The basic stance taken here is that our understanding advances most rapidly when we alternate between theoretically-driven, experimental approaches on the one hand, and the processing of naturally occurring data on the other.

The inadequacy of some theoretically evolved concepts for the handling of behavior and experience of everyday life was demonstrated by early experience in ecological psychology. Before they became "ecological psychologists," pioneers in the field had been highly involved in issues of success and failure and of frustration and regression. When records of the daily lives of children became available, these two theoretical issues were studied to determine how they looked in "real life," not in theoretically shaped experiments. What was learned by this juxtaposition of theory and naturally occurring phenomena?

The success and failure ideas had been developed from the "level of aspiration" investigations of Lewin and others (Lewin, Dembo, Festinger, & Sears, 1944); the psychological situation and the behavioral reaction aspects of success and failure had been well honed and their fit into a larger theoretical context was promising. The possibilities with regard to frustration and regression also appeared favorable: Experiments which became classics in child psychology texts showed very strong and psychologically intriguing relationships between experimentally induced frustration and a variety of regressive behaviors (Barker, Dembo, & Lewin, 1941).

What happened when the success and failure ideas were put to the specimen records of 12 boys and girls aged 2 to 11 years behaving for a full day each in their natural habitat? For the thousands of episodes analyzed, success (as defined from experimental research) occurred less than 1.5% of the time. It was not that failure was frequent, however. The data here were even more minuscule. Failure—again as defined from the theory—occurred at a median percentage of zero. It was possible to speak of positive and negative outcomes of various types but for these records of real children acting in their real worlds, success and failure were not "ecologically valid" descriptors (Wright, 1967).

The specimen record data on frustration and regression were even more disappointing. An investigation by Fawl (1963) showed that, even with a liberal interpretation of frustration, that phenomenon occurred infrequently in the real lives of children. Further, when all of the samples of frustration were analyzed in terms of the consequences for behavior, regression was *not* significantly related to frustration. In fact, the chosen definition of frustration—goal blockage—resulted in many instances in which frustration, as a psychological disturbance, was not present; further, there were many disturbances which did not require an antecedent goal blockage. Clearly, some rethinking was required.

We have selected these two examples of naturally occurring data failing to support the relevance and/or the relationships of concepts derived from theoretically driven experiments because they show how such ideas can become inadequate even when the researchers wanted very much for them to prove productive. The obtained data simply do not fit the researchers' conceptual framework. All social scientists would subscribe to the dictum, "Let the data decide." But data only from theoretically driven experiments may be insufficient for decision. Could it be that we need atheoretical, nonexperimental data in large and frequent doses, if we are to answer questions about children's behavior in their real-life situations?

What is the present situation with regard to psychologists' research on play? A kind of narrowing of the data base seems to have taken place, uncorrected by naturalistic research as suggested above. Calls for such naturalistic research have surfaced, usually recommending ethnographic approaches to problems in child play. For example, Susan McBride recently had the following to say regarding toy research:

> The culture of toy research needs to become more scientific in developing theory, while toy play needs to be taken from the scientific laboratory and examined first in its natural cultural context . . . children should be observed in their own daily play settings on a long-term-basis, free from experimental constraints. (1981, p. 216)

McBride calls for ethnographic research for toy play problems. I assert that the ecological stance has something to offer the naturalistic methodology for play research. And I would add that one reason naturalistic approaches are avoided is that experimental researchers are skeptical that the primary data of naturalistic research can be adequately conceptualized and quantified. More fundamentally, experimental investigators may doubt that any kind of regularity, any demonstrated relationships can be obtained in nonexperimental research. This chapter will point to some ecological possibilities regarding these issues.

The promise of naturalistic research was described early in eco-behavioral work (Barker & Wright, 1955; Gump & Kounin, 1959; Willems, 1965). Ecological psychology offers some general ideas and some specific concepts and methods for the recording and analysis of children's behavior in the natural habitat. Although the primary data taken and methods employed for their analysis are atheoretical, the findings generated are systematic, quantitative, and—at their level—comprehensive.

RESEARCH ON THE STREAM OF BEHAVIOR

A basic challenge in ecological research is the delineation of inherent units within more global phenomena. The wider spans may be an individual's stream of behavior or an environmental array. Adequate unitization of either behavior or environment yields not only the smaller parts of the phenomenon—which parts are often necessary for research analysis—but the unitization can provide a picture of the phenomenon's structure. The methods employed by ecological psychologists to unitize the behavior stream are fully described by Wright (1967); for our purposes here it may be sufficient to indicate that the basic criterion for identifying the beginning and end of a behavior unit is the start and the cessation of a behavioral direction. Such an unit has been labeled an episode and may vary in duration but for children aged 6 to 10 it averages about a minute. Descriptive material offered later will illustrate the results of the episoding operation.

Once episoding has marked the changes in behavioral direction, an interesting question is: What are the circumstances, the forces, which initiate a new direction? Most simply, directions can change with or without manifestly impinging external events. With units identified, it is also possible to categorize the quality of the units. Some units of a child's stream of behavior will involve social activity, others not. Some episodes will show a playful action and others show routine or serious actions. If play is present, one can ask which form of play is being exhibited.

Finally, ecological research would, almost as a matter of course, relate the quality of the behavioral units to qualities of the context or the setting in which the units occurred.

The four issues of episoding, influences at episode change, forms of play, and the relations of play to setting can be illustrated by excerpts from two day-long specimen records. These accounts describe the situation and behavior of 9-year-old Wally O'Neill at summer camp and at home. (Gump, Schoggen, & Redl, 1963). Play within the records was defined as action following interest, not necessity, as seeking stimulation, behaving "just for fun." Nonplay episodes involved chores, self-care behavior, necessary locomotions, following established routines. Three excerpts from the records together with notes on their analysis follow. The first two accounts come from the camp experience, the third from Wally's home. Wally and several cabinmates are on a "nature hike." Wally has been ambling along without looking up. The ground here is quite damp with many twigs lying upon it.

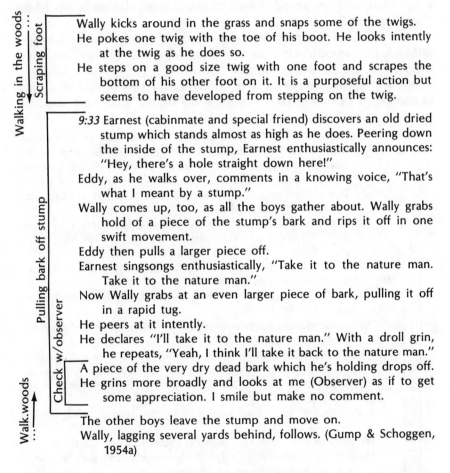

Wally kicks around in the grass and snaps some of the twigs.
He pokes one twig with the toe of his boot. He looks intently at the twig as he does so.
He steps on a good size twig with one foot and scrapes the bottom of his other foot on it. It is a purposeful action but seems to have developed from stepping on the twig.

9:33 Earnest (cabinmate and special friend) discovers an old dried stump which stands almost as high as he does. Peering down the inside of the stump, Earnest enthusiastically announces: "Hey, there's a hole straight down here!"
Eddy, as he walks over, comments in a knowing voice, "That's what I meant by a stump."
Wally comes up, too, as all the boys gather about. Wally grabs hold of a piece of the stump's bark and rips it off in one swift movement.
Eddy then pulls a larger piece off.
Earnest singsongs enthusiastically, "Take it to the nature man. Take it to the nature man."
Now Wally grabs at an even larger piece of bark, pulling it off in a rapid tug.
He peers at it intently.
He declares "I'll take it to the nature man." With a droll grin, he repeats, "Yeah, I think I'll take it back to the nature man."
A piece of the very dry dead bark which he's holding drops off.
He grins more broadly and looks at me (Observer) as if to get some appreciation. I smile but make no comment.

The other boys leave the stump and move on.
Wally, lagging several yards behind, follows. (Gump & Schoggen, 1954a)

Episode structure in the above specimen record shows a general direction of "walking in the woods," interrupted by a highly involved and different direction of "pulling bark off stump." Other occasions of an overlapped episode may not show so much an interruption of, as a parallel action to, the overarching unit. Thus the little byplay with the observer is marked as not interrupting the "pulling bark . . ."

Since the episode of interest to us—"Pulling bark off stump"—is a naturally occurring unit it makes sense to ask about the circumstance of its initiation. Clearly, the vigorous and curious actions of Wally's peers stimulated his behavior. Initiation of the episode was coded as "Instigated." Other possibilities for initiation would be "Pressured" if the outside circumstances coerced a direction change. If no outside event manifestly triggered the direction change, the code would be "Spontaneous."

The quality of the play here was coded "Investigation and Exploration." The woods, with decomposing logs and stumps, provided support to these curious camper actions.

A second specimen example of the camp day occurred during swimming at the waterfront, where Wally noted something exciting.

Two older boys are playing a game in which one person stands with his back to the water, heels just over the edge of the dock. His opponent in the game stands opposite him and tries to upset his balance by pushing at his palms-up hands. The person poised on the edge tries to elude the thrusting hands of this opponent.

After watching this game, Wally enthusiastically tries to enlist three different peers in playing the game with him. None are willing.

Wally's shoulders droop a little as he turns and walks back from the dock towards the shore.

He sees Addie (counselor) sitting on the bank. He breaks into a run.

As he approaches he calls eagerly, "Will you come and play that game with me?"

Addie asks interestedly, "What game?"

"The one where one guy tries to push another guy in the water."

Addie laughs and asks, "What if I fall in?" She sounds as if she might play.

Wally assures her, "You won't. I'll be the one standing on the edge of the dock."

He runs to the edge of the dock, grinning from ear to ear.

He puts his heels off the edge of the dock so that he's balancing on the balls and toes of his feet.

He stands expectantly, waiting for Addie.

Addie, moving more slowly, nears Wally.

She makes a feint toward his outstretched hand.

Swimming

Playing water game with Addie

Splashing Floyd

Wally eludes her thrusting hands.

After six or eight attempts, Addie topples Wally.

Wally is laughing even as he goes down.

He comes up sputtering and laughing.

He immediately runs to the shallow area on his way back.

Floyd is playing in the sand up on the shore.

Wally deliberately goes out of his way to kick water on Floyd.

Addie calls a warning to him.

Wally, ignoring Addie, kicks more water on Floyd.

Addie calls a firmer warning.

Wally runs back to his old position on the dock, clearly ready to go again.

He giggles as he places his feet in the proper position.

Addie feints several times, Wally evading her thrusts.

Wally is grinning and giggling.

Addie connects.

Wally tries hard to right himself but only succeeds in twisting and going in the water head first.

He comes up sputtering, and announces, "Fun! Let's do it again." . . .

The game continues for several more cycles, then Wally comes up sputtering, floating on his back.

He appears to be satisfied, saying, "That's enough."

Oscar, on the dock, throws a mousetrap (made in crafts) to Wally in the water.

Wally, grinning, catches it. . . . (Gump & Schoggen, 1954a)

The overarching episode is Swimming; one unit within swimming is sufficiently involving and delineated to be identified as an episode in its own right: "Water Game." Since the "Water Game" was judged as a bounded part of the "Swimming" episode, it is not an interruption. The episode structure at one point is judged to present three episodes relatively simultaneously: Swimming, Water Game, and Splashing Floyd. The initiation of "Water Game" is clearly related to the events which preceded it and would be coded as *instigated*.

The play episode here was labeled Informal Active Game, a type of activity frequently found in the swimming setting. The physical milieu is very crucial for this kind of activity. On land, being toppled over backwards results in painful contact with an unyielding surface; over water, however, the accepting medium causes no pain. Much of the exuberance noted in water play at camp seemed related to this freedom from the usual pain involved in falling.

Wally's pleasure and full involvement in the Water Game provide data that invite relatively confident analysis that the behavior is indeed playful. However, if one includes all of a child's behavior for play analysis, it must be admitted that manifest pleasure and high involvement are often *not* present in activities which would seem, nevertheless, to represent kinds of play.

At home Wally has been around the TV set for 2½ hours. He watches but he gets other things done as well (teases baby brother, converses with other brother, etc.). These interruptions and the many restless movements may indicate that he is finding the TV presentation insufficiently active for his state but he can't seem to separate himself completely from the TV setting.

Watching TV

Getting new position . . .

Wally squirms into a new position on the davenport. He is now sitting open-legged, one leg under a cushion, another stuck way out.

Evidently this position is not comfortable for long. He plops around on the davenport and eventually lies back with his head at the end near me (observer), resting on the arm of the davenport.

Fingering string

As he lies back, Wally catches hold of a scrap of davenport trimming cloth which is about half an inch wide, very thin, and over 2 feet long.

Wally takes off his glasses and watches TV without them. (The daily serial, "The Return of Jesse James," is showing. This is a regular part of the "Happy Hank Children's Show.")

R—Wally fingers his glasses.

Then he grasps the long string and wraps it around his neck in a self-choking gesture.

He tugs on it but not hard.

Then he just lies there watching TV and absently fingering the

R——string around his neck.

(There follows a 20-minute period in which Wally checks the TV happenings, exhibits many restless movements, and does things with the string; the latter are sequenced; in abbreviated form, below.)

Now the string is again extended full length and Wally fingers the end of it . . .

Wally wraps the string twice around his neck making it fit snugly. . . .

Wally unwinds the string and immediately rewraps his neck.

He tugs gently at the string as it is wrapped twice around his neck. . . .

Wally puts the string across the middle of his head and on down over his face. . . .

Wally wraps the string around his head like an Indian headband. . . .

Wally pulls the string taut with one hand and then runs his other hand the length of string. The string is passing through the sensitive "V" where the index and the middle finger join the hand. He runs his hand back the opposite direction.

He repeats this back-and-forth movement now with the string between the pads of the index finger and the thumb. . . .

With the string held taut, Wally "walks" the fingers of his free hand from the free end to the attached end. . . .

Wally puts the string between his lips and pulls so it wriggles in his mouth. . . .

Wally makes a "bridge" of the string so that it crosses from its attachment up and over his head and back to the davenport. . . .

Wally begins to wind the string in and out of his fingers. Wally no longer holds the string.

He checks the TV picture as he has intermittently for the last 20 minutes. Happy Hank explains how Sequoia invented a symbol system for the Cherokee language. . . . (Gump & Schoggen, 1954b)

The episode structure again shows more than one unit operating. Wally keeps tracks of TV events by periodic glances at the screen (and, presumably, by listening to the sound track). At the same time, he fiddles with the string in a somewhat purposeful fashion. Actions which appear to be made without awareness and purpose are coded restless movements or *R* (e.g., Wally fingers his glasses). While Wally's involvement with the string is not high or continuous, it was usually judged not to be simply restless movement but part of an episode of doing various things with the string.

The initiation of the string episode was not directly related to some active event in Wally's environment and was coded Spontaneous. Content of this activity was coded Manipulative Amusement; such play seemed related to Wally's need for activity and stimulation which was not satisfied by the TV watching.

The preceding material relating to episode structure is pertinent to the very real problems involved in describing naturally occurring behavior. Although behavior units may appear in a single uncomplicated sequence, frequently two or three units operate simultaneously with some larger episodes enclosing smaller ones, with smaller ones sometimes interrupting larger ones, and so forth. The investigation of behavior in a manner which preserves natural temporal differentiations is a significant challenge. I have tried to illustrate that ecological psychology offers conceptual resources in meeting that challenge (see Wright, 1967, for full explication).

With a coding of circumstances around changes in behavior direction, one can ask whether camp or home was the more stimulating environment. Wally engaged in slightly more than 1,000 episodes on each day. For all of these (play and nonplay), a significantly larger proportion were instigated at camp. Camp was more stimulating. On the other hand, freedom from coercion was the norm in both environments; only 1 in 20 episodes were pressured.

The proportion of play episodes among all episodes was substantially similar at camp and home (27% and 30% respectively). The kinds of play manifest on the 2 days were quite different. To present this material it is necessary to indicate the kinds of play that were noted in the two situations. The major categories identified are listed below. Full definitions for each category are available in the basic reference (Gump, Schoggen, & Redl, 1963). The categories are listed from the most to the least frequently identified.

Watching	Stunts
Teasing	Rough and Tumble
Investigation and Exploration	Informal Active Games
Drama (Histrionics)	Construction
Unorganized Sport	Stationary Game
Manipulative Amusement	Formal Active Game

One persisting issue in our field is that of situational versus personal determination of behavior. In this study, behavior of one person occurs in two very different molar environments: camp and home. If play is mostly determined by the person variables, the play on both days should show similarity; if situational factors are paramount, the play at home should not be congruent with play at camp.

A simple operation for testing similarity is to rank the play forms from most to least utilized for each day and determine the correlation between the rankings. However, the concept of "most utilized" can refer to number of episodes in each category or to the amount of time of these episodes. It can be inferred that the number of episodes represents the number of occasions a particular form was attempted, whereas the amount of time in episodes of various types reflects the amount of environmental support given these attempts. An example of this inference supported by the records is Watching behavior. Wally was sensitively tuned to the passive intake of conflict and aggression. At camp, he watched intently the numerous counselor–camper and camper–camper conflicts; however, such events were of short duration. At home, the TV set presented prolonged doses of aggressive behavior and took up much of Wally's time. The result was that Watching (for "fun") was more frequent at camp but much more prolonged at home.

When frequency of episodes was the measure of category utilization, Wally's play was somewhat similar at camp and home (Tau = .49, $p < .01$). However, when amount of time in episodes was ranked, the correlation between play in the two environments disappeared (Tau = −.16, $p > .40$). It was inferred that camp and home permitted similarity in play attempts but supported the attempts quite differentially.

What then, were major differences in play form for the camp and the home days? At camp, Investigation and Exploration was much more frequent and of much greater duration than at home. Also, Drama, Unorganized Sport, and Construction (Wally built a dam) showed decidedly greater duration at camp. Home was marked by more frequent episodes and longer durations of Manipulative Amusement. Durations for Watching, Formal Stationary Games, and Formal Active Games were much longer at home. In sum, play time at camp was less formal or constrained and more physically active. Only one kind of free-wheeling active play was more important at home: Rough and Tumble. This exception did not change the balance, however.

These camp–home differences can be related to differences in the settings available to Wally. The woods yielded 27 Investigation and Exploration play episodes (all home and neighborhood settings yielded only 10). The woods and its tree hut was also the support for many of the Drama episodes; these included pretend ambushes on the ground, and histrionic challenges from the tree hut to peers below. Unorganized Sport (action simply for action's sake) was frequent at the waterfront, on the paths through the woods and on the trees in the woods.

In contrast, Manipulative Amusement at home was mostly a correlate or by-product of extended TV watching. Rough and Tumble play was safe for Wally at home where all four siblings were younger than he. Attempts at rough housing with peers at camp resulted in actual hostilities and was therefore not safe and not "play." The predominance of traditional sedentary and active games at home reflected the frequent provision of these action structures, in the home, in the street, and in the park. The camp did not offer formal competitive games.

The material on Wally's 2 days in contrasting environments shows that naturally occurring units in the behavior stream not only can be identified but that they can be used to answer, in a quantified manner, questions about the impact of the different environments upon the initiation of behavior, and the quality of behavior, in this case the contrasting qualities of play behavior.

RESEARCH ON PLAY SETTINGS

The strong influences of settings upon camp behavior has been confirmed in other camp studies. The social and physical behaviors of cabin groups were recorded with short specimen records as the same groups experienced swimming, crafts, cookouts, and dining hall suppers. (Gump & Kounin, 1959; Gump, Schoggen, & Redl, 1957; Gump & Sutton–Smith, 1955).

Setting-behavior associations were also convincing in the day-long specimen records of children in their small town. Barker (1968) summarized the aspects of this setting-behavior relationship. First, it was repeatedly documented that several aspects of the behavior of a child often changed dramatically as that child moved from one setting to another. Secondly, the behaviors of different children in the same setting were more similar than the behavior of any one in different settings. Third, the congruence of child behavior and setting is most substantial between the major configurations of behavior and setting, not between momentary and specific child behaviors and immediate and varied inputs from the setting environment. A child in a circle game setting may tease a neighbor, pay attention to out-of-game events, break a single rule about taking turns, and so forth, but, in the usual case, the overall requirements of game play from the setting and the overall trends of the child's behavior will fit. The setting, in the large, "has its own way."

The coercivity of settings is of course recognized by everyone at the level of what might be called "program enactment." That is, if a child is in a running game, the child will run; a child in an art group will most likely draw. The coercivity however, extends beyond these obvious associations to influence the amount and quality of social interaction, and the emotional experience of setting participants.

Before examining some of the evidence for setting coercivity, it is necessary to define what is meant by settings and to indicate how settings qualities—as they relate to this shaping of their inhabitants behavior—might be described.

The setting is a *context* for behavior but of a very specific kind. Current uses of *context* are varied, sometimes amorphous, and often tautological.

In anthropological studies, context is often described with variables from tradition or culture; specific observed behaviors become meaningful when "viewed in context." *Context* here is not a first-order reality but a summary abstraction of many realities. (See Cheska's *Play as Context* for examples.) On the other hand, cognitive psychologists use context in the most minute sense; specific situational inputs are "context" and the debate is between input-behavior "interactional approach" and a so-called "contextual event" conception of person-situation relationships. (Rogoff, 1982).

The tautological issue arises when we describe an external ecological context by targeting only those aspects of that context that the subject selects and gives meaning to. In this case, we describe a phenomenon by a subject's reaction to it (perception and interpretation) and then we may explain the subject's action by referring to this perception and interpretation as causing the action. What we are doing is relating one kind of subject response to another kind. This circularity may give us an understanding of the individual but it does not let us learn about the effects of ecological realities upon psychological ones.

The setting used by ecological psychologists has a physical locus, is bounded in space and time, operates according to a program of actions or a "standing pattern of behavior," which is congruent with and enclosed by its physical milieu (Barker, 1968). Settings are places with programs; settings are ecological—not psychological or social—phenomena. Nursery school playground times, dodge-ball games, block play in operation, folk dancing sessions—all are examples of play settings. Although these ecological contexts are ubiquitous and successfully utilized by ordinary people in their daily lives, they have been given inadequate attention by social scientists. In psychology, if the context becomes a part of the environment, it frequently is reduced to aspects of the physical milieu. For example, the chapter titled "Play" in the *Handbook of Child Psychology* offers a section on "Ecological Influences" in which objects, enclosures, or population density are the samples of ecological influences (Rubin, Fein, & Vandenberg, 1983). No mention is made of the way program, or the nature of the "standing pattern of behavior" might contribute to play. The result is that play, in these studies, is seen as influenced only by the physical milieu aspects of its context.

One of the difficulties in appreciating the reality of the setting is probably related to the fixation upon it only as a context. From the point of view of a psychologist centering upon an individual subject, the setting *is* a context. But the setting, approached from an ecological level, is an *entity*. Settings are bounded systems—perhaps not as tightly bounded nor as internally integrated as the systems we call persons—but systems nonetheless. Therefore on its own level, the setting is an entity, not a context. Communities have been described as assemblies of setting entities (Barker & Schoggen, 1973). Ecological psychologists would maintain that such description provides essentials about the community as environments for people not available when other units or entities are employed (persons or groups, for example).

Since settings appear often in assemblies, the question of where to draw boundaries arises. A baseball game is one part of setting operations in a playground, which itself is only one section of a public park, which is a portion of a neighborhood environment, and so on. Where does one draw the line? (Experience shows that finding boundaries is not the difficult part; these are clear to common perception. But *which* of the discernible boundaries to employ is more problematic.)

The first level of setting identification is intuitive; townspeople and psychologists can identify the local drugstore as a setting; spatial and temporal boundaries of a drugstore operation are clear. However, two questions about boundaries arise. First, the drugstore manifestly has within it three different setting operations: a fountain area with seating accommodations, a complete pharmacy, and a merchandise area. Shall each of these be identified as settings? Secondly, the drugstore is just one of a complex of retail establishments around the town square. Should any or all of these be seen as joining the drugstore setting?

The problem of internal and external differentiation of units can be solved by proposing a setting unit of a specified degree of independence from settings seemingly related to it. Operations for measuring degrees of independence have been developed. One can note the extent of overlap between settings which might be related. Do the same leaders operate in both settings? Does the same population use the two settings? Are the settings contiguous in space and time? In all, seven observable and measurable dimensions of overlap can be quantified as measures of independence. If the sum of independence goes beyond a set point, the settings are separate, or independent; if the sum drops below the set point, the settings are two subsettings of one larger setting entity. (See Barker, 1968; or Schoggen, in press.)

Persons responsible for habitats for children establish settings and setting clusters for their care and development. Some of these settings are intended to enable, possibly enhance, children's play. To illustrate the use of setting units and setting variances in the study of play, the work of Kounin and his associates can be useful (Kounin & Sherman, 1979).

The Kounin group carried out a variety of researches based on videotapes taken in a university nursery school. The primary data were of two types; first, session-long records of 37 children, aged 29 to 65 months. A persisting question for different studies employing these specimen records was: How are the various settings of the school associated with behavior variables of the individual child occupants? The second type of primary data was 596 videotapes of "lessons" for the same nursery children. These short, teacher-led periods occurred in a small room where an elevated camera could cover almost all of the action space.

Employing the 37 videotaped individual child records, Rosenthal (1973) developed a unit for the individual behavior streams called an "activity chapter." These segments resembled episodes but were less fine grained. Activity chapters continued as long as the general play activity at one of the subsettings remained the same. Interspersed smaller units of behavior (e.g., interpersonal episodes) were not considered as activity starters or stoppers, unless, of course, they resulted in substantially different activities. Changes in activity chapters usually coincided with changes in site or sets of behavior objects. While episodes often average less than half a minute for children of this age, activity chapters averaged 3 minutes in duration. Once activity chapters were identified, description of their initiation and termination became feasible. Specifically, one could answer a question about child freedom: "To what extent was 'free play' really free?" Persons acquainted with day-care centers and nursery schools are aware that periods labeled "free play" often contain much teacher direction about what to play or how to play. Rosenthal examined the beginnings and endings of activity chapters to determine whether these molar units were self or teacher-directed; she found that only 9% of the beginnings and 12% of the terminations were teacher-instigated. In this institution the free play was, by and large, truly free.

Perhaps more important than this finding is the development of a method which provides an operational definition for child freedom. To an important extent, play is free when its units are begun and ended without intervention by authority figures.

Rosenthal also applied her data to the problem of the use of the nursery school subsettings. She considered two issues: Attraction power, that is, how many children use a subsetting? and Holding power, that is, how much time does a child spend at a setting? Although these variables are correlated, they are also logically and empirically distinct. Block play was a subsetting which yielded high attraction (visited by many children) but only moderate holding power (visitors did not stay for long periods). The art and the role play sites were examples of settings with high holding power while the vehicle area manifested low holding power. Holding power, Rosenthal noted, is to a setting as attention span is to a child.

What qualities of a play subsetting contribute to high holding power? A post facto analysis suggested several dimensions. Two may serve as examples: number of constituent performances and number and clarity of "progress point outs." Vehicular play, as carried out here, involved simple leg-pumping actions with some arm movement. Role play, for example, involved talking, motoric action, thinking (fantasizing) and so on. Progress point outs occur rarely in vehicular play (one just goes "round and round") but in art there were repeated feedbacks indicating that one was changing the environment and was closing in on creating "a picture." The variety of constituent actions and the presence of progress point outs are just two of a larger group of variables that one might apply to play activities which may determine child response to various play settings and formats (Rosenthal, 1973).

The same 37 videotaped records used by Rosenthal were also employed by two other researchers for different questions. Houseman (1972) studied interpersonal conflict in relation to demographic variables (age, gender, race) and to setting factors; the latter turned out to be much more predictive of behavior than the former. Fisk (1975) identified imitation behaviors in nursery school and found them more frequent in some settings (e.g., pathways and role play sites) and less frequent in others (e.g., art easels, puzzle table).

All of the individual record investigations pointed to the differential effects of subsettings on children's actions and emotions in the free play sessions.

The tapes of the 596 lessons provided research challenges and opportunities different from those associated with the individual records. Most fundamentally, the target of analysis could be the setting entity itself with its particular physical milieu and its standing pattern of behavior. The nature of the lesson and the simultaneous and continuous behavior of teacher and children could be examined with such tapes. The replay possibilities in the tapes mean that events could be isolated and then the behaviors and conditions either leading up to or following from the event could be studied. Of course, such replay is possible with the individual records, but the span of action and actors was much more limited.

The group activities provided by lessons were not nearly so academic as the word "lessons" might imply. Many represented kinds of directed play. Examples would include a short arts or crafts activity, a teacher-led story time, group discussion of "what parents do at work," a music and movement session with chanting and marching, or dancing. Lessons were usually short (5 to 15 minutes) and involved four to eight children. No specific learning outcome was customarily sought; rather the goal was exposure to different enriching objects and activities.

After considerable viewing of tapes and reflection upon them, a method of characterizing the lessons was evolved (Kounin & Gump, 1974). The key conception was that participants are guided by the *signal systems* inherent in these group action structures. As a part of its standing pattern of behavior, each lesson setting has a characteristic stimuli pattern which tells participants what to do and when to do it. Some signal systems are simple and emphatic. For example, when the teacher reads a story, the signal originates from a single emitter and the child participant is to focus upon that emission. Furthermore, the signal is predominately continuous. At certain points in the story reading, child participants may be asked for contributions and at these times the dominant pattern of single source continuous signal changes to one of multiple signal sources. This latter pattern is typical throughout the child discussion lessons. Here children, who at this age, often communicate in a hesitant and unclear fashion, provide multiple and often discontinuous signals for one another.

Another dimension of lesson signal system is its insulating capacity. In individual construction, for example, participants attend to their own materials, to actions with the materials, and to the results of their actions upon the materials. For example, a child in an art lesson may be given a paper pie plate, pieces of colored paper, scissors, and paste. The goal is to produce a "pie-plate face." As the child cuts a bit of blue paper and pastes it to the plate, the one-eyed plate shows a child-caused change in the object plus a suggestion for a next act—the adding of another eye. The resulting plate with eyes show more child-caused change and suggests the need for a nose. The cycle of child action, changed objects, and suggestion for further change continues. Not only are the signals continuous—given appropriate child competences and project supplies—but they form a kind of closed behavior–environment circuit.

One more aspect of signal sources can be the intensity of the stimulation involved. The music and movement activity structures involve double stimulations created by strong external sources (e.g., the "beat" of music) and by vigorous internal sources (e.g., the gross motor activity and the stimulation of singing). For children, these are exciting and possible "loosening" signal qualities.

With the dimensions just described in mind, it was possible to relate the qualities of lesson signal systems to play involvement. (Involvement here was the proportion of time that child participants were engaged in the actions appropriate to the activity. Thus, children who were stimulated by the setting but engaged in inappropriate behaviors would be scored "low" in involvement.) Results showed that the high continuity single source signal systems (e.g., teacher reads, or record plays) produced significantly more child involvement than the multiple and often discontinuous signal sources (e.g., discussion) or the music and movement activities. The high insulation or "closed circuit" activities (e.g., crafts) showed even more involvement being significantly higher than all other types. As noted, the music and movement or vigorous stimulation activities were relatively low in involvement. Although the official signals for music and movement were continuous, they were also highly stimulating. Further, inspection of the tapes showed that children with their focus upon the wider scene, took one another as signal sources and imitated or elaborated upon one another's often "unofficial" behaviors. The music and movement action structures clearly lacked insulation. Additional proof of this lack of insulation and of high stimulation was provided by Davenport (1976) who showed that deviancy contagion was highest for the music and movement activity and lowest for the individual construction lessons.

While the music and movement signal system was productive of less involvement and more deviancy contagion, it also yielded another behavior of interest to those who are interested in children's pleasure. Sherman (1975) identified a form of child reaction which he labeled "group glee." When more than half of the group engaged in joyful screaming, loud laughter, or expressive motoric gyrations, group glee was said to operate. These gleeful outbursts were several times more frequent in the music and movement activities than in the individual construction formats.

Sherman (1975) exploited the replay possibilities of the TV tapes by observing and analyzing events both prior to and subsequent to the gleeful incident. One question of interest was the extent to which gleeful outbursts represented spontaneous and simultaneous individual reactions or a chain reaction in which one child initiator "contages" another child and this child another, and so on. A review of the taped microhistories of the glee incidents indicated that most glee was not a spontaneous and simultaneous reaction of individuals; rather, 70% of the outbursts were contagious; that is, they started with one glee initiator and then spread throughout the group.

Observed events just subsequent to the gleeful incident showed that teachers intervened more often when contagion was operating but that with or without intervention, the incidents were usually short (one-half lasting less than 10 seconds) and 7 times out of 10 group glee created no significant disruption of the planned activity.

The Kounin group has provided us with ample demonstration of the relation of ecological variables to those of child play behavior. The methodology of this project and of those described earlier can illustrate that naturalistic data can be made amenable to systematic and quantitative research. It is not necessary to view naturalistic data as merely "suggestive" or "exploratory." Further, to ecological psychologists it is quite improper to equate naturalistic investigation to that current favorite, "qualitative research."

SUMMARY AND PERSPECTIVES

Possible contributions of ecological psychology to play research can deal with research *stance,* or to more specific resources involved in concepts and methods. By *stance,* we refer to the general position taken about what the basic question of the researcher shall be. For ecological psychologists the basic question is "What goes on here?" (Barker, 1965). "Here" in this case refers to individual behavior and to setting operations in naturally occurring situations. Ecological research takes its basic direction from that simple question, in contrast to leads derived from experimentally driven theories. Admittedly, theories from whatever source are necessary for our science; furthermore, they often serve as useful guides in analyzing naturalistic data. But, for ecological psychologists, the "What goes on here" query takes precedent over efforts to prove a set of theory-derived hypotheses.

Focus upon children's behavior in their natural habitats turns out to pose problems which were of no or minor importance in tightly controlled experimental research. A foremost problem is unitization. In the more experimental studies, both behavioral and environmental units are much determined by the investigators' intrusions. An environmental unit may be a short session in a highly defined situation or an input from the experimenter (a question, a rating scale). Behavioral units, then, easily become subjects' reactions to these inputs.

If researchers are to study the real worlds of children and how children deal with them, concepts and methods for the description of both environmental units and behavioral units will be necessary and those from experimental research are likely to be insufficient. Particularly, the experimental method of deriving units will likely obscure or destroy the inherent structure available in the naturally occurring behavior or setting operation. The contribution of such units as episodes or activity chapters makes it possible to preserve behavior structure as well as to derive interesting findings regarding the initiation of behavior and its play content.

If we are to study play behavior in complex and investigator-free environments, we need methods of mapping, of unitizing that environment. The use of settings, as defined by ecological psychologists, is a feasible method to create such natural world units and maps of units. Of even more value may be the developing systems of describing these units, as opposed to simply naming them. Descriptions limited to such labels as "nursery school free play" or "active playground games" provides no precise identification of the ecological dimensions which might impinge upon children's behavior and experience.

The ecological task of describing settings in systematic dimensions is incomplete. Available are general variables such as the setting's social purposes (action patterns) or its use of behavior mechanisms (Barker, 1968; Schoggen, in press). A more fine-grained and activity-focused system is still being developed. This kind of program characterization is analogous to some of the dimensions developed from the signal system concept (Kounin & Gump, 1974). A more recent attempt (Gump, 1987) analyzes settings' programs in terms of their activity requirements. For example, the program of a setting may be such that it offers very active or relatively passive input to participants; it may call for highly active and overt participant response (e.g., game of tag) or it may emphasize quiet and covert reaction (e.g., listening to a story).

This same system can describe the action relationships set up by the program. Some settings call for cooperative relationships, some ask for competitive responses, some ask for both (as in team games), and some prescribe parallel or even independent participant orientation and action.

Researchers active in play phenomena will, of course, make their own decisions about what aspects of ecological psychology described here they will find useful or they wish to see developed. My own perspective is that there are several areas that should receive research attention.

We need studies which describe and analyze children's activity throughout their territorial ranges (not just studies in experiments or in convenient but limited natural areas such as nursery schools and playgrounds). Once such studies are available we need taxonomic effort. Within the extensive variety of children's activity, what shall we call play? Can a system of dimensions—rather than categories—of play behavior be developed?

Finally, with advances in descriptions of the programs of settings as indicated above, what can be learned about how variations in settings' action structures shape play behaviors, and developments within the child?

REFERENCES

Barker, R.G. (1965). Explorations in ecological psychology. *American Psychologist, 20*(1), 1–14.

Barker, R.G. (1968). *Ecological psychology.* Stanford, CA: Stanford University Press.

Barker, R.G., Dembo, T., & Lewin, K. (1941). Frustration and regression: A study of young children. *University of Iowa Studies in Child Welfare, 18*(1).

Barker, R., & Schoggen, P. (1973). *Qualities of community life.* San Francisco: Jossey Boss.

Barker, R.G., & Wright, H.F. (1955). *Midwest and its children.* New York: Harper & Row.

Cheska, A.T. (1981). *Play as context.* New York: Leisure Press.

Davenport, G.G. (1976). The effects of lesson's signal systems upon the duration and spread of deviancy. Doctoral dissertation, Wayne State University, Detroit. *Dissertation Abstract International, 37,* 2736A.

Fawl, C.L. (1963). Disturbances experienced by children in their natural habitats. In R. Barker (Ed.), *Stream of behavior* (pp. 99–126). New York: Appleton-Century-Crofts.

Fisk, W.T. (1975). An ecological study of imitation in preschool children. Doctoral dissertation, Wayne State University, Detroit. *Dissertation Abstract International, 36,* 7289A.

Gump, P. (1987). School and classroom environments. In I. Altman & D. Stokols (Eds.), *Handbook of environmental psychology* (pp. 691–732). New York: Wiley.

Gump, P., & Kounin, J. (1959). Issues raised by ecological and "classical" research efforts. *Merrill–Palmer Quarterly of Behavior & Development, 6,* 145–152.

Gump, P., & Schoggen, P. (1954a). *Wally O'Neill at camp.* Unpublished manuscript. (available on loan from senior author)

Gump, P., & Schoggen, P. (1954b). *Wally O'Neill at home.* Unpublished manuscript. (available on loan from senior author)

Gump, P., Schoggen, P., & Redl, F. (1957). The camp milieu and its immediate effects. *Journal of Social Issues, 13*(1), 40–46.

Gump, P., Schoggen, P., & Redl, F. (1963). The behavior of the same child in different milieus. In R. Barker (Ed.), *Stream of behavior* (pp. 169–202). New York: Meredith Publications.

Gump, P., & Sutton–Smith, B. (1955). Activity settings and social interaction. *American Journal of Orthopsychiatry, 25*(4), 755–760.

Houseman, J.A. (1972). An ecological study of interpersonal conflict among preschool children. Doctoral dissertation, Wayne State University, Detroit. *Dissertation Abstract International, 33,* 6175A.

Kounin, J., & Gump, P. (1974). Signal systems of lesson settings and task related behavior of preschool children. *Journal of Educational Psychology, 66,* 554–562.

Kounin, J., & Sherman, L. (1979). School environments as behavior settings. *Theory Into Practice, 18*(3), 145–151.

Lewin, K., Dembo, T., Festinger, L., & Sears, P. (1944). Level of aspiration. In J. McV Hunt (Ed.), *Personality and the behavior disorders.* New York: Ronald.

McBride, S.R. (1981). The culture of toy research. In A.T. Cheska (Ed.), *Play as context.* West Point, NY: Leisure Press.

Piaget, J. (1951). *Play, dreams, and imitation in childhood.* New York: Norton.

Rogoff, B. (1982). Integrating context and cognitive development. In M.E. Lamb & A.L. Brown (Eds.), *Advances in developmental psychology* (Vol. 2). Hillsdale, NJ: Erlbaum.

Rosenthal, B.L. (1973). An ecological study of free play in the nursery school. Doctoral dissertation, Wayne State University, Detroit. *Dissertation Abstract International, 34,* 4004A.

Rubin, K.H., Fein, G.G., & Vandenberg, B. (1983). In P. Mussen (Ed.), *Handbook of child psychology* (Vol. 4, pp. 693–774). New York: Wiley.

Schoggen, P. (in press). *Behavior Settings: A revision of Barkers's Ecological Psychology.* Stanford, CA: Stanford Press.

Sherman, L. (1975). Glee in small groups of preschool children. *Child Development, 46,* 53–61.

Willems, E.P. (1965). An ecological orientation in psychology. *Merrill–Palmer Quarterly, 11,* 317–343.

Wright, H.F. (1967). *Recording and analyzing child behavior.* New York: Harper & Row.

4
Issues in the Study of Children's Rough-and-Tumble Play*

MICHAEL BOULTON AND PETER K. SMITH
University of Sheffield, England

INTRODUCTION

The main focus of this chapter is a consideration of some of the methodological issues in the naturalistic study of children's play. We shall concentrate on rough-and-tumble play (r/t); however, the issues raised should be applicable to other forms of play as well. Of particular concern will be the issue of studying this form of behavior in its proper ecological context. Such an approach clearly enhances the general ecological validity of the data obtained; more specifically, it enables the researcher to record certain aspects of behavior which only reveal themselves when the behavior is studied as it occurs in natural settings. For example, it is only through studying play in realistic situations (such as the school playground) that we can see who children play with. Is it only with people they like or dislike, who are stronger or weaker than themselves? This information, which can be obtained by combining observational and sociometric data, would be missing from studies carried out in artificial settings. Moreover, by recording prolonged periods of playground behavior, we are able to carry out sequential analyses and determine which other behaviors, if any, characteristically occur in close temporal proximity to the kinds of play we are interested in. This may be important in considering the causes of the behavior and its likely functions (for

* We are grateful to Rivka Glaubman and Louise Stout for their help with reliability checks, and to the headmaster, children and staff at Athelstan Middle School in Sheffield, England. Michael Boulton also acknowledges the financial support of the Science and Engineering Research Council, London.

example, the nonaggressive or aggressive causation or function of r/t).

This chapter will use our current project on r/t as an example of a study concerned with the ecological context of children's play. Although constructive (object) play and symbolic (fantasy) play have received much research attention over the last decades, r/t has had only a handful of publications specifically devoted to it (see Humphreys & Smith, 1984, for a discussion). Yet r/t takes up some 10% of natural playground activity throughout the infant and middle school years. The impetus for our project came from a desire to extend previous research which had only examined ecological issues to a limited extent. Studies by Blurton–Jones (1967, 1972), Smith and Connolly (1972), and DiPietro (1981) gave us much important information, revealing such things as structural details and time spent on the behavior, as well as age and sex differences in occurrence, but much less about "deeper" contextual issues. For example, a sequential approach to the study of this form of play has been lacking in previous research, yet instances of r/t do not simply occur in isolation, but as part of a much wider temporal and social context, with antecedent and consequent behaviors, and in a matrix of other people. The same is true of other forms of play occurring in natural settings, and there is no reason why some of the points mentioned will not be of use to researchers studying these as well.

The term r/t is generally applied to playful activities that appear to mimic more aggressive behaviors. Common actions are play fighting and chasing in various forms as well as a wide variety of other physical contact activities, such as colliding. Although outwardly these behaviors may appear aggressive in nature, research has indicated that this is not usually the case. Children and adults, in the main, reliably distinguish between the two types of behavior, drawing on various criteria to do so, for example, strength of blow, facial expression, and prior knowledge of the children involved.

R/t can be a fairly frequent activity, taking up something of the order of 5% to 10% of children's free-play time. It is seen in children from the age of 2 right through to adolescence and beyond (Humphreys & Smith, 1984). Cross-cultural studies have revealed its occurrence in a wide variety of cultural settings, some very different from our own. Whiting and Whiting (1975), for example, have reported it in Japan, the Philippines, India, Kenya, and Mexico as well as the United States.

After a long period of neglect, researchers are becoming more aware of the importance of understanding this form of play. An initial aim of our current project is a detailed structural analysis of r/t, to arrive at a clearer idea of the various forms this behavior may take. The project can be envisaged as consisting of four stages. First, an initial or pilot stage involving informal observation. Second, the collection of a permanent video record of discrete bouts of r/t, used to develop a taxonomy. Third, the collection of sequential data in the form of spoken commentaries on audiotape. This provides the bulk of our data for analysis, the fourth stage of the project.

In the first of the five sections in this chapter, we shall consider the importance of defining or offering criteria to distinguish the play behavior(s) in question and the ways this has been and can be done. We would argue that this is the essential starting point in a sequence of methodological steps. It is important because coworkers in a particular field use terms and concepts every day and come to, implicitly if not explicitly, know where they are applicable. Workers in different institutions and settings do not have this advantage of continuous contact and thus it is essential that clear definitions or criteria are included in published work. We shall mention briefly some of the consequences of failing to do this.

The second section will look at more traditional methodological issues associated with studying play in naturalistic settings. Initially we shall look at methods of recording data, focusing on the advantages and disadvantages of video, film, and portable tape recorders. Going on from this we shall mention some factors which may reduce the reliability and validity of the data, illustrating how we tackled them.

The third section will consider some of the issues associated with the development of a behavioral taxonomy. Relating to issues raised in the first section, we shall mention some of the reasons for wanting a taxonomy, steps in its creation, its limitations, and checks on its reliability in use.

The penultimate section will briefly consider what we feel has been an underrepresented form of analysis, sequential analysis. Again, rather than focusing on analysis per se, we shall concentrate on how various methodological considerations both influence and are influenced by the type of questions about sequences asked by the researcher. Finally a short, concluding section summarizes the main points.

WHAT IS ROUGH AND TUMBLE: DEFINITIONS AND CRITERIA

Recent writers working in the field of play have found it necessary to distinguish between r/t and other forms of play. It is probably true to say that both theoretical and empirical considerations have exerted an influence. With respect to theory, by breaking play down into discrete subcategories (e.g., r/t, fantasy, object, active physical, language) the functional and causal aspects of each can be considered separately.

Empirical studies have also found evidence to support the view that r/t should be seen as a separate play category. These have been heavily influenced by ethological theories and methods in that the majority were observational in nature and were conducted under naturalistic conditions (classrooms and school playgrounds). Some preliminary studies concentrated on a fine-grained analysis of the structure of play, based on molecular behavioral action patterns, and incorporated statistical techniques such as factor analysis (e.g., Blurton–Jones, 1967, 1972) and principal component analysis (e.g., Smith, 1973; Smith & Connolly, 1972). These studies identified r/t as a separate behavioral factor. In particular, Blurton–Jones identified a cluster of behaviors—"laugh," "jumps," "run," "open beat," and "wrestling"—that tended to co-occur within 5-minute intervals at separate times from "work," and Smith's analysis supported this picture. He found that "laugh," "smile," "chase/flee," "wrestle/tumble," and "play noise" co-occurred significantly within half-minute intervals.

One problem with the level of analysis reported in these studies is that they do not fully clarify the distinction between the (proto-typical) behaviors of r/t (fighting or chasing) and more general physical activity play. After considering this point, Humphreys and Smith concluded that "despite some overlap, it seems to us sensible to distinguish 'vigorous activity play' from 'rough and tumble play'" (1984, p. 245).

Given that it is meaningful to look at r/t as a separate taxonomic component of play, it is necessary to propose a definition or at least offer some criteria which would help us agree that a particular behavior was or was not r/t. This is important for a number of reasons, not least in connection with conceptual clarity. The best illustration of this can perhaps be made using the very influential set of studies by Bandura and his associates (e.g., Bandura, Ross, & Ross, 1961, 1963) which looked at the influence of models on children's aggression. Later evidence suggests that these studies confounded r/t and aggression. This was almost certainly due to the two types of behavior being made up of structurally similar action patterns. For example, Blurton–Jones (1972) points out that aggression was not defined in these studies nor was a distinction made between play fighting and real fighting. Consequently, some playful behaviors may have been mistakenly classified as aggressive. This is further suggested by some of the accompanying photographs, which show a clear play face ("smiles with open jaws, with or without laughing noises," Blurton–Jones, p. 106). Many play researchers, and probably most lay persons as well, would accept this as one of the strongest and most unambiguous criteria for indicating that an interaction is playful. It could be argued that stating publicly the appropriate definitions or criteria to distinguish r/t and aggression would greatly reduce the likelihood of confounding them in the future. Even some recent studies (e.g., Ladd, 1983; Potts, Huston, & Wright, 1986) have still treated these two kinds of behavior as if they can be meaningfully scored together under one category.

However, as with play itself, defining r/t has proved extremely difficult. Essentially the problem is one of obtaining a definition that is at once both general enough to incorporate all behaviors which most observers would agree are r/t play and specific enough to exclude those which seem nonappropriate. This objective has not yet been completely satisfied.

A pragmatic approach to this problem is the paradigm case approach, suggested by Matthews and Matthews (1982). This involves identifying a set of prototypical instances which almost everyone would agree are examples of the behavior concerned. For example, a paradigm case approach to r/t might describe it as play fighting or grappling to achieve superior position. However, the paradigm case approach, while helpful in signifying what are obvious cases of the behavior, is not so helpful in clarifying more borderline instances which might or might not qualify (e.g., shadow boxing or colliding). This difficulty can be alleviated by specifying certain criteria which identify r/t; the more criteria are present, the more sure the identification. Smith and Vollstedt (1985) used this approach in considering the definition of play generally. As far as r/t is concerned, Humphreys and Smith (1984) implicitly adopted this approach in part in describing r/t as "agonistic behaviors, specifically wrestling, hitting and chasing, in a playful mode as indicated primarily by laughter and children staying together through and after the episode." The latter part of this quote highlights two criteria which may distinguish r/t from aggression. The results of studies by Humphreys and Smith (1984) and Smith and Lewis (1985) suggest that outcome and facial/vocal criteria when used in conjunction are useful in indicating whether an encounter is playful or aggressive, even though the other actions are seemingly similar. However, they also highlight the fact that a small but noteworthy number of exceptions do exist. Although such criteria may be useful for separating r/t from aggression, they may not be so useful in distinguishing r/t from other forms of activity (e.g., other forms of play, or vigorous physical activity). In any event, it may be useful to combine the use of identifying criteria, with attempts to subdivide the type of behavioral domain we are considering to some extent. After all, different criteria might differentially apply to different kinds of r/t. Laughter may be more characteristic of some types than others, for example. Therefore, while not denying the use of identifying criteria, we feel it is also worthwhile to develop a more comprehensive behavioral taxonomy, and at present we are engaged in such an endeavor.

Before presenting the details it may be useful to consider how this approach fits in with previous work. In the early 1970s the focus of research was on identifying discrete action patterns that temporal analysis suggested tended to co-occur within specified intervals. These studies may best be viewed as providing the behavioral foundation upon which subsequent work has been based (i.e., suggesting rather than testing hypotheses). Following on from this work were attempts to see r/t in more ecologically valid terms, so that factors such as context, outcome, and children's perceptions were examined in relation to these action patterns. With respect to contextual features, Humphreys and Smith (1987) looked at whether r/t was initiated by challenge, such as a fight, or by invitation, such as sociable games. They also looked at outcome data to see whether r/t led to the participants staying together or separating at the end of an encounter.

The present approach is, we believe, a logical extension of these two empirical trends. It attempts to break down behavior labeled r/t into discrete types and then relate each back to those ecological factors which have been shown to be important as well as identifying new ones. This would enable the following sorts of questions to be tackled; Would one type of r/t be more likely to lead to the participants separating after the end of an encounter than another? Is one type of r/t engaged in more often by one sex than another? Do children engage more in one type of r/t with people they like rather than those they dislike?

Besides specific questions such as these, we argue that a taxonomy is a vital step toward the difficult goal of answering functional questions about r/t. Behaviors which in the past have been lumped together as r/t very often are dissimilar in structure. Thus, functional hypotheses presented in the past may stand little chance of becoming verified in the future since, essentially, they have been applied to a heterogeneous set of behaviors which, for convenience purposes only, have been placed in the same category. To bring this point home, we would like to consider perhaps the most prevalent functional hypothesis to date concerning r/t, that it provides practice in specific skills such as those of fighting or hunting (Humphreys & Smith, 1984; Symons, 1978).

Humphreys and Smith (1987) attempted to scrutinize this hypothesis by looking at evidence from a number of sources, but particularly the nature of partner choices in r/t bouts. Specifically, they found that 11-year-old children chose partners whom they perceived as closer to themselves in strength than chance would have predicted. This was taken as supportive evidence for the practice-fighting hypothesis, since it was argued that the best person to practice fighting skills with is someone who is closely matched with you for strength. A problem lies with the fact that the only measure of r/t made was quantitative and not qualitative (i.e., absolute frequency of r/t as a whole). Thus, going back to our taxonomy, it is possible that some proportion of these encounters involved nonfighting forms of r/t (e.g., chasing, swinging, running past and/or colliding), as well as those which are more like the behaviors seen during real fights. It could be argued that a more rigorous test of the practice fighting hypothesis would concentrate on those types of r/t which could, in their execution, directly prepare the individual for better combat performance. By so doing we would not introduce irrelevant data which could erroneously be taken as supportive or not supportive of the hypothesis.

Some caution is called for in this line of reasoning since, as Martin and Caro (1985) have pointed out, two behaviors may have similar structures but have different functions, or have different structures but serve the same functions. The consequence of this is "the disheartening possibility that play could be a developmental determinant of adult behavior patterns which look entirely different." (Martin & Caro, 1985, p. 91). This intriguing potentiality should be borne in mind but it should not curtail the search for a close match between structure and function. Just because something is theoretically possible does not mean that the most direct avenue of investigation should not be pursued in the first instance.

The achievement of a clear understanding of various forms of play in terms of function is notoriously difficult. We are just as interested in proximate causational processes, described by Fagen (1981, p. 54) as including "contexts and situations; eliciting, inhibiting and terminating stimuli (both internal and external); motivation; and developmental causation on the long time scale of an entire life history or on the shorter time scale of development of a particular sequence of behavior." Besides their intrinsic interest, an understanding of proximal processes may go a long way to achieving a better understanding of evolutionary functions. A taxonomy would, we argue, be useful on both levels. We can also see the value of studying the ecological context of r/t here, since many of the factors listed by Fagen will only be revealed in natural settings.

Before going on to look at the taxonomy we have developed, the next section will consider some general methodological aspects of studying play in naturalistic situations and of gathering data on which a taxonomy can be based and later used. We shall illustrate some of these aspects with examples from our current research project.

OBTAINING DATA ON ROUGH AND TUMBLE

There are a number of alternative methods of obtaining data on rough-and-tumble play. It is our intention to consider some of the more important ones here along with some very broad guidelines for indicating when one approach may be more appropriate than the other.

One decision facing researchers concerns the degree to which he or she will constrain the conditions which will prevail. Experimental studies, whether field or laboratory experiments, by their very nature involve manipulation of contextual variables of which Ss may or may not be aware. In contrast, naturalistic studies do not on their own involve any such manipulation of variables, but instead involve systematic observation and recording of behavior under "normal" conditions, that is, conditions which the researcher has not significantly changed or interfered with. Such an approach is ideally suited to a study of the ecological context of a particular behavior. The methods of observation and recording to be considered below are most usual in naturalistic studies, but they are in fact relevant to both types of study, since it is not critical whether the researcher has played a part in "setting up" the situation or not. For example, an experiment might change the configuration of the playground, or the timing of playground breaks, and examine their impact on r/t.

For many studies an observational approach is the obvious one. If so, the next decision concerns how the observations themselves are going to be recorded. It is likely that some of the methods available will be applicable at different stages of a research project. Flexibility is the key here, the researcher should be free (and willing) to switch from one to the other in order to provide data of appropriate detail and/or fit the constraints of the situation. In our study, we wished to preserve behavioral detail above the "simple" level of whether or not a particular behavior occurs within a set of sample periods, as in, for example, one–zero sampling. Although these latter methods are appropriate in some situations and with some research questions, they have disadvantages notably in the loss of information about frequency, duration, and structure of the behavior, and the loss of any flexibility in subsequently reclassifying behavioral episodes. Two methods which preserve this information, and which we shall concentrate on, are the use of video/film cameras and the use of portable tape recorders.

Perhaps the most important technological innovation for observational research has been the widespread availability of portable video recording equipment. Hutt and Hutt (1974) have outlined five situations in which videotapes are particularly useful: (1) swift action, (2) complex action, (3) subtle behavioral changes, (4) complex behavioral sequences, and (5) the need for precise measurements of parameters.

Most pertinent to our present discussion is that videotaping of live playground action preserves maximum information about the structure of the behavior. Thus absolute frequency scores and absolute duration scores are available as is information concerning temporal sequences. Moreover, by reducing the playback speed or even analysing the record frame by frame, a rich source of information concerning the detailed structure of the behavior emerges. This method is so powerful that even aspects of structure which are not immediately apparent at normal speed may reveal themselves. The rich detail it provided was used by us early on in our project, in developing the taxonomy. Furthermore, through analyzing recorded sequences it is possible to achieve very high reliability, both within and between observers. By using the consensus coding method (see Sackett, Ruppenthal, & Gluck, 1978, p. 7) two or more researchers can review the tape until they agree that the behavior fits one or other category.

A further advantage of having a video record of the behavior is that it enables us to play it back to the subjects themselves. Such a procedure may provide information that can usefully complement that from observational recordings. This approach was used by Smith and Lewis (1985) who played video recordings of both r/t and aggressive episodes to preschoolers with the aim of determining whether children of this age could reliably discriminate between these two types of behavior, (essentially they could), and what criteria they used to do so.

All this may suggest that video recording is a panacea for play researchers. Unfortunately this is not the case. Despite these advantages, there were a number of reasons why video was not employed in the latter stage of our current study, and why, moreover, it may not be appropriate in other situations. We shall consider the drawbacks associated with the use of video.

One of the most important of these for the play researcher is that the presence of a video camera may seriously influence children and their behavior, considerably reducing the internal validity of the data. This may be less of a problem with preschool-age children, who usually are less familiar with this equipment and what its function is. However, it remains a serious problem with older children who, in our experience, find it very attractive to be filmed. A common reaction is for them to approach the camera, waving their arms in the air and shouting very loudly (unusual behavior even for children). One way around this problem would be to conceal the camera in some way. In practice, though, we found that this presents many problems. Our approach was to film from between closed curtains in an upstairs classroom. However, the word soon got out that this was happening, from children retrieving things from their desks, and it seemed that the lure of the camera was so great for many children that they did not mind acting in the way described just in case the camera was present. The extent of this problem is further revealed by our finding that there was little if any sign of the children becoming habituated to the camera even after 3 months of filming.

An alternative way around this problem of children behaving in an artificial way in front of the camera is to film children in the middle and far distance. This proved successful during the pilot stage of our study, but introduced further problems, notably the absence of any information concerning what the children said to each other. Although this was not of primary interest in our study, it was nevertheless an important drawback. One way around this problem would be to use a directional microphone in conjunction with a video camera. However, this equipment is fairly unwieldly and, in addition to the logistical humanpower difficulties, it may increase the degree of intrusion imposed upon the Ss. Alternatively, radio-microphones might be employed, but we found these too difficult to operate in practice.

A further problem of using video recorders in the playground environment lies with the fact that many children are highly mobile and thus for much of the time are likely to be out of sight of the camera. From our point of view, because an important part of our study was the analysis of extended sequences of playground action, this further ruled out its use in the latter stages.

Before leaving the problems associated with the use of video, it is also important to keep in mind the time required for analysis. This may be many times the duration of the behavior on film. Thus, for example, 2 or 3 hours of film may require up to a week to analyze.

In summary, the great strength of video lies in the preservation of the maximum amount of structural and temporal information of behavior and the flexibility that this provides in analysis. The researcher must, however, weigh this up against its relative inflexibility in actually getting the data and its often intrusive nature.

An alternative to video is the method of dictating comments about children's behavior into a portable tape recorder. This method was used by Humphreys and Smith (1984) to provide quantitative data on rough and tumble in middle-school children. By using a portable tape recorder, the observer is able to work in the playground itself and is free to follow a focal child for considerable lengths of time even if that child is highly mobile. This flexibility was one reason why we decided to adopt this approach in the latter stages of the project. The observer's presence in the playground, though, introduces further problems, an important one being that the children's behavior may be changed as a result of this presence. The only way around this problem is for the observer to spend considerable periods becoming so familiar to the children in the playground that eventually they habituate to his or her presence. By neither initiating interactions with children nor responding to their initiation attempts we found, as did Connolly and Smith (1972) and Sluckin (1981) with preschoolers and 5- to 13-year-olds, that they fairly soon lost interest in the observer. This procedure was so effective that the observer was able to stand within a few feet of the children and quietly record their verbal and nonverbal behavior, without apparently influencing them in any appreciable way, something which would have been out of the question with video. Of course, the phrase 'in any appreciable way' may be questioned, but some aspects of our data suggest it is appropriate. As an example, middle-school children very largely refrain from swearing or fighting in front of adults who, after all, wield considerable powers of sanction against children displaying such behaviors. However, we have observed both behaviors in the current study while in close proximity, suggesting that the children are behaving "naturally" and thus attesting to the internal validity of the data. A potential problem though could be that of individual differences in the degree to which a child's behavior is changed by the observer's presence. Thus, for example, while some children may be impervious to an observer and behave the same whether he or she was there or not, some may respond by displaying increased antisocial behaviors, while others may be "on their best behavior."

This would seem to be an important issue and one which calls for empirical inquiry.

There are other reasons for believing that most children are behaving naturally in front of the observer; during the initial stages of the habituation process, they very often came over to the observer and made comments, either directly at him or indirectly about him to their friends. Moreover, at this time even when they were several yards away, they very often looked over at the observer with interest or curiosity, stopping what they were doing in the process. Both of these behaviors soon disappeared, suggesting that the observer had become a normal part of the playground scene and thus not worthy of attention.

In general then, from the point of view of the behavior being observed, it seems that the validity of data obtained in this way would not seriously be in question.

Two further and related advantages of using a portable tape recorder concern the verbal behavior of children. As already mentioned, this was not one of the primary areas of focus of our research but one which we felt merited some attention. By being in the playground itself and close to the children involved, any verbalizations related, in our case to rough and tumble, could be recorded (albeit not verbatim). This has proved especially useful in relation to our understanding of the strategy that children sometimes adopt for initiating rough and tumble, that of quasi-threat, challenge, or mock. A related point is that the observer's presence in the playground facilitates on-the-spot interviews. These have proved very valuable to us in situations where children behaved in unusual or unexpected ways. To illustrate, on one occasion we were baffled by a particular sequence of rough and tumble which was unusual in a number of ways; it was especially boisterous, involved an unusually large number of participants (up to 10) of both sexes, was made up of unusual physical actions and lasted longer than normal. It was only when one of the participants was asked what they were doing that a clearer picture emerged. Apparently they were playing "miners and pigs (police)." Armed with this information we were better able to make sense of some of the unusual actions manifested, something which would have been virtually impossible if we had filmed the sequence from an upstairs classroom window.

An important problem with using a portable tape recorder is that structural detail of behavior is lost. The main concern for any researcher should be that this is at an acceptable level and obviously this will vary from study to study. In our case we had to be sure that the data obtained were of sufficient detail to enable r/t encounters to be classified on the basis of our taxonomy. This was tested in the following way. The usual observer (MB) recorded the behavior of a focal child in the same way as would be employed to collect data in our study. This entailed a verbal description of the child's behavior in terms of physical actions (such as "grabs," "kicks," "chases") spoken into a portable tape recorder. Simultaneously, this child's behavior was recorded by a second observer on videotape. In the laboratory, the two records were analyzed separately (but by the same person each time) so that each episode of r/t was classified as being of one or other type from the taxonomy. By comparing the data produced by these two records, we were able to ensure that the information from audiotape in our study would be of sufficient detail.

An important issue when using observational methods is that of reliability, a concept basically referring to the reproducibility of the measurements. In our particular study, at least three different measures of reliability were or are being undertaken, illustrating the need to ensure that neither data collection nor data analysis processes are unduly influenced by limitations of methodology or the idiosyncrasies of the person carrying them out. One kind of reliability check was made on the principal observer. Any observer may be biased by their personal expectancies. Lehner (1979, p. 129) sums up this problem by saying "in truth, research hypotheses are really personal prophecies and to strengthen confidence in our ethological insight most of us would like to see them come true." Observer bias would seem to be related intimately to experimenter effects reported by Rosenthal (1976). Unfortunately, the former cannot be eliminated by ensuring that the researcher is blind to any manipulation of variables, which often goes a long way to reducing biases associated with experimenter effects. Very often observational studies do not involve manipulation of variables. Consequently, it is important to attempt some measure of this bias, usually by obtaining some measure of interobserver reliability, checking that the data obtained by two independent observers reach some agreed-upon level of concordance. By doing so, we can ensure that the observer is accurately recording, at the appropriate level of abstraction, what is "out there."

The other two reliability checks were carried out in relation to our taxonomy and it is to these issues that we now turn in the next section.

DEVELOPING A TAXONOMY OF ROUGH AND TUMBLE

An essential beginning to creating a behavioral taxonomy is informal observation. For us, this initial phase was coupled with the collection of an extensive video record of playground action. These video records were replayed over and over again, enabling us to "get a feel" for r/t and providing a foundation on which to develop the taxonomy.

Lehner (1979, p. 44) has pointed out that there are two basic types of description upon which a taxonomy may be based; "empirical description—description of the behavior in terms of body parts, movements and postures (e.g., baring the teeth), and functional descriptions—incorporation of reference to the behavior's function, proximally or ultimately (e.g., bared teeth threat)." Although the latter has several advantages (see Rosenblum, 1978, p. 22), there were numerous reasons to suggest that it would be premature for us to adopt such an approach here. Notably, this would have required us to make as yet unwarranted inductive leaps from purely behavioral descriptions to functional descriptions which are far from intuitively obvious at this stage. A practical example may illustrate the problem. At an initial stage, the category "trial of strength" was included in our taxonomy. However, it soon became apparent that this placed too heavy a burden on the observer in terms of having to make inferences about the aims/objectives of the children. Specifically, in an ongoing sequence of a wrestling encounter, very often it would be almost impossible for the observer to say whether the two participants were testing each other's strength, whether one participant was struggling to escape, or whether one person was self-handicapping. One way round this problem, in theory at least, could be to record the episode on video and then ask the children involved what they were doing. However, this would be impossible if other methods of data collection were employed (e.g., a portable tape recorder) and practical constraints would rule it out as a general procedure in many situations since the time required to ask the children would probably disrupt their school routine to an unacceptable extent. This is not to say that at no stage would we be willing to make any inferences about the behaviors seen, but we felt it premature and inappropriate to make them at the data collection stage of the project.

We therefore decided to base the taxonomy on empirical description, or the form of the behavior. Preliminary analysis of the video record suggested to us that a bottom–up, or molecular, approach to the formulation of a behavioral taxonomy would not be the most appropriate. This would have involved defining categories, as far as possible, in terms of very specific motor actions. The problem is that we have identified more than 30 distinct motor actions occurring in r/t, such as "grabs leg" and "shoves with both hands" (and there is no reason to believe that this list is exhaustive). The potential number of categories which could be based on these behavior's alone, (e.g., "grabs leg" r/t) and even simple combinations and permutations of them, (e.g., "grabs leg, then shoves with both hands" r/t) is very large. Even if the researcher could remember and record all these types of r/t in situ, it is doubtful whether the data in this form would do anything more than "name rather than explain" the behaviors seen. Greater explanatory power would arguably come from a taxonomy with much fewer categories, such as, at a basic level, "combat" and "noncombat" forms of r/t. These could be more readily used to test functional hypotheses, such as the practice fighting hypothesis.

We chose to formulate a molar taxonomy which employs a higher level of abstraction in that the categories developed were able to contain much larger combinations of specific or molecular actions. Consequently the number of categories in the system is lower than would be the case in a molecular taxonomy. This is an important consideration because to be useful practically, a taxonomy must be manageable; one which contains an unwieldy number of items would be of little use.

Once this decision as to the empirical basis of the taxonomy was reached, a further criterion to be met was that of the categories being mutually exclusive. Thus a particular bout labeled r/t could be placed in one and only one category. Much effort was expended in attempting to satisfy this criterion.

Table 1 includes the taxonomy developed to date. A cursory examination of this shows the great variety of forms r/t can take and this, in a sense, provides some justification for its creation. Moreover, when this is related to previous research, we begin to see that much of the complex structure of r/t may have been overlooked. For example, Smith and Connolly's (1980) definition was "play fighting, play chasing, running in a group." This definition was appropriate for the questions they were seeking to answer in their particular study, but, as the taxonomy reveals, play fighting may be in the form of boxing, kung fu, brief blows/contact, restrain or grapple; lumping all these behaviors together may have obscured some interesting and important phenomena. This aspect of the taxonomy also reveals the possibility that any general definition and/or taxonomy may be culturally specific or at least contain culturally specific components. For example, the occurrence of kung fu behavior is likely to be influenced by both media presentation and the general popularity of this or other forms of martial arts. The extent of cultural or even historical specificity in our definition is perhaps particularly noticeable in this

Table 1. A Taxonomy of Rough and Tumble Play

Brief blows/contact: One or some blows, kicks, pulls, grabs, shoves, and so forth, lasting 3 seconds or less; for example, smack bottom, single punch or one person pulls the other's arm briefly before letting go.

Grab at: One person unsuccessfully attempts to seize the other.

Restrain: One person, who may or may not try to escape, has their movements limited in some way; for example, one person holds the other in a bear hug or one person holds the other's arm to prevent their running away. Lasts more than 3 seconds.

Grappling: Involves one, some or all of the following actions. Punch, pull, shove, kick, swing, grab or grapple. Lasts more than 3 seconds.

Boxing: Conventional western boxing; for example, clenched fists and sparring stance (legs apart, fists raised and gaze directed at opponent). Lasts more than 3 seconds.

Kung-fu: Actions specific to this type of oriental combat. Lasts more than 3 seconds.

Colliding: One or both partners barges into the other.

Spinning and swinging: One or both partners swing or spin the other. Both cooperate. Lasts more than 3 seconds.

Hit and run: One person approaches unseen or attempts to approach unseen and/or unexpectedly delivers a blow before withdrawing quickly; for example, a child runs up to another from behind, pushes them in the back and runs away.

Chasing: One person pursues or begins to pursue another but excluding conventional chasing games such as "tag."

Runs past: One person runs past another close by, often looking back.

type of play, but is certainly not unique to it, and is a problem the researcher needs to be aware of from the outset.

The taxonomy includes both core behaviors (such as "grappling") as well as more borderline ones (such as "spinning and swinging" and "runs past"). The latter have been included because they were seen fairly frequently in the pilot study, often in association with the more paradigm cases, and are similar in form to other behaviors such as "grappling" and "chasing." However, their status within a r/t taxonomy remains to be determined empirically.

It would be wrong to present our taxonomy of r/t as being a finished product, but we hope that it proves to be a useful step in elaborating our research findings and directing some aspects of future studies. The acid test for any taxonomy is its usefulness across researchers and research teams—it ought to provide a useful tool for any one wishing to employ it. Consequently, it must yield high interuser reliability scores. There are a number of ways of computing these scores, but it is not our intention to consider the actual computations themselves. Rather, we shall look at how the methodology employed in a given study goes a long way to dictating which reliability check will be the most meaningful. As in previous sections, this can be illustrated with examples from our current study. We began by checking how two observers used the taxonomy to classify sequences of action recorded on videotape. In other words, on its use under "ideal" circumstances. Two observers watched a number of r/t bouts, and independently scored them in terms of the taxonomy by stating in each case what type of r/t they thought had occurred.

A number of different factors led to our using video recordings for the basis of the initial reliability check rather than truly live action. Firstly, the taxonomy itself was fairly extensive and would have required a familiarization period of considerable length to ensure that the observers would not be overloaded in trying to use it in the field. The use of video recordings made this unnecessary, since they could be replayed a number of times and/or at reduced speed to allow observers to make their decisions.

Similarly, the behaviors seen in r/t are sometimes complicated and/or of short duration. Again, this could lead to an untrained observer becoming overloaded unless the behaviors could be seen several times and/or at reduced speed. This problem would be compounded if the observer had to pay attention to these sometimes complex and rapid behaviors and then, in situ, classify them on the basis of a fairly extensive taxonomy.

It was because of the latter problem that the observer did not, during the main data collection stage of our project, attempt to classify the behaviors seen in terms of the taxonomy, but stopped at "mere" descriptions themselves. In our case, it was only later, in the laboratory, that this was attempted. Specifically, the verbal descriptions obtained in the field were transcribed and then decisions as to the type of r/t displayed were made on the data in this form. Consequently, it was important for us to check the reliability of the taxonomy at this coding stage as well, since this was where it was applied to the data. We are in the process of assessing this aspect of reliability by having two persons work independently through the transcript for a particular S. and break this down into episodes of r/t, in each case stating what type of r/t they think has occurred. The two records would then be checked for their reliability in the usual way.

In summary, the following three steps were used to assess reliability in our study; the first check looked at the principal observer to ensure that he or she was collecting accurate data; the second ensured that two independent raters agreed that bouts of r/t, seen on video, were one or other type from the taxonomy; and the third that two independent raters agreed on the type of bouts when the data were in the form of transcripts of verbal descriptions obtained by the principal observer.

SEQUENTIAL ANALYSIS OF ROUGH AND TUMBLE

In the final section, we will discuss one type of analysis which concerned us and which could conceivably concern other play researchers—sequential analysis. This type of analysis involves behavioral sequences and very often looks at sequential dependencies among specific behavioral acts, for example, whether the occurrence of a particular behavior is contingent upon the preoccurrence of another.

Rather than considering the computational aspects, we discuss here those decisions which must be made prior to, and implemented during, the study in order for a meaningful sequential analysis to be conducted. One concerns the method of data collection. In our particular case we have seen how the high degree of mobility in our sample ruled out the use of video and led to our use of a portable tape recorder in order to preserve the sequential nature of the data. This is an important point, because the larger the gaps in the behavioral record, the more errors may be introduced and the less meaningful a sequential analysis would be.

A second important decision to be reached which both influences and is influenced by the method of data collection, concerns what could be called the "type" of data collected. Two dimensions are important in this respect. The first is whether the researcher is primarily interested in behavior that is sequential or concurrent. The former are data which describe behavior from moment to moment and the latter describe behaviors occurring simultaneously. Put another way, sequential data always involve mutually exclusive coding categories, whereas concurrent data involve nonmutually exclusive coding categories (although of course concurrent data allow for behaviors to occur on their own).

The second dimension concerns whether behavior is recorded on an event base or a time base. The former notes the order that behaviors occur in and the latter notes this and their duration. These two distinctions give rise to four data types; event base/concurrent; event base/sequential; time base/concurrent, and time base/sequential.

The method of data collection and type of data the researcher is interested in exert a reciprocal influence over each other. We can illustrate this two-way influence with decisions made in our own study. Initial observation had indicated that on hard surfaces, the vast majority of r/t encounters involved two participants, and only occasionally three or more. Moreover, since an important prerequisite for our taxonomy was that the categories should be mutually exclusive (children couldn't be involved in two types of r/t at the same time) and since we were focusing on one child at a time, sequential data were "adequate"; in our study, concurrent data were not required. This influenced the method of data collection, since a portable tape recorder would provide this sequential information. In situations where the researcher is interested in numerous behaviors occurring simultaneously, a portable tape recorder may be unsatisfactory, since the observer would probably be overloaded. Some other method of data collection would have to be used.

Similarly, we wanted our data to be recorded on at least an event base and a portable tape recorder would yield this. In some situations this method may also be able to produce time base data at some acceptable level of reliability. For more rigorous time base data, especially with complicated behaviors of short duration, a video/film record may be required to enable more precise temporal information to be obtained.

Event base/sequential data were of primary concern to us in our project. Before going on to consider two sorts of analyses that can be performed on data in this form, we must first mention how the stream of spoken commentaries was transformed into a sequence of events. To this end, it was important for us to ensure that our coding scheme was exhaustive, meaning that no observation time could pass in which behavior could not be placed in one or other category. This meant that we needed one or some other categories in addition to those in the taxonomy, especially since research has indicated that r/t 'only' takes up about 5% to 10% of children's free-play time (Humphreys & Smith, 1984). At the simplest level, this could be achieved by including a "non-r/t" or "other" category, a strategy which may be sufficient in some studies. For simplicity, this is what we have done in the two examples presented below, but in our final analysis we intend to extend this by breaking down inter-r/t bout activities into a number of categories with the aim of identifying any particular non-r/t behaviors which characteristically precede and/or follow r/t bouts.

The next decision concerned the r/t bouts themselves, or more specifically, what constitutes a r/t bout. At this, albeit preliminary, stage of our analysis we have defined a bout as having an identifiable onset, continuing with behavior of one type from the taxonomy and ending with one of the following; the occurrence of some non-r/t activity lasting more than 5 seconds, the occurrence of some other type of r/t by the same participants within 5 seconds of the first type (the two bouts would be seen as consecutive in this case) or the occurrence of the same type of r/t within 5 seconds of the first but involving someone else other than the person the Target was initially interacting with (these, too, would be seen as consecutive bouts). By employing these criteria, we were able to produce a sequence of events which could form the basis for analysis.

In the first of two sorts of sequential analyses to be considered, we have taken data from one of our Ss. A "criterion" behavior was selected, in this case "chasing," in order to see which other behaviors (known as "matched" behaviors) characteristically precede or follow it. As a consequence of the sequential nature of our data, we were not restricted to simply looking at immediate antecedent and/or following matches, but could also look at behavioral relationships various steps removed from the criterion behavior, that is, between behaviors with different behaviors occurring in between them.

The upper half of Table 2 contains the frequency data obtained in this way. Thus, chase followed itself five times at lag step 2 (i.e., with one other behavior occurring in between), twice at lag step 3 (i.e., with two others occurring in between), and so on. The lower half of the table represents probability of event matches or lag conditional probabilities. To obtain these values, each matching frequency score is divided by the total number of occurrences of the criterion at each lag step. For example, at lag step 1, "restrain" followed "chase" four times out of a total of 15 "chase" occurrences. Thus, the conditional probability is $4/15 = 0.27$. These conditional probabilities can be compared with the unconditional probabilities, the latter being derived in the usual way, that is, number of occurrences of a given behavior divided by the number of behavior changes in the sequence. In this way we can investigate the temporal relationships among the different types of r/t occurring in an extended sequence (see Sackett, 1978, p. 41, for a method of assessing statistical significance of lag probabilities).

At this stage, the important issue of how many data points (i.e., behavioral transitions) are "sufficient" should be mentioned. Although less of a problem if the investigator stops at the simple level of computing conditional probabilities, it becomes a matter of much greater consequence if significance is to be determined. The crucial question concerns the minimum number of events which can justify assigning significance. A detailed discussion of this point is outside the scope of the present chapter but it has been covered recently

Table 2. Event Sequential Analysis for Lagged Probabilities for 7 Behaviors Preceding and Following Chase. Illustrative Data from 1 Subject.

Frequency of Event Matches	Match Follows Chase			Match Precedes Chase		
	1	2	3	1	2	3
Chase	0	5	2	0	5	2
Restrain	4	2	1	1	3	1
Grab at	0	2	1	1	1	1
Brief blows or contact	0	0	1	1	2	0
Colliding	0	1	0	0	0	0
Threat, challange, and/or mock	0	2	0	0	1	0
Non-rough and tumble	11	2	9	12	2	10
Total	15	14	14	15	14	14

Probability of Event Matches	Match Follows Chase			Match Precedes Chase		
	1	2	3	1	2	3
Chase (0.22)	0.0	0.36	0.14	0.0	0.36	0.14
Restrain (0.13)	0.27	0.14	0.07	0.07	0.21	0.07
Grab at (0.04)	0.0	0.14	0.07	0.07	0.07	0.07
Brief blows or contact (0.06)	0.0	0.0	0.07	0.07	0.14	0.0
Colliding (0.04)	0.0	0.07	0.0	0.0	0.0	0.0
Threat, challenge, and/or mock (0.06)	0.0	0.14	0.0	0.0	0.07	0.0
Non-rough and tumble (0.45)	0.73	0.14	0.64	0.80	0.14	0.71

by Bakeman and Gottman (1986). They stress two aspects which must be considered prior to data collection. Firstly, the number of categories within a coding system, and secondly, the length of sequences in which the investigator is interested. As each increases, so too does the amount of data required. In some cases, this may be to prohibitive levels. If so, the researcher must either change one or both of these aspects or even consider an alternative method of analysis.

The method described above is a useful tool for looking at sequences with respect to one particular behavior—that is, the criterion

Table 3. First-order Contingency Table for 11 Behaviors, Using Pooled Data from 10 Subjects. Upper Values in Each Cell Represent Frequency of Behavior in the Column Following Behavior in the Row Represented. Lower Values Represent Probability.

Preceding Acts	Following Acts											
	Chase	Restrain	Grab at	Brief blows or contact	Threat, challenge, and/or mock	Hit and run	Runs past	Aggression	Grapple	Swinging	Non-rough & tumble	Total
Chase	[8] 0.13	[8] 0.13	[3] 0.05	[5] 0.08	[1] 0.01	[1] 0.01	[3] 0.05	[0] 0.0	[0] 0.0	[0] 0.0	[34] 0.54	63
Restrain	[4] 0.23	[0] 0.0	[1] 0.06	[2] 0.12	[0] 0.0	[1] 0.06	[0] 0.0	[0] 0.0	[0] 0.0	[0] 0.0	[9] 0.53	17
Grab at	[3] 0.23	[0] 0.0	[0] 0.0	[0] 0.0	[0] 0.0	[0] 0.0	[0] 0.0	[1] 0.08	[0] 0.0	[0] 0.0	[9] 0.69	13
Brief blows or contact	[6] 0.19	[1] 0.03	[0] 0.0	[2] 0.06	[0] 0.0	[1] 0.03	[1] 0.03	[1] 0.03	[0] 0.0	[0] 0.0	[20] 0.63	32
Threat, challenge, and/or mock	[8] 0.42	[1] 0.05	[4] 0.21	[1] 0.05	[1] 0.05	[0] 0.0	[0] 0.0	[1] 0.05	[0] 0.0	[0] 0.0	[3] 0.16	19
Hit and run	[3] 0.37	[0] 0.0	[0] 0.0	[1] 0.13	[0] 0.0	[0] 0.0	[0] 0.0	[0] 0.0	[0] 0.0	[0] 0.0	[4] 0.50	8
Runs past	[2] 0.29	[0] 0.0	[3] 0.43	[1] 0.14	[0] 0.0	[0] 0.0	[0] 0.0	[0] 0.0	[0] 0.0	[0] 0.0	[1] 0.14	7
Aggression	[1] 0.17	[0] 0.0	[0] 0.0	[0] 0.0	[1] 0.17	[1] 0.17	[0] 0.0	[1] 0.17	[0] 0.0	[0] 0.0	[2] 0.33	6
Grapple	[0] 0.0	[0] 0.0	[0] 0.0	[1] 0.11	[1] 0.05	[0] 0.0	[0] 0.0	[0] 0.0	[1] 0.11	[0] 0.0	[7] 0.78	9
Swinging	[0] 0.0	[0] 0.0	[0] 0.0	[0] 0.0	[0] 0.0	[0] 0.0	[0] 0.0	[0] 0.0	[0] 0.0	[3] 0.21	[11] 0.79	14
Non-rough and tumble	[28] 0.28	[7] 0.07	[2] 0.02	[20] 0.20	[7] 0.17	[3] 0.03	[2] 0.02	[2] 0.02	[9] 0.09	[11] 0.11	—	101

behavior. A useful alternative is to construct a contingency table in which all behaviors are considered. Table 3 is a first-order contingency table, in which the frequency that all r/t behaviors immediately precede and follow all other r/t behaviors are noted. Data are pooled from 10 Ss. For simplicity, interbout activity has been grouped into a single category, with the exception of a "threat/challenge/mock" category and an "aggression" category. From this table we can construct diagrammatic representations of sequential relationships, to see at a glance numerical values for these relationships. One such diagrammatic representation can be seen in Figure 1.

Since the number of Ss in this example was small, it should not be taken as normative in any way. Nevertheless, it does reveal some interesting things about how bouts of r/t occur in lengthy free-play periods, which are an integral part of the school day for the child. Most apparent is how bouts of r/t are predominantly followed by non-r/t activity, rather than being "chained" together in a sequence of various types of the behavior. By examining this aspect in much larger samples, we could see whether this episodic quality is an important characteristic of r/t.

Where different types of r/t do occur consecutively, we can see, for example, that "threat/challenge/mock" is a fairly productive strategy for eliciting a chase (which children seem to enjoy and engage in frequently), more so than "runs past" and "hit and run."

A separate finding shown in Figure 1, and from which we can draw a modicum of comfort, is how r/t and aggression do not occur in close temporal proximity. Again, this could be looked at in data from larger samples since it has something to add to the debate concerning the relationship between them.

It could be argued that playful behaviors such as r/t can be much better understood by considering them in their full ecological context, and in part this would entail a consideration of their occurrence in the complex nexus of activities that is so characteristic of children's free play. The examples given above illustrate how this goal might be approached.

SUMMARY

In this chapter we have outlined our current research project on r/t with the aim of illustrating methodological principles relevant to future studies of play.

The importance of producing clear definitions or criteria for a given behavior was stressed in the light of some earlier research

Figure 1. Sequential Relationships Among 11 Behaviors. Magnitude is Indicated by Arrow Thickness.

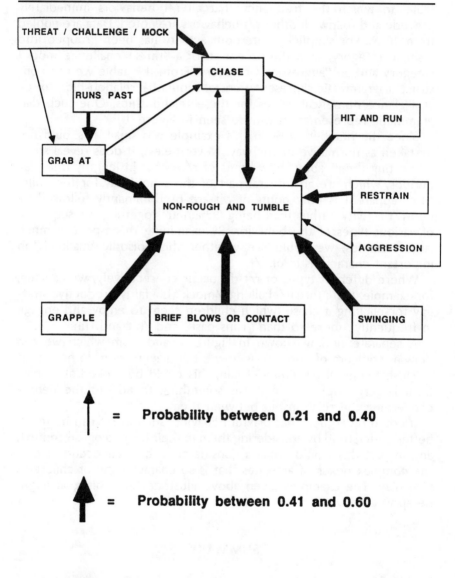

which failed to do this. Not only is this important for conceptual clarity among and between research teams, it also represents the starting point in a logical sequence of methodological steps.

In relation to data collection, the relative merits and limitations of two methods were discussed, video recording and using a portable tape recorder. By employing each at the appropriate stage of a study such as ours, the researcher can have the complementary benefits of the structural detail provided by video recordings and the flexibility in application of a portable tape recorder.

The development of a taxonomy and the advantages which may result from its application were also considered. In our project, we were able to extend previous studies by applying the taxonomy to those ecological factors (such as play partner choice) which have been shown to be important.

Assessing reliability at various stages of a project was also stressed in relation to the observer, the data obtained and the subsequent classification of that data, in our case, on the basis of the taxonomy.

An illustration of a sequential analysis was undertaken, mentioning how this is intimately related to the method(s) of data collection employed. Specifically, we noted how the type of data obtained influences the sorts of sequential analyses that can be performed. Consequently, we recommend that researchers should consider this point prior to data collection.

Finally, the implications of these methodological issues for our own and other researchers' future efforts revolve around increasing our knowledge about the various forms of play in their social, temporal, and broadly ecological context. Such an understanding is essential in our endeavors to answer difficult causal and functional questions about play. By tightening and refining methodologies, in the widest sense of the word, we place ourselves in a better position to do just that.

REFERENCES

Bakeman, R., & Gottman, J.M. (1986). *Observing interaction: An introduction to sequential analysis.* Cambridge: Cambridge University Press.

Bandura, A., Ross, D., & Ross, S.A. (1961). Transmission of aggression through imitation of aggressive models. *Journal of Abnormal Social Psychology, 63,* 575–582.

Bandura, A., Ross, D., & Ross, S.A. (1963). Imitation of film-mediated aggressive models. *Journal of Abnormal Social Psychology, 66,* 3–11.

Blurton-Jones, N.G. (1967). An ethological study of some aspects of social behavior of children in nursery school. In D. Morris (Ed.), *Primate ethology.* London: Weidenfeld & Nicolson.

Blurton–Jones, N.G. (1972). Categories of child–child interaction. In N.G. Blurton–Jones (Ed.), *Ethological studies of child behaviour.* Cambridge, England: Cambridge University Press.

Connolly, K.J., & Smith, P.K. (1972). Reactions of pre-school children to a strange observer. In N.G. Blurton–Jones (Ed.), *Ethological studies of child behavior.* Cambridge, England: Cambridge University Press.

DiPietro, J.A. (1981). Rough and tumble play: A function of gender. *Developmental Psychology, 17,* 50–58.

Fagen, R.M. (1981). *Animal play behavior.* New York: Oxford University Press.

Humphreys, A.P., & Smith, P.K. (1984). Rough and tumble in preschool and playground. In P.K. Smith (Ed.), *Play in animals and humans.* Oxford, England: Basil Blackwell.

Humphreys, A.P., & Smith, P.K. (1987). Rough and tumble, friendship and dominance in school children. Evidence for continuity and change with age. *Child Development, 58,* 201–212.

Hutt, S.J., & Hutt, C. (1974). *Direct observation and measurement of behavior.* Springfield, IL: Charles C. Thomas.

Ladd, G.W. (1983). Social networks of popular, average and rejected children in school settings. *Merrill-Palmer Quarterly, 29*(3), 283–307.

Lehner, P.N. (1979). *Handbook of ethological methods.* New York: Garland STPM.

Martin, P., & Caro, T.M. (1985). On the function of play and its role in behavioral development. *Advances in the Study of Behavior, 15,* 59–103.

Matthews, W.S., & Matthews, R.J. (1982). Eliminating operational definitions: a paradigm case approach to the study of fantasy play. In D.J. Pepler & K.H. Rubin (Eds.), *The play of children: Current theory and research.* Basel, Switzerland: Karger.

Potts, R., Huston, A.C., & Wright, J.C. (1986). The effects of television form and violent content on boys' attention and social behavior. *Journal of Experimental Child Psychology, 41,* 1–17.

Rosenblum, L.A. (1978). The creation of a behavioral taxonomy. In G.P. Sackett (Ed.), *Observing behavior: Vol. 2. Data collection and analysis methods.* Baltimore: University Park Press.

Rosenthal, R. (1976). *Experimenter effects in behavioral research.* New York: Halsted Press.

Sackett, G.P. (1978). Measurement in observational research. In G.P. Sackett (Ed.), *Observing Behavior: Vol. 2. Data collection and analysis methods.* Baltimore: University Park Press.

Sackett, G.P., Ruppenthal, G.C., & Gluck, J. (1978). Introduction: An overview of methodological and statistical problems in observational research. In G.P. Sackett (Ed.), *Observing behavior: Vol. 2. Data collection and analysis methods.* Baltimore: University Park Press.

Sluckin, A. (1981). *Growing up in the playground: The social development of children.* London: Routledge & Kegan Paul.

Smith, P.K. (1973). Temporal clusters and individual differences in the behaviour of preschool children. In R.P. Michael & J.H. Crook (Eds.),

Comparative ecology and behaviour of primates. London: Academic Press.

Smith, P.K., & Connolly, K.J. (1972). Patterns of play and social interaction in preschool children. In N. Blurton–Jones (Ed.), *Ethological studies of child behaviour.* Cambridge, England: Cambridge University Press.

Smith, P.K., & Connolly, K.J. (1980). *The ecology of preschool behaviour.* Cambridge, England: Cambridge University Press.

Smith, P.K., & Lewis, K. (1985). Rough-and-tumble play, fighting and chasing in nursery school children. *Ethology & Sociobiology, 6,* 175–181.

Smith, P.K., & Vollstedt, R. (1985). On defining play: An empirical study of the relationship between play and various play criteria. *Child Development, 56,* 1042–1050.

Symons, D. (1978). *Play and aggression: A study of rhesus monkeys.* New York: Columbia University Press.

Whiting, B.B., & Whiting, J.W.M. (1975). *Children of six cultures: A psycho-cultural analysis.* Cambridge, MA: Harvard University Press.

5

The Influences on the Play of Infants and Toddlers*

MARGUERITE B. STEVENSON
University of Wisconsin-Madison

Lewin (1931) proposed a model in which human behavior was seen as a function of the person and the environment. More recently, Darvill (1982) applied this model to the consideration of children's play. In his application, the child's play behavior becomes a function of the child and the play environment. With this model, it becomes important to consider as the context of the child's play both the setting for play and the social environment provided by the child's play partners. Further, understanding of play must recognize the role of the child's own input into play.

For infants and toddlers, the usual play setting is the home, and the usual play partner is the mother. However, researchers are beginning to learn about the play of infants and toddlers in other settings and with other partners. This chapter will review three major influences on the play of infants and toddlers: (a) The ways in which the play of infants and toddlers is influenced by ecological contexts including the immediate setting for play—home, day care, or laboratory—as well as the macrosystems of culture and social class. (b) The ways in which early play is influenced by the young child's play partner—young partners, including peers and siblings as well as adult partners. (c) The ways that the play of infants and toddlers is influenced by characteristics of the children themselves. Finally, a more mi-

---

* Portions of this chapter were presented at a colloquium during the author's term as a research fellow at the Women's Studies Research Center, University of Wisconsin. The research reviewed here was supported in poart by NIH Grant HD-13352 to the Waisman Center on Mental Retardation and Human Development. Address correspondence to M. B. Stevenson, 204 Child and Family Studies Building, 1430 Linden Drive, University of Wisconsin, Madison, WI 53706.

croanalytical examination of the social environment that children's play partners provide in the home will be used to suggest the aspects of play that may be most facilitating for the development of infants and toddlers.

SETTINGS FOR EARLY PLAY

Settings at Home and Away

Day care. Today almost half of the mothers of 1-year-old infants are working outside the home (National Commission on Working Women, 1985). As a consequence, a common setting for the infant and toddler is that of substitute care—a day-care center, or more commonly, a family day-care home. Yet most studies of day care focus on the preschool child (Clarke–Stewart, 1982; Ruopp, Travers, Glantz, & Coelen, 1979). Researchers who have observed infants and toddlers in these settings find that the experiences are not always the same as the experiences infants and toddlers have with their own mothers. For example, the research of Rubenstein and her colleagues (Rubenstein, Pedersen, & Yarrow, 1977) compared the care provided by mothers with the care provided by other caregivers (relatives and babysitters). The care provided by mothers was more stimulating and responsive than the care provided by other caregivers. However, caregivers who had more months of caring for these infants gave care that was more similar to the care provided by mothers than did caregivers who had fewer months of experience with the particular infant. Despite the different environments, whether cared for by mother or by a substitute caregiver, infants explored their environments similar amounts and performed similarly on cognitive assessments.

Comparison of infant experiences in day-care centers and homes indicated that there was more adult–infant play and more positive affective exchange in day-care centers than in homes (Rubenstein & Howes, 1979). Perhaps as a consequence of this and as a consequence of the exposure to peers, the day-care infants showed greater maturity in their play than did the infants who were at home with their mother. Infants at home, in contrast, experienced greater restrictiveness than did the infants in day care. Howes (1983) found that caregivers in day-care centers who have more experience and training spent more time playing with children than less well-qualified caregivers. In summary, not only the type of care—center care or family day care—but also the qualifications and experience of the caregiver influence the play experiences of infants and toddlers in substitute care.

Laboratory. Another setting that infants find themselves in, albeit at the request of the researcher, is that of the laboratory playroom. Although the playroom setting is frequently criticized for its lack of ecological validity, it is, nevertheless, a common setting for research on infants and it does serve to standardize the play environment across families. Comparisons of parents' behavior in the home and laboratory settings indicate differences in play (Power & Parke, 1982), in attentiveness and responsiveness (Belsky, 1980; Moustakas, Sigel, & Schalock, 1956), in restrictiveness (Moustakas et al., 1956), and in vocal behavior (Stevenson, Leavitt, Roach, Chapman, & Miller, 1986). Comparisons of infants in home and laboratory settings indicate differences in attachment and emotional expression (Brookhart & Hock, 1976; Klein & Durfee, 1979; Ross, Kagan, Zelazo, & Kotelchuck, 1975; Sroufe, Waters, & Matas, 1974) and differences in cognitive performance (Horner, 1980). These findings readily combine to suggest an important influence of the microsystem—the infant's immediate play environment—on both the play partner and the young child.

Within the laboratory setting, materials available for play clearly influence the quality of young children's play. Bretherton and her colleagues (Bretherton, O'Connell, Shore, & Bates, 1984) examined the effects of contextual variation on symbolic play. The toddler's ability to engage in and model symbolic play varied with the props and scenes available. The toys that are available also influence the peer play of toddlers in the laboratory; more numerous and more complex toys decrease interaction (Mueller & Vandell, 1979).

Culture

The comparison of the home environments of infants and toddlers with day-care environments or with laboratory environments suggests some uniformity in home environments. But young children, in fact, find themselves in a wide variety of homes. Culture is one large source of variation in home environments of infants, and research documents the effects of culture on the infant's day-to-day experiences (Field, Sostek, Vietze, & Leiderman, 1981; Leiderman, Tulkin, & Rosenfeld, 1977). For example, infants in Yugoslavia are held less than infants in the United States (Lewis & Ban, 1977); infants in the

Kalahari Desert San (Botswana and Namibia) are held more than infants in the United States (Konner, 1977).

Opportunities for play are restricted by the swaddling that Mayan infants experience (Brazelton, 1977) or by the extensive holding that Gandan infants experience (Ainsworth, 1977). However, confinement does not necessarily limit opportunities for play; infants in the Kalahari Desert San play with their mothers' jewelry even though confined to a sling on their mothers' hips. As suggested by Fenson (1986), the symbolic play of toddlers finds expression in the materials available in the culture. Although few of the cross-cultural studies have given close attention to play during infancy, there is evidence that Yugoslavian infants spend considerably more time alone in quiet play than do American infants, even though Yugoslavian and American mothers spend similar amounts of time playing with their infants (Lewis & Ban, 1977). The report by Super (1981) offers an important reminder that cultural differences in infancy overlap with racial differences; racial/cultural differences in infant development are reflected in early play.

Social Class

Even within homes in the United States, there is considerable variability in the experiences provided to infants and young children. Socioeconomic status is one consistent source of variation in early experiences. A recent review of research on the early home environments of infants suggests that social class accounts for about half of the variation in early home environments (MacPhee, Ramey, & Yeates, 1984). Examination of mothers' responses to infant play within a range of social classes suggests that responsiveness is influenced by social class (Lewis, 1972). In this research, middle-class mothers responded to their infants' vocalizations with vocalizations of their own. In contrast, lower-class mothers were more likely to respond to infants' vocalizations with touch. Tulkin (1977) has also suggested social class differences in responsiveness; he found more reciprocity in the interaction of middle-class mothers and their infants than in working-class dyads.

Not only does responsiveness during play vary with social class, the amount of the mother's play with her infant also varies with social class (Lewis & Wilson, 1972). In a study of newborns, mothers with higher and lower socioeconomic status were found to play with their infants for similar amounts of time, but the mothers with higher socioeconomic status were more verbal (Kilbride, Johnson, & Streissguth, 1977). The amount of infant solitary play also varies with social class (Tulkin, 1977). Tulkin found that infants in middle-class homes played more and had longer individual play episodes than infants in working-class homes. Field and Widmayer (1981) offer an important reminder of the considerable variability in culture within lower socioeconomic status groups in the United States.

ROLE OF THE PLAY PARTNER

One of the important conclusions of the Whiting's Six Cultures studies (Whiting & Whiting, 1975) was that the identity of the child's partner—whether peer, sibling, parent, or other adult—played a major role in determining the child's behavior. For example, in Kenya and Ganda the number of people in the household determines the likelihood that infants will be held and have their cries responded to (Munroe & Munroe, 1971). In a more recent study of Navajo residence patterns, Chisholm (1981) found that infant's opportunities for interaction with others was a major determinant of mother–infant interaction. Thus it becomes important to examine in more detail the infant's play with the various child and adult play partners.

Young Play Partners

Although early observers of infants and toddlers concluded that peer play was rare and usually negative, recent observers have described a sequence in the development of peer play that begins very early and includes rich interactions (Mueller & Vandell, 1979). The infant peer as play partner has the power to elicit smiling, approach, vocalization, and exchange of toys. The affiliative behaviors that infant and toddler peers direct toward one another during play are more frequent with familiar peers and for infants and toddlers with greater peer experience. The recent increase in the use of substitute care for infants and toddlers brings these young children into increased contact with peers—though peer relations in substitute care settings have been little studied to date.

Other common young play partners of infants and toddlers are siblings (Dunn & Kendrick, 1982). Young children have great interest in their older siblings, but this interest is largely expressed through watching the activities of the older sibling and following the older sibling (Lamb, 1978; Vandell & Wilson, 1983). Interactions between infants and their slightly older siblings show much lower-level play than interactions between infants and their mothers or fathers (Stevenson, Leavitt, Thompson, & Roach, 1983). Similarly, the experiences that infants have during play with their peers are characterized by less reciprocal exchange than are the experiences that infants have with their mothers (Roach, 1982). These studies suggest that play with young partners is a common social context for infants and toddlers, but that it cannot serve as a substitute for the richer interactions that adults can orchestrate.

Adult Play Partners

Characteristics of the parents may influence the play environment that they provide for their infants. For example, mothers and fathers may differ or younger mothers and older mothers may differ. Parental responsiveness during play may also be influenced by parental psychopathology. Though less frequently discussed, infants and toddlers also play with other adults, and researchers have begun to examine these interactions. Clearly the play of young children with adult partners differs from their play alone (O'Connell & Bretherton, 1984).

Parent gender. Comparison of the play of mothers and fathers with their 1-year-olds has helped to answer the question about the role of parent gender in creating play environments for infants and toddlers. Mothers do more of the caregiving than fathers; fathers spend more of their time playing with infants (Lamb, 1976). But when parents play, do mothers and fathers play similarly? In a laboratory study where each parent played independently with their 1-year-old, interactions were examined for frequencies of behaviors and for contingencies of responsiveness (Stevenson & Roach, 1984). Examination of frequencies indicated that mothers were more vocal than fathers and that mothers were more likely to smile at their infants and stay near their infants. In contrast, examination of contingencies of responsiveness during play indicated substantial similarity in the responsiveness of mothers and fathers to their infants' vocalizations, smiles and offers of toys. Despite the lower levels of several behaviors shown by fathers in comparison with mothers, both parents were similarly responsive—the role of parent gender in responsiveness during play appeared to be minimal. Infant behavior during these play sessions was substantially similar with mothers and fathers, although 1-year-olds were more vocal during play with fathers.

Other research comparing the play of mothers and fathers with their infants suggests that mothers are more didactic and verbal with their infants than are fathers (Clarke-Stewart, 1978; Killarney &

McCluskey, 1980) and that fathers are more physical than mothers (Lamb, 1976; Yogman, 1982). In a comparison of parent–infant interaction in Germany and the United States, mothers were found to be more involved in caregiving than fathers, but fathers were nevertheless active participants with their newborns (Parke, Grossmann, & Tinsley, 1981). Recent reports emphasize the similarities in the play of mothers and fathers with their infants rather than the differences (Pedersen, 1980; Power, 1985; Stevenson, Leavitt, Thompson, & Roach, 1983).

Parent age. It is often suggested that adolescent mothers may not provide adequate interactive environments for their infants (McAnarney, 1983). Earlier suggestions in the literature indicate that young mothers may respond less sensitively to their infants than older mothers (Lissovoy, 1973; Williams, 1974). However, recent investigation of the responsiveness of adolescent single mothers to infant signals during play at home suggests similar responsiveness in younger and older mothers (Stevenson & Roach, 1987). In this research, comparison was made between adolescent single mothers and adult single mothers matched on the basis of social class. With any possible effects of marital status and social class thus controlled for, results may be more clearly attributable to differences in mothers' ages. Results suggested more interaction, particularly verbal interaction, in the adult mother–infant dyads than in the adolescent mother–infant dyads. Nevertheless, adolescent and adult mothers showed similar responsiveness to infant signals during play.

Parent psychopathology. Ainsworth's early reports on the Baltimore sample of mothers who were observed during their infants' first year raised the possibility of psychopathology in the handful of mothers who were especially insensitive to signals from their infants (Ainsworth, 1973). More recent investigation of the role of possible mental illness in parenting suggests that mothers with psychopathology may play less optimally with their small children than mothers without psychopathology (Musick & Cohler, 1983).

Specific research studies detail this association: Depression of upper socioeconomic status mothers during pregnancy has been found to be associated with less smiling and talking by the mother during play with their infants (Moss & Jones, 1977). Infants with depressed mothers mirror their mothers' affect during play by showing less positive affect, more negative affect, and less activity (Field, 1984). In the case of maternal schizophrenia, both mothers and infants show heightened reactivity during play (Schachter, Elmer, Ragins, Wimberly, & Lachin, 1977). In summary, maternal psychopathology impacts on the mother and infant during their play interactions.

Other adults. Consideration of infant interaction with unfamiliar adults has been part of the study of attachment. Ainsworth's Strange Situation includes assessment of the infant's reaction to an unfamiliar adult as part of determining the quality of the infant's attachment to the mother. (Ainsworth, Blehar, Waters, & Wall, 1978). Other researchers emphasize the infant's wariness with strangers (Sroufe, 1977). Infants, however, also exhibit a number of positive reactions during their play with unfamiliar adults (Bretherton, Stolberg, & Kreye, 1981; Ross & Goldman, 1975). Infants tend to reserve attachment behaviors for their interactions with parents, but affiliative behaviors are commonly directed toward a stranger (Lamb, 1979). Assessment of infant sociability through a few minutes of play between an infant and an unfamiliar adult has indicated not only considerable infant sociability, but also that sociable infants who were willing to play with a stranger performed better on cognitive assessments than less sociable infants (Stevenson & Lamb, 1979).

Infant play with adults who are a part of the infant's social world other than parents is seldom described, though there has been a recent focus on the role of grandparents in the development of children (Tinsley & Parke, 1984). In other cultures, the social world of the infant includes numerous other adults (Goldberg, 1977; Konner, 1977), and social interaction has been reported to be similar with parent and nonparent caregivers (Sostek et al., 1981). Detailed descriptions of mother–infant interaction in the Marquesas Islands (Martini & Kirkpatrick, 1981) indicate the many ways in which mothers encourage their infants' interactions with others.

Second-order effects. The play of an infant and a parent is not only influenced by characteristics of the parent, but also by others who may be present at the time (Lamb, 1979). When both parents are present, the infant directs fewer behaviors to a given parent than during dyadic play with only that parent; in other words, during triadic interaction, the infant plays less with either parent than during dyadic play. In a cross-cultural comparison, Sostek and colleagues (Sostek et al., 1981) found that the size of the group influenced infant behavior in Fais Island (Micronesia) and the United States. This phenomenon of second-order effects provides yet another influence of social context on the play of infants and toddlers.

INFLUENCES OF THE CHILDREN THEMSELVES

Clearly there are individual differences in the play of parents and their sensitivity to infant signals during play. Parent characteristics such as responsiveness and sensitivity during play are influenced by characteristics of the infant such as risk, infant responsiveness, and disability.

Low Birthweight

Low-birthweight, prematurely born infants are at risk for developmental delays (Parmelee, Sigman, Kopp, & Haber, 1975). Associated with their prematurity is often a heightened parental concern with infant well-being. Infants' risk status might be expected to influence parental sensitivity or responsiveness to infant signals during play and during everyday activities. Examination of the feeding exchange between 8-month-old infants and their mothers indicated that the patterns of contingency were different for low-birthweight, prematurely born infants and for normal birthweight, full-term infants (Stevenson, Roach, & VerHoeve, 1984). For example, only mothers of low-birthweight infants fed their infants in response to infant vocalization and vocalized in response to infant eating. Mothers of normal birthweight infants responded to their infants' eating with a more predictable sequence of touching, looking away, looking back, and proffering another spoonful of food. This finding of differences in mothers' responsiveness during the everyday activity of feeding with the risk status of infants suggests the possibility of differences in responsiveness in play settings also.

Infant Traits

The responsiveness of parents to infant signals during play may be influenced by infants' responsiveness to parents. Evidence suggesting this comes from a study of low-birthweight and normal birthweight, 4-month-old infants seen playing at home with their mothers (Leavitt & Stevenson, 1983). Interestingly, in these infants, higher levels of mothers' responsiveness to infant vocalization were associated with higher levels of infant responsiveness to mothers. Others suggest the role of the infant's individual temperament or intelligence in shaping the environment that the infant experiences (MacPhee et al., 1984).

Disability

Another infant characteristic that may influence parent responsiveness during play is disability. Case study examination of play interactions between Down Syndrome infants and their mothers at home has addressed this issue (Stevenson, Leavitt, & Silverberg, 1985). Analyses of patterns of vocal responsiveness indicated reduced levels of responsiveness during play in the mothers of Down Syndrome infants in comparison with mothers of nondelayed infants. This reduced responsiveness during play may have come about in several ways: Evidence suggests that it may have been a response to the reduced level of responsiveness characteristic of these infants. Perhaps it was a result of the mothers' expectations of the delays that accompany the label of Down Syndrome. Finally, because these mothers were participating in an infant stimulation program, the lowered level of responsiveness may have derived from mothers' efforts to provide stimulation during play without regard to signals from the infants.

Further speculation about the source of mothers' lowered levels of responsiveness during play with Down Syndrome infants derives from Redditi's work with developmentally delayed infants (Redditi & Stevenson, 1985). During free play at home, mothers of developmentally delayed infants were particularly likely to direct their infants' play. This directiveness may be a lower limit control strategy (Bell & Harper, 1977) designed to elicit more mature behavior patterns. For example, when the mother sees her infant's play as being below the level that she would expect, her directiveness may be designed to elicit infant play. As a consequence, the mother's directiveness during play may take precedence over her responsiveness.

WHAT ASPECTS OF PLAY ARE FACILITATING?

Theoretical Positions

Theorists suggest that the home environment of infants and toddlers can be characterized by the amount of stimulation provided, the variety and appropriateness of experiences provided, and the responsiveness of the environment to signals from the child (Stevenson & Lamb, 1980). These views each argue that different aspects of parental behavior during play at home are of primary importance for facilitating the development of the young child.

In support of the importance of the amount of stimulation, Casler (1961) argues that infants who do not receive sufficient input will show delayed development. An intervention program was developed in which additional stimulation provided for orphanage infants served to accelerate development (Casler, 1965); however, subsequent interventions based on the same ideas proved less successful (Casler, 1975). The idea that "more is better" continues today with the proliferation of "infant stimulation" programs for developmentally delayed infants and infants at risk for developmental delays (Office of Maternal and Child Health, 1980). The assumption that disadvantaged children suffered from a lack of stimulation was later revised to suggest that these children may, in fact, be experiencing overstimulation (MacPhee et al., 1984).

Evidence for the importance of the variety and appropriateness of maternal stimulation is derived largely from the work of Caldwell and her colleagues (Bradley, & Caldwell, 1984). Caldwell's Home Observation for Measurement of the Environment (HOME; Caldwell & Bradley, 1984) assesses the variety of experiences that infants are provided with, and evidence supports relations between these experiences and later cognitive outcomes. Hunt (1961) and later Wachs and Gruen (1982) additionally stressed the importance of the age appropriateness of young children's play experiences for their development.

These theorists' suggestions about the importance of the amount of stimulation provided and of the variety and appropriateness of the experiences share the view that infants and young children are the passive recipients of stimulation during play. However, Bell and Harper (1977) offer a less passive view of infants. They emphasize the bidirectional nature of play interactions between parents and children. When infants are seen as active partners in play, then another important characteristic of the early social environment is responsiveness to infants during play (Bruner, 1977; Schaffer, 1977). The focus on reciprocity during the play of parents and young children at home has become one of the new focuses in the field of child development (Rutter, 1979).

The responsiveness or sensitivity of parents of very young children during play is seen as important from four theoretical perspectives (Lamb & Easterbrooks, 1980). Psychoanalysts emphasize the role of early maternal sensitivity in later personality development (Brody & Axelrad, 1978). Ethological-attachment theorists explain that adults' responsiveness to infant signals is innate, and that this responsiveness leads to a secure attachment of infants to their mothers (Ainsworth et al., 1978; Bowlby, 1969). Organismic theorists (Brazelton, Kowlowski, & Main, 1974) emphasize the early capacities of infants to communicate with sensitive parents. Social learning theorists suggest that infants' competencies and sense of competency are derived from parental behavior that is contingent upon the infant's own behavior (Watson, 1979; Gewirtz, 1977).

Documenting Responsiveness

Evidence documents parental responsiveness to infant signals as early as the first days of life. When infants pause in their sucking, mothers respond by jiggling the bottle (Kaye, 1977). Examination of the feeding of newborn infants by mothers and fathers indicates that both parents respond similarly to signals from their infants (Sawin & Parke, 1979). Clearly the care-giving context has power to elicit responsiveness in parents very early.

Not until infants are 4 months old is there evidence documenting responsiveness in the context of naturally occurring play (Stevenson, VerHoeve, Roach, & Leavitt, 1986). From hour-long observations of mothers and infants at home, periods of attentiveness were examined. Within these periods of attentiveness, microanalytical techniques were used to characterize the structure of the communication of mothers and infants. To examine the mother's vocal responsiveness to her infant, the probability of a mother's vocalization following an infant's vocalization was compared with the ongoing likelihood of the mother's vocalizing. There was a positive association between infant's vocalization and subsequent mother's vocalization. Furthermore, during periods of infant's attentiveness, infants also responded to the vocalizations of mothers. Restated, patterns of vocal exchange between mothers and 4-month-old infants during play were structurally similar to patterns of adult conversation. These conversational exchanges are clearly an important part of the play of young infants and their parents at home.

Empirical Support

Beyond documenting responsiveness, there is considerable empirical support for the importance of responsiveness during play for very young children's social and cognitive growth. The research of Ainsworth (Ainsworth, 1969; Ainsworth & Bell, 1974) emphasizes the importance of maternal responsiveness for infants' social development. It is from infants' experiences with sensitive and responsive mothers that secure attachment develops. Yarrow and his colleagues (Yarrow, Rubenstein, & Pedersen, 1975) found that infants' experiences during play with responsive mothers and with responsive toys were both related to the development of cognitive competence.

And finally, in the research of Lewis and Coates (1980), the input of infants' social environments was assessed by measuring the frequency of input and by measuring responsiveness to infant signals. Only the measure of responsiveness was related to infant cognitive competence.

With this theoretical and empirical support for the importance of responsiveness in the early environment of the child, parents are not only actors who shape their infant's world by structuring the play environment, but parents also influence infant development by responding to signals from infants and toddlers during play at home. An interesting intervention program for developmentally delayed infants encouraged increased responsiveness by mothers during play interactions (Seitz & Hoekenga, 1974). Not only was the intervention successful at increasing mothers' responsiveness, but the program reduced the appearance of retardation in the young children (Wikler, Stevenson, & Seitz, 1984). When naïve observers viewed videotapes of trained mothers playing with their developmentally delayed young children, observers reacted as positively to the children of trained mothers as to nondelayed children. This was in sharp contrast to observers' more negative reaction to the developmentally delayed children's play with their mothers before training.

CONCLUSION

In summary, this chapter has examined the ecological context of the play of infants and toddlers in terms of the social and setting characteristics of the microsystem and the macrosystem influences of culture and social class (Bronfenbrenner, 1979). Early theorists considered the infant to be a passive observer of a world constructed by parents through play. According to this framework, the role of the parent was to provide stimulation of sufficient quantity and appropriate quality to the passive infant. More recent theory recognizes infants' contributions in shaping their own world. According to this framework, parents make a special contribution to infant development as they respond to signals from the infant during play. This responsiveness to infant signals during play becomes the crucial aspect of early play for facilitating development.

Individual parents differ in the success with which they are able to respond to infant signals within the context of play. Evidence reviewed here suggests that the sensitivity of individual parents is influenced by characteristics of the infant including risk status, infant responsiveness to the parent, and disability. Evidence suggests that parent characteristics such as age or gender may have little influence on parental sensitivity to infant signals, although they do influence other aspects of play behavior. Rather, the cultural context of child rearing, and possible parental psychopathology, may contribute to the sensitivity and responsiveness of parents during play and to the infants' opportunity to play with a variety of partners.

REFERENCES

Ainsworth, M.D.S. (1969). Object relations, dependency, and attachment: A theoretical review of the infant–mother relationship. *Child Development, 40,* 969–1025.

Ainsworth, M.D.S. (1973). The development of infant–mother attachment. In B.M. Caldwell & H.N. Ricciuti (Eds.), *Review of child development research* (Vol. 3, pp. 1–94). Chicago: University of Chicago Press.

Ainsworth, M.D.S. (1977). Infant development and mother–infant interaction among Ganda and American families. In P.H. Leiderman, S.R. Tulkin, & A. Rosenfeld (Eds.), *Culture and infancy: Variations in the human experience* (pp. 119–150). New York: Academic.

Ainsworth, M.D.S., & Bell, S.M. (1974). Mother–infant interaction and the development of competence. In K.J. Connolly & J.S. Bruner (Eds.), *The growth of competence.* New York: Academic.

Ainsworth, M.D.S., Blehar, M.C., Waters, E., & Wall, S. (1978). *Patterns of attachment: A psychological study of the strange situation.* Hillsdale, NJ: Erlbaum.

Bell, R.Q., & Harper, L.V. (1977). *Child effects on adults.* Hillsdale, NJ: Erlbaum.

Belsky, J. (1980). Mother–infant interaction at home and in the laboratory: A comparative study. *Journal of Genetic Psychology, 137,* 37–47.

Bowlby, J. (1969). *Attachment and loss: (Vol. 1). Attachment.* New York: Basic Books.

Bradley, R.H., & Caldwell, B.M. (1984). Children: A study of the relationship between home environment and cognitive development during the first 5 years. In A.W. Gottfried (Ed.), *Home environment and early cognitive development* (pp. 5–56). New York: Academic.

Brazelton, T.B. (1977). Implications of infant development among the Mayan Indians of Mexico. In P.H. Leiderman, S.R. Tulkin, & A. Rosenfeld (Eds.), *Culture and infancy: Variations in the human experience* (pp. 151–188). New York: Academic Press.

Brazelton, T.B., Koslowski, B., & Main, M. (1974). The origins of reciprocity: The early mother–infant interaction. In M. Lewis & L.A. Rosenblum (Eds.), *The effects of the infant on its caregiver.* New York: International Universities Press.

Bretherton, I., O'Connell, B., Shore, C., & Bates, E. (1984). The effect of contextual variation on symbolic play: Development from 20 to 28 months. In I. Bretherton (Ed.), *Symbolic play: The development of social understanding* (pp. 271–298). New York: Academic Press.

Bretherton, I., Stolberg, U., & Kreye, M. (1981). Engaging strangers in proximal interaction: Infants' social initiative. *Developmental Psychology, 17,* 746–755.

Brody, S., & Axelrad, S. (1978). *Mothers, fathers, and children.* New York: International Universities Press.

Bronfenbrenner, U. (1979). *The ecology of human development: Experiments by nature and design.* Cambridge, MA: Harvard University Press.

Brookhart, J., & Hock, E. (1976). The effects of experimental context and experimental background on infants' behavior toward their mothers and a stranger. *Child Development, 47,* 333–340.

Bruner, J.S. (1977). Early social interaction and language acquisition. In H.R. Schaffer (Ed.), *Studies in mother–infant interaction.* New York: Academic.

Caldwell, B.M., & Bradley, R.H. (1984). *Administration manual: Home observation for measurement of the environment* (rev. ed.). Little Rock: University of Arkansas.

Casler, L. (1961). Maternal deprivation: A critical review of the literature. *Monographs of the Society for Research in Child Development, 26*(2, Serial No. 80).

Casler, L. (1965). The effects of extra tactile stimulation on a group of institutionalized infants. *Genetic Psychology Monographs, 71,* 137–175.

Casler, L. (1975). Supplementary auditory and vestibular stimulation: Effects on institutionalized infants. *Journal of Experimental Child Psychology, 19,* 456–463.

Chisholm, J.S. (1981). Residence patterns and the environment of mother–infant interaction among the Navajo. In T.M. Field, A.M. Sostek, P. Vietze, & P.H. Leiderman (Eds.), *Culture and early interactions* (pp. 3–20). Hillsdale, NJ: Lawrence Erlbaum.

Clarke-Stewart, K.A. (1978). And daddy makes three: The father's impact on mother and young child. *Child Development, 49,* 466–478.

Clarke-Stewart, K.A. (1982). *Daycare.* Cambridge, MA: Harvard University Press.

Darvill, D. (1982). Ecological influences on children's play: Issues and approaches. In D.J. Pepler & K.H. Rubin (Eds.), *The play of children: Current theory and research* (Vol. 6, pp. 144–153). Basel, Switzerland: S. Karger.

Dunn, J., & Kendrick, C. (1982). *Siblings: Love, envy, and understanding.* Cambridge, MA: Harvard University Press.

Fenson, L. (1986). The developmental progression of play. In A.W. Gottfried & C.C. Brown (Eds.), *Play interactions: The contribution of play materials and parental involvement to children's development.* Lexington, MA: Lexington.

Field, T.M. (1984). Early interactions between infants and their postpartum depressed mothers. *Infant Behavior & Development, 7,* 517–522.

Field, T.M., Sostek, A.M., Vietze, P., & Leiderman, P.H. (1981). *Culture and early interactions.* Hillsdale, NJ: Erlbaum.

Field, T.M., & Widmayer, S.M. (1981). Mother–infant interactions among lower SES Black, Cuban, Puerto Rican and South American immigrants. In T.M. Field, A.M. Sostek, P. Vietze, & P.H. Leiderman (Eds.), *Culture and early interactions* (pp. 41–62). Hillsdale, NJ: Erlbaum.

Gewirtz, J.L. (1977). Maternal responding and the conditioning of infant crying: Directions of influence within the attachment acquisition process. In B.C. Etzel, J.M. LeBlasnc, & D.M. Baer (Eds.), *New developments in behavioral research: Theory, method, and application.* Hillsdale, NJ: Erlbaum.

Goldberg, S. (1977). Infant development and mother–infant interaction in urban Zambia. In P.H. Leiderman, S.R. Tulkin, & A. Rosenfeld (Eds.), *Culture and infancy: Variations in the human experience* (pp. 211–244). New York: Academic.

Horner, T.M. (1980). Test–retest and home–clinic characteristics of the Bayley scales of infant development in nine- and fifteen-month-old infants. *Child Development, 51,* 751–758.

Howes, C. (1983). Caregiver behavior in center and family day care. *Journal of Applied Developmental Psychology, 4,* 99–107.

Hunt, J. McV. (1961). *Intelligence and experience.* New York: Ronald.

Kaye, K. (1977). Toward the origin of dialogue. In H.R. Schaffer (Ed.), *Studies in mother–infant interaction.* New York: Academic.

Kilbride, H.W., Johnson, D.I., & Streissguth, A.P. (1977). Social class, birth order, and newborn experience. *Child Development, 48,* 1686–1688.

Killarney, J., & McCluskey, K. (1980, April). *Interactional styles and teaching strategies in families with one-year-old infants.* Paper presented at the International Conference on Infant Studies, New Haven, CT.

Klein, R.P., & Durfee, J.T. (1979). Comparison of attachment behaviors in home and laboratory. *Psychological Reports, 44,* 1059–1064.

Konner, M. (1977). Infancy among the Kalahari Desert San. In P.H. Leiderman, S.R. Tulkin, & A. Rosenfeld (Eds.), *Culture and infancy: Variations in the human experience* (pp. 287–328). New York: Academic.

Lamb, M.E. (1976). Interactions between 8-month-old children and their fathers and mothers. In M.E. Lamb (Ed.), *The role of the father in child development* (pp. 307–327). New York: Wiley.

Lamb, M.E. (1978). Interactions between eighteen-month-olds and their pre-school-age siblings. *Child Development, 49,* 51–59.

Lamb, M.E. (1979). The effects of the social context on dyadic social inter-action. In M.E. Lamb, S.J. Suomi, & G.R. Stephenson (Eds.), *Social interaction analysis: Methodological issues* (pp. 253–268). Madison, WI: University of Wisconsin Press.

Lamb, M.E., & Easterbrooks, M.A. (1980). Individual differences in parental sensitivity: Origins, components and consequences. In M.E. Lamb & L.R. Sherrod (Eds.), *Infant social cognition: Empirical and theoretical considerations* (pp. 127–153). Hillsdale, NJ: Erlbaum.

Leavitt, L.A., & Stevenson, M.B. (1983, May). *Individual differences in mother and infant vocal responsiveness: Low birthweight and normal birthweight infants.* Paper presented at the second International Workshop on the "At Risk" Infant, Jerusalem, Israel.

Leiderman, P.D., Tulkin, S.R., & Rosenfeld, A. (1977). *Culture and infancy: Variations in the human experience.* New York: Academic.

Lewin, K. (1931). Environmental forces in child behavior and development. In C. Murchison (Ed.), *A handbook of child psychology.* Worcester, MA: Clark University Press.

Lewis, M. (1972). State as an infant–environment interaction: An analysis of mother–infant interaction as a function of sex. *Merrill–Palmer Quarterly, 18,* 95–121.

Lewis, M., & Ban, P. (1977). Variance and invariance in the mother–infant interaction: A cross-cultural study. In P.H. Leiderman, S.R. Tulkin, & A. Rosenfeld (Eds.), *Culture and infancy: Variations in the human experience* (pp. 329–356). New York: Academic.

Lewis, M., & Coates, D.L. (1980). Mother–infant interaction and cognitive development in twelve-week-old infants. *Infant Behavior & Development, 3,* 95–106.

Lewis, M., & Wilson, C.D. (1972). Infant development in lower-class American families. *Human Development, 115,* 112–127.

Lissovoy, V.D. (1973). Child care by adolescent parents. *Children Today, 2*(4), 22–25.

McAnarney, E.R. (1983). *Premature adolescent pregnancy and parenthood.* New York: Grune & Stratton.

MacPhee, D., Ramey, C.T., & Yeates, K.O. (1984). Home environment and early cognitive development: Implications for intervention. In A.W. Gottfried (Ed.), *Home environment and early cognitive development* (pp. 343–377). New York: Academic.

Martini, M., & Kirkpatrick, J. (1981). Early interactions in the Marquesas Islands. In T.M. Field, A.M. Sostek, P. Vietze, & P.H. Leiderman (Eds.), *Culture and early interactions* (pp. 189–214). Hillsdale, NJ: Erlbaum.

Moss, H.A., & Jones, S.J. (1977). Relations between maternal attitudes and maternal behavior as a function of social class. In P.H. Leiderman, S.R. Tulkin, & A. Rosenfeld (Eds.), *Culture and infancy: Variations in the human experience* (pp. 439–468). New York: Academic.

Moustakas, C.E., Sigel, I.E., & Schalock, H.D. (1956). An objective method for the measurement and analysis of child–adult interaction. *Child Development, 27,* 109–134.

Mueller, E.C., & Vandell, D. (1979). Infant–infant interaction. In J.D. Osofsky (Eds.), *Handbook of infant development* (pp. 591–622). New York: Wiley.

Munroe, R.H., & Munroe, R.L. (1971). Household density and infant care in an East African society. *Journal of Social Psychology, 83,* 3–13.

Musick, J.S., & Cohler, B.J. (Eds.) (1983). *Parental psychopathology and infant development: A special issue of the Infant Mental Health Journal, 4,* 135–286.

National Commission on Working Women. (1985). *Working mothers and children* (Child Care Fact Sheet). Washington, DC: NCWW.

O'Connell, B., & Bretherton, I. (1984). Toddlers' play, alone and with mother: The role of maternal guidance. In I. Bretherton (Ed.), *Symbolic play: The development of social understanding* (pp. 337–368). New York: Academic Press.

Office for Maternal and Child Health. (1980). *Guidelines for early intervention programs.* Based on a conference: Health issues in early intervention programs. Office of Maternal and Child Health, Department of Health and Human Services.

Parke, R.D., Grossmann, K., & Tinsley, B.R. (1981). Father–mother–infant interaction in the newborn period: A German–American comparison. In T.M. Field, A.M. Sostek, P. Vietze, & P.H. Leiderman (Eds.), *Culture and early interactions* (pp. 95–114). Hillsdale, NJ: Erlbaum.

Parmelee, A.H., Sigman, M., Kopp, C.B., & Haber, A. (1975). The concept of a cumulative risk score for infants. In N. Ellis (Ed.), *Aberrant development in infancy: Human and animal studies* (pp. 113–121).

Pedersen, F.A. (1980). *The father–infant relationship: Observational studies in the family setting.* New York: Praeger.

Power, T.G. (1985). Mother–and father–infant play: A developmental analysis. *Child Development, 56,* 1514–1524.

Power, T.G., & Parke, R.A. (1982). Play as a context for early learning: Lab and home analysis. In I.E. Sigel & L.M. Laosa (Eds.), *Families as learning environments for children.* New York: Plenum.

Redditi, J.S., & Stevenson, M.B. (1985). Mother–infant interaction in families with infants who are developmentally delayed, developmentally delayed with physical handicaps, or developmentally normal. *American Journal of Mental Deficiency, 90,* 513–520.

Roach, M.A. (1982). *Relationships between infant–mother and infant–peer interaction systems.* Unpublished master's thesis, University of Wisconsin–Madison.

Ross, G., Kagan, J., Zelazo, P., & Kotelchuck, M. (1975). Separation protest in infants in home and laboratory. *Developmental Psychology, 11,* 256–257.

Ross, H.S., & Goldman, B.D. (1975). Establishing new social relations in infancy. In T. Alloway, P. Pliner, & L. Krames (Eds.), *Advances in the study of communications and affect* (Vol. 3, pp. 61–79). New York: Plenum.

Rubenstein, J.L., & Howes, C. (1979). Caregiving and infant behavior in day care and in homes. *Developmental Psychology, 15,* 1–24.

Rubenstein, J.L., Pedersen, F.A., & Yarrow, L.J. (1977). What happens when mother is away: A comparison of mothers and substitute caregivers. *Developmental Psychology, 13,* 529–530.

Ruopp, R., Travers, J., Glantz, F., & Coelen, C. (1979). *Children at the center: Summary findings and their implications.* Cambridge, MA: Abt.

Rutter, M. (1979). Maternal deprivation, 1972–1978: New findings, new concepts, new approaches. *Child Development, 50,* 283–305.

Sawin, D.B., & Parke, R.D. (1979). Fathers' affectionate stimulation and caregiving behaviors with newborn infants. *Family Coordinator,* 509–513.

Schachter, J., Elmer, E., Ragins, N., Wimberly, F., & Lachin, J.M. (1977). Assessment of mother–infant interaction: Schizophrenic and non-schizophrenic mothers. *Merrill–Palmer Quarterly, 23,* 193–206.

Schaffer, H.R. (1977). Early interactive development. In H.R. Schaffer (Ed.), *Studies in mother–infant interaction.* New York: Academic.

Seitz, S., & Hoekenga, R. (1974). Modeling as a training tool for retarded children and their parents. *Mental Retardation, 12,* 28–31.

Sostek, A.M., Vietze, P., Zaslow, M., Kreiss, L., van der Waals, F., & Rubinstein, D. (1981). Social context in caregiver–infant interaction: A film study of fais and the United States. In T.M. Field, A.M. Sostek, P. Vietze, & P.H. Leiderman (Eds.), *Culture and early interactions* (pp. 21–40). Hillsdale, NJ: Erlbaum.

Sroufe, L.A. (1977). Wariness of strangers and the study of infant development. *Child Development, 48,* 731–746.

Sroufe, L.A., Waters, E., & Matas, L. (1974). Contextual determinants of infant affective response. In M. Lewis & L.A. Rosenblum (Eds.), *The origins of fear.* New York: Wiley.

Stevenson, M.B., & Lamb, M.E. (1979). Effects of infant sociability and the caretaking environment on infant cognitive performance. *Child Development, 50,* 340–349.

Stevenson, M.B., & Lamb, M.E. (1980). The effects of social experience on cognitive competence and performance. In M.E. Lamb & L.R. Sherrod (Eds.), *Infant social cognition: Empirical and theoretical considerations* (pp. 375–393). Hillsdale, NJ: Erlbaum.

Stevenson, M.B., Leavitt, L.A., Roach, M.A., Chapman, R.S., & Miller, J.F. (1986). Mothers' speech to their one-year-old infants in home and laboratory settings. *Journal of Psycholinguistic Research, 15,* 451–461.

Stevenson, M.B., Leavitt, L.A., & Silverberg, S.B. (1985). Mother–infant interaction: Down's syndrome case studies. In S. Harel & N.J. Anastasiow (Eds.), *The at-risk infant: Psycho-socio-medical aspects* (pp. 379–388). Baltimore: Paul H. Brookes.

Stevenson, M.B., Leavitt, L.A., Thompson, R.H., & Roach, M.A. (1983, April). *Play in the family: Mothers and fathers with their infants and preschoolers.* Presented at the biennial meeting of the Society for Research in Child Development, Detroit.

Stevenson, M.B., & Roach, M.A. (1984, April). *Fathers' and mothers' interactions with their one-year-olds: Analyses of behavioral frequencies and contingencies.* Paper presented at the International Conference on Infant Studies, New York.

Stevenson, M.B., & Roach, M.A. (1987, April). *Adolescent and adult single mother's interaction with their four-month-olds: Analyses of behavioral frequencies and contingencies.* Paper presented at the biennial meeting of the Society for Research in Child Development, Baltimore.

Stevenson, M.B., Roach, M.A., & VerHoeve, J.N. (1984, April). *Behavioral contingencies during feeding of 8-month-old low birthweight infants.* Paper presented at the International Conference on Infant Studies, New York City.

Stevenson, M.B., VerHoeve, J.N., Roach, M.A., & Leavitt, L.A. (1986). The beginning of conversation: Early patterns of mother–infant vocal responsiveness. *Infant Behavior & Development, 9,* 423–440.

Super, C.M. (1981). Behavioral development in infancy. In R.H. Munroe, R.L. Munroe, & B.B. Whiting (Eds.), *Handbook of cross-cultural human development.* New York: Garland STPM.

Tinsley, B.R., & Parke, R.D. (1984). Grandparents as support and socialization agents. In M. Lewis (Ed.), *Beyond the dyad* (pp. 161–194). New York: Plenum.

Tulkin, S.R. (1977). Social class differences in maternal and infant behavior. In P.H. Leiderman, S.R. Tulkin, & A. Rosenfeld (Eds.), *Culture and infancy: Variations in the human experience* (pp. 495–538). New York: Academic.

Vandell, D.L., & Wilson, K.S. (1983, April). *The relationship between infants' interactions with mother, sibling, and peer.* Paper presented at the biennial meeting of the Society for Research in Child Development, Detroit.

Wachs, T.D., & Gruen, G.E. (1982). *Early experience and human development.* New York: Plenum.

Watson, J.S. (1979). Perception of contingency as a determinant of social responsiveness. In E. Thoman (Ed.), *The origins of social responsiveness.* New York: Erlbaum.

Whiting, B.B., & Whiting, J.W.M. (1975). *Children of six cultures: A psychocultural analysis.* Cambridge, MA: Harvard University Press.

Wikler, L., Stevenson, M.B., & Seitz, S. (1984, May). *Reducing visibility of mental retardation through parent training.* Paper presented at the meeting of the American Association of Mental Deficiency, Minneapolis.

Williams, T.M. (1974). Childrearing practices of young mothers: What we know, how it matters, why it's so little. *American Journal of Orthopsychiatry, 44,* 70–75.

Yarrow, L.J., Rubenstein, J., & Pedersen, F. (1975). *Infant and environment.* New York: Wiley.

Yogman, M.W. (1982). Development of the father–infant relationship. In H. Fitzgerald, B. Lester, & M.W. Yogman (Eds.), *Theory and research in behavioral pediatrics* (Vol. 1, pp. 221–229). New York: Plenum.

6

Play With Peers in Child Care Settings

CAROLLEE HOWES
OLIVIA UNGER
University of California, Los Angeles

INTRODUCTION

While the development of pretend play and of social pretend play is often considered to be motivated by underlying cognitive changes in the capacity of the child to manipulate symbols (McClune–Nicolich, 1981), all of children's development, including play, occurs within a particular ecocultural context. The ecocultural context or the social ecology of the child includes environmental features which directly affect the child, for example, patterns of interaction with significant caregivers, and environmental features which only indirectly affect the child, for example, the education of the care-giving adult (Bronfenbrenner, 1979; Weisner, 1984).

The particular ecocultural context provides the child with a structure for the expression of newly developing competencies. Thus as described by Bruner (Bruner & Sherwood, 1976), the care-giving adult's social and verbal behaviors directed to the child provide a structure or scaffold for emerging play skills. Aspects of the ecocultural context such as caregivers, materials and peers may foster or inhibit the emergence of competent behaviors. Finally, the ecocultural context may influence the content of the child's play. For example, children in age-graded child care centers may spend their days playing elaborated versions of superhero games while children in more traditional societies really care for younger siblings in real-life mommy and baby games (Weisner, 1984).

The purpose of this chapter is to examine the influences of a particular ecocultural context, child care, on a particular domain of children's development, social pretend play. Social pretend play is a form of play in which nonliteral or symbolic material is integrated into social play interactions. That is within the context of social play with a peer, children add elements of fantasy and communicate to the partner that the nature of the play is pretend.

Preschool children, who are usually quite accomplished at social pretend play, often begin social pretend play with such markers as "Let's pretend we are going shopping and there is a lion in our path" or "You be the Mommy and I'll be the sister" (Garvey, 1977). However, the focus of this chapter will be on the emergence of social pretend play in younger children, between 18 and 30 months of age. Children in this age group usually lack the language flexibility and vocabulary to initiate social pretend play with verbal markers. Recent research suggests, however, that if the children have been in relatively stable peer groups since infancy, and if they are observed in familiar settings with familiar peers, toddler-age children are found to use actions and one-to-two-word phrases to communicate the nonliteral nature of social pretend play (Howes, 1985).

Although Vygotsky did not study children under the age of 3, a Vygotskian perspective is useful in examining the development of social pretend play in toddler-age children. A Vygotskian (1978) perspective supports the notion that social pretend play emerges from the experience of social interaction between the child and a play partner. In order to explain how the child's individual development occurs within social interactions, Vygotsky (1978) has introduced the notion of the zone of proximal development or ZPD. The ZPD is "the distance between the actual developmental level as determined by independent problem solving" and the child's developmental level "under adult guidance or in collaboration with more capable peers" (Vygotsky, 1978, p. 86). Thus adult–child play or child–child play with a more capable partner allows the child to extend skills to produce more complex behavior than the child would have accomplished on one's own.

Empirical research on the ZPD in other domains of development find that more experienced play partners facilitate development by arranging appropriate sequences of materials and task, and by transmitting information and strategies to the child as they participate together in an activity (Rogoff, Malkin, & Gilbride 1984; Wertsch, 1979; Wood, 1980). Therefore, the emergence of social pretend play in toddler-age children would be expected to be facilitated by experiences in constructing play with more experienced play partners.

Vygotsky (1978) suggests that within play, freed from situational constraints whereby one object can now represent another, children create their own ZPD. This allows children's conceptual and imaginative activities to be extended beyond their average abilities. From this it follows that same age children engaging together in social pretend play might also each be stimulated to engage in more complex behavior than could be accomplished by the child outside of play or in solitary play. Furthermore, the collaborative activity of constructing the play may serve to stimulate still more complex behavior (Rubenstein & Howes, 1976).

Strategies used by same-age toddlers to construct social pretend play support the view that collaborating children may produce complex play. Fifteen to thirty-three month old children were observed within same-age dyads. The children used strategies that both accommodated the partner's pretend action and required a response from the partner; for example, Child A said, "Rock your cradle," as Child B placed his doll in the cradle. Child A's doll was in her cradle and the two children engaged in the game of "putting the babies to sleep."

The Vygotskian perspective will be used to frame this chapter. The goal of the chapter is to identify social agents within the child care ecocultural setting that facilitate collaborative pretend play. Two major social agents are to be found within the child care setting: care-giving adults and peers. As has been outlined from a Vygotskian perspective, each of these social agents could potentially facilitate the construction of collaborative social pretend play. In the subsequent sections of the chapter, the contributions of care-giving adults and peers to social pretend play in toddlers will be reviewed. The extant research on early social pretend play is small, therefore, as well as reviewing the existing literature, suggestions for future research will be made.

CARE-GIVING ADULTS

From a theoretical point of view, care-giving adults might contribute to the emergence of social pretend play in toddlers in several different ways. First of all, by directly interacting with the children in their care they may provide a framework or a ZPD for the child's emerging social pretend play. Second, care-giving adults might facilitate and structure encounters between play would be enhanced. Third, as care-giving adults are responsible for the construction of space within the child care center and for the provision of materials, they might facilitate social pretend play by the particular arrangements of space and objects selected. In the ideal world there would be a body of research studies to support each of these functions of caregivers. In fact, there is almost no empirical literature on how care-giving adults facilitate social pretend play in toddlers. There is, however, a body of related literature to support the outlined functions of caregivers. In subsequent sections, this literature will be reviewed.

Within the field of child care, there has been a debate concerning the training of adult caregivers for child care. While many caregivers are well educated in child development, most states do not require extensive training for teachers in child care. It seems reasonable to assume that if caregivers are trained in child development they would be more likely to interact directly with the children, facilitate and structure encounters with peers, and arrange space and provide objects so that opportunities for toddler social pretend play would be maximized. In other words, caregiver training would serve as a marker of the knowledge and ability to facilitate social pretend play. This assumption was tested in the final section of the discussion of the role of the care-giving adult in facilitating social pretend play.

Care-Giver–Child Interaction

Rubenstein & Howes (1979) report that within child care centers toddlers spend 53% of their time interacting with a care-giving adult. About 3% of this interaction is social play (mutual game playing such as peek-a-boo) and another 23% is object play (the adult participates in play or games with the toddler and an object, e.g., ball play). Howes (1979) reports similar proportions for toddlers in family day-care home child care. In both settings adult caregivers are more likely than mothers who are engaged full time in child care to involve the toddler in mutual game playing (Howes & Rubenstein, 1985; Rubenstein & Howes, 1979). While we know that care-giving adults are engaging in mutual play activity with the children in their care we can only speculate about the nature of the play, literal or pretend.

Studies of parent–toddler play support the Vygotskian perspective that adults guide children to more competent performance. Studies which describe the play of parents and children suggest that parent's interaction with the child does facilitate the construction of social pretend play (Seidner, 1984; Miller & Garvey, 1984; Sachs, 1980). By playing pretend with the child the parent communicates the structure of social pretend play. Sachs (1980) suggests that the adult plays pretend for the child before the child has completely mastered the pretend form. By manipulating objects as if they were animate the parent communicates that objects can be used in nonliteral ways and that these symbols can be incorporated into the social play.

Since previous research suggests that care-giving adults in child care are more likely to play with children than are mothers, we might assume that care-giving adults in child care also provide experiences in constructing social pretend play. Future research is needed to describe such interactions within child care settings and to examine which aspects of the wider ecocultural context of child care support such adult–child encounters.

Caregiver Facilitation of Encounters with Peers

There is little extant literature to describe how caregivers facilitate toddlers' encounters with their peers. Research on preschool classroom structure suggests that with more children per adult there is less adult–child contact and more peer contact (O'Connor, 1975), and within more teacher-directed curriculum models there is less peer contact than within child-directed curriculum models (Reuter & Yunik, 1973). (However, peer contact can be of many different forms, for example, aggressive encounters, out-of-control running, or collaborative problem solving in constructing social pretend play.) Peer contacts which involve collaborative interactions could be structured by a sensitive caregiver who would have the skills to organize the encounter and also to remove oneself when the children were able to continue without adult support. Future research in this area could describe such teacher strategies and then compare strategies experimentally.

Construction of Space and Provision of Objects

Caregiving adults in child care are responsible for the arrangement of space and the provision of material for the children. There is a fairly extensive literature on space and object influences on play. (For a review of this literature see Rubin, Fein, & Vandenberg, 1983). In this section the portion of the literature which applies to play between toddlers and their peers will be reviewed. There is only limited literature on the influence of space arrangements and objects on social pretend play in the toddler period. We will review the literature on the influences of space and objects on both social and social pretend play in toddlers. The complementary and reciprocal structure of toddler social play, is similar to the structure of social pretend play (Howes, 1985). Therefore, spacial arrangements and objects which facilitate social play may be assumed to also facilitate social pretend play.

Toddler-age children are more likely than preschool children to use large concrete objects in their social pretend play (Gowen, 1978). This supports Vygotsky's (1978) notion that younger children, as opposed to older children, are less likely to sever thought from object and require concrete pivots or links to support conceptualizations. This finding is also consistent with the observations that toddler social pretend play is communicated via actions on objects rather than verbal markers of pretend.

Laboratory investigations of early peer interaction found that peer play was increased when there were no objects or only large nonportable objects present (DeStefano & Mueller, 1982); Eckerman & Whatley, 1977). A study of toddler peer play in child care centers and family day-care homes (Howes & Rubenstein, 1981) found that not only the nature of the objects that were available to the children but also the spatial arrangement of objects and rooms provided for peer-interaction-influenced peer play. In child care centers, which more often than family day-care homes had large nonportable play equipment, the most complex peer social play occurred when the children were using this equipment. Children in family day-care homes achieved the same level of complex social play by using the spatial arrangements of the home to structure the play. The authors conclude that complex social play in toddler-age children is facilitated by inanimate environments which organize space so that toddlers can focus on each other and respond to the action of the other. The spaces for these encounters must be large enough to keep the toddlers from physically intruding on each other and shaped to provide paths for complementary actions. Examples of these arrangements include corners, hallways, and connecting rooms, with permission to play "run chase"; climbing structures that provide paths to go in, out and around; and playhouses that can be circled and peeped into.

These studies suggest that social pretend play in toddlers might be best facilitated by large objects that suggest pretense and provide spaces for dyads to focus on the action of the other. For example, cooking material, a stove, and a small table with chairs might be set up under a climbing structure. A kitchen area under a climbing structure would provide a protected space and focus peer encounters. The cooking materials and stove would provide realist props for the children's pretend. Similar play might be facilitated by a large, two-seater, wooden car, complete with steering wheel, ignition, and seatbelts. The two seats would both limit peer play to a dyad, and focus the attention of the partner on the other. The equipment would suggest pretend activities.

Caregiver Training

The emergence of social pretend play in toddlers is enhanced by care-giving adults who engage with the child in pretend play, facilitate collaboration between peers, and organize the space and objects so that play is facilitated. An increasingly large literature on quality indicators in infant and toddler child care (Howes, 1987) suggests that children's development within child care settings is influenced by the training of care-giving adults. Specifically, caregivers in both center and family day-care home child care who have more child development training are more likely than caregivers with less training to engage in play with the infants and toddlers in their care (Howes, 1981). Similarly, care-giving adults with more training in child development arranged classrooms which receive higher scores on the Prescott Environmental Inventory, a measure of developmentally appropriate child care environments (Olenick, 1986). Perhaps with greater training, caregivers are more sensitive to the developmental needs of the children and provide a framework which encourages social pretend play.

To examine directly the influence of caregiver training in child development on the emergence of social pretend play, the social pretend play of 64 two-year-olds enrolled in six different child care centers was compared (Howes & Farver, 1985). In three of the child care centers ($n = 35$ children) the director of the center had a PhD or Master's degree in a child-related field and the teachers had received both formal postsecondary and in-service training in child development. In the remaining centers ($n = 29$ children) the director of the center had postsecondary training in child development but the teachers had no formal training and there was no in-service program. The centers were comparable in adult–child ratio, group size, and socioeconomic background of the children served.

All of the children in the study were from low-income families. Fifty-two percent were Anglo, 16% Latin, 16% Asian, and the remaining 14% Black. Equal numbers of boys and girls participated in the study. There were no demographic differences in the children in the two samples.

Each toddler was observed with a randomly selected same-sex partner as the two children played with the Fisher–Price camping set, a toy designed to facilitate social pretend play. Social behavior used to construct social pretend play and the complexity of the social pretend play were coded every 30 seconds for a total of 15 minutes.

The following behaviors were coded. Metacommunications about

play were coded as either verbal or nonverbal. Verbal metacommunications included utterances that established a script for the
pretense, made explicit how other verbalizations and behavior should
be interpreted, or clarified the organization of the pretense, the
rules that govern pretense, or whether a pretense state existed.
Nonverbal metacommunications were gestures, eye gazes, or objects
offered that directed fantasy actions to the partner. Teaching behaviors were defined as giving explicit instructions regarding the use
of the toy, and imitation was defined as the immediate imitation of
the other's fantasy action or verbalization.

The complexity of the social pretend play was rated, using a coding
scheme developed by Howes (1985). In order for social pretend play
to be rated, the children had to engage in social interaction with at
least two turns, that is, the social bids of Child A received contingent
social responses from Child B. Social pretend play was rated as either
simple social pretend play or cooperative social pretend play. In
simple social pretend play, both children performed pretense actions,
which although temporally related or involving similar objects, did
not include complementary roles. In cooperative social pretend play
the fantasy actions and/or verbalizations of both partners indicated
that children had assumed complementary pretend roles, for example,
mother–baby or bus driver–passenger.

Comparisons between the social pretend play activities of children
in the centers with high and low trained caregivers were made using
t-tests. These comparisons are presented in Table 1. Children in

**Table 1. Comparisons of Frequencies of Social Pretend Behaviors in
Children with and Without Trained Caregivers**

| | Caregiver Training | | | | | | |
| | High | | Low | | | | |
	M	SD	M	SD	t-Test	DF	Prob.
Social Behaviors							
Metacommunication							
verbal	3.8	1.9	.8	.5	2.09	52	.04
nonverbal	1.3	.8	.3	.2	2.80	62	.03
Teach	1.2	.6	1.3	.5	.55	62	.58
Imitate	1.0	.3	.4	.7	1.17	29	.25
Social Pretend Play							
Simple	4.6	1.3	3.6	3.7	.49	19	.63
Cooperative	11.47	9.6	3.5	1.4	4.67	34	.01

centers with trained caregivers used more verbal and nonverbal metacommunications about play and engaged in more cooperative social pretend play than children in centers with untrained teachers.

This study suggests that trained care-giving adults facilitate social pretend play in toddlers. It does not explain why such a relationship exists. Perhaps a knowledge of the capacities of a toddler assists the caregiver in structuring the environment, peer encounters, and his or her own interactions with the child so that the child's emerging understanding of social pretend is elaborated and maintained. With knowledge of child development, the caregivers may recognize the value of children's play thereby encouraging and supporting the development of play behaviors. Future studies should address the issue of caregiver training and social pretend play.

In summary, the care-giving adult in child care provides the eco-cultural context from which social pretend play may emerge. Within this context caregivers play with children and provide appropriate space and materials to facilitate social pretend. Although training was associated with children's more complex social pretend play, the mechanisms whereby caregiver–child interactions influence social pretend play are not understood at this time.

PEERS

Peers, of course, are important social agents in the emergence of social pretend play, for it is usually with peer partners that the child constructs social pretend play. Three aspects of the peer ecocultural context are important in the emergence of social pretend play: the familiarity of the peer, friendships with peers, and the age of the peer. Each of these aspects will be discussed in subsequent sections.

Peer Familiarity

Toddler-age children's peer interaction, due to their sensorimotor period of development, is initially based on actions which come to have social meaning (Hay, 1985). As toddlers approach their second birthdays they begin to "share meaning," that is, their peer interaction is based on symbols as well as action (Brenner & Mueller, 1982; Howes, 1985). The transition from action based interaction to inter-action based on shared meaning is facilitated by familiarity. With time toddlers construct games and routines, known and understood by each participant but difficult to communicate to the unfamiliar child.

For example, a small group of toddlers may understand a game that is signaled by putting on hats but is beyond the language capacity of the children to initiate by saying "let's play . . ." Unless the child is familiar with the game signal he or she will have trouble playing the game.

Further support for a relationship between peer familiarity and early capacities to use symbolic communication comes from Dunn and Kendrick (1979) who report that infant–preschool sibling dyads, who of course are familiar peers, are less dependent on objects than unrelated familiar peers to sustain complex interaction. Furthermore, some of the most complex examples of social pretend play in toddlers reported in the literature are to be found in the sibling pairs studied by Dunn and Dale (1984).

Several studies of preschool-age children have explicitly tested the relationship between peer familiarity and social pretend play. Doyle, Connolly, and Rivest (1979) compared 3-year-olds playing with familiar and unfamiliar age mates. With familiar peers, children engaged in more social pretend play. Matthews (1977) paired previously unacquainted 4-year-old children for three sessions of play with play materials suggestive of fantasy. Between the first and the third sessions, the proportion of time spent in social pretend play and number of ideational transformations increased.

FRIENDS

If the construction of social pretend play between age mates is facilitated by familiarity then toddler-age friends should be particularly adept in constructing social pretend play. Toddlers in stable peer groups such as those found in child care settings are reported to form stable friendships, and the social play of children within friendship pairs is more complex than the play of children with acquaintances who are not friends (Howes, 1983). Through repeated play experiences, friends develop a large repertoire of shared meanings and games. Support for friends greater facility in constructing social pretend play comes from work with preschool-age children. Gottman and Parkhurst (1980) report greater communication clarity and frequency of fantasy play between preschool-age children who were friends rather than strangers.

In order to examine directly the social pretend play of toddler-age friends, 43 children ranging in age from 16 to 33 months were observed over 4 months in their community-based child care centers. The children were enrolled in groups consisting of 14 to 16 toddlers;

there were no group differences in age range, or sex composition. All of the children were well acquainted and had been in the same peer group for at least 6 months.

For purposes of data analysis, the sample was divided into four age groups (defined by age at the onset of the study): (1) 16–17m., (n = 9), (2) 21–23m., (n = 14), (3) 27–28m., (n = 12), (4) 32–33m., (n = 8).

There were four data collection periods over a 4-month period; each period of data collection lasted for about 2 weeks. Four complete 5-minute play episodes were collected for each child during each data collection period. Play episodes were defined as an interactive unit between two children containing an initiation or social bid, the partner's response or lack of response, the content and order of subsequent social bids, and the termination of peer play or contact. At each data collection period, teachers were asked to identify friend pairs.

Brenner and Mueller's (1982) concept of shared meaning was expanded in this study to include social pretend play themes. Shared meanings are defined as a social interaction in which both participants used the same behavioral theme. The following shared meanings identified by Brenner and Mueller were observed: vocal prosocial, positive affect as a meaning shared, vocal copy, motor copy, run chase, peek-a-boo, object exchange, object possession struggle, aggression/rough and tumble, and shared reference. The following additional shared meanings were also observed: ballgame, giving rides (one child sits in a wagon or cart and is pulled by the other child), crash game (the children ride their bikes into each other and laugh and vocalize), reading (the children sit together holding a book, point out pictures to each other, and vocalize), cooking or eating, fix cars (one child sits in a wagon or cart and is pulled by the other child, then the wagon is stopped, the rider gets out, and both children use plastic hammers to pound on the wheel of the wagon), dress up, talk on the phone, be animals (the children crawl on hands and knees, growling at one another, or one child acts like an animal and the other child acts like the animal's master by feeding the animal), put baby to sleep, doctor, and gunfight.

Eight of the shared meanings (cooking or eating, fix cars, dress up, talk on phone, be animals, put baby to sleep, doctor, and gunfight) were considered pretend themes. Each child was assigned the following scores: frequency of engaging in each of the identified pretend play themes with friends and with nonfriends; and frequency of play episodes with friends and nonfriends.

The distribution of pretend theme shared meanings by age group is presented in Table 2. A larger proportion of children in the oldest two groups shared pretend meanings than in the younger two groups, and a large proportion of 21- to 26-month-old children shared pretend meanings than the proportion in 16- to 20-month-old children (x^2 (3) = 15.67, p < .01). Frequencies of pretend shared meanings also differed across the four age groups $F(3,39)$ = 4.42, p< .01. Twenty-seven to 31-month-old and 32- to 35-month-old children had higher frequencies of pretend theme shared meanings than 16- to 20-month-old children (Scheffe = .01).

Forty-one children, or 95%, had at least one teacher-identified friend. Children in all four age groups were equally likely to have at least one friend, although children in the oldest age group had more friends than children in the three youngest age groups, ($\bar{x}$(group 4) = 3.75, $\bar{x}$(groups 1,2,3) = 2.5, $F(3,41)$ = 4.05, p = .01). There were no age differences in the overall frequency of play episodes ($F(3,41)$ = .32 n.s.) with friends and with nonfriends.

The frequency of engaging in pretend play themes with friends and nonfriends at each age level was compared by dependent t tests. These comparisons are presented in Table 3. Children in the middle two age groups (21 to 31 months of age) were more likely to engage in pretend play themes with friends than with nonfriends.

The primary role of a friendship appeared to be one of facilitating

Table 2.   Proportion of Each Age Group Exhibiting Pretend Theme Shared Meanings

			Age Group			
			1	2	3	4
		Age Range When				
Themes	n[a]	Observed	16–20m.	21–26m.	27–31m.	32–35m.
Any Pretend	27	17–37	.25	.54	.92	1.00
Dress up and go out	15	17–36	.13	.23	.39	.71
Gunfight	6	19–28	.13	.23	.15	.00
Cooking or eating	16	19–28	.13	.23	.61	.31
Doctor	4	21–34	.00	.15	.00	.29
Put baby to sleep	6	23–32	.00	.08	.23	.29
Talk on phone	2	24–26	.00	.08	.08	.00
Fix cars	2	27–29	.00	.00	.08	.14
Be animals	2	32–36	.00	.00	.00	.57

[a] Number of children out of a possible 43 who demonstrated theme.

Table 3.   Comparison of Frequencies of Pretend Play Themes with Friends and Nonfriends in Each Age Group

Age Groups	Friends		Nonfriends		t	DF	Prob.
	M	SD	M	SD			
1. 16–20 months	.26	.23	.33	.26	.68	8	n.s.
2. 21–26 months	2.27	.87	1.05	.98	2.75	13	.02
3. 27–31 months	2.53	.61	1.15	.64	2.65	11	.05
4. 32–35 months	2.50	.57	2.25	1.92	.25	7	n.s.

pretend play when children were beginning to engage in social pretend rather than when social pretend play was well established. Twenty-one to 31-month-olds were less likely than older children to engage in pretend play themes but when they did engage, they were more likely to engage with a friend than with a nonfriend. Thirty-two to 37-month-old children were more likely than the younger children to engage in pretend play themes, and they were as likely to engage in these with nonfriend as with friend partners. Perhaps the greater communicative capacities of the older children allowed them to choose nonfriends as well as friends as social pretend play partners. The child with the ability to say, for example, "Let's play firefighter," can communicate a desire to play pretend to a greater number of partners than the child whose ability to play social pretend is dependent on a shared understanding of an idiosyncratic preverbal routine.

Therefore, one function of the friendship context appears to be to facilitate the emergence of more complex social behaviors, including social pretend play. As was suggested, friends and familiar peers may serve to facilitate the emergence of social pretend play because the nature of the play does not have to be communicated in a purely symbolic manner. Friends and well-acquainted children have developed rituals and game structures that serve to frame or support the imperfect and presymbolic communication attempts of toddler age children.

Age of the Peer

According to the Vygotskian perspective outlined in the introduction, mixed-age dyads of peers would be expected to facilitate the construction of social pretend play. The older child in the dyad would be expected to provide a scaffold for the younger child's attempts, and perhaps to transmit information and strategies to the younger child.

Literature on sibling interactions suggests that, at least within this domain of mixed-age peer interaction, play is facilitated. The sibling pairs reported by Dunn and Dale (1984) who actively constructed social pretend play were toddlers and preschool-age mates. While the preschoolers may have attempted to manage the game, the 2-year-old siblings actively cooperated within the shared framework, and disputed and negotiated the rules of pretend, suggesting that the social pretend play was constructed by both participants. The literature on the sibling interaction in general suggests that older siblings play a leadership role but the younger siblings tend to maintain the interaction by responding positively to prosocial behavior and submitting to aggressive behaviors (Pepler, Corter, & Abramovitch, 1982).

REFERENCES

Brenner, J., & Mueller, E. (1982). Shared meaning in boy toddler's peer relations. *Child Development, 53,* 380–391.

Brody, G., Graziano, & Musser, L. (1983). Familiarity and children's behavior in same age and mixed age peer groups. *Developmental Psychology, 19,* 568–576.

Bronfenbrenner, U. (1979). *The ecology of human development.* Cambridge, England: Harvard University Press.

Bruner, J., & Sherwood, V. (1976). Peek-a-boo and the learning of rule structures. In J. Bruner, A. Jolly, & K. Sylva (Eds.), *Play—Its role in development and evolution* (pp. 277–285). London: Penguin.

DeStefano, C., & Mueller, E. (1982). Environmental determinants of peer social activity in 18-month-old males. *Infant Behavior & Development, 5,* 175–183.

Doyle, A.B., Connolly, J., & Rivest, L.P. (1979). The effect of playmate familiarity on the social interactions of young children. *Child Development, 51,* 217–223.

Dunn, J., & Dale, N. (1984). I a Daddy: Two-year-olds' collaboration in joint pretend with sibling and with mother. In I. Bretherton (Eds.), *Symbolic play* (pp. 131–158). New York: Academic.

Dunn, J., & Kendrick, C. (1979). Interaction between young siblings in the context of family relationships. In M. Lewis & L. Rosenblum (Eds.), *The child and its family* (pp. 143–168). New York: Plenum.

Eckerman, C., & Whatley, J., (1977). Toys and social interactions between infant peers. *Child Development, 51,* 217–223.

Furman, W., Rahe, D.F., & Hartup, W.W. (1979). Rehabilitation of socially

withdrawn preschool children through mixed age and same age socialization. *Child Development, 50,* 915–922. Cambridge, MA: Harvard
University Press.

Garvey, C. (1977). *Play.* Cambridge, MA: Harvard University Press.

Gottman, J., & Parkhurst, J. (1980). A developmental theory of friendship and
acquaintanceship processed. In A. Collins (Ed.), *Minnesota Symposium
on Child Psychology.* Hillsdale, NJ: Erlbaum.

Gowen, J. (1978). *Structural elements of symbolic play of preschool children.*
Paper presented at the meeting of the American Psychological Association, Toronto.

Hay, D. (1985). Learning to form relationships in infancy. *Developmental
Review, 5,* 122–161.

Howes, C. (1979). *Toddler social competence in family and center day care.*
Unpublished doctoral dissertation. Boston University.

Howes, C. (1981). Caregiver behavior in center and family day care. *Journal
of Applied Developmental Psychology, 4,* 99–107.

Howes, C. (1983). Patterns of friendship. *Child Development, 43,* 1041–1053.

Howes, C. (1985). Sharing fantasy: Social pretend play in toddlers. *Child
Development, 56,* 1253–1258.

Howes, C. (1987). Quality indicators for infant and toddler child care. In P.
Phillips (Ed.), *Predictors of Quality Child Care.* Washington, DC: National
Association for the Education of Young Children.

Howes, C., & Farver, J. (1985). *Social pretend play in two-year-olds: Effects
of teacher training.* Unpublished manuscript, University of California,
Los Angeles.

Howes, C., & Farver, J. (1987). *Social pretend play in two-year-olds: Effects
of older partners. Early Childhood Research Quarterly, 2,* 305–314.

Howes, C., & Rubenstein, J. (1981). Toddler play in two types of day care.
Infant Behavior & Development, 4, 387–393.

Howes, C., & Rubenstein, J. (1985). Determinants of toddlers' experiences in
day care. *Child Care Quarterly, 14,* 140–151.

Howes, C., & Unger, O. (under review). *Collaborative construction of social
pretend play between toddler age partners.*

Matthews, W.S. (1977). Modes of transformation in the initiation of fantasy
play. *Developmental Psychology, 13,* 212–216.

McClune–Nicolich, L. (1981). Toward symbolic functioning: Structure of early
pretend games and potential parallels with language. *Child Development, 52,* 785–797.

Miller, P., & Garvey, C. (1984). Mother–baby role play. In I. Bretherton (Ed.),
Symbolic Play (pp. 101–130). New York: Academic.

O'Connor, M. (1975). The nursery school environment. *Developmental Psychology, 11,* 556–561.

Olenick, M. (1986). *Child care quality and social policy.* Unpublished doctoral
dissertation. University of California, Los Angeles.

Pepler, D., Corter, C., & Abramovitch, R. (1982). Social relations among
children: Comparison of sibling and peer interaction. In K. Rubin &

H. Ross (Eds.), *Peer relationships and social skills in childhood* (pp. 209–228). New York: Verlag.

Reuter, J., & Yunik, G. (1973). Social interaction in nursery schools *Developmental Psychology, 9,* 319–325.

Rogoff, B., Malkin, C., & Gilbride, L. (1984). Interaction with babies as guidance in development. In B. Rogoff & J. Wertsch (Eds.), *Children's learning in the zone of proximal development.* San Francisco: Jossey Bass.

Rubenstein, J., & Howes, C. (1976). The effects of peers on toddler interaction with mother and toys. *Child Development, 47,* 597–605.

Rubenstein, J., & Howes, C. (1979). Caregiving and infant behavior in day care and homes. *Developmental Psychology, 15,* 1–24.

Rubin, K., Fein, G., & Vandenberg, B. (1983). *Play.* In P.H. Mussen (Ed.), *Handbook of Child Psychology: (Vol. 4): Personality, socialization, and social development* (4th ed.). New York: Wiley.

Sachs, J. (1980). The role of adult–child play in language development. In K. Rubin (Ed.), *Children's play* (pp. 33–48). San Francisco: Jossey Bass.

Sneider, L. (1985, April). *Mothers and toddlers: Partners in early pretend.* Paper presented at the biennial meeting of the Society for Research in Child Development, Toronto.

Vygotsky, L. (1978). *Mind in society: The development of higher mental processes.* Cambridge, MA: Harvard University Press.

Weisner, T. (1984). The social ecology of childhood. In M. Lewis (Ed.), *Beyond the dyad* (pp. 43–58). New York: Plenum.

Wertsch, J. (1979). From social interaction to higher psychological processes. *Human Development, 22,* 1–22.

Wood, D. (1980). Teaching the young child: Some relations between social interaction, language, and thought. In D.R. Olson (Ed.), *The social foundations of early language and thought.* New York: Norton.

7

Young Boys' and Girls' Play at Home and In the Community: A Cultural-Ecological Framework*

MARIANNE N. BLOCH
Department of Curriculum and Instruction, University of
Wisconsin–Madison

A CULTURAL-ECOLOGICAL FRAMEWORK

Anthropological, ethological, and psychological theories (e.g., Barker & Associates, 1978; Barker & Wright, 1955; Blurton–Jones, 1972; Gump, 1975; Lewin, 1935; McGrew, 1972) have long emphasized the importance of studying the ecological context in which children develop and the influence of specific setting characteristics on behavior. The definition of "ecological setting," however, as well as the specific features of settings appropriate for study, have been the subject of some debate and continuing controversy (see the chapter by Gump, for example, in this volume).

Recent cultural-ecological theories have enlarged some of the earlier frameworks and have re-emphasized the complexity of studying the ecological context and its relation to child development. Such cultural-ecological models emphasize the effect of cultural or macrosystem level variables on children's behavior and development, as well as the effect of intracultural systems and settings (e.g., Bronfenbrenner, 1979, 1986; Cochran & Brassard, 1979; Ogbu, 1981; Whiting, 1980). In the models of the Whitings and Ogbu (e.g., Ogbu,

* The Senegalese research reported in this chapter was conducted while the author was an NIMH postdoctoral fellow at the Laboratory of Comparative Human Development, Harvard University. Support for the American research and data analysis was provided by the Wisconsin Alumnae Research Fund, University of Wisconsin–Madison. Daniel J. Walsh provided essential assistance in the collection of data on the American sample.

1981; Whiting, 1980; Whiting & Whiting, 1975). History, climate, terrain, architecture, normative ideologies, and economic, social, and political maintenance systems are examples of cultural factors that define and limit children's immediate settings. Cultural factors are defined at the macrosystem level in Bronfenbrenner's (1979) four-nested ecological system (micro-, meso-, exo-, and macrosystems); he suggests that culture can be operationally examined by looking at the "form and content of the lower-order systems (micro-, meso-, and exo-) that exist, or could exist, at the level of the subculture or the culture as a whole, along with any belief systems or ideology underlying such consistencies" (p. 26).

The model's lowest level is the microsystem, which is a "pattern of activities, roles, and interpersonal relationships experienced by the developing person in a given setting with particular physical and material characteristics" (ibid., p. 22). Whiting's and Ogbu's concep- tions of children's immediate settings resemble Bronfenbrenner's microsystem; they are defined by the people children encounter in various physical settings, the specific activities in which people par- ticipate, and the standing pattern of behavior or interaction that occurs in the settings.

While recent cultural-ecological models are not identical, they seem to view the following factors as generally important: (1) cultural, historical, social, and economic factors outside children's direct ex- perience that constrain their experience to a subset of all possible settings and to a subset of people within these settings; (2) the physical opportunities available to children within the immediate settings they occupy (e.g., play terrain, play materials, physical proximity to different age/gender children, danger from roadways, etc.); (3) the social net- work of people children encounter directly, and the resulting re- lationships, interactions, and experiences children have with these people.

This chapter uses the Whiting (1980) cultural-ecological model as a framework to examine children's play in two communities—one in the United States and one in West Africa—and the effect of the ecological context on children's play within these two cultures. The Whiting (1980) model emphasizes the social and physical aspects of children's most typical settings and analyzes how these affect their activities and the social behavior they learn over time. It also requires consideration of the larger cultural-ecological setting (e.g., climate, architecture, socioeconomic systems) that constrains the settings chil- dren experience. Although play is only one aspect of child activity, it is considered an essential expressive activity that incorporates important learnings and reflects cultural values and behavioral norms.

While the Whiting model has been criticized as overly deterministic (cultural factors affect play) (e.g., Schwartzman, 1978; see discussion by Slaughter & Dombrowski, this volume), recent elaborations on the model (e.g., Konner, 1981; Weisner, 1984) acknowledge the interactive relationship between children's behavior—their environment and culture.

The Whiting model was also selected because of its focus on the emergence and maintenance of sex differences in child and adult behavior in a variety of cultural contexts. Whiting (1980) suggested that age and sex differences in children's behavior should be related to age and sex differences in the physical and social settings they occupy, and, especially, in the "company children keep" (Whiting & Edwards, in press). Whiting and Edwards suggest that cross-cultural differences and similarities in the ages at which boys and girls participate in specific play and nonplay activities reflect differences and similarities in the settings they experience across cultures. Differences may occur, for example, because of cross-cultural differences in the locations in which boys and girls spend time, and the people with whom they interact in these settings.

This chapter explores these theoretical ideas by examining the emergence of sex differences in young children's play activities in home and community contexts within two very different cultures. The intent of this examination is not the comparison of two cultures (middle-class American Caucasian families vs. rural West African families) but the illustration of how play is affected by varying cultural-ecological contexts.

Four general and four specific questions were posed. At the most general level: First, how does children's play vary cross-culturally? Second, to what extent do young boys' and girls' physical and social settings for play vary cross-culturally? Third, what relationships exist between setting characteristics and boys' and girls' play within a culture? And, fourth, are relationships similar across cultures?

Four specific questions also guided this chapter. They relate, in particular, to several areas identified by Schwartzman (1986) as questionable givens in cross-cultural research. First, in cultures in which children engage in frequent work, to what extent does that work affect the amount or type of play in which they can engage? Second, do children in "less economically complex" societies play less frequently and also less imaginatively than children from more economically advantaged families living in economically complex societies (ibid., p. 16)? Third, what is the role of adults in children's play cross-culturally? Fourth, what is the role of peers in children's play, and, in light of recent discussions (e.g., Bloch, 1987; Harkness & Super,

1985; Konner, 1975), does the availability or unavailability of same- and different-age children, as well as same- and different-sex children, affect the way children engage in social play of different sorts?

YOUNG CHILDREN'S PLAY IN TWO CULTURAL CONTEXTS: CONTEXT EFFECTS

The literature on children's play in various contexts suggests that both physical and social aspects of children's settings vary, and, to the extent that research findings are available, these setting differences affect children's play (see review in Bloch & Walsh, 1985; Bloch, 1987; Rubin, Fein, & Vandenburg, 1983; Schwartzman, 1978). Despite increasing research in this area, however, we still know surprisingly little about the most common physical settings young children experience, the effect of children's most typical physical settings on play, the typical company they keep, and the impact of the social network of people they encounter in play and other activities.

Rubin et al. (1983) call for more research on children's play at home and in the community (outside of school or laboratory contexts). While a number of research studies have begun to fill the gap, only a small number on preschool-age American and English children have been done in natural home/community settings where children's most "typical" play and play settings have been observed (e.g., Blurton–Jones & Konner, 1972; Coates & Sanoff, 1972; Dunn & Kendrick, 1982; Ellis, Rogoff, & Cromer, 1981; Hart, 1979; Littlewood & Sale, 1973; Munroe, Munroe, Michelson, Koel, Bolton, & Bolton, 1983; Newson & Newson, 1968, 1976). While more of the anthropological literature has focused on children's activities within their natural contexts, only a few have described the typical settings and activities of very young children (Blurton–Jones & Konner, 1973; Draper, 1976; Munroe et al., 1983; Whiting & Edwards, in press).

RESEARCH ON YOUNG AMERICAN AND SENEGALESE CHILDREN

In 1976, 1979, and again in 1981, the author collected information on young children's play and nonplay activities within two distinct cultural contexts: an American Midwestern middle-class, suburban community and a rural West African village in Senegal. The 1976 study (Bloch, in press; Bloch & O'Rourke, 1982) examined the effect of maternal absence due to wage employment on 3–5-year-old Senegalese children's nonsocial and social behavior with other children and caretakers in a setting in which shared care-taking was traditional. In 1979, this study was extended to examine the activities, settings, and interaction of children up to 6 years old during the summer, a season when parents were, in general, at home, or at work in traditional agricultural jobs near the village. In 1981, data on American middle-class children of the same age were gathered, using similar techniques (see below) in order to provide an American-based data set that could be used to investigate patterns of children's play and settings within and across cultures. In the following section, data from the 1981 American study (reported in Bloch & Walsh, 1985; Bloch, 1987) will be summarized in order to illustrate important features in an American context that can then be contrasted to the 1979 Senegalese sample.

THE AMERICAN STUDY

Whiting's (1980) cultural-ecological model was applied in exploring the relationships between age and sex differences in American children's play and nonplay activities and their typical physical and social settings at home. Bloch and Walsh (1985) predicted that age and sex differences in the location and social and nonsocial settings of children would be similar to age and sex differences in their activities. In Bloch (1987), the age, sex, and relationship of people in children's settings and activities were examined; age and sex differences in activities were related to age and sex differences in the social network of people children encountered in their typical settings and activities. The methodology and findings of these two studies are presented below in order to provide a description of the ecological context of young American children's play in a middle-class suburban community, and as a frame of reference for the Senegalese study discussed in the following section.

Method

The American sample consisted of 83 children from 38 two-parent families living in middle-income suburban residential areas in a Midwestern city. All but one of the children's parents were Anglo–American. Each family had two or more children, one of whom was under 2 years of age. The modal number of children in a family was two (25 of 38 families; number of children ranged from 2 to 6).

Families with 2 or more young children were selected to examine care-taking patterns and responsibilities in families with very young children, as well as for comparing the results with data from families in other cultures where family size was larger and the presence of a baby in a family was typical.

The sample was initially selected from newspaper birth announcements. Parents who agreed to participate (nearly 100% of those contacted) were selected for the study if at least one caretaker expected to be at or near home during most of the summer; specifically, families that expected to be on vacation during a significant part of the summer and families with preschool-age children in school or day care outside the home much of the day were not included. The sample consisted of twelve 5–6-year-olds, thirty-three 2–4-year-olds, and twenty-eight 0–1-year-olds; 45 boys and 38 girls, evenly divided across the three age groups, participated. All but one family were white, and all were classified as middle-class, following Hollingshead's measures (1975). All but one father were engaged in full-time paid employment outside of the home during the summer of the study; most of the mothers were at home with their children. Thirty-five of the 38 families in the study lived in single-family houses in suburban, middle-class family neighborhoods.

An adaptation of a "spot observation" technique used in a number of cross-cultural studies (e.g., Ellis et al., 1981; Munroe & Munroe, 1971; Munroe et al., 1983; Whiting & Edwards, in press) was used to obtain a composite picture of children's typical activities and settings during the course of a single summer. Rogoff (1978) suggests that the spot observation technique approximates taking multiple pictures of children and compiling them to produce a broad view of children's activities and settings within a given culture. The spot observation method has been used in the United States and in a number of third world societies (see Munroe et al., 1983; Whiting & Edwards, in press) where low literacy rates inhibit use of time diary techniques for obtaining time allocation information. It has also been used to record the typical pattern of daily activities of young children, where recall errors and reporting biases of caretakers have made time diary methodology less useful. Most often, this technique involves trained observers who enter a setting, typically outdoors, locate a child or adult at play or work, and unobtrusively and quickly record the targeted person's activity, location, and the people involved in the activity and setting at the moment that the observer first enters the setting.

In the American study reported here, spot observations of 0–6-year-old children were made by a parent, or another caretaker, after a randomly timed telephone call by one of two interviewers working in the project; the telephone method was used with American families in order to minimize the intrusiveness of a visitor to houses and has been used for similar reasons in several earlier studies (e.g., Ellis et al., 1981; Munroe et al., 1983).

In the current study, interviewers telephoned families across 7 days of the week (although a given family received calls over 5 days of any given week) based upon a random numbers schedule. Calls were made between 8 A.M. and 8 P.M. (or during all-daylight and normal child-waking hours) over a 2-month summer season. Interviewers were randomly assigned to one of three 4-hour periods each day during their 5-day workweek (8 A.M.–12 P.M.–4 P.M.–8 P.M.). Families were contacted once each day. Those absent from the home at the time of the original call received callbacks; in this case, caretakers were asked about children's activities and settings at the time of the earlier call.

Caretakers were typically asked about only one child per call, in order to maximize the independence of information. Interviewers asked about the child and his or her setting; when necessary, caretakers were directed to find the child and observe him or her or, if the child were absent, to provide as much information as possible on his or her activities, locations, and social settings. Caretakers who received instructions before the beginning of the study, were always asked to provide precise and low-inference, full descriptions.

Telephone interviewers recorded narrative responses on coding sheets and coded information as soon after each telephone call as possible. Coding was carefully checked by one researcher and spot checked by another; intercoder agreement on activity categories was 85%, while location and social context information was coded directly as reported.

A total of 2,012 telephone interviews were completed during the 2-months. Of these, approximately 1,500 yielded complete information on children's locations and activities and 1,474 of these produced social setting information and were used in the analyses; on average, 20 observations per child were considered "complete" with location and activity information and an average of 18 per child were complete with location, activity, and social setting information.

A variety of activity and setting variables were coded and analyzed. Variables reflected those examined in other cross-cultural research on children's settings and their activity patterns (see, e.g., Blurton–Jones & Konner, 1973; Medrich, Roizen, Rubin, & Buckley, 1982; Munroe et al., 1983; Whiting & Edwards, in press). In addition, because the Parten–Smilansky (see Rubin et al., 1983) play categories (nonsocial and social functional, constructive, and pretend play) have been used in a variety of recent studies of young children's play, these categories were included to facilitate data comparison.

Variables included several aspects of children's physical setting (room location, distance from home, materials children used in their activities), social settings (particularly, the number, age, sex, and relationship of other people in these settings, and play and nonplay activities. While detailed definitions are provided in Bloch and Walsh (1985) and Bloch (1987), brief descriptions are provided below.

Locations were defined by room type or by distance from home. Distance from home was categorized as: in the home, in the yard (front or back), in the neighborhood (within one block), or out of the neighborhood. People in children's settings, which included up to six people who could see the child, were identified by age, sex, relationship to child and activity. Children were considered to be involved in social activities if one or more persons were coded as doing the same activity as the child or activities with the child; nonsocial or solitary activities were defined as activities that were done by a child by himself or herself, regardless of whether others were present in the child's setting or not. Coded play activities included: gross motor, functional, constructive, pretense, exploratory, rough and tumble, art, music, and dance (music, dance, and art were combined in tables presented here). Finally, a number of nonplay activities were examined, including sleeping, eating, personal hygiene, care by others, self-reliant care for self, responsible housework, observing others, watching TV, sociable interaction, school-related work (e.g., math or reading activities, being read to), and transitional activities.

Two proportion scores were calculated to estimate the proportion of time children spent in different types of activities, in different locations, and with different people: Total (T) scores (frequencies of observations in which children were reported in an activity, location, or with one or more activity partners, divided by all completed activity, location, or social setting observations) and Waking Time (WT) scores (frequencies of observations in which children were in an activity, location, or with an activity partner, divided by all completed activity, location, or social setting observations conducted while children were awake). While earlier papers report information on all 0–6-year-olds, this chapter summarizes the results on the 2–6-year-old children's time in different activities, locations, and with different activity partners in order to illustrate differences in context and activities between American and Senegalese 2–6-year-olds.

Results

Children's Activities. The results of multivariate and univariate analyses of variance on activity scores showed, first, that 2–6-year-olds spent about 30% of their Total (T) time in play (all types) during the summer period of the study and spent approximately 70% of their time engaged in all other, nonplay activities (See Table 1). While no age and sex differences were identified in the total time children spent in play, age differences in nonplay categories were significant: Younger, 2–4-year-old children slept more than did 5–6-year-olds, and age by sex differences suggested older 5–6-year-old boys spent more time in self-care, while 5–6-year-old girls spent more time in responsible work and school-related work than did boys or younger girls (see Table 1 and detailed results in Bloch & Walsh, 1985). Additional analyses of types of play unexpectedly showed that there were no significant age or sex differences in 2–4 vs. 5–6-year-old American children's play.

Physical context: Locations and materials. Interviewers requested information about children's toys and play materials, as well as their

Table 1. Mean Proportion (T) of All Observations Allocated to Major Activities (American Sample)

Activities (n)	2–4 Years		5–6 Years	
	Males (16)	Females (17)	Males (6)	Females (6)
Sleeping	.10	.10	.04	.02
Eating	.11	.12	.17	.15
Personal hygiene	.02	.02	.03	.03
Care by others	.02	.02	.00	.00
Care for self	.05	.02	.05	.01
Responsible work	.03	.03	.03	.13
Observes others	.04	.01	.04	.02
Watches TV/objects	.11	.11	.12	.10
Sociable interaction	.08	.10	.05	.03
Play	.30	.29	.32	.30
School-related	.02	.03	.01	.08
Transitions	.08	.05	.08	.09
No information	.02	.04	.07	.04
At school (preschool)	.02	.02	.01	.02

locations. While the frequency of reports was lower than expected and may not represent all play materials that were used, the type of materials reported for all children in the study, in the order of reporting frequency, were: food, blankets, utensils, books, clothing, cars or trucks, dolls, toy animals, bottles, cups and glasses, bikes, blocks, and swings; the books, cars/trucks, dolls, toy animals, bikes, blocks, and swings were used primarily by 2–6-year-olds.

Children's locations (See Table 2) showed that the 2–6-year-olds studied in this research spent more than 60% of their Total (T) time in the house, and approximately three fourths of their time in the house or yard. While there were no statistically significant sex differences in children's locations in this age category, significant age differences were identified: 2–4-year-olds spent more time in their yards than did 5–6-year-olds, while 5–6-year-olds spent more time outside their own yards and in their neighborhood than did the 2–4-year-olds.

Locations inside the house were not calculated separately by age and sex of child. However, for the total sample of 0–6-year-olds, children's locations within the house were examined. Children spent the greatest amount of time in their own bedrooms (326/1,535 valid location observations, including sleeping and nonsleeping time). The frequency of observations in living rooms (180), common or family rooms (126), kitchens (102), dining rooms (62), parents' bedrooms (54), bathrooms (40), and siblings' rooms (14) suggested that, first, there are many common family rooms in which American children do activities, and, second, that the majority of children's indoor activities were done in their own rooms or in common family spaces; in general, siblings did not go into each others' rooms to do activities.

Table 2. Mean Proportion (T) of Observations in Different Locations [a] **(American Sample)**

Location	2–4 Years		5–6 Years	
	Males	Females	Males	Females
In house	.70	.68	.63	.65
In yard	.13	.14	.06	.10
In neighborhood	.09	.08	.12	.13
Outside neighborhood	.08	.09	.15	.09
(n)	(16)	(17)	(6)	(9)

[a] Does not include time in school.

Finally, with regard to location, Bloch and Walsh (1985) reported relationships between children's locations (in and out of house) and their activities. With age partialed out of correlation analyses, indoor locations were associated with functional play ($r = 26$), watching television ($r = .22$), school-related activities ($r = .22$), eating ($r = .35$) and sleeping ($r = .35$). In-the-yard locations were associated with gross motor play ($r = .26$), exploratory play ($r = .32$), and pretense play ($r = .26$). Gross motor play also was associated with in-the-neighborhood locations ($r = .45$), which would have included neighborhood playground play as well as sports, bicycling, and so forth. This study found no correlation between any activity and outside-the-neighborhood locations.

Social context and children's play partners. With the exception of the time spent sleeping, the 2–6-year-old American children in this study were rarely alone; in 92% of children's waking-time observations, children were in the company of at least one other person. Despite this, children's activities were done independently almost as often as with others. Fifty-two percent of children's activities were considered social (at least one other person participated with the child), while 48% of the activities were solitary (40% with others in the setting, 8% with the child alone in the setting) (see Table 3).

Further analyses were conducted to identify the people in children's settings and activities. These analyses showed that an average of two people were present *in children's settings,* and that 90% of the time, these people were immediate family members. Most often, the people in children's settings or in their most typical "social network" (using Lewis, Feiring, & Kotsonis's 1984 terminology) were the children's mothers and one other sibling (For 2–6-year-olds, mothers were present in an average of 52% of the observations, and at least one sibling was present in 38% of the observations.) While results showed that children were with their mothers more often than their fathers, it is surprising to note that mothers and fathers were in girls' settings as frequently as they were in boys' settings. While there also were no significant sex or age differences in time spent with male or female children, by ages 5–6, the descriptive results suggested that boys were beginning to spend less time in settings with their sisters (a mixed-sex setting for the boys) or with other female children than girls were. No similar trends were observed in girls' time with their brothers or with other male children.

When specific attention was given to children's play activities, findings were similar. Nearly half of the 2–6-year-old children's time in all play activities (See top row, Table 3) was spent in solitary play (mean percentage of observations was 16%), and half was spent in

Table 3. Mean Proportion of Major [a] Play Activities (All Categories) Solitary and Social with Mother, Father, and Other Child Activity Partners (WT) (American Sample)

Solitary Social or Activity	2-4 Years (n = 33)						5-6 Years (n = 12)					
	Total		Solitary		Social Play with Diff. Partners		Total		Solitary		Social Play with Diff. Partners	
Child Sex	M	F	M	F	M	F	M	F	M	F	M	F
All Play	.33	.32	.17	.17	.16	.15	.32	.30	.14	.14	.18	.16
Mother					.05	.02					.03	.03
Father					.00	.01					.03	.01
Children					.12	.12					.14	.14
Functional	.06	.05	.03	.03	.03	.03	.06	.05	.03	.02	.03	.03
Mother					.01	.00					.00	.01
Father					.00	.00					.02	.00
Children					.01	.03					.02	.02
Constructive	.02	.01	.01	.00	.01	.01	.05	.02	.02	.01	.03	.01
Mother					.00	.00					.00	.00
Father					.00	.00					.00	.00
Children					.00	.01					.03	.01
Pretense	.05	.06	.02	.04	.03	.02	.02	.06	.01	.02	.01	.04
Mother					.01	.00					.00	.00
Father					.00	.00					.00	.00
Children					.03	.02					.01	.04
Gross Motor (excl. R&T, Sports Games)	.13	.12	.06	.07	.07	.05	.11	.11	.03	.08	.08	.03
Mother					.03	.01					.02	.01
Father					.00	.01					.01	.01
Children					.07	.02					.07	.03

[a] Activities listed account for at least 5% of all waking time observations in one or more age/sex group.

social play with others (mean percent of observations: 17%). There were no age or sex differences identified. When 2–6-year-old children's social play was examined for typical play partners, child partners were most frequent (Mean Number of Play Partners was 1). Based upon the sample and social setting information (see above), the typical play partner of children between the ages of 2 and 6 was a younger sibling.

Social and nonsocial play of different types also was examined. When children under the age of 2 were excluded, none of the play categories appeared to involve primarily social or solitary play. However, in the overall age and sex analyses reported in Bloch (1987), a trend ($p < .08$) was identified toward a significant sex difference in gross motor play when children did this type of activity with others; boys were more likely to engage in gross motor play with others than were girls. Follow-up analyses, by play partner supported this trend. In particular, boys' gross motor play with other children was significantly greater than girls' gross motor play with children.

Finally, the study examined children's play with their parents. Somewhat surprisingly, 2–6-year-old children spent relatively little time in any sort of play with their mothers and/or fathers, and there were no age or sex differences in the time children spent in different types of play with their parents.

Discussion

This study of young American children suggests that, during a summer at home, young children played approximately one third of their waking time; play was, therefore, one of their major activities. Despite this, individual play types did not account for much of children's time. The major play activity during the summer season of observation was gross motor play, with functional and pretense play accounting for, on the average, only 5% of children's waking-time activities at home and in the community; because some pretense play, particularly social pretense play, has received considerable theoretical and empirical attention, the low frequency of its occurrence in this study merits note.

The study's findings also help to define the settings in which children's play occurs, to define some of the factors that affect the kind of play that takes place, and to suggest what children may learn from their play within these settings. In this sample of 2–6-year-olds, more than 70% of children's play occurred in or near the home (typically in the yard or within one block's distance); functional play frequently occurred indoors, while gross motor, pretense, and exploratory play were more likely to occur outside the house, or, in the case of gross motor play, within the neighborhood, where more male and female children probably were available.

Much of children's play was done in a narrow, and somewhat isolated, social situation. While children rarely were entirely alone, they were most frequently with members of their immediate family— most typically with their mother and one (often younger) sibling. Perhaps as a result of their limited social network, children spent a surprisingly large amount of time in solitary activities, indeed, as much time in solitary activities and play (an average of 48% and 16% of their waking-time observations, respectively) as they did in social activities and play (52% and 17%, respectively).

The large amount of solitary time spent in play and nonplay activities may have been related to a number of factors, including the small number of older (same or even near-age) play partners available to children. The typical presence of only one parent in the household limits the single parent or caretaker's time for direct involvement in play or other activities; household work, including baby care, demands much of parent time. In addition, the space and privacy available in many middle-class American residences and yards supports or elicits more independent or solitary activities by children. Finally, Sutton–Smith's (1985) suggestion that American manufactured toys encourage independent play, and are given to children to encourage such play, should be considered as a possible influence on children's "choice" to play alone.

The study's results also suggest that while a small amount of play occurred with parents, children's typical play partners were other children (usually a younger sibling) or, given the frequency of their solitary play, the toys they played with when they played alone. The results reinforce previous research that indicates the importance of mothers and siblings to children in small American families (e.g., Bryant, 1985; Dunn & Kendrick, 1982; Fischer & Fischer, 1966; Lewis et al., 1984), but fail to support research that suggests that children experience frequent direct play with their parents. Thus, while current theory (e.g., Vygotsky, 1978) suggests the potential importance of adult input in play, the results of this study, supported by those of Dunn and Kendrick and Carew (Carew, 1980; Dunn, 1986; Dunn & Kendrick, 1982), show that direct parent initiation and participation in play may be rare. Dunn (1986), for example, found that children usually initiate play encounters with parents, with parent involvement frequently consisting of momentary feedback, reinforcement, or instruction, rather than direct reciprocal play. The American results reported here, based upon spot observations without detailed interaction data, fail to shed light on this type of moment-to-moment interaction during play.

Cultural-ecological factors of importance. The picture of children's play activities within their typical physical and social settings highlights the importance of many of the factors described in the Whitings' cultural-ecological model (Whiting & Whiting, 1975; Whiting, 1980). It also highlights the need to identify the cultural-ecological context in which children engage in activities in order to make sense of children's development within these contexts. Similar issues were explored in a second study of children's play within a particular cultural-ecological context. Discussion of this study highlights similarities and differences in individual (age, sex of child) and context effects on children.

THE SENEGAL STUDY

In 1979, a study similar but not identical to the American study was conducted in a rural village in Senegal. In this study, trained Senegalese observers identified children, generally in outdoor locations (see results below), performed spot observations, and wrote 10-minute narrative records of their social and nonsocial behavior and activities. While the Senegalese study had multiple objectives, this chapter reports its findings on children's play and play contexts, based primarily on the spot observation data. Because narrative records of children's solitary and social play also were available, information from these records are also included where appropriate.

The principal purpose of the following analysis is to describe the cultural-ecological context of young Senegalese children's play at home; a second purpose is to suggest differences in the effect of ecological variables on young children's behavior within two quite different cultural contexts. With minor exceptions, direct statistical comparisons of American and Senegalese data and results have not been made, due to differences in the telephone and observation methods, as well as to the complexity of the differences in the two cultures (e.g., ethnicity, class, geography, economic systems). However, questions stimulated by the American study but specific to children's play in Senegal were asked: 1) How much play did Senegalese children do relative to other activities? Was play as dominant an activity, in terms of time allocation, as it was for American children?; 2) What factors are related to the frequency and the type of play in which Senegalese children are engaged in (e.g., age and sex differences; relationship between play and other activities, such as workload, cultural emphases on certain types of play rather than others)?; 3) What were the physical characteristics of children's play settings (distance from home, availability and use of certain play materials)? Were certain types of play more likely to occur in certain physical settings than in others?; 4) What were the characteristics of children's social settings? Within those settings, how much solitary and social play did children do, and with whom? Were certain types of play done with certain partners and not with others? Finally, based upon questions generated in the American study, the Senegalese study explored the relationship between the number of male and female children present in children's home compounds and the type of play in which they engaged.

Method

The original Senegalese sample consisted of nearly all 0–6-year-old children living in a rural village about 1 hour inland from the capital of Dakar. Ninety-two 0–6-year-old children of 47 mothers were involved; data on the sample's fifty-four 2–6-year-olds are described in this chapter.

The children and their mothers lived in 29 households (defined as kin-related eating and working groups) in 13 of the 24 village compounds. Thirty-eight 2–4-year-olds (17 males and 21 females) and sixteen 5–6-year-olds (9 males and 7 females) were studied. The majority of children were middle-born children (neither oldest nor youngest).

The majority of the 700 village residents belonged to the Lebou ethnic group, a traditional coastal fishing group in Senegal; one large, extended family was Wolof, the major ethnic group in Senegal. The Lebou families in this study had moved inland and adopted farming in the early 1920s. All families were Moslem and polygynous, and an extended family patrilocal (housing was with the father's family) residence system was the norm.

Each family had two or more children, with at least one child under the age of 2. The average number of children born to a given mother in our sample was four (ranging from two to eight). While children's own siblings were available for play (average number of male siblings = 1.57, range = 0–5; Average number of female siblings = 1.63, range = 0–4, with an average of one sibling within the 2–6-year-age range), additional children living in children's village "compounds" also were available. Calculations (Kalu, 1985) made by compounds (one or more kin-related households clustered together within the village) showed that an average of nine 2–6-year-olds (4 males and 5 females, on the average) also were within easy range of sample children.

Children lived in extended-family, polygamous households ranging in size from four people living in a single room to 25 household members living in multiple rooms and multiple dwellings within a compound; in almost all cases, a mother, father, and the youngest children shared one or two rooms at most, while any older children lived in other rooms or with other household relatives. Most families lived in small, concrete-block dwellings, while some lived in the more traditional, square straw huts of the Lebou. Compounds also ranged from one or two families living in clusters to compounds of multiple extended families of up to 150 people.

During the summer season, when this study was conducted, regular economic activities of women and men included subsistence and cash crop agriculture, petty trade, and wage labor in agriculture, and, for some men, employment in cities within a 60-mile range of the village. Mothers of the sample children spent approximately 2 hours each day engaged in such economic activities as agriculture or petty trade near the village (Bloch, 1980), and during the winter seasons, many worked at seasonal wage labor at a nearby agribusiness (Bloch, 1988).

The study, which assessed the specific educational and occupational backgrounds of family members, found that mothers and fathers had 1.64 (S.D. = 2.39) and 2.79 (S.D. = 3.49) mean years of schooling, respectively. Sixty-one percent of mothers and 45% of fathers had never attended a Western-type school; of those with some Western (as opposed to Koranic) schooling, 16% and 9% of mothers and fathers, respectively, had completed primary schooling, and 11% of fathers had completed secondary school. Paternal occupations varied with educational level and age; many of the older fathers were traditional farmers and had never attended school. Younger fathers and mothers were more likely to have attended some school, and the better-educated fathers frequently were employed in nearby cities.

Procedure. Random spot observations, followed by 10-minute written narrative records, were made by four trained Senegalese female observers. These observers were trained to record detailed notes and narrative records of children's behavior; reliability of recording on both spot observation and narrative records was assessed before data collection began. Subsequently, observers following a prearranged random schedule, visited village households, identified children (usually out of doors), and quickly and unobtrusively noted their activities, locations, and social settings. Ten-minute narrative records of children's activities were written after the spot observations were completed and recorded. As in the American study, observers made their observations across 7 days of the week, and during daylight hours (in this case 7 A.M. to 8 P.M.) during a 3-month (July–September) summer season; the summer season was selected because it is the traditional agriculture season, and research questions concerning child-care organization during a traditional work season could be best answered at this time. As in the American study, observations were made at random within three daily time periods: 7 A.M.–12 P.M.; 12 P.M.–4 P.M.; and 4 P.M.=8 P.M.

When children were out of their family compounds, observers were directed to ask someone in the original setting where the child might be found, and to go to as many as two different locations in an attempt to locate the child; in fact, on occasion, observers walked across the entire village and back again in order to find children. When children could not be located, observers asked caretakers for information about the children's whereabouts and about their activities. Information from caretakers was recorded and used in analyses when that information was considered complete and accurate (e.g., a caretaker reports that the child was taken to a clinic in the next town by his mother for medical care).

An average of 20 observations were made on each of the 54 children in the Senegalese sample. Of these, an average of 18 provided complete information on a child's location and activities. Narrative information recorded during spot observations and in the 10-minute narratives was coded by American coders following the author's return to the United States. Coders were trained to code spot observations using the same activity, location, and social setting information codes described earlier for the American study. During reliability tests, intercoder agreement was 85% on activity codes, and nearly 100% on the low-inference information concerning locations, toys, and social settings.

Results

Mean proportion scores representing time children spent in all activities (total time), in locations (total time), and in different solitary and social play activities (waking time) are presented in Tables 4, 5, and 6. Findings from multivariate and univariate analyses of these results are presented, by section, below.

Children's activities. Results of the analyses of the time Senegalese children spent doing different activities showed that, as in the American study, 2–6-year-olds spent more time in play than in any other single type of activity (see Table 4). Total time analyses showed that play accounted for 18% to 27%, or about one-quarter, of children's total time and when out-of-school waking-time was analyzed, children's play accounted for one-third of their time, a result remarkably similar to the results obtained in the American study; there were no significant age or sex differences in this result.

Table 4. Mean Proportion (T) of All Observations Allocated to Major Activities (Senegalese Sample)

Activities (n)	2–4 Years		5–6 Years	
	Males (17)	Females (21)	Males (9)	Females (7)
Sleeping	.04	.05	.02	.06
Eating	.12	.15	.08	.15
Personal hygiene	.02	.03	.02	.01
Care by others	.00	.02	.00	.01
Care for self	.03	.01	.03	.01
Responsible work	.03	.05	.13	.15
Observes others	.11	.13	.08	.07
Observes TV/objects	.03	.02	.02	.01
Sociable interaction	.08	.10	.06	.03
Play	.21	.27	.22	.18
School-related	.00	.01	.03	.01
Transitions	.06	.05	.08	.06
No information	.15	.05	.10	.04
At school (Koranic)	.12	.06	.13	.21

Table 5. Mean Proportion (T) of Observations in Different Locations [a] (Senegalese Sample)

Location	2–4 Years		5–6 Years	
	Males	Females	Males	Females
In house	.12	.13	.13	.12
In yard or compound	.49	.64	.51	.50
In village/outside compound	.13	.09	.07	.12
Outside village	.04	.05	.08	.05
Elsewhere [b]	.07	.02	.05	.00
(n)	(17)	(21)	(9)	(7)

[a] Does not include time in school.

[b] Observers were unable to find child and no adult or child asked could identify child location.

Table 6.   Mean Proportion of Major [a] Play Activities, Total, Solitary and Social with Child Activity Partners[b] (Senegalese Sample)

Solitary or Social Activity	2–4 Years (n = 38)						5–6 Years (n = 16)					
	Total		Solitary		Social Play with Children		Total		Solitary		Social Play with Children	
Child's Sex	M	F	M	F	M	F	M	F	M	F	M	F
	(n = 17)	(n = 21)					(n = 9)	(n = 7)				
All Play	.38	.32	.19	.13	.19	.19	.32	28	.02	.06	.30	.22
Functional	.06	.09	.05	.07	.01	.02	.02	.00	.00	.00	.01	.00
Constructive	.04	.02	.02	.00	.02	.00	.04	.00	.00	.00	.03	.00
Pretense	.05	.10	.03	.03	.02	.06	.01	.09	.00	.03	.01	.07
Gross Motor (excl. R&T, Sports Games)	.17	.05	.05	.01	.11	.04	.17	.08	.00	.03	.16	.06
Dance, music, art	.03	.03	.01	.01	.01	.02	.03	.04	.00	.00	.03	.04

[a] Activities listed account for at least 5% of all waking time observations in one or more age/sex group.

[b] Because there were so few (< 2%) observations in which adults played with children, *all* social play is with child partners.

Children's other major nonplay activities, in order of their quantitative importance, also were examined. For 2–4-year-olds, they included eating, observing others, and attendance at the local Koranic school; and for 5–6-year-olds, attendance at Koranic school, responsible work, and eating were, in order of importance, their major activities. In the nonplay category, several activities showed evidence of age and sex differences: (1) Girls engaged in responsible work more than boys (F(Sex) = 6.74; $p < .05$); (2) older children engaged in responsible work more than younger children (F(Age) = 8.97, $p < .05$); (3) and boys engaged in self-reliant self-care significantly more than girls (F(Sex) = 6.04, $p < .05$).

When play types were analyzed (data are presented in the left-hand columns for each age group in Table 6), it was interesting to note that the time Senegalese children spent in different types of play also was very similar to results from the American sample. In fact, in one direct comparison of data across the two samples of 2–6-year-olds (Bloch, 1984a), there was only one significant difference: While American children engaged in more gross motor play (total time) than did Senegalese children, both groups were virtually identical in time spent in pretense, functional, constructive, exploratory, rough-and-tumble, and music/art play.

As in the American study (Bloch & Walsh, 1985), the Senegalese study examined age and sex differences in the various types of play that accounted for at least 5% of children's waking time. Age differences in waking-time functional play were significant (F(Age) = 2.27, p < .05); younger children engaged in more functional play than older children. Sex differences in gross motor and pretense activities also were significant (F(Sex) = 16.39 and 5.84, p < .01, respectively). Boys engaged in more gross motor play than girls, and, though not analyzed statistically, the spot and narrative records indicated boys also engaged in more constructive play than girls. In contrast, girls engaged in more pretense play than boys; this result was particularly evident in the 5–6-year-period, when both spot and narrative records indicated girls' pretense was fairly high (mean proportion of waking-time spots = .09) while boys' pretense was almost nonexistent (mean proportion of spots = .01).

Relationships between nonplay and play activities. While the Senegalese children spent a great deal of time playing, the fact that they spent less total time in play than American children was of some interest. Various factors—seasonal variations in play across the sample, different cultural values assigned to play, nutritional and health effects on children's activities, school or housework requirements that infringed on play—might account for this cultural difference. While most of these factors could not be explored across the two cultures, the health status of the Senegalese children and its effect on their play time could be explored with available data, and relationships between Senegalese children's play and nonplay activities could be examined.

Correlations between the proportion of observations children spent in play and their nutritional status (rudimentary assessments of height/weight per age) and summer health status (days in which spot observations reported children as ill with malaria or diarrhea) were examined, and results were nonsignificant. Correlations between children's play and nonplay activities also were generally nonsignificant, with one important exception: The time children spent in household or responsible work activities was negatively correlated with play time (r = .397, p < .01).

Table 4 shows that Responsible Work accounted for an average of 14% of 5–6-year-olds' total time during the summer observations. The negative correlation obviously indicates that children with heavier work assignments played less. Ten-minute narrative records confirm that children frequently were involved with such activities as sweeping, small-animal care (feeding chickens), carrying small amounts of water from the village well, some supervision of younger siblings, and, most frequently, running errands in and out of the household and compound for caretakers. They also show: (1) that parents or other adults frequently interrupted children's play for work, but that (2) children frequently returned to play, or combined play and work activities; one example from the narrative records of one child illustrates the most typical pattern:

> Ibra gathers together a small group of boys to play soccer with just outside his compound. He gets them together and begins to kick the ball; just then his brother calls him to run to the small store in the center of the village to buy sugar; the other boys continue to play soccer while he runs the errand, and when he returns, he gives his brother the sugar, the change, and immediately rejoins the game.

This example illustrates the play–work–return-to-play pattern that children used as a means of maintaining play as a dominant activity during their preschool years. A second example, more typical for girls than for boys during the 5–6-year period, shows that play and work frequently were combined as girls played at learning the tasks for which they would soon take full responsibility:

> Binta (age 6) has just returned from the village well with a small basin of water on her head. She pours some of it into the drinking water jar, and her mother says, take the rest and go wash your clothes. She puts the basin down and fetches her clothes and soap. She starts to wash her clothes, singing while washing. Then Demba (another 6-year-old girl) comes and calls her to come play. Binta tells Demba she can't go now, that she's "learning" to wash the laundry. Demba comes over to Binta and starts to wash the laundry (several of Binta's cloth skirts) with her.

Physical settings: Locations and materials. In an earlier article (Bloch, 1984b), Senegalese children's toys and play materials were described as "scrounge" materials. Children used leftover fishbones for pretense, made toys (e.g., wire can cars) from leftover purchased materials, or found play materials in the garbage heaps or the "bush" country outside the village boundaries. Parents occasionally made toys (e.g., a corncob doll with fabric scraps for clothes), or children themselves made or scrounged for their own materials (e.g., a tin can and scrounged wire was fashioned into sophisticated push cars with wheels). Children's play involved rolling wire hoops, playing marbles with rocks and sand, and soccer with balls or rolled pieces of cloth.

Materials differed by play type to some extent: Functional play usually consisted of play with sand, sticks, and rocks; constructive play frequently involved making a doll, a wire car, truck, or slingshot; pretense play involved play with store-bought or homemade dolls wrapped and strapped to children's backs, or scrounged tin cans, sand, leftover food scraps, and so forth, to play at food preparation or marketing; gross motor play involved climbing trees, playing soccer or throwing balls, running, and chasing roaming sheep and chickens, or swimming in a small infectious pond outside the village; dance, music and art involved village-fabricated toy "tam-tams" (tin cans with bits of sheepskin stretched on top), space, and, on occasion, radio music or, even more rarely, adult music making. While structured games with rules were rare, 2–6-year-olds played marbles with sand and stones, or hide and seek; while soccer was included as a gross motor activity in our analyses, it also was identified as a "game."

Children's location data (see Table 5) also were analyzed. In this warm climate in which much activity took place in compounds out of doors and even behind houses in the bush country, it was not surprising to find that children spent little time inside. Nonetheless, in support of the results of the American study, as well as other research (e.g., Newson & Newson, 1968) that suggest young children spend much of their time close to home, the Senegalese results showed that children spent the majority of time in the yard and compound near their children's homes. As the village was compact and circular, and populated almost exclusively by relatives and other people familiar to the children, time spent in the village can be considered similar to time spent by American children in their "neighborhoods." Time spent by children outside the village was recorded, but it was the least frequent of the location categories. Age differences existed in two categories: older children spent more time outside the compound in the village and outside of the village than did younger (2–4-year-old) children. No sex differences were identified in the inside the house, in compound, in-village, or outside-village location data. However, when the proportion of observations simply coded "elsewhere" (the observer could not find the child) were analyzed, sex differences were significant; observers had more trouble locating boys than girls.

As in the American study, relationships between children's locations (in and out of the house) and children's activities were calculated. With age partialed out of correlation analyses, indoor locations were associated with sleeping ($r = .56$), transitional activities or waiting (r

= .27), and sociable interactions (particularly anger) (r = .26). In the compound locations were associated with observing adults (r = .35), but no other activities. In the village/outside compound locations were associated with eating, personal hygiene, and dance/music activities (r = .38, .35, .25, respectively). Locations outside the village were associated with gross motor, constructive, and exploratory play (r = .33, .33, .39, respectively).

Social context and children's play partners. In contrast to the more isolated nature of American children's settings, the Senegalese children's play typically took place in settings in which a number of male and female adults and children were present; indeed Kalu's (1985) thesis, mentioned in the methods section of this chapter, showed that the typical family household had several kinship-related smaller families living in it, that compound membership could reach 150, and that many adults and children were available for play (for example, an average of nine other 2–6-year-olds, 4 males and 5 females, were available to a sample child in a typical compound).

While many other adults or children (10 or more in many of the spot records), might be in a compound and within play or supervisory range, calculations of the average number of people in children's more immediate settings (defined as being within seeing and hearing distance of the child) showed that typically 4 or 5 others were in children's more proximate settings—frequently 2 adults and several children.

In contrast to the limited nature of the American children's social network (mother, father, one or two siblings, and some friends and relatives), the age, sex, and precise relationship of the people in Senegalese children's settings was more difficult to characterize. Wide variations in family and household type and size meant that some children lived in small compounds consisting of two nuclear-type families, while others lived in large compounds where grandparents, aunts, uncles, parents, adult and child male and female cousins and siblings were available for supervision, instruction, or play. Within this context, children most frequently were in their more immediate settings with a number of their closer female and male adult relatives (mothers, grandmothers, aunts, the father's other wives, older sisters, all typically occupied by cooking, talking, washing clothes, caring for a baby; older adult brothers, grandfathers, uncles, or fathers). Typically, two other children (e.g., older and younger siblings, half-siblings, cousins, or friends) were in children's immediate settings, while, for most children, others were readily available in neighboring houses or in the compound, if play required more partners.

With such a contrast between the number of people available for play in the Senegalese and American studies, the proportion of time children spent in social and solitary play was of interest. When Senegalese children's scores for solitary and social play were calculated (See Table 6), clear age, but no sex differences were observed (F(Age) = 4.17, $p < .05$). As in the American sample, 2–4-year-old children engaged in approximately equal amounts of social and solitary play; in contrast to the American sample, however, 5–6-year-old Senegalese children's waking-time play was almost entirely social (see Table 3 and Table 6).

Proportion scores representing the time children spent on social and solitary play were examined to determine whether some activities were more likely to be done in social or solitary contexts than others; whether age or sex differences could be identified in the time children spent in particular social or solitary play activities; and who their play partners were.

As in the American study (Bloch & Walsh, 1985), results across age groups were examined to see whether certain activities were typically done with others or alone. As in the American study (Bloch & Walsh, 1985), functional play was usually done alone (Pair-wise $t = 2.899$, $p < .001$) while gross motor play was done primarily with others, usually children, (Pair-wise $t = 4.33$, $p < .001$). In addition, in the Senegalese results, dance and music play, generally done by 5–6-year-olds, also was a social activity ($t = 2.03$, $p < .05$).

Age, sex and age by sex interaction effects were examined for each of the major (5% or more in one age/sex group) solitary and social play categories (waking-time scores presented in Table 6). Age differences were observed in solitary functional play (younger more than older) (F(Age) = 2.76, $p < .05$), while age by sex differences were observed in solitary gross motor play (boys engaged in less solitary gross motor play as they got older) (F(Age $\times$ Sex) = 4.50, $p < .05$).

Although the amount of social play children did increased with age no age differences were identified in any of the individual social play categories; thus, age differences appeared to be spread across social play types. There were two significant sex differences: girls engaged in more social pretense play than boys, and boys engaged in more social gross motor play than girls (F(Sex) = 11.07, $p < .01$, and 9.15, $p < .01$, respectively).

The study examined the number and type (age, sex, relationship) of children's typical play partners. As suggested above, and in Table 6, most of the Senegalese children's social play involved other children, not parents or other adults. In fact, 179/191 or 94% of the social play spot observations showed children playing with other children. Play between 2–6-year-old sample children and their parents was reported in only four of the waking-time observations (3 with father, 1 with mother) and play between sample children and all other adults was recorded in eight spot observations.

Adult–child play. In order to verify that play with parents was rare, spot observations and 10-minute narrative records were examined to determine the frequency of play between adults and children and the type of play that did occur. The spot observations and narrative records verified that collaborative play of long duration between parents and other adults and children was indeed rare, and that it frequently involved ball play, rough-and-tumble play, dancing or music activities (See examples 1–8 below). In addition, there were examples of adults responding to children's comments or questions during play (e.g., "come see this"), and there were examples of adults providing materials for play or encouragement of play; example 9 below provides a good illustration of this pattern, in the context of a little girl's pretense play.

> Ex. 1 (Child 02109)—17-year-old male relative throws a ball with a 2-year-old boy.
>
> Ex. 2 (Child 02109)—27-year-old uncle throws a ball with 2-year-old boy.
>
> Ex. 3 (Child 12016)—2-year-old boy dances to radio music by self, while three female relatives sitting nearby clap their hands for him to encourage his dancing.
>
> Ex. 4 (Child 12016)—Grandpa throws ball with 2-year-old boy.
>
> Ex. 5 (Child 13026)—4-year-old girl dances with a female adult relative and other little girls.
>
> Ex. 6 (Child 14005)—Three-year-old boy taps on grandma's feet as though they were a tam-tam (African drum); singing.
>
> Ex. 7 (Child 17018)—Four-year-old boy plays soccer with other 4–7-year-old boys and one 23-year-old male relative.
>
> Ex. 8 (Child 18010)—Four-year-old boy does rough-and-tumble play (playful wrestling) with 27-year-old uncle.
>
> Ex. 9 (Child 02126)—(one example of play that was coded as social pretense; a 3-year-old girl with both of her parents in their family field outside of the village):
>
> At first, Sacou is observed under a tree, planting some grass; her mother is within one yard of her planting bissap (a plant made into a drink when ripe) and her father is a little farther away weeding his garden. Sacou goes up to her mother and picks up some of the weed grass and

says to her mother, "Take this" and gives the grass to her mother. She goes away a few feet and returns and asks her mother to give her back the grass, that she is going to make a garden of her own like her father's field. She returns to her original "garden" and plants some of the grass in a hole. She watches her father working and says "my father works well but I can work like he does." She gets more grass and plants it in her garden. Her mother calls her to say they are returning to the village. She gets up and says to her mother "Mais je labourerai bien mon champ" ("but I was working well in my garden"). Her mother asks her what she was planting. She says "bissap and corn", and that it will soon be ripe and she will harvest it soon.

Child–child play. In the discussion of the American study results, it was hypothesized that children's limited social network (primarily their siblings) affected the extent of solitary vs. social play (more solitary play), the type of play (e.g., when other children were available, more gross motor play occurred), and the people with whom they played (e.g., when fewer children were available, mixed-age, mixed-sex play was more likely to occur). In contrast to the American sample, and other African studies in which few children have been available for play (e.g., hunter-gatherers described by Konner, 1975; the Kipsigis described by Harkness & Super, 1985), the Lebou children in the Senegalese study had access to numerous child play partners. The hypothesis that the availability of more children affects the extent and type of social play in which children engage could therefore be explored.

The availability of child play partners was related to the amount of time children did social play, social play of different types (e.g., social gross motor), and the extent to which children did same-age, same-sex play. These relationships were explored further by looking at children's play partners, and through regression analyses where scores representing play (proportion of social play, proportion of social gross motor play, etc.) were separate dependent variables, and child age, sex, and *number* of 0–12- and 2–6-year-old male and female child play partners in the compound (multiple households), household (multiple families living together) and family were independent variables.

Results of the regression analyses were disappointing in that no significant relationships emerged between any of the variables.

The number and type of child play partners also were examined.

Because the number of spot observations per child was too small to examine individual child data by different child age and sex groups, boys' and girls' play partners were examined by looking across the sample of boys' and girls' spot observations, and by examining children's play and play partners in the 10-minute narrative records of play. These analyses showed, first, that boys and girls' social play typically involved an average of two other play partners (or three in an average play group, with a range from two to nine) and that there were no sex or age differences in the average size of the play group. Second, these analyses suggested there were age and sex differences in the composition of children's peer groups. While 2–4-year-olds were more likely to engage in cross-age play (2 or more years difference in children's ages in the group) with mixed-sex partners, 5–6-year-old children were more likely to be in same-sex groups. In addition, 5–6-year-old boys and girls spent time with children of somewhat different ages; boys were more likely to be in groups of "near-age" (1-year spread in child ages) or cross-age groups of children who were older (e.g., 5–9-year-olds), while girls were likely to be in near-age groups or cross-age groups that were younger (e.g., 6–2-year-olds) and were more likely to be with babies than were boys.

Girls and boys' social play, within these types of child groups, was also different by the ages of 5–6. The statistical results reported above showed that girls did more social pretense with other children while boys did more social gross motor play with peers. The closer examination of the spots and narratives confirmed these results, and suggested that 5–6-year-old boys rarely did any pretense play (while it was common among 2–4-year-old boys). Compared with girls, boys engaged in more gross motor (soccer, ball throwing, etc.), active games such as hide and seek, rough-and-tumble play, constructive play (building a wire truck), and exploratory play (roaming the countryside, exploring termite mounds, etc.); older boys (usually 7–10-years) were most frequently involved in soccer games and building activities where skills such as wood carving or car building were taught. Five- to 6-year-old girls spent a significantly greater proportion of their play time in social pretense (marketing, baby care, learning to do laundry, carrying water, cooking, farming) than boys, and younger children were frequently involved. Girls also spent some time in gross motor activities (e.g., swimming, climbing trees, active games such as hide and seek), and all children did ritual dances and played toy or real tam-tams (categorized as music/dance, though some might call it pretense). Quiet games, such as marbles or cards, also were played by both boys and girls.

Discussion

The results of the study of 2–6-year-old Senegalese children's play at home and in their rural village community suggest that play was a dominant activity for these children, as it was for the American children described earlier. This result was particularly interesting given the heavier workload of the Senegalese children, and the significant negative relationship observed between work time and play time. The magnitude of the Senegalese children's time at play, despite work demands, attests to the intrinsic power of play for young children, and to its probable developmental importance (see discussion on this last point by Slaughter & Dombrowski, this volume).

During the agricultural summer season of the study, Senegalese boys and girls spent most of their play time in active (swimming, sports, climbing, rough-and-tumble play), pretense, functional, and dance and music (ritual dance/drumming play). Some constructive and exploratory play was also done by boys. There were significant age differences in functional play (2–4-year-olds more than 5–6-year-olds) and significant sex differences in gross motor and pretense play (boys more than girls, and girls more than boys, respectively).

Play was typically done outdoors. Like the American children, however, the majority of play was done close to home—around the house, in children's own compound, or inside the kin-related village. Five-to-6-year-old boys were sometimes seen outside the village, or coded as being "elsewhere" (unlocatable by the observers), but, in general, being this far removed from the home was an infrequent occurrence.

While some activities, like pretense or functional play, were no more likely to be done in one location than another, some activities were associated with certain locations; gross motor, constructive, and exploratory play, for example, were more likely to be done outside than inside the village. Interestingly, these three activities also were more associated with boys.

Although 2–4-year-old Senegalese children spent similar amounts of time in solitary and social play, by 5–6 years the children's play was almost exclusively social. Given the number of children and adults available to sample children, the solitary time spent by 2–4-year-olds was almost more surprising than the large proportion of social play common among 5–6-year-olds. Age-related differences in social competence in general, or specific to social play, may account for these differences.

The large number of adults and children available for play, up to 10 in many of the observations, did not result in particularly large play groups (average size was 3 in Senegal and 2 in the American study). Nor did the variations in the number of children in the Senegalese families, households, or compounds relate to the incidence of social play that occurred.

Sex differences in children's play and play partners were observed, particularly for 5-6-year-olds; this difference may have been related to the availability of boys and girls of different ages. Five-to-6-year-old boys spent more time playing with near-age and older boys than girls did, while girls spent more time playing with near-age girls, and younger boys and girls. The availability of a number of boys and girls of different ages may have facilitated the beginning of these sex differences in play partners and in the play activities children did with their partners (e.g., boys' gross motor, constructive, and exploratory play); however, other age-or gender-related changes may have also been influential.

Little adult–child play was observed in the Senegalese study, despite the relatively large numbers of male and female adults in children's settings. The Whitings and their colleagues (Whiting & Whiting, 1975; Whiting & Edwards, in press) suggest that this may be due to the heavy adult workload in societies such as Senegal. In such societies, children are more likely to be socialized to be independent of adults. In addition, adult–child interaction in such societies is more likely to be characterized by requests for obedience than in low-workload societies (the Whitings' cite a middle-class American society by example) where adult–child socializing appears to occur more frequently.

The spot and narrative observations of Senegalese children's play showed that child play frequently was interrupted for work, although adults supported children's play when possible. Adults provided play materials, such as food scraps for cooking pretense activities, and, on occasion, developed play materials, such as carving a child-sized mortar and pestle, or helping a child make a doll or truck. They also modeled adult gameplaying, and good-naturedly supported, sometimes through simple noninterference, children's play. Nonetheless, direct playful interaction with 2-6-year-olds was rarely observed.

Cross-cultural conclusion. In both cultural contexts, play was a dominant activity. In both the American and Senegalese samples, children engaged in direct play with children more often than with adults, and engaged in reasonably similar types of play, despite the wide differences in the cultural-ecological contexts of play, the space in which children played, the materials available for play, or the differences in adult–child interaction and activities.

The results showed that there were several consistent factors related to play in the two cultures. First, two nonecological factors were related to play patterns. *Age* was related to several types of play; in Senegal, for example, 2–4-year-olds did functional play more than 5–6-year-olds, while in the American study (Bloch & Walsh, 1985), this difference was observed in the 0–1 vs. 2–6-year-old comparisons. *Sex* differences were observed in both cultures in social gross motor play with other children (boys more than girls), and, in Senegal, in pretense play (girls more than boys).

A number of physical factors (materials, locations) were examined. Differences in toys were observed, but the difference in manufactured versus scrounged materials had no obvious effect on play between the two cultures, perhaps because there were adequate, though different, materials in both contexts.

Differences in locations consisted primarily of time spent inside larger American houses, and time spent outside, but nearby, the Senegalese houses. In both cultures, older children were significantly more likely to spend some time farther from home, and, in both cultures, summertime large motor play was more likely to occur in out-of-door locations. Despite these similarities, different locations were associated with somewhat different types of play in the two cultures. Thus, while *location* or "distance from home" was a significant ecological factor in both cultural contexts, location, by itself, could not be used to predict children's play.

Functional play was most likely to occur in solitary contexts, and sex differences in gross motor play were associated with away-from-home physical contexts, as well as social contexts in which other child play partners were available. No other play type was done consistently alone or with others, in either culture. While the number of boys and girls available for play may be an important factor in children's selection of play partners (e.g., same-sex), play type (e.g., gross motor or pretense), and play context (solitary/social), the correlational analyses reported in this chapter failed to provide a firm answer to this question.

Finally, both the American and Senegalese research showed that child–child play within home and community contexts was much more frequent than adult–child play. Therefore, if the quantity of time children spend in play with others has any developmental importance, these results indicate that further research on child–child play at home (with siblings, relatives, and friends) is warranted and, perhaps, less attention should be given to parent–child play. On the other hand, to the extent that even infrequent adult–child play, interactions during play, adult responses to play, or adult encouragement of play is important, as Vygotsky (1978) and others suggest, this type of play should continue to receive researchers' attention, and should be encouraged to become more frequent.

In conclusion, it was clear that the ecological contexts in which the young children played were very different, but that important similarities as well as differences occurred in children's play within these different contexts. Work that can continue to explore both the continuities and discontinuities in children's play and play contexts, along with their developmental implications is critical for the future.

REFERENCES

Barker, R.G., & Associates. (1978). *Habitats, environments, and human behavior.* San Francisco: Jossey Bass.

Barker, R.G., & Wright, H.F. (1955). *Midwest and its children.* New York: Harper & Row.

Bloch, M.N. (1980, December). *Senegalese mothers and their children: Proximity related to child sex, age, and maternal activity.* Paper presented at the meeting of the American Anthropological Association, Washington, DC.

Bloch, M.N. (1984a, April). Young Senegalese Children's Social Play. In J. Johnson (chair). *Cultural influences on play, education, and socialization.* Symposium conducted at the meeting of the American Educational Research Association, New Orleans.

Bloch, M.N. (1984b). Play materials: Considerations from a West African setting. *Childhood Education, 60*(5), 345–348.

Bloch, M.N. (1987). The development of sex differences in young children's activities at home: The effect of the social context. *Sex Roles, 16*(5/6), 279–301.

Bloch, M.N. (1988). The effect of seasonal maternal employment on young Senegalese children's behavior. *Journal of Comparative Family Studies,* Vol. XIX (3), 397–417.

Bloch, M.N., & O'Rourke, S. (1982). The nonsocial play of young Senegalese children: Sex differences and the effect of maternal employment. In J. Loy (Ed.), *Paradoxes of play.* West Point, NY: Leisure Press.

Bloch, M.N., & Walsh, D. (1985). Young children's activities at home: Age and sex differences in the activity, location, and social context. *Children's Environment Quarterly, 2*(2), 34–40.

Blurton–Jones, N.G. (1972). *Ethological studies of child behaviour.* Cambridge, England: Cambridge University Press.

Blurton–Jones, N.G., & Konner, M.J. (1973). Sex differences in the behavior of Bushman and London two- to five-year olds. In J. Crook & R. Michael (Eds.). *Comparative ecology and behavior of primates.* New York: Academic Press.

Bronfenbrenner, U. (1979). *The ecology of human development.* Cambridge, MA: Harvard University Press.

Bronfenbrenner, U. (1986). The ecology of the family as a context for human development. *Developmental Psychology, 22,* 723–742.

Bryant, B.K. (1985). The neighborhood walk: Sources of support in middle childhood. *Monographs of the Society for Research in Child Development, 50*(3) (Serial No. 210).

Carew, J. (1980). Experience and the development of intelligence in young children. *Monographs of the Society for Research in Child Development, 45*(12, Serial No. 183).

Coates, G., & Sanoff, H. (1972). Behavioral mapping: The ecology of child behavior in a planned residential setting. In W.J. Mitchell (Ed.), *Environmental design: Research and practice.* (Proceedings of the EDRA, Vol. 1). Raleigh, NC: Environmental Design Research Association.

Cochran, M.M., & Brassard, J.A. (1979). Child development and personal social networks. *Child Development, 50,* 601–616.

Draper, P. (1976). Social and economic constraints on child life among the !Kung. In R.B. Lee & I. DeVore (Eds.), *Kalahari hunter-gatherers.* Cambridge, MA: Harvard University Press.

Dunn, J. (1986). Pretend play in the family. In A.W. Gottfried, & C.C. Brown (Eds.), *Play interactions: The contribution of play materials and parental involvement to children's development* (pp. 149–162). Lexington, MA: Lexington Books.

Dunn, J., & Kendrick, C. (1982). *Siblings.* London: Grant McIntyre.

Ellis, S., Rogoff, B., & Cromer, C.C. (1981). Age segregation in children's social interactions. *Developmental Psychology, 17*(1), 399–407.

Fischer, J., & Fischer, A., (1966). The New Englanders of Orchard Town, U.S.A. In B. Whiting (Ed.), *Six cultures: Studies of child rearing.* New York: Wiley, pp. 869–1010.

Gump, P. (1975). *Ecological psychology and children.* In E.M. Hetherington (Ed.), *Review of child development research.* Chicago: University of Chicago Press.

Harkness, S., & Super, C.M. (1983). *The cultural structuring of children's play in a rural African community.* Paper presented at the meeting of the Association for the Anthropological Study of Play, Baton Rouge, LA.

Harkness, S., & Super, C.M. (1985). The cultural context of gender segregation in children's peer groups. *Child Development, 56,* 219–224.

Hart, R. (1979). *Children's experience of place.* New York: Irvington.

Hollingshead, A.B. (1975). *Four-factor index of social status.* Unpublished manuscript. (Available from Department of Sociology, Yale University, New Haven, CT).

Konner, M.J. (1975). Relations among infants and juveniles in comparative perspective. In M. Lewis & L. Rosenblum (Eds.), *The origins of behavior: Vol. 3. Friendship and peer relations.* New York: Wiley.

Konner, M.J. (1981). Evolution of human behavior development. In R.H.

Munroe, R.L. Munroe, & B.B. Whiting (Eds.), *Handbook of cross-cultural human development* (pp. 3–51). New York: Garland Press.

Kalu, N.J.N. (1985). *The effect of social class on children's play: A look at 2–6 year old Senegalese children.* Unpublished master's thesis. University of Wisconsin–Madison.

Leacock, E. (1976). At play in African villages. In J.S. Bruner, A. Jolly, & K. Sylva (Eds.), *Play—Its role in development and evolution* (pp. 466–473). New York: Basic Books.

Lewin, K. (1935). *A dynamic theory of personality.* New York: McGraw Hill.

Lewis, M., Feiring, C., & Kotsonis, M. (1984). The social network of the young child: a developmental perspective. In M. Lewis (Ed.), *Genesis of behavior: Vol. 4. Beyond the dyad* (pp. 129–160). New York: Plenum Press.

Littlewood, J., & Sale, R. (1973). *Children at play. Design Bulletin, 27.* London: Department of the Environment.

McGrew, W.C. (1972). *An ethological study of children's behavior.* New York: Academic Press.

Medrick, E.A., Roizen, J.A., Rubin, V., & Buckley, S. (1982). *The serious business of growing up.* Berkeley, CA: University of California Press.

Munroe, R.L., & Munroe, R.H. (1971). Effect of environmental experience on spatial ability in an East African society. *Journal of Social Psychology, 83,* 15–22.

Munroe, R.H., Munroe, R.L., Michelson, C., Koel, A., Bolton, R., & Bolton, C. (1983). Time allocation in four societies. *Ethnology 22*(4), 255–270.

Newson, J., & Newson, E. (1968). *Four years old in an urban community.* Harmondsworth, England: Pelican.

Newson, J., & Newson, E. (1976). *Seven years old in the home environment.* London: Allen & Unwin.

Ogbu, J. (1981). Origins of human competence: A cultural-ecological perspective. *Child Development, 52*(2), 413–429.

Rogoff, B. (1978). Spot observations: An introduction and examination. *Quarterly Newsletter of the Institute for Comparative Human Development, 2*(2), 21–26.

Rubin, K.H., Fein, G.G., & Vandenberg, B. (1983). Play. In P.H. Mussen (Ed.). *Handbook of child psychology: Vol. 4. Socialization, personality, and social development* (4th ed., pp. 693–774). New York: Wiley.

Schwartzman, H. (1978). *Transformations: The anthropology of children's play.* New York: Plenum Press.

Schwartzman, H.B. (1986). A cross-cultural perspective on child-structured play activities and materials. In A.W. Gottfried, & C.C. Brown (Eds.), *Play interactions: The contribution of play materials and parental involvement to children's development* (pp. 13–30), Lexington, MA: Lexington Books.

Sutton-Smith, B. (1985). *Toys as culture.* New York: Gardner Press.

Vygotsky, L.S. (1978). *Mind in society: The development of higher psychological processes.* Cambridge, MA: Harvard University Press.

Weisner, T.S. (1984). The social ecology of childhood: A cross-cultural view.

In M. Lewis (Ed.), *The genesis of behavior: Vol. 4. Beyond the dyad.* New York: Plenum Press.

Whiting, B.B. (1980). Culture and social behavior. *Ethos, 2,* 95–116.

Whiting, B.B., & Edwards, C.P. (Eds.). (in press). *The company they keep: The effect of age, gender and culture on social behavior of children aged two to ten.* Cambridge, MA: Harvard University Press.

Whiting, B.B., & Whiting, J.M.W. (1975). *Children of six cultures.* Cambridge, MA: Harvard University Press.

8

Parental Distancing Strategies and Children's Fantasy Play*

JANE C. PERLMUTTER
Early Childhood Education

ANTHONY D. PELLEGRINI
Institute for Behavioral Research and Early Childhood Education,
University of Georgia

One of the major accomplishments of the preschool period is being able to think and talk about things that are not physically present in the immediate environment. According to Vygotsky (1976), children's interaction with more competent others, particularly adults, facilitates the growth of this ability. This ability to use language to refer to things which are not present has been defined by Sigel, McGillicuddy-Delisi, and Johnson (1980) as one attribute of representational competence. Sigel and Cocking (1977) have explicated the construct of distancing whereby parents help children develop representational thinking. Certain distancing strategies are assumed to facilitate the growth of representational competence in children because they are utterances that have children attend to things which are not immediately present. Distancing behaviors are assumed to form a continuum from least demanding to more demanding. The more demanding, or higher level, distancing strategies require children to function more abstractly and at higher cognitive levels.

* This study is based on a dissertation submitted by the first author under the direction of the second author to the University of Georgia in partial fulfillment of the requirements for the degree of Doctor of Education. We acknowledge the invaluable statistical help provided by Supoat Charenkavanich. The authors wish to thank the children, parents and teachers at the McPhaul Center for their generous participation. Requests for reprints should be sent to Jane C. Perlmutter, Department of Early Childhood Education, 427 Aderhold, University of Georgia, Athens, GA 30602.

155

Like distancing, fantasy play also involves movement from the here and now to symbolic understanding. Because of this aspect of fantasy, major theorists, such as Piaget (1951/1962) and Vygotsky (1976), have linked the growth and development of fantasy play to the development of representational competence. Both parental distancing behaviors and fantasy play then may facilitate the growth of children's more general representational competence. Since distancing behaviors and fantasy are theoretically related, we might expect to find relationships between the two types of behaviors. Because of the hierarchical nature of the distancing strategies, we would expect to find a stronger relationship between children's fantasy and the higher level distancing strategies (Sigel & Cocking, 1977).

As parents interact with their children, they exhibit a wide range of behaviors with their children. To some extent the context of the parent–child interaction may determine the type of parental behavior exhibited (Pellegrini, Brody & Sigel, 1985). Sigel (Sigel et al, 1980) and his colleagues have identified distancing strategies that parents use with their children in a variety of situations (e.g., paper folding tasks and book reading). The first objective of this study was to see if the distancing strategies that parents used in a fantasy play situation varied according to parent (father vs. mother), age and sex of their preschool children. The research evidence comparing mother–father behavior is mixed. In a recent study comparing mother–father play with three- and four-year-old children, MacDonald and Parke (1984) did not find mothers and fathers differing on verbal behavior. On the other hand, Sigel and McGillicuddy-DeLisi (1984) found a cross-sex pattern of differences with mothers of sons and fathers of daughters using more higher level distancing strategies than mothers of daughters and fathers of sons.

The second objective of the study was to assess the relations of parental behaviors to children's fantasy play. The research evidence concerning parental (particularly mothers') influence on children's play is inconclusive, however. Some authors (i.e. DeLoache & Plaetzer, 1985) have reported direct improvement in the level of children's play when mothers are present. Johnson (1978), however, minimized the influence of mothers' play. Other authors have cited indirect effects of parental involvement in children's play. Fein (1979) described an elaborative style of mothers' involvement, that is similar to Wootton's (1974) description of the way middle-class parents extend children's knowledge of a particular topic through fantasy play. These parents used children's fantasy to encourage their cognitive operations and to provide information for their children. This is similar to the parent role that Sachs (1980) reported assuming with her daughter. These studies are intriguing but they do not explicate the mechanisms by which parents may affect their children's play. In this study we wanted to investigate the possibility that particular parental behaviors might be related to increased levels of fantasy play in children.

METHOD

Subjects

The subjects in this study were 20 preschool children (32- to 68-months-of-age), each attending a University preschool, and their mothers and fathers. Equal numbers of boys and girls participated. Children's ages were ranked chronologically and divided by a median split procedure into two age groups. The ages of the children in the younger age group ranged from 32 to 46 months ($M = 40.4$) and the ages of the children in the older group ranged from 48 to 68 months ($M = 54.3$). Each age group contained equal numbers of boys and girls. Mother's ages ranged from 26 to 41 years ($M = 32.8$) and father's ages ranged from 31 to 68 years ($M = 35.75$). Educational levels reported by parents were generally high, with mothers reporting educational experiences between college graduate and "some post-graduate experience" and fathers reporting averages between post-graduate and masters. All families recruited had two biological parents in the home and one, two, or three children.

Sessions

Play sessions were held in a small playroom in a university preschool. The materials in the playroom were chosen to facilitate dramatic play production and consisted of two doctor's kits and related materials (two stethoscopes, two blue plastic doctor's bags, three play syringes, a plastic "doctor's hammer", an otoscope, two pairs of blue plastic eye glasses, two baby dolls, two white men's shirts and a small baby bottle). Each parent came to the center for two 10 minute sessions. Sessions were scheduled at the parents convenience. Otherwise the order of sessions was random. The average number of days between sessions was 22.88. When each parent and child entered the playroom, they were told to play as they normally would at home. While the parents and children played, running notes were made of activities and audiotapes were used to record language.

Measures

Transcripts were prepared with reference to running notes and audiotapes. Transcripts were coded for fantasy transformations following McLoyd (1980). Each speaker's turn was broken down into the set of his/her utterances. Each utterance was defined as a word or word-string which communicated one idea. Those utterances that expressed nonliteralness or make-believe were identified. Seven individual fantasy categories were adapted from McLoyd's work and used in coding transcripts of play. Animation involved the attribution of living or human characteristics to a nonliving object, most often a doll. Reification involved taking an existing object (e.g., play syringe, blood pressure cuff, stethoscope, etc.) and pretending that it really worked. It was also coded when someone pretended the existence of an imaginary substance related to an actual object (pretend medicine in a toy medicine bottle). Attribution of object or person property included references to pretend physical conditions associated with real people and pretend noises made by instruments. Substitution involved giving a new identity to an existing object. Object realism was coded when there was pretense that an imaginary object or material existed. Situational attribution involved pretense that an imaginary situation existed. Role attribution was coded when there was portrayal of an imaginary character or role (i.e. nurse, doctor, mother, patient). Numbers of children's fantasy utterances from each category for each session were summed to produce a total fantasy score for each child.

Reliability of fantasy coding was determined by examination of 10% of the 80 transcripts. These transcripts were randomly chosen and were coded independently for fantasy transformations by the researcher and a doctoral student. Percentage agreement was calculated by dividing the total agreements minus disagreements and omissions by the total number of fantasy transformations. A reliability of 92.8% was achieved.

Following Sigel, McGillicuddy-DeLisi, and Johnson (1980), each parental utterance was coded for use of distancing strategies. There were six superordinate categories into which an utterance might be coded. Those were Directiveness, High Mental Operational Demands (distancing), Medium Mental Operational Demands (distancing), Low Mental Operational Demands (distancing), Positive Verbal Support, and Negative Verbal. An utterance was coded as task management/ directiveness if the parent told the child what to do. This included suggestions made in the course of the play. The category of low distancing or mental operational demands included the following parental demands: that the child observe, produce information, label, describe, interpret, demonstrate, or describe usage. Medium distancing or mental operational demands included the following demands: that the child sequence, represent, compare, describe similarities, describe differences, infer similarities, infer differences, classify symmetrically, estimate, classify asymmetrically, enumerate, or synthesize. High distancing or mental operational demands included the following demands: that the child evaluate consequences, evaluate his own competence, evaluate affect, evaluate performance, evaluate necessity, infer cause and effect, infer affect, infer effect, generalize, propose alternatives, resolve conflict, plan, or conclude. An utterance was coded as positive support if parents gave positive feedback, answered questions, or reflected the child's utterance. Numbers of instances in each category were summed over the two sessions so that each parent had a task management, a high distancing score, a medium distancing score, a low distancing score, and a positive support score.

Reliability for the coding of parental distancing behaviors was determined by an examination of 10% of the 80 parent transcripts. Eight transcripts were randomly chosen and were coded independently by the first author and a doctoral student. A total of 802 coding decisions measuring distancing behaviors and structuring behaviors were made. Using the formula of agreements divided by agreements plus disagreements and omissions, an inter-rater reliability of 98% was calculated.

Design

The study was designed to test the main and interactive effects of children's age and gender and parental status on parental interaction strategies in a fantasy play situation. A child gender (2) × child age (2) × parent (2) with the last factor repeated experimental design was used. The dependent measures were the parents' three levels of distancing behaviors, positive support, and directiveness. In order to test the effects of our model of parent–child interaction, a multivariate analysis of variance (MANOVA) using Wilkes criterion was utilized. We planned to use only those variables identified by the MANOVA as having significant main or interactive effects in the second series of analyses which were to be analyses of variance (ANOVA) on each dependent measure. The third series of analyses was comprised of Pearson correlations calculated to determine the relations between children's fantasy and parental behaviors (high, medium, and low distancing, positive support and directiveness).

RESULTS

The first objective of the study was to examine the extent to which our model affected parent-child interaction. This objective was tested with a (2) gender × 2 (age of children) × 2 (parents) Multivariate Analysis of Variance (MANOVA). The MANOVA detected no significant main or interactive effects. Means and standard deviations for dependent variables are listed in Table 1.

The second objective of the study was to examine the relation between individual parent interaction variables to children's fantasy

Table 1. Means and Standard Deviations of Parental Distancing and Task Management Behaviors by Sex and Age of Child

	Girls		Boys	
Variables	Younger	Older	Younger	Older
M's Lo Distancing	85.2	82.0	91.0	96.6
	(25.48)	(19.49)	(21.67)	(27.4)
F's Lo Distancing	87.2	83.2	105.0	98.0
	(38.6)	(18.66)	(43.57)	(26.29)
M's Med. Distancing	18.6	12.8	15.0	21.4
	(19.6)	(8.4)	(6.96)	(14.84)
F's Med. Distancing	14.4	19.4	12.8	17.2
	(10.45)	(9.93)	(4.76)	(7.49)
M's Hi Distancing	66.2	53.2	68.6	62.0
	(20.81)	(14.31)	(10.50)	(17.13)
F's Hi Distancing	63.8	59.0	58.8	63.0
	(17.28)	(9.69)	(16.67)	(27.61)
M's Directiveness	43.8	26.6	49.4	64.2
	(18.13)	(15.85)	(17.72)	(30.76)
F's Directiveness	53.4	33.0	44.0	28.8
	(27.8)	(14.43)	(12.86)	(12.19)
M's Positive Support	82.4	61.4	78.0	51.6
	(29.53)	(30.31)	(17.46)	(10.13)
F's Positive Support	74.4	73.4	57.4	78.0
	(36.47)	(35.54)	(18.80)	(29.29)

Note. M = mother, F = father.

production. Results are displayed in Table 2. Children's fantasy was negatively and significantly correlated with parental use of medium distancing strategies. In contrast, children's fantasy was positively and significantly correlated with high levels of distancing strategies, positive support, and directiveness.

DISCUSSION

Parental use of different distancing strategies did not vary as a function of child or parent status variables. Mothers and fathers did not differ significantly in the amounts of distancing behaviors they exhibited with their children. Neither mothers nor fathers made differential use of higher, medium, or lower level distancing behaviors. This result is congruent with MacDonald and Parke's (1984) findings of no significant differences in mothers' and fathers' verbal behavior in a play context. Research by Pellegrini, McGillicuddy-DeLisi, Brody, and Sigel (1985) suggests that the demand characteristics of an experimental playroom situation may mask mother–father differences. Both parents may react to the researcher's request to play by following their children's lead in observational laboratory settings. Pellegrini's (Pellegrini et al., 1985) research in experimental settings has not shown the mother–father differences that other researchers have noted in home settings. Indeed, both parents adjusted their levels of interaction to their child's level of competence thus minimizing between parent differences.

The props provided by researchers may also have been responsible for masking parent and parent by sex differences because parent's self-selection of props was controlled. Eisenberg, Wolchik, Hernan-

Table 2. Correlations Between Parental Distancing Strategies and Children's Fantasies

Distancing Strategy	r
Low distancing	− .02
Medium distancing	− .44 *
High distancing	.60 **
Positive support	.56 **
Directiveness	.45 *

* p < .05
** p < .01

dez, and Pasternack (1985) note a "channeling" effect of the children's play as a result of differential toy selection. As such, in studies where parents and children choose toys, parents' selection of toys and the toys themselves may produce differences between parents that would not be found where toys were experimentally determined. The point is that some reported mother–father differences may be as much a function of context as a function of real differences between parental interaction styles or toy selection preferences.

In the present study, the preselected toys used may have restricted the possible differences between parents. Mothers and fathers may have been responding in similar ways to the implicit scripts suggested by the doctor props. More ambiguous materials or a greater variety of materials might have elicited differential prop selection and responses from mothers and fathers. In fact, when context is controlled there may be fewer differences between parental behaviors than are seen in more naturalistic uncontrolled situations.

Medium level distancing strategies were significantly and negatively correlated with children's fantasy play. The medium level distancing strategies occurred less frequently than either high or low strategies. These medium level strategies require that children sequence, represent, compare, describe, and infer similarities or differences, estimate, and classify. Examination of the transcripts reveals that these strategies tended to occur in more didactic parent sessions, particularly when parents and children discussed uses of materials. For example, a father examining a toy stethoscope said, "It's a pretty good toy. It works like a real one." A mother discussing a piece of equipment said, "It doesn't seem to belong in there. It came from someplace else." These comments and challenges may be nonfacilitative of pretending to the extent that they are didactic in that they are concerned with means not ends.

The three types of parental strategies that were positively and significantly correlated with children's fantasy play were high level distancing strategies, positive support and directiveness. Higher level strategies include evaluating, inferring, proposing alternatives, planning, and resolving conflict. These strategies, along with directiveness, suggest parental scaffolding of the play scripts. Examinations of transcripts reveal numerous examples of parental suggestions that extend the children's fantasy stories. The doctor props elicited many varied yet similar stories of hospitals, sick children, busy doctors and nurses. In creating and extending the stories, parents challenged their children's interpretations of events and uses of materials. Children were asked to consider whether babies really needed shots in their toes and noses or whether it would not be best to examine patients before treatment. Thus, many of the higher level distancing strategies appeared to set up situations of cognitive conflict. Parents challenged their children to evaluate and plan. It appears that when parents challenge children through higher level cognitive demands their children produce more fantasy. Fantasy is an open-ended affair, involving divergent thinking. The higher level strategies encourage divergent thinking also. If we assume that fantasy play is related to higher levels of representational competence then these findings are consistent with Sigel's distancing hypothesis. Higher levels of distancing strategies do encourage children to look beyond the present.

Parents' positive verbal support, which included positive verbal feedback, informational feedback, and reflection of the child's utterances, was also positively and significantly correlated with children's fantasy. This category appears to reflect facilitative behavior on the part of parents. Using positive verbal feedback and reflection, parents followed their children's leads and encouraged play. This approach was related to more fantasy with our sample. A positive environment is necessary to support play (Rubin, Fein, & Vandenberg, 1983).

The combination of these factors (high distancing, directiveness, and positive support) seems to represent an active, encouraging parental role. Parents and teachers who suggest and challenge as well as support their children may have children who feel free to pretend more. The combination of support and suggestion suggests that both parents and children are playing active roles in creating fantasy.

REFERENCES

DeLoache, J.S., & Plaetzer, B. (1985, April). Tea for two: Joint mother–child symbolic play. In J. DeLoache & B. Rogoff (Chairs), *Collaborative cognition: Parents as guides in cognitive development.* Symposium conducted at the meeting of the Society for Research in Child Development, Toronto.

Eisenberg, N., Wolchik, S.A., Hernandez, R., & Pasternack, J.F. (1985). Parental socialization of young children's play: A short term longitudinal study. *Child Development, 56,* 1506–1513.

Fein, G.G. (1979). Play with actions and objects. In B. Sutton-Smith (Ed.), *Play and learning* (pp. 69–82). New York: Gardner Press.

Johnson, J.E. (1978). Mother–child interaction and imaginative behavior of preschool children. *Journal of Psychology, 100,* 123–129.

MacDonald, K., & Parke, R.D. (1984). Bridging the gap: Parent–child play interaction and peer interactive competence. *Child Development, 55,* 1265–1277.

McLoyd, V. (1980). Verbally expressed modes of transformation in the fantasy play of Black preschool children. *Child Development, 51,* 1133–1139.

Pellegrini, A.D., McGillicuddy-DeLisi, A., Brody, G.H., & Sigel, I. (1985). The effects of children's communicative status and task on parent's teaching strategies. *Contemporary Educational Psychology, 11,* 240–252.

Piaget, J. (1962). *Play, dreams and imitation in childhood* (C. Gattengno & F.M. Hodgson, Trans.). New York: W.W. Norton. (Original work published 1951).

Rubin, K.H., Fein, G., & Vandenburg, B. (1983). Play. In E.M. Hetherington (Ed.), *Carmichael's manual of child psychology: Vol. 4. Social development.* New York: Wiley.

Sachs, J. (1980). The role of adult–child play in language development. In K. Rubin (Ed.), *Children's play* (pp. 33–48). San Francisco: Jossey-Bass.

Sigel, I., & Cocking, R.R. (1977). Cognition and communication: A dialectic paradigm for development. In M. Lewis & L. Rosenblum (Eds.), *Interaction, conversation and the development of language.* New York: Wiley.

Sigel, I.E., & McGillicuddy-Delisi, A.V. (1984). Parents as teachers of their children: A distancing behavior model. In A. Pellegrini & T. Yawkey (Eds.), *The development of oral and written language in social contexts.* Norwood, NJ: Ablex.

Sigel, I.E., McGillicuddy-DeLisi, A.V., & Johnson, J.E. (1980). *Parental distancing, beliefs and children's representational competence within the family context.* Princeton, NJ: Educational Testing Service.

Vygotsky, L. (1976). Play and its role in the mental development of the child. In J.S. Bruner, A. Jolly, & K. Sylva (Eds.), *Play: Its role in development and evolution* (pp. 537–554). New York: Basic Books.

Wootton, A.J. (1974). Talk in the homes of young children. *Sociology, 8,* 277–295.

9

Children's Use of Time in Their Everyday Activities During Middle Childhood*

C. JAN CARPENTER
Department of Human Development and Family Ecology, University of Illinois

ALETHA C. HUSTON
Department of Human Development, University of Kansas

LAURA SPERA
University of Illinois

How children use their time and the social ecology within which they spend it during the middle childhood years is the focus of this chapter. Although we know the types of leisure and nonleisure after-school activities in which children participate, we know little about the quantity or type of interactions they have with adults, siblings, or peers while in these activities. Even less is known about the correlates of children's time use. These issues are addressed in this chapter in the context of a theoretical framework that views the social milieu of the activity in which a child participates as one of the important influences on children's social and cognitive behaviors. This study of children's time use is one of several studies testing a research model (Carpenter, 1983, 1987; Carpenter & Huston-Stein, 1980).

The rationale for the research model was to document the social

* This research was supported by grants (MH 33082) from the National Institute of Mental Health and the Institute of Child Health and Human Development (5T32 HD 07173). Requests for reprints may be sent to C. J. Carpenter, Department of Human Development, University of Illinois, Urbana, IL 61801.

165

and environmental process by which sex-typed cognitive and social behaviors develop. One key component of the model is the presence of adults in the activity settings. The child's activity is the unit of analysis and it includes both the physical setting and the adults, siblings, and peers who occupy it with the child. The decision to focus on the activity as the unit of analysis was guided by the fact that children's routine daily experiences occur in activities, for example, playing doll house, riding a bike in the neighborhood, or taking a ballet lesson. Differential exposure to adults occurs through participation in activities that differ in content, but that also differ in the amount of adult supervision associated with them. The amount of socialization input received from adults in these activities is empirically measured by quantifying the intervals of adult feedback received by a child, and by measuring the child's exposure to adult modeling. Adult feedback and modeling are conceptualized as *adult-supplied structure* since both supply information, rules, and expectations to the child about appropriate behavior in tasks and activities. In this sense, adult feedback and modeling "structure" the experiences of children exposed to them. Exposure to adult-supplied structure provides cultural norms for appropriate or expected behaviors that children can adopt. If little adult information is supplied about appropriate or expected behaviors, a child must supply his or her own rules, relying on current repertoire levels of expertise, or those of peers around him or her.

The framework guiding the present investigation shares the basic assumptions of an ecological approach—namely that the behavior of the participants in activities is related to the physical and social qualities of particular settings (Barker, 1968; Bronfenbrenner, 1979; Gump, this volume; Gump, 1975; Whiting, 1980). The physical milieu of the behavior setting, its social program, and participants' levels of involvement in the program encourage or coerce specific behaviors elicited by that behavior setting. Children's activities can be viewed within this perspective. Each activity has a physical and social milieu unique to it. Over time, the behaviors developed by children are partly a function of the settings in which they spend their time. Children are active participants in their choice of activities. But once in them, there is ongoing interactive influence between aspects of the setting and the child's social and cognitive behaviors. Once a specific behavioral repertoire has developed from the activity-specific experiences, future activity choices are influenced.

A series of studies have tested the above research model. Six major findings emerged: (1) Children's routine preschool activity experiences differ in the amount of exposure to adult-supplied structure, (Carpenter, 1984; Carpenter & Huston–Stein, 1980). (2) Boys and girls differ in exposure to high or low amounts of adult-supplied structure because they participate differentially in activities. Boys preferred low structure more than girls, while girls preferred high adult-structured activities, regardless of the overall classroom structure level, or the specific activities ranked as low or high adult-structure (Carpenter, 1984; Carpenter & Huston–Stein, 1980; Huston & Carpenter, 1985). The preschool finding was replicated with a sample of 7- to 11-year-olds who participated in a summer day camp (Huston, Carpenter, Atwater, & Johnson, 1986). (3) Activity participation encourages the development of behaviors and skills that are specific to the adult-structure level of the activity. In preschool classrooms, children who received high levels of adult-supplied structure exhibited feminine social behaviors, such as compliance to adults or asking for help, task persistence, and attempts at mastery that reflected adaptation to the adult rules and expectations. Low levels of adult-supplied structure encouraged masculine self-initiated, assertive, and peer-oriented behaviors (Carpenter, 1984; Carpenter & Huston–Stein, 1980). (4) Adult rules or information about appropriate behavior supplied directly, or abstracted by children influenced their behavior by participation in high- or low-adult structured activities. Children's rates of sex-typed behaviors increased and decreased, depending on the structure of the activity in which they were placed (Carpenter, Huston, & Holt, 1986). Similar results were found when children were randomly assigned to high or low structure in an experimental laboratory study (Carpenter, Huston, & Petrowsky, 1982); when their motor behaviors were observed in the natural environment (Carpenter, Logman, Roots, Cahoon, & Lewis, 1987), and when children were exposed to modeled video-experimental conditions and then allowed to play with the materials viewed (Carpenter, Miller, & Lewis, 1987). (5) The presence of warm, interacting adults precludes most interactions with peers also present in the activity setting (Carpenter et al. 1982; Huston et al., 1986). (6) Childrens' preference for high or low adult-structured activities is stable from the preschool to the early elementary-age period (Carpenter, Huston, Atwater, & Johnson, 1986). The children's social behaviors were also relatively stable, with their choice of activity predicting the type of social behavior they would exhibit.

TIME-USE

In the research reported in this chapter, the conceptual focus on the social and physical ecological setting is combined with documentation of the actual amount of time middle-childhood children spend daily in different settings. Following the tradition of time use studies on adults, recent studies have documented the variety of activities in which children spend time, (Medrich, Roizen, Rubin, & Buckley, 1982; Timmer, Eccles, & O'Brien, 1985). A few time use studies have also employed an ecological approach to time use. These studies elaborated an ecological theory (Whiting, 1980) which also proposes that patterns of behavior are developed in relation to the settings that people frequent (Bloch, 1987; Bloch & Walsh, 1985).

Out-of-school time use for early elementary-age children is viewed differently by children, by parents or adults, and by researchers. From a child's perspective, time is endless, something that one fills with various activities, in part to provide entertainment. Adults, particularly middle- and upper-class adults, appreciate time, and lament the increasing speed with which it appears to pass. Their view of the quality of time has an economic ring to it; time becomes more precious the less they have. Regularity of schedule helps to fit in the necessary elements of work, sleep, and nonwork activities. This view of time use, as a "fixed sum resource" is often expressed by researchers in quasieconomic terms (Rubin, 1978). Some time budget research examined household routines of working women, or contrasted daily activity schedules of single- and dual-parent families (Nickols, Powell, Rowland, & Teleki, 1983; Walker & Woods 1976). An element of incentives and constraints, and consequent reflection of priority underlies many theories on adult time use (Chapin, 1974; Robinson & Converse, 1972). Other investigators have been interested in single activity time studies—how much time is devoted to particular activities, such as television (Meyersohn, 1968). Others have elaborated the profile of activities engaged in, rather than the duration of time spent in them (Robinson, 1977). Children have not frequently been the topic of time use studies, in part because their use of time does not imply the same sense of priority that it does for adults (Medrich et al., 1982).

Time use studies with middle childhood-age children have described activities for a day or week, often by reconstructing the day from an interview (Medrich et al., 1982; Miller, 1970); a phone interview (Timmer, Eccles, & O'Brien, 1985); a booklet (Long & Henderson, 1973); an interview with the mother (Lawson & Ingleby, 1974), or an hourly log kept by parents (Winett & Neale, 1981). In the study reported in this chapter the child subject and his or her parent were trained to record the child's daily activities in 15-minute intervals for an entire week. The level of routine detail captured in the 15-minute interval diary may be greater than that obtained when respondents are asked to recall a past day's activities in a 20–30-minute interview. In the study reported in this chapter the child subject and his or her parent were trained to record the child's daily activities in 15 minute intervals for an entire week. Although comparison research was not conducted, it was hypothesized that the 15-minute recording approach would elicit more detail about routine, ordinary daily events than might be obtained in other methods, for example, from recall of a past day's events in a 20–30-minute phone interview.

PURPOSE OF STUDY

A major purpose of the present study was to analyze children's daily activities in middle childhood within the conceptual framework outlined above. Frequent participation in activities where adults are present encourages specific behaviors. Thus, one purpose was to analyze daily activities on this dimension. The daily activities of children were classified on the basis of the amount of adult supervision or involvement and on the basis of inherent organization in the form of specific rules or procedures (e.g., a baseball game) as indexes of the amount of structure provided for participants. When adults are present in children's daily activities, they are likely to provide a structure or an organization for children to follow. Adults may give direct instruction (as in lessons or team sports), take responsibility for decisions, give praise or reprimands, or offer cognitive and intellectual stimulation that may promote children's own cognitive development. Experience in adult-structured activities may provide practice in verbal and other intellectual skills and in being compliant to adults.

Activities in which peers are present without adults may provide opportunities for children to engage in peer structuring, independence, and leadership attempts. Children's activities were classified by peer involvement to provide an index of opportunities for this type of behavior.

A second purpose of the study was to investigate gender differences in daily activities. It was expected that girls would spend more time than boys in activities with adults present (i.e., those structured by adults). Observations of very young children have shown that girls spend more time in close proximity to adults than boys do as early as 20 months of age (Fagot, 1978). In a large survey of British 7-year-olds, girls received more "chaperonage" (i.e., close adult supervision) than boys (Newson & Newson, 1976). In a sample of American fifth graders, girls spent more time in organized activities, such as lessons, scouts, and shopping trips with mother, while boys spent more time in unorganized activities such as free play and watching television (Long & Henderson, 1973). Timmer et al. (1985) found that girls spent more time than boys doing household work, in personal care activities, eating, and spent less time playing sports. Several investigations have shown that girls devote more time to household chores than boys do (Long & Henderson, 1973). Girls' greater experience with structured daily activities may contribute to their greater compliance to adult rules and their generally higher levels of verbal and reading skills in the early school years (Maccoby & Jacklin, 1974); boys' greater experience in peer-guided activities may provide opportunities for learning leadership skills and aggression, as the cross-cultural work of Whiting and Whiting (1975) also suggests.

A third purpose was to investigate how children's daily activities vary as a function of social status and family structure. Several time use studies of children have investigated differences related to SES (Benson, Medrich, & Buckley, 1980; Lawson & Ingleby, 1974; Medrich et al., 1982; Miller, 1970; Nickols et al., 1983). Socioeconomic status is positively correlated with school achievement (Benson et al., 1980; Long & Henderson, 1973; Miller, 1970) while the amount of time watching television is not. Benson et al. (1980) found that for low SES families, the amount of time the family spent eating together was positively associated with school achievement.

In a national survey of adult time use, Hill and Stafford (1980) demonstrated that maternal education was positively related to time spent in child care, particularly in playing with children, teaching them, and in child-related travel activities which may be especially likely to contribute to children's cognitive and social development. Similar results were reported by Benson, et al. (1980). The difference between high- and low-educated mothers increased as children got older. Maternal education was a more important predictor of the time spent with children than was maternal employment. College-educated women who were employed more than 20 hours a week spent more time with their school-age children than the average mother with a high school education or less. Similarly, among English 7-year-olds, the amount of adult supervision increased with social class (Newson & Newson, 1976). It might be expected, therefore, that children's participation in adult organized activities would be positively related to maternal and paternal education.

The fourth purpose of the study was to investigate how daily time use was related to children's intellectual and personal development. Previous investigations suggest that reading achievement is positively related to the time children spend in leisure reading (Long & Henderson, 1973), and to an "optimum" daily schedule which involves variety and stimulation (Miller, 1970). There is also some evidence that reading achievement and IQ are negatively related to the amount of time spent watching television (Morgan & Gross, 1982; Peterson & Zill, 1980).

In summary, children's after-school and weekend time use was expected to differ in the amount of time spent in activities that were organized by adults, or that were predominantly self-directed, or peer-oriented. Girls were expected to spend more time in adult-directed activities, while boys were expected to spend more of their leisure time in nonadult structured activities. Family demographic variables such as SES or parent educational would predict intellectual measures, such as school achievement. Finally, the amount of time children spent in activities where adult modeling and feedback routinely occurred, was expected to relate to intellectual and cognitive performance.

METHOD

Subjects

Participants were 117 boys and girls who ranged in age from 7 to 11 years of age. All lived in or near a small Midwestern city. The majority ($n = 75$) were recruited as part of a longitudinal follow-up of children who had been studied in preschool (Carpenter, 1983; Carpenter & Huston–Stein, 1980). They had attended a university laboratory preschool or a university-based day-care center in the city where the study was conducted for at least one semester when they were 3 to 5 years old. Each family was contacted by letter and a follow-up phone call to request their participation in the follow-up.

The remaining children were recruited, from second, third, and fourth-grade classrooms in the public schools of the city through flyers sent to all children. The flyers offered a free 1-week day camp in connection with participation in a research project. If families agreed to consider participating, an interviewer explained the entire project (which included the diary, day camp, individual psychological measures, and permission to obtain school achievement scores from the public school) to the parent and the child.

A consent form was read and signed by both parent and child. Each child was offered an incentive payment of $15 for completion of the 7-day diary, and another $15 for completion of the day camp and psychological measures.

Most of the children were from middle-class families, although there was some variation in social status. The average level of education for both parents was a bachelor's degree. Approximately one-third of the mothers were employed full time outside the home, one-third half time, and the final third were full-time homemakers. Eighty-seven percent of the children had two parents in the home (either original or stepparents); the remainder had single parents. The average number of siblings was 0.83. Ninety-seven children were white, and 20 were nonwhite. The nonwhite category included children of Afro-American, Asian Indian, Japanese, Chinese descent.

Most of the children lived in or near a city in northeastern Kansas with a population of about 60,000. The great majority lived in single-family homes with outdoor play areas readily accessible. Most neighborhoods in the community are relatively free of traffic hazards and crime and are considered safe by parents. (Parents were asked how safe their neighborhood was for children. On a 7-point scale ranging from 1 = not at all safe to 7 = absolutely safe, the mean rating was 5.31.) However, there is no public transportation system, so children can travel alone only as far as their legs or a bicycle will take them.

Diary Measure

The principal measure was a time use diary which each child completed for out-of-school activities for 7 consecutive days. The diary was specifically designed to elicit the maximum amount of information about routine, daily events from the children rather than highly salient ones. The form of the diary was a printed booklet with spaces to record each 15-minute interval from 3 P.M. to 12 P.M. on weekdays and from 6 A.M. to 12 P.M. on Saturday and Sunday. A total of 81 hours were accounted for in the diary. For each interval, there were columns to write where the child was, with whom (adults, siblings, peers), primary activity, and secondary activity. When entries continued over several intervals, the respondent simply drew a vertical line through the relevant intervals.

Extensive training and a financial incentive were used to ensure quality of diary information. In the initial home visit, the interviewer spent approximately 1 hour instructing the parent and child about how to fill out the diary and helping the child fill in the activities for that day. Although the child was encouraged to be responsible for the diary, parents were asked to help, either by reminding the child to fill it out or by writing in the entries as the child described them. For the younger children in the sample, the parental help appeared essential. The same interviewer returned at the end of the week to collect the diary. She checked it for completeness, and questioned the child or parent about any vague or blank sections. On occasion, children were asked to do additional days if they had been sick or if there were blank sections for some days. When the completed diary was returned, the child received $15.

One validity check was conducted by telephone for each child. The family was informed that sometime during the week an interviewer would call and ask to speak to the child. The interviewer asked the child what he or she was doing at that time. This reliability method, while not without potential flaws, was selected as the best of those practically available. Although it might have been possible for parents to influence the reliability check by immediately recording the activity reported by the child, anecdotal examples from parents about when and how the diaries were filled out gave us confidence in the accuracy of this reliability check.

One week-long diary was randomly collected from each subject during the latter part of the spring school semester (April and May) and the first part of the following fall semester (September and October). These times were selected because school was in session, the weather was generally mild, and there was daylight for substantial periods after school.

Diary Coding

After completion of the diaries, trained coders placed each 15-minute interval in one of 20 categories, which were exhaustive and mutually exclusive. The categories were derived from three sources: a priori definitions based on the theoretical framework guiding the study, categories used in previous time use studies, and categories suggested by the nature of the entries made in the diaries. Once the 20 activity categories were established, coders assigned one category to the primary and secondary activities each of the 15-minute diary intervals. Reliability checks were conducted to ensure that coders agreed on assignment of individual activities to the 20 categories. Overall agreement among coders was 98%.

The 20 activity categories are:

> *Chores:* Errands, housework, jobs.
> *Personal hygiene:* Personal care.
> *Sleep:* Morning or evening sleep, or napping. The sleep

category does not reflect 6 hours during the night for the 7-day period.

Transportation: Car, bike or leg transport from one place to another.

Pets: Care of or playing with pets.

Interaction: Interactions with other people. Since interaction occurred during most of the categories, it was not entered as a separate category unless it was the only activity recorded for the interval.

Reading/homework: Reading, being read to, doing homework or lessons that involved written or verbal exercises, such as Hebrew or French.

Music: Listening to music on the radio, tape recorder, or stereo.

Lessons: Any type of lesson, except those that were primarily written in form, and including taking or practicing for musical lessons.

Television: Watching television. A qualification to this category occurred when the child recorded TV watching and some other activity. When other categories, such as homework, chores, personal hygiene, or reading, occurred with TV, they were coded as the primary activity. These intervals were coded as occurring simultaneously with watching TV.

Video games: Using home video games on the family computer, TV, or hand held game, or playing video games in a commercial location, such as those found in shopping centers.

Shopping: Shopping at stores.

Meals and snacks: Regular meal times with the family. This category did not include such items as "doing homework and eating apple." This example would have been coded as "homework."

In-the-home organized activity: A game or activity that had a prescribed set of rules, method, or procedure for completing the game or activity.

In-the-home unorganized activity: Activity in a home where there appeared to be opportunity for the child to generate or promote his or her own version of, or rules for the activity.

Loafing: Doing no activity in particular, waiting for an activity to begin, and so forth.

Out-of-the-home unorganized activity: Activities outside the home that were organized by the child, and not by a group or leader. Examples included bike riding, roaming around the neighborhood, or shooting baskets (with a few peers. An organized game with a team and coaches would be classified in "sports").

Out-of-the-home organized activity: Activities that were organized, suggested, or promoted by someone other than the child, as in organized trips by the Girl Scouts, church or school activities, or going to a Royals ballgame in Kansas City.

Sports: Organized sports involving a degree of group organization, prescribed rules or team play, for example, baseball or team swimming. Unorganized ball games or "sandlot ball" were included in the out-of-home unorganized category.

Undetermined: Intervals that could not be categorized in other areas were included here. This category was not included in any of the analyses.

COGNITIVE AND PERSONALITY MEASURES

The following pencil-and-paper measures of cognitive skills and personality attributes were administered once per day during the summer day camp:

1. The Children's Embedded Figures Test is a measure of field dependence–independence.
2. The Spatial Relations subtest of the Primary Mental Abilities Tests is a measure of children's visual-spatial ability. An IQ equivalent score is based on age-graded norms.
3. Three figural subtests of the Torrance Tests of creativity are designed to measure fluency, flexibility, originality, and elaboration.
4. The Harter Scale of Intrinsic versus Extrinsic Orientation in the Classroom (Harter, 1981) measures individual differences in children's orientation toward independent mastery versus dependence on adult evaluation and guidance.
5. The Harter Perceived Competence Scale for Children (Harter, 1982) measures children's self-evaluations or self-esteem. It contains four subscales: the child's perceived competence in cog-

nitive, social, and physical skill domains, and general feelings of self-worth.

6. The Children's Personal Attributes Questionnaire (Simms et al., 1978) measures children's self-perceptions of masculine and feminine personality characteristics. It contains three subscales: masculine, feminine, and MF (bipolar masculine–feminine).

7. School Achievement. The most recent scores on standardized achievement tests administered by the schools were obtained for 106 of the children. The majority of children had taken the SRA Achievement Tests the previous fall. A minority took the Iowa Tests of Basic Skills. Scores for the remaining children were unavailable. Normal curve equivalent scores for reading, math, and combined achievement were obtained for all children.

TIME IN ACTIVITIES

The total time spent in each of the 20 activity categories appears in Table 1. Only primary activities were included in this tabulation. The totals reflect childrens' time allocations over an entire week from 3 P.M. to 12 midnight, and 6 A.M. to 12 midnight on Saturday and Sunday. They do not include the hours between midnight and 6 A.M., or 6 A.M. and 3 P.M. on Monday through Friday, (most of which is in school or preparing to leave for school).

Children devoted more time to television than to any other activity except sleep. Watching television was a primary activity for slightly more than 9 hours per week on the average; and the total amount of television viewing (as a primary or secondary activity) was 11.44 hours. The next most frequent categories were out-of-home unorganized activity, meals and snacks, chores, transportation, and in-home unorganized activities. Children, on average, spent the small amounts of time listening to music, playing video games, playing with pets, or in organized sports. For sports, and video games, the low mean is due to zero participation for many children. Those who participated in sports, spent much more time than 1.2 hours per week in organized team sports.

Time with Adults

Overall, children spent 68% of their waking after school and weekend hours in the presence of adults. In the analysis reported in this

Table 1. Mean Number of Hours in Each Activity

	Total Time			With Adults Present N = 118			With Siblings Present N = 100			With Peers Present N = 118		
	Female	Male	Both	Female	Male	Both	Female	Male	Both	Female	Male	Both
In-home organized	1.88	1.50	1.68	1.67	1.39	1.52	0.84	0.79	0.81	0.44	0.30	0.37
Team sports	0.49	1.84	1.19	0.49	1.59	1.06	0.13	0.38	0.26	0.49	1.65	1.10
Out-of-home organized	3.96	2.90	3.41	3.69	2.56	3.10	2.10	1.48	1.77	3.05	1.96	2.48
Lessons & practice	2.16	0.55	1.32	1.77	0.59	1.15	0.66	0.31	0.47	0.84	0.18	0.50
Shopping	1.44	1.36	1.40	1.30	1.28	1.29	0.71	0.76	0.73	0.25	0.24	0.24
Meals & snacks	6.09	6.11	6.10	5.18	5.32	5.25	4.72	4.51	4.61	1.19	0.91	1.05
Interaction	2.08	1.84	1.96	1.73	1.46	1.59	1.30	0.97	1.13	0.57	0.46	0.51
Transportation	4.47	4.85	4.67	3.31	3.82	3.58	2.48	2.60	2.53	1.72	2.06	1.90
Video games	0.52	0.72	0.62	0.43	0.49	0.46	0.22	0.32	0.27	0.19	0.42	0.31
Chores	5.25	5.16	5.21	3.61	4.00	3.81	2.64	2.60	2.50	0.74	0.42	0.57
Homework & reading	2.77	2.61	2.69	1.60	1.87	1.74	1.30	1.05	1.16	0.28	0.10	0.19
TV (primary activity)	8.24	10.07	9.19	5.30	7.03	6.20	5.80	6.98	6.41	1.38	1.27	1.32
TV (including secondary)	10.53	12.28	11.44									
Personal hygiene	3.04	2.38	2.70	1.94	1.62	1.77	1.63	1.21	1.41	0.29	0.12	0.20
Loafing	0.58	0.70	0.65	0.37	0.40	0.39	0.28	0.33	0.31	0.11	0.16	0.14
In-home unorganized	4.90	4.30	4.59	2.61	2.81	2.72	3.19	2.50	2.84	1.86	1.45	1.65
Pets	1.10	0.65	0.86	0.55	0.35	0.45	0.40	0.25	0.32	0.28	0.21	0.25
Music	0.44	0.32	0.37	0.24	0.12	0.18	0.18	0.14	0.17	0.09	0.10	0.10
Out-of-home unorganized	7.65	9.91	8.83	2.82	3.65	3.25	3.89	4.32	4.12	5.11	7.00	6.10
Miscellaneous	2.46	2.46	2.46	0.11	0.12	0.11	0.01	0	0.01	0.13	0.11	0.12
Sleep	21.54*	20.95	21.23	0.18	0.33	0.26	1.24	2.57	1.93	0.78	0.23	0.49
TOTAL				38.89	40.79	39.88	33.78	33.83	33.81	19.80	19.34	19.56

*Note.** Children's mean number of 15-minute intervals per 20 activity categories was divided by 4 to obtain the hourly figures. Total time in the activity was the total number of hours per week in the activity. Time with adults, siblings, and peers present was the amount of time spent in each activity category with adults, siblings, or peers.

chapter, adult presence was defined as either being involved in the activity with the child, or being present in the same room. More fine-grained analyses were collected, but are not reported in this chapter. Adults were present 80% or more of the time when children participated in in-home organized activities (90%), out-of-home organized activities (91%), team sports (89%), lessons (87%), shopping (92%), meals (86%), and social interaction (81%). These activities probably entailed a considerable amount of adult-provided structure. Activities in which adults were present 50% to 75% of the time were predominantly those involving routine activities such as chores (73%), transportation (76%), personal hygiene (65%), homework (65%), loafing (60%), and watching television (67%). Activities where adults were least often present included out-of-home unorganized activities (37%), in-home unorganized activities (59%), music (49%), and pet care (52%).

Time with Siblings

Those children who had siblings ($n = 100$) spent 56% of their waking hours with siblings. As one might expect, most of the activities with high levels of sibling presence were routine, and home-oriented. The majority of time with siblings was spent watching television (5.4 hours per week) and siblings watched together 69% of the time. Meals (3.9 hours) were the next most frequent activity, and were conducted with siblings 75% of the time. Children spent 46% of their time with siblings in out-of-home unorganized activities, 61% during in-home unorganized activities, 48% during chores and 53% during transportation, 52% during personal hygiene and 52% during out-of-home organized activities.

Time With Peers

Overall, children spent 33% of their time with one or more peers. Peer contacts occurred more than 70% of the time children were engaged in out-of-home unorganized activities, out-of-home organized activities, organized sports.

SEX DIFFERENCES IN ACTIVITY PARTICIPATION

The mean number of hours spent in each category by females and males was significantly different for six of the activities. A multivariate analysis of variance was performed with gender as the independent variable and 18 activities as dependent variables (excluding sleep and miscellaneous). The main effect of sex was significant, Wilks Lambda = 0.635; $F(18, 98) = 3.13$, $p < 0.001$. Univariate F tests were performed to determine which activities differed significantly by sex. Girls spent more time than boys in away-from-home organized activities, lessons and practice, and personal hygiene. Boys spent more time than girls in team sports and out-of-home unorganized activities. There was a borderline ($p < .06$) tendency for boys to watch more television than girls.

In order to test the prediction that girls' time would be spent in high structure activities and boys' time in low structure activities, the 18 activities were grouped into three levels of structure on the basis of the amount of time adults were present. A sex (2) $\times$ structure (3) analysis of variance demonstrated a significant interaction, $F(2,114) = 3.15$, $p < 0.05$. Girls spent significantly more time than boys in high-structure activities, (Means: girls = 16.0; boys = 14.2). Boys spent more time than girls in medium-structure activities (girls = 23.6; boys = 25.0). Contrary to prediction, however, girls spent slightly more time in low-structure activities (girls = 18.5; boys = 17.4).

Time with adults. Initial analyses demonstrated that there were no overall sex differences in the amount of time spent with adults, but there were differences in the distribution of that time across activities. Multivariate analyses of variance performed for the time spent with adults in each activity demonstrated significant effects of child sex, Wilks Lambda = 0.672, $F(18,98) = 2.65$, $p < .01$. Univariate F tests indicated that girls spent more time than boys with adults in away-from-home organized activities and lessons and practice; boys spent more time with adults than girls did in organized sports; they tended to spend more time with adults watching television, and in out-of-home unorganized activities. These results are generally parallel to those for total time.

Because the total time with adults in an activity depends largely on the time in the activity, the proportions of time in each activity with adults were examined. They were not subjected to multivariate analyses because they could not be computed for any activity in which the child did not participate; therefore, there were a large number of cells with missing data. Girls spent a higher proportion than boys of their time with adults during out-of-home organized activities (Females = 0.92; Males = 0.87; $F(1,100) = 2.40$, $p < 0.01$) and organized sports ($F = 1.00$ M = 0.86). Girls never participated in organized sports without adults. Boys spent a higher proportion of their time than girls with adults during lessons and practice (0.80; M = 0.96; F (1,53) = 5.30, $p < 0.001$).

Time with peers. There were no significant sex differences in total time spent with peers, but again, there were differences in the distribution of time across activities, Wilks Lambda = 0.65, $F(18,98)$ = 2.87, $p < 0.01$. Girls spent more time than boys with peers in away-from-home organized activities, lessons, homework and reading, and personal hygiene. They also tended to spend more time with peers during chores. Boys spent more time than girls with peers in organized sports, and they tended to spend more time with peers in transportation and away-from-home unorganized activities.

PREDICTORS OF TIME IN ACTIVITIES

Some of the 20 activity categories were collapsed into seven groupings on theoretical, conceptual, or empirical grounds: Study (lessons, reading, and homework); meals and snacks; out-of-home organized activities (out-of-home organized activities and sports); indoor organized activity; out-of-home unorganized activity; indoor unorganized interaction (indoor unorganized activities and interaction); television.

Family structure variables, personality attributes, and intellectual skills were examined as predictors of children's total time in each activity, time in each activity with adults, and time in each activity with peers in a series of multiple regressions. For each dependent variable, the first regression included seven individual and demographic variables as predictors: gender, parent education, age or grade, parent occupational status, maternal employment, number of younger and older siblings. The mean of mother's and father's educational, and occupational status was used for each measure respectively in two-parent families. In single-parent families, the parent's score was used. Then, a second regression was performed entering gender and parent education first and the personality and intellectual variables second. This two-step procedure was used so that the total number of predictors in each analysis would not exceed a reasonable limit. The results are summarized in Table 2.

Total time with adults. The only predictor of children's total time with adults (summed over all activities) was grade level, $F(1,107)$ = 4.71, $p < 0.05$, Beta = −0.21. Children in lower grades spent more time with adults than those in higher grades.

Study. Gender and parent education were positive predictors related to the amount of time children spent in lessons, reading and homework. When personality and intellectual measures were entered

Table 2. Predictors of Time Spent in 7 Activity Categories

Activity	Predictors	Total Time			Time with Adults			Time with Peers		
		Beta	F	R	Beta	F	R	Beta	F	R
Study	Sex	.11[a]	1.78		—	—		.31	13.36**	
Lessons, reading & homework	Parent education	.23	6.97**		.20	5.04*		—	—	
	Perceived competence in athletics	-.31	14.97***		-.33	14.00**		—	—	
	Intrinsic motivation	.21	6.16*		.29	8.64***		.21	6.27*	
	Elaboration	.28	11.17**		—	—		—	—	
	Fluency			.57	—	—	.45	-.17	4.13*	.45
Meals & snacks	Parent education	.07[a]	0.46		—	—		—	—	
	School achievement	.27	9.02**		—	—		—	—	
	Spatial relations (PMA)			.27	.27	8.59**	.27			
Out-of-home organized	Sex	.24	6.49*		.21	5.28*		.29	9.43**	
	Masculinity (Mf score)	.19	4.12*	.26	—	—	.21	.22	5.69*	.31
In-home organized	Intrinsic motivation	—	—		—	—		.27	7.96*	
	School achievement	—	—		—	—		-.19	3.99*	.28

Table 2. (continued)

Activity	Predictors	Total Time			Time with Adults			Time with Peers		
		Beta	F	R	Beta	F	R	Beta	F	R
Out-of-home unorganized	Sex	-.21	5.29*		—	—		—	—	
	Perceived competence in athletics	—	—		—	—		.23	6.30*	
				.21						.23
Indoor unorganized	Field independence (EFT)	-.27	8.97**		-.31	12.67**		—	—	
				.27			.31			
Television	Age	.20	4.76*		—	—		—	—	
	Number of older siblings	.20	5.03*		—	—		—	—	
	School achievement	—	—		-.20	4.94*		—	—	
				.29			.20			

* **Note.** Results of multiple regressions predicting the seven summary activity categories from personality and family demographic characteristics

ᵃBeta in final step before variable dropped from equation

Variable initially entered equation at $p < 0.05$.

as predictors, gender no longer accounted for a significant proportion of the variance. Intrinsic motivation and creative elaboration were positively related to study time; perceived competence in athletics was negatively related. Gender was dropped from the equation after perceived competence in athletics entered, suggesting that self-concepts about athletic skill accounted for some of the gender differences in study time.

In summary, children who spent a lot of time in lessons, reading, and homework most often were girls and those with well-educated parents. They had high levels of school achievement, nonverbal cognitive skills, and intrinsic motivation, and they did not consider themselves good at athletics.

Meals and snacks. Parent education was a significant predictor of meal and snack time in the analysis of individual and demographic variables. However, when the cognitive and personality variables were entered, the only significant predictor in the final equation was school achievement. Children who did well in school spent relatively large amounts of time in meals and snacks with their family.

Out-of-home organized activities. Girls spent more time than boys in out-of-home organized activities. This difference held even though sports activities were collapsed into this variable. The only other significant predictor was the Mf score from the CPAQ. Children with high Mf scores spent relatively large amounts of time in organized activities away from home, particularly with their peers.

In-home-organized activities. There were no significant predictors of total time in in-home organized activities or time with adults. Time with peers in home-based organized activities was positively related to intrinsic motivation and negatively related to school achievement.

Out-of-home organized activities. The total time spent in unorganized activities out of the home was predicted only by gender; boys spent more time than girls in the neighborhood or yard in unsupervised activities. Time with peers in this category was positively related to perceived competence in athletics; that personality variable accounted for much of the variance associated with gender.

Indoor unorganized activities. The only predictors of this category were intellectual measures. Field independence was negatively related to time spent in indoor unorganized activities (including social interaction), as was school achievement.

Television. Total time spent watching television as a primary activity was predicted by age and number of older siblings. Older children and those with older siblings watched the most television. School achievement was not significantly related to total television viewing time, but was negatively related to time spent watching television with adults. There were no predictors of time watching television with peers.

DISCUSSION

One theoretical dimension for differentiating leisure time activities is the amount of structure supplied to the participants. Structure can be provided by adults when they are involved in an activity, or it may be provided by well-defined rules for the activity. In the present study, adults were present during a majority of the children's time. During the week-long diary collection, children devoted 6 hours a week to organized meals and snacks, and about 4.5 hours to organized activities away from home (including team sports). Children spent 1-2 hours in organized activities at home, another hour or so in lessons and practicing, and not quite 3 hours in reading and homework.

A sizable portion of childrens' time was devoted to "maintenance" of self and environment: shopping, transportation, chores, and personal hygiene. These activities were usually performed with adults present, but it seems likely that the adults are not focusing their principal attention on directing the child's behavior during much of this time.

Unorganized activities provide potential opportunities for children to create their own structure. When peers are present, they experience group efforts to decide what to do and how to do it. Children spent sizable amounts of time in out-of-home unorganized activities, usually with peers, and in unorganized activities at home.

Television is difficult to classify on a structure dimension. Adults are present during the majority of viewing, and there are some guidelines about appropriate behavior while watching television. The viewer is not required to structure the activity. Children in this sample devoted more time to television than to any other waking activity except school. Nevertheless, the amount of viewing is lower than that reported in some other studies (e.g., Timmer et al., 1985). One reason for this discrepancy may be a difference in measurement method. Most other estimates are based on rating services diaries or on checklists of television programs filled out by children (Comstock, Chaffee, Katzman, McCoombs, & Roberts, 1978). The respondents know that the focus is television when they complete the questionnaires. In addition, "viewing" is often recorded if the person is in a room with a functioning television set even though they may not be attending to it very often. In the present study, television was not emphasized. It was one of any number of activities that could be recorded. Therefore, children probably did not record television as either a primary or secondary activity when it was peripheral to other activities. Most are filled out fairly soon after viewing.

Another reason for the relatively small amount of television viewing is probably the season of the year. Viewing is typically more frequent in winter and less frequent in warm weather. The diaries were collected in late spring and early fall when the weather was mild and when there were many weekend and after-school activities available.

Girls spent more time in highly structured activities than boys did. In particular, girls devoted more time to lessons and to out-of-home organized activities such as clubs, organized outings, and parties. The one highly structured activity in which boys spent more time was organized sports. Boys spent more time than girls in the least structured activity—unorganized out-of-home activity. Much of the time included peers, suggesting that boys get more practice in the social skills of creating structure within a peer group. Boys tended to watch slightly more television than girls, a finding consistent with earlier literature (Comstock et al., 1978).

The sex difference findings conform in some instances with social stereotypes for males and females. Even at ages 8 to 10, girls spent more time on personal hygiene than boys. There were no differences, however, in household chores.

There is some suggestion in the data that when children engage in sex atypical behavior, they are more apt to do so with an adult involved than when the activity is typical for their gender. When girls participated in sports, adults were always present; boys sometimes engaged in organized sports without adult leadership. When boys participated in lessons, an adult was more likely to be present than was the case for girls. Adults were more likely to help boys with their homework than girls. Girls more often engaged in lessons and practicing for lessons without an adult present.

Very few age differences in activities occurred. Younger children spent more time generally with adults than older children, but the only activity for which there were age differences was television. The finding that older children watched more television is consistent with other literature on television viewing showing that viewing peaks in late childhood (Comstock et al., 1978). Of course, the range of ages in the sample is relatively narrow (7 to 11), but it is great enough that more age differences might have been expected than were found.

Parent education was related to children's time allocations, and it was a better predictor than occupational status. Children of highly educated parents spent more time in study (lessons, reading, and homework) and in organized meals and snacks than those with less-educated parents. This is consistent with earlier findings that maternal education was related to the total amount of time spent in child care (Benson et al., 1980; Medrich et al., 1982).

Neither maternal employment nor family structure was strongly related to children's time allocation. As the distribution of maternal employment in this sample was wide, the negative results have meaning; children with employed mothers have similar activity patterns to children whose mothers are not employed. The only activity that was related to family composition was television viewing. Children with older siblings watched more television than those who were firstborn. Direct social influence from older siblings' viewing is the most likely explanation for this result.

Childrens' intellectual skills were among the most consistent predictors of their time allocation. Both nonverbal cognitive skills—field independence, spatial relations, and two scores on figural (nonverbal) tests of creativity—and performance on standardized tests of school achievement were related to time in activities. High achievers spent more time in study and in organized meals and snacks; low achievers spent more time in unorganized indoor activities and in watching television with adults. These findings are independent of parent education and gender. It is particularly striking that time spent with adults in television and unorganized indoor activity is associated with low school achievement, because it is often recommended to parents that they view television with their children.

There are problems of causal direction in this argument. One could argue that intelligent children do better in school and choose "intellectual" activities. However, time spent in meals and snacks is unlikely to result from children's intelligence or cognitive competence. Having a regular meal time may be an index of family organization. It may also be the one occasion in which the family interacts in an active way, converses, has give and take among parents and children. By contrast, watching television or other unorganized activities where adults and children are in same room may not be occasions in which conversation or intellectually challenging interchanges are likely. It is noteworthy that unorganized out-of-home activity was not related, positively or negatively to school achievement. In that activity, children more often interact with peers, and they may also practice spatial and nonverbal skills.

Personality variables were also related to some activity categories independently of cognitive and demographic variables. Perceived competence in athletics was the only self-concept index to be related to time allocation. It accounted for much of the variance associated with gender. Children who considered themselves skilled at athletics spent more time in outdoor unorganized activity and less time in study than those with lower perceived competence in athletics.

Intrinsic motivation predicted "intellectual" activities—study, and in-home organized activities such as board games. Children who gain satisfaction from mastery, defining their own goals, and meeting challenges in school might also be expected to engage in intellectually challenging activities during their free time. It is noteworthy that this pattern of motivation contributes to prediction of time allocation independently of gender and cognitive skills.

None of the measures of sex-typed personality attributes were related to time allocation except the Mf scale of masculinity, which predicted out-of-home organized activity. The items on that scale appear to tap independence, a characteristic that might facilitate the children's willingness to participate in activities away from home.

CONCLUSION

In general, the findings from this study of children's out-of-school time use provide additional support for the theoretical model documenting the process by which adult-supplied structure influences children's social and cognitive behaviors. Previous studies by the authors were conducted in preschool or middle-childhood day camp environments, settings away from the child's home. These studies found that spending time in activities characterized by adult–child interactions or peer–peer interactions leads to very different social behaviors in the immediate as well as long-term context. Differential participation in activities by boys and girls promotes different opportunities for skill learning. Boys preferred peer activities, those with low amounts of adult-supplied information and rules, while girls preferred activities where adult presence controlled and directed the interactions. This was also the case in the home environment. Girls spent more time than boys in activities such as lessons and out-of-the-home organized activities where adults provided high levels of information about appropriate or expected behaviors. Boys spent more of their out-of-school leisure time in activities organized by themselves. Also consistent with the authors' previous studies was the finding that school performance and spatial abilities were related to spending time with adults. The amount of time spent by the family in meals predicted school achievement and other cognitive abilities. Organized and routine meal times are probably a fairly accurate measure of the overall organization of the family system. In addition, meal times provide an arena in which to observe complex and more advanced adult language, intellectual, and social skills. This finding could provide an insight into the well-demonstrated advantage for school performance of middle-class children. Organized time use and established activity routines are also associated with middle- and upper-class rather than lower-class populations. Spending time with adults while watching television was the exception to this notion. Children with low academic performance spent more time watching television with their parents.

REFERENCES

Barker, R.G. (1968). *Ecological psychology: concepts and methods for studying the environment of human behavior.* Stanford, CA: Stanford University Press.

Benson, C.S., Buckley, S., & Medrich, E.A. (1980). A new view of school efficiency: Household time contributions to school achievement. In J. Guthrie (Ed.), *School Finance Policy in the 1980's: A Decade of Conflict.* Cambridge, MA: Ballinger.

Bloch, M.N. (1987). The development of sex differences in young children's activities at home: The effect of the social context, *Sex Roles, 16,* 279–301.

Bloch, M.N., & Walsh, D.J. (1985). Young children's activities at home: age and sex differences in activity, location, and social context. *Children's Environment Quarterly, 2*(2), 34–40.

Bronfenbrenner, U. (1979). *The ecology of human development: Experiments by nature and design.* Cambridge, MA: Harvard University Press.

Carpenter, C.J. (1983). Activity structure and play: Implications for socialization. In M. Liss (Ed.), *Social and cognitive skills, sex roles and children's play* (pp. 117–145). New York: Academic Press.

Carpenter, C.J. (1984). *Patterns of behavior and sex differences associated with preschool activity structure.* Doctoral dissertation, University of Kansas. (Available through Dissertation Abstracts).

Carpenter, C.J. (1987). Boys and girls why they behave differently, *Health & Medical Horizons,* New York: Macmillan Educational Co.

Carpenter, C.J., Huston, A.C., Atwater, J., & Johnson, L. (1986, August). *Early social experiences as predictors of school achievement.* Paper presented at the American Psychological Association, Washington, DC.

Carpenter, C.J., Huston, A.C. & Holt, W. (1986). Modification of preschool sex-typed behaviors by participation in adult-structured activities. *Sex Roles, 14*(11/12), 603–615.

Carpenter, C.J. Huston, A.C., & Petrowsky, K. (1982, August). *An experimental investigation of the effects of activity structure on sex-typed behaviors.* Paper presented at the American Psychological Association meeting, Washington, DC.

Carpenter, C.J., & Huston–Stein, A.C. (1980). Activity structure and sex typed behavior in preschool children. *Child Development, 51*(3) 862–872.

Carpenter, C.J., Logman, D., Cahoon, B., & Roots, L. (1987). Adult-supplied Structure and Childrens' Activity Levels. *Society for Research in Child Development Abstracts* (Vol. 6, pp. 317–318). Chicago: University of Chicago Press.

Carpenter, C.J., Miller, K., & Lewis, E. (1987). Modeled Adult-structure and Preschool Activity Levels. *Society for Research in Child Development Abstracts* (Vol 6, pp. 317–318). Chicago: University of Chicago Press.

Chapin, F.S. (1974). *Human activity patterns in the city.* New York: Wiley.

Comstock, D., Chaffee, S., Katzman, N., McCoombs, M., & Roberts, D. (1978). *Television and human behavior.* New York: Columbia University Press.

Fagot, B.I. (1978). The influence of sex of child on parental reactions to toddler children. *Child Development, 49,* 30–36.

Gump, P.V. (1975). Ecological psychology in children. In E.M. Hetherington, J. Hagen, R. Kron, & A.H. Stein (Eds.), *Review of Child Development Research* (Vol 5). Chicago: University of Chicago Press.

Harter, S. (1981). A new self-report scale of intrinsic versus extrinsic orientation in the classroom: Motivational and Informational components. *Developmental Psychology, 17,* 300–312.

Harter, S. (1982). The Perceived Competence Scale for Children. *Child Development, 53,* 87–97.

Hill, C.R., & Stafford, F.P. (1980). Parental care of children: Time Diary estimates of quantity, predictability and variety. *Journal of Human Resources, 15,* 220–239.

Huston, A.C., & Carpenter, C.J. (1985). The Effects of Sex-Typed Activity Choices. In L.C. Wilkinson, & C.B., Marrett (Eds.), *Gender differences in preschool classrooms.* New York: Academic Press.

Huston, A.C., Carpenter, C.J., Atwater, J., & Johnson, L. (1986). Gender, adult structuring of activities, and social behavior in middle childhood. *Child Development, 57,* 1200–1209.

Lawson, A., & Ingleby, J.D. (1974). Daily routines of preschool children: effects of age, birth order, sex and social class, and developmental correlates. *Psychological Medicine, 4,* 399–415.

Long, B.H., & Henderson, E.H. (1973, January). Children's use of time: Some personal and social correlates. *Elementary School Journal,* 193–199.

Maccoby, E.E., & Jacklin, C.N. (1974). *The psychology of sex differences,* Stanford, CA: Stanford University Press.

Medrich, E., Roizen, J., Rubin, V., & Buckley, S. (1982). *The serious business of growing up.* Berkeley, CA: University of California Press.

Meyersohn, R. (1968). *Television and the rest of leisure. Public Opinion Quarterly,* Spring, 102–112.

Miller, W.H. (1970). An Examination of children's daily schedules in three social classes and their relation to first-grade reading achievement. *California Journal of Educational Research,* 21(3), 100–110.

Morgan & Gross, (1982). *Correlates of achievement and amount of time watching television.* National Institute of Mental Health.

Newson, J., & Newson, E. (1976). *Seven years old in the home environment.* London: Allen & Unwin.

Nickols, S.Y., Powell, J.A., Rowland, V.T., & Teleki, J.K. (1983). *Resources and relationships in one-parent and two-parent households: An Oklahoma study.* Family Study Center, Stillwater, OK: Oklahoma State University.

Peterson, J.L., & Zill, N. (1980, May). *Television viewing and children's intellectual, social, and emotional development.* Paper presented at the meeting of the American Association for Public Opinion Research, Delavan, WI.

Robinson, J. (1977). *How Americans use time,* New York: Praeger.

Robinson, J.P., & Converse, P. (1972). Social change reflected in the use of time. In A. Campbell & P. Converse (Eds.), *The human meaning of social change.* New York: Russell Sage.

Rubin, V. (1978, September). The time budget research tradition: Lessons for planning with young people. *Children's Time Study.* Schools of Law and Education, University of California, Berkeley.

Simms, R.E., Davis, M.H., Foushee, H.C., Holohan, C.K., Spence, J.T. & Helmreich, R.L. (1978, April). *Psychological masculinity and femininity in children and its relationship to trait stereotypes and toy preference.* Paper presented at the meeting of the Southwestern Psychological Association, New Orleans.

Timmer, S.G., Eccles, J., & O'Brien, K. (1985). How children use time. In F.T. Juster & F.P. Stafford (Eds.), *Time, goods, and well-being.* Ann Arbor: University of Michigan, Institute for Social Research.

Walker, K., & Woods, M. (1976). *Time use: A measure of household production of family goods and services.* Washington, DC: American Home Economics Association.

Whiting, B.B. (1980). Culture and social behavior: A model for the development of social behavior. *Ethos,* 100–110.

Whiting, B., & Whiting, J. (1975). *Children of six cultures: A psycho-cultural analysis.* Cambridge, MA: Harvard University Press.

Winett, R.A., & Neale, M.S. (1981). Flexible work schedules and family time allocation: Assessment of a system change on individual behavior using self-report logs. *Journal of Applied Behavior Analysis, 14,* 39–46.

10
Before and After Asphalt: Diversity as an Ecological Measure of Quality in Children's Outdoor Environments

ROBIN C. MOORE
School of Design, North Carolina State University

INTRODUCTION

On February 2, 1972, a great D6 bulldozer plowed back-and-forth across the schoolyard of Washington Elementary School (K–3) in Berkeley, Calif. Before its massive blade, slabs of asphalt cracked and heaved like pie crust scraped from the life-giving earth, hidden from view since the rebuilding of the school in 1958. This erstwhile soulless monoculture of asphalt (Figure 1) was located near downtown, in a residential area of small single- and multifamily homes and apartments.

Eventually, the 1.5-acre Washington Environmental Yard that took shape contained two ponds, a small stream and waterfall, woodland, meadows, clubhouses, gardens, sand, learning stations, climbing structures, swings and slides. About half the site remained as asphalt when the final phase of major construction was completed in 1979. The project was codirected by Herb Wong, Washington School principal, and the author, working with a parent–teacher core group, and a fluctuating cadre of community volunteers and college students, mainly from the University of California at Berkeley.

As a research and development effort, the main purpose of the Yard was to demonstrate how school grounds, through physical diversification, could become significant educational environments able to support a wide range of playing and learning activity (Moore, 1978a; Moore & Wong, 1977). The asphalt monoculture was assumed to have a low child development value, if not severe *negative* impact on child development.

191

Figure 1.   The original asphalted yard (1972).

From the beginning, the site was designed with a strong emphasis on community participation. Through surveys, workshops, classroom exercises, and events conducted on the Yard, children, teachers, parents and residents took an active part in the development process (Moore, 1978b, 1980). Every child in the school completed a simple questionnaire, saying what they liked about the old yard, what they disliked and what they would like to see added or changed. Some classroom groups made designs for parts of the Yard (Figure 2) and built models.

Children made proposals for three types of setting: conventional play equipment (slides, swings, climbing structures, etc.); settings that already existed (asphalt for ballgames, traditional bars, jungle gym, etc.); and natural settings (plants, trees, flowers, water, birds, fish, etc.). Children and adults all agreed on one thing: the importance of nature. As later studies showed (Moore, 1986a, 1986b), natural settings supported a great variety of imaginative and dramatic play, primarily because of their great diversity and ease of manipulation. These primary setting types defined the ecological structure of the Yard as it evolved over the years (Figures 3 and 4).

Educational program potentials were greatly extended by the diversity of Yard settings, as discussed in detail elsewhere (Moore &

Figure 2.   Children's design for part of the Environmental Yard.

Wong, in press), covering three domains of recreational/educational activity:

1. Extended classroom, environmental education programs covering interdisciplinary activities in math, language arts, science, and social studies, conducted through topics such as gardening, pond studies, weather and climate, seasonal change, animal life (Figure 5).
2. After-school and summertime recreation programs, the most successful of which was Project PLAE (Iacofano, Goltsman, McIntyre, & Moreland, 1985), ongoing since 1980 to integrate disabled and nondisabled children (Figure 6).
3. Free play during recess and after school (the Yard was open 24 hours a day) (Figures 7–9).

Figure 3.   The mature Environmental Yard landscape (1984). A community-oriented play area and sand pit appear in the center of the picture, with asphalt ball-playing areas at either end. The natural resource area lies beyond.

MEASURING THE IMPACT

How could the impact of different outdoor settings on children's behavior and development be measured? An earlier review of research (Moore & Young, 1978) indicated an ethnographic approach as the best means of learning what the world of the Yard was like to its users. We wanted to understand the culture of the Yard, to know what the physical changes meant. To do so required an investigation of relationships between the children's behavior, knowledge, and artifacts (Spradley, 1980).

For this "postconstruction evaluation," a cohort of just over 50 children was identified as especially qualified to judge and reflect on their experiences. This was the generation who attended the school during the heyday of Yard development. Most had entered kindergarten just prior to ground breaking and had lived through an engaging, educationally rewarding period (so much so that in 1976 their parents had petitioned to add a fourth-grade class to reap an extra year's benefit from the program).

This 1977 graduating class was a truly expert group of "consultants,"

Figure 4.   Ecological structure of the Environmental Yard, based on behavior-mapping studies conducted in 1977. There are three primary zones (natural resource area, 33% of site, 38% of use; the main yard community areas, 23%of site, 33% of use; and the asphalt, 44% of site, but only 29% of use—USR, Use/Space Ratio is shown for each zone.
The zones subdivide into 10 major types of physical setting or behavior-environment ecosystems, which in turn subdivide into 58 activity places or specific settings. These latter were studied in great detail, using participant observation methods (Moore & Wong, in press).

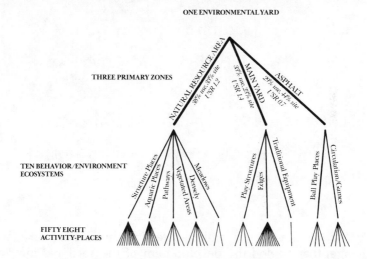

knowledgeable about their innovative learning environment that had been part of their lives for up to 5 years. In other respects, however, it is important to note that they were, as far as we could tell, an unremarkable sample of the socioeconomically mixed, multiracial Washington neighborhood.

Information was gathered in a series of 20–30-minute, tape-recorded personal interviews, conducted with each child during school hours in a corner of the library. Reflecting Spradley's (1980) principles of "structural," "descriptive," and "contrast" questions, children were asked what the Yard used to look like, how they would describe it to a friend, what they had learned there, what difference it had made to them individually, and what would be the result if it was taken away and the site returned to asphalt.

A careful selection has been made from the transcripts to highlight differences in the children's social and emotional reactions to the monoculture of asphalt compared with a diversified, ecologically viable environment. The concept of "ecologically viable" was based

Figure 5.   Classroom work stimulated by the Environmental Yard.

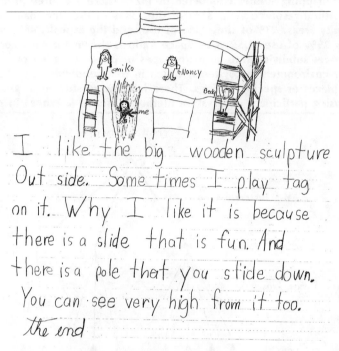

I like the big wooden sculpture
Out side. Some times I play tag
on it. Why I like it is because
there is a slide that is fun. And
there is a pole that you slide down.
You can see very high from it too.
the end

on the four ecological principles: diversity, interaction, adaptation and change, that guided the development of the Yard and informed its educational programs (Wong 1976, 1977). Material has been organized to reflect the most commonly occuring themes illustrating the benefits of diversified outdoor playing and learning settings.

THE CHILD'S RIGHT TO A HEALTHY, SAFE ENVIRONMENT

The initially appalling conditions were vividly described:

> Kids were always tripping and falling, hitting their heads on the concrete [asphalt] and hurting themselves. It's dangerous to have just concrete. Kids get bored, so they mess around a lot, more than they would if they had something to play with. Kids even smash glass, not because they're bad but just because they need something to do. People get hurt. There's nothing to do on concrete. You can sit down. You can play jump rope. Maybe you can play ball, or tag, or jacks, but you can't have fun.
>
> People get bored when there's nothing to do, and they get real

Figure 6.   Project PLAE music workshop in the Redwood Grove, integrating disabled and nondisabled children.

irritable and cranky. When someone asks you something, you're rude. You say, "Get outta here!" And then a fight can start. It's dangerous to fight on asphalt, you can easily fall down and crack your skull.

These observations about the hurtful, pre-Yard environment were backed up by the accident records kept by the school. Many recorded the bumps caused by children running into each other and grazes caused by blacktop falls. Many so called "accidents" were the result of physical conflict (usually described vaguely to avoid even further conflict between the parents of the warring children).

If schoolchildren were unionized they would surely organize walk-outs and strikes against such atrocious working conditions. The fact that they are still prevalent in a majority of schools, where supposedly children should learn understanding and respect for their surroundings, is a measure of adults' disregard for children's basic right to a safe environment, one that is life enhancing and developmentally supportive.

Figure 7.   Free play on the Yard. Girls and boys help each other build a clubhouse in the bushes.

Figure 8.   The environment can be a friendly companion.

Figure 9.   Playing in the weeping willow tree by the ponds.

According to the school secretary, the day redevelopment started, tearful children stopped lining up at her desk with bumps and grazes. The children knew why:

> There was more fighting over things before [the changes], because there was not much stuff. It was all bare. Just ball courts, bars, and cement. It was easy to slip and fall and hurt yourself. There's not so many knee injuries now because there's not so much asphalt, if you fall it's not likely that you'll get all scratched up.
>
> The pressure's off now. There's not so many arguments and maybe only about 10 big fights a year when somebody gets hurt.

BANISHING BOREDOM AND HAVING FUN

"Boring!" was the most common description of the undeveloped yard, with related comments like "a regular flat school yard with basketball courts and painted hopscotches. . . ." "not enough to play with so there was more fighting. It was scary."

Blacktopped school yards have become such a stereotypical aspect of the American public school, they are no longer seen as inhuman environments; yet we wouldn't even keep domestic pets in them, so why children? With a little diversification, however, their playing and learning potential can be dramatically improved, as suggested by this description of the rebuilt Yard.

> You can do a million things here, like collect fossils," the child says, matter of factly, as if emphasizing that there were thousands of activities just as exotic as "collecting fossils." In their eyes a fossil could be something as commonplace as a decomposed leaf with the rib structure remaining—commonplace because of the Yard's well-appreciated natural setting:
>
> It has two ponds and a river. It has dirt and trees and plants and bushes. You can eat in there. You can watch frogs and fish, and tadpoles, and . . . it's neat. There's swings and a slide and sand and the bars and there's so much stuff to play on it's real fun.

Boredom is the result of an absence of playing and learning opportunities. It extracts a high cost in missed learning opportunities—benefits lost forever, if not captured in early childhood. Boredom is seldom considered a social disease; yet some of its crippling symptoms—graduation to drugs and antisocial behavior—are issues of national concern. Boredom negates motivation. Washington students understood the issue well:

> Other schools just have huge blocks of cement—5 miles of boring cement. This one has cement *and* nice, pretty places, where animals and butterflies live. At other schools I never wanted to go out, I didn't even want to go to school. But here I just love coming to school every day.

Boredom presents a great barrier to individual development, self-sufficiency, and social integration. Bland, hard surfaces breed animosity. They injure body and spirit.

Environmental diversity banishes boredom, supports the development of each child's personality and skills and provides essential opportunities for learning through playful exploration and manipulation of ones surroundings. The quality of social interaction is directly affected by the quality of the physical setting.

> It's so much fun. We learn lots of things there. We catch fish and put 'em back. We pretend we're in a jungle. You can play tag, swing and play house in the trees. It's really nice, like a country place, a natural place, with ponds you can throw things into. It's fun to float things down the river and to bust dams.

The children's testimony demonstrates the value of improving educational environments so that imaginations and creative potential can be stimulated. Diversity generates FUN! For children this is an indicator of well being, often resulting from a manipulative setting supplying many forms of "play prop":

> I make little horses out of pieces of wood and sit under the willow tree by the stream with one of my friends. It feels good there. Really quiet. Lots of kids just like to sit there and talk.

In having fun, children feel good about themselves, their friends, their school, their environment. Animals small and large played an important role. "The most fun thing that ever happened was the time we had pigs, goats and chickens here" (an experimental "farmyard" set up during the spring of 1974).

Too often adults look at fun as somehow devaluing straight-faced education. Yet it is happy times that people remember best. Laughing faces are a powerful symbol of well-being, of education too: "It [the Yard] is like a gym, fun, playful, real active, groovy, out of sight, fantastic. I LIKE IT."

Picture this child laughing his head off as he describes "jumping across streams . . . playing rock games [hopping from one rock to another without falling off] . . . spying on people we hate . . . playing tag where there's lots of bushes to hide behind."

Another form of fun, very different from this laugh-your-head-off behavior, was signaled by a quiet smile, a pensive look, slow movement:

"It's really fun to explore the little paths. We used to go on trips and look at things . . . hunt bugs . . . collect rocks . . . discover places we didn't know about . . . it was like a maze."

Fun is also something social, involving the whole community at social events:

"I like it when we have festivals and everyone comes to have a good time. We set up stalls and sell stuff we've made and invent games for people to play. We sell plants from the garden."

FEELING AT HOME

Being welcomed, feeling at ease, having the option of being private or sociable, are attributes of a good home environment. Home should be is a friendly companion, a place of contemplation, full of reminders of happy times, of friends and relations and souvenirs, of exciting trips; a treasure house of nonverbal communication, a cultural repository. For a refugee child, the Yard in some way helped bridge the great distance between the old home lost forever and the new home being adapted to:

When I first came to school from my country [Vietnam] last year, I thought the Yard looked friendly. It made me feel at home. There's a little stump under the willow tree beside the pond where I can eat lunch and talk with my friends. In the trees you can be alone. You can wander along little pathways and find lots of different places where you can feel private. It's a good place to come if you want to be by yourself.

For children who have no one to play with, environmental diversity can be an antidote to sadness, a reliable companion:

It was lonely before we had the sandbox. Being alone doesn't bother me now, I can always wander around looking at stuff and watch people play.

You go on trips. Sometimes I pick flowers to take home to my mother. Yeah, you go on trips and see the sunlight through the trees just like a forest. I think the Yard gives me all the sunshine I need. I love the back path through the redwoods. The pond reminds me of a swamp that we went to when I was 4 or 5. Sometimes when I look at the sky, it reminds me of the Yard. And when I look at the clouds it reminds me of the ponds. When I look at the birds it reminds me of the kids.

PRIDE OF PLACE

It is important that people feel a strong attachment to the places where they have to spend so much of their time. Without this "sense of belonging" we feel alienated, unhappy, unable to work. This is especially true of children and schools. Schools need to be attractive in every sense of the word—not only with cosmetic planting along their public "fronts" but with private "backs" that each day make children eager to return:

It kinda gives me something to brag about. Other kids have to play on cement every day. Same old thing, cement, cement. When I see another school I think, too bad, they've just got a cement yard and we've got trees and a river and ponds with fishes, frogs, tadpoles, snakes and a turtle. It makes me feel good to tell other people about our school and what we have. It used to be a normal school. I played on the cement like everybody else. Now it's different. It's got a wildlife area with lots of birds.

When I first came to Washington School I thought the nature part was somebody's [private] yard. Ooo, I thought, I'm going to tell on you guys for playing in there. Then I started going there and saw lots of kids and the Yard teachers, and so I asked my cousin, "What's that great beautiful yard?" "That's what we call the Environmental Yard," he said. It looked beautiful, just beautiful, like blossoms in the spring. There's so many things, I can't say them all. It's my favorite part of the school. I'm going to miss it when I leave. It seems like one big family playing out there.

How would you describe the Yard to a friend?" we asked, trying to get at the children's most persistent images.

It makes you feel like you're in a special place. You can hide around in the bushes and spy on people or play hide-and-go-seek, which at any regular school you can't do. It's just neat . . . the only place in the whole world like this, with pretty ponds and trees and birds that come out. It's just a good-natured place. It gives me a new idea every

day. It makes me feel like I can make skyscrapers and buildings out of
sticks and sand. It's not too hot either, it's cool but not cold. The trees
make shade. Kids learn about birds and trees and fish. And maybe they
learn they can't push other people around.

On the cement, boys feel like playing kick ball . . . in the nature
area it seems like you're in the woods. People don't get hurt so much
because everyone is careful with everyone else. There's running water
and picnic benches in the shade in a little kind of enclosed area with
birch trees and pussy willows. The ground is covered with plants,
flowers, leaves and soil. There's wood chips all over. It's just perfect.
There's a little pasture surrounded by pine trees with needles and
wooden fences to bounce on. There's a lake with a little creek that
goes over a waterfall, under two bridges made of stone and wood.
One pond has a fountain in it. The other is crowded with fish and is
almost overgrown with cattails and rushes. And there's a sort of island
with a weeping willow in the middle. There's lots of big trees and tiny
animals like snails, potato bugs, leaf hoppers, pill bugs, bees, beetles,
ants, ladybugs. . . . I remember seeing a grasshopper being eaten by
a spider once.

There's a kind of structure where kids play house and have club
meetings and eat lunch, or it can be a fort. And there's other little
buildings with crooked branches where kids meet. There's lots of color,
mostly green with bluebirds. There's a big mound with a bunch of
bushes all over it and another part with redwood trees we call Sherwood
Forest. There's a garden place, too.

The other part of the Yard is a big place that's covered with asphalt
and surrounded by gardens and flowers. There's structures and stuff
to climb, a wide metal slide and a big net, a fireman's pole, swings
and a tunnel that's all the same structure. There's a big sandbox with
a tall fence around it and a structure made of giant spools, and a
compass with North, South, East and West painted on the ground.

Here we have the barefaced expression of the Yard in language,
a veritable thesaurus, a place where children went with John Simon,
a Poet in the Schools, "hunting for poems":

ME AND THE TREE

I am setting in between three
green pine trees and a rock,
with grass surrounding me and
my friends the trees. When I
listen to the cars zoom by I feel
in my body a faint cry.
                                        —*Brendan*

ENVIRONMENTAL LEARNING

When asked what they had learnt from the Yard, children talked about the natural environment, how it had affected their behavior and how they had learnt "environmental stuff":

> The Yard has gotten the whole school to think environmentally. We do all sorts of stuff with nature. I used not to care about the environment or know about plants and animals. Now I've learnt a lot . . . how caterpillars turn into butterflies . . . about redwings and swallowtails . . . about marshes and wet places. We've learnt a lot about trees. If I hadn't been to the school I would never have thought about different environments. Now I think of my own backyard as an environment and I've noticed that some private schools have planted areas.
>
> I know how it *feels* to have ponds. . . . I've studied them a lot. I know what lives there . . . water bugs, frogs, and fish. They multiply fast, almost as fast as rabbits. I've seen the way the ponds change. I've tried to sail pieces of wood across them.
>
> I've learnt that plants are very special. I've learnt to recognize them. What's good to eat, taste, and smell. I like to walk around looking at them. There's lots of insects and spiders' nests in the trees. I know how plants grow, what makes them survive, which seeds to plant, which grow faster, how to plant redwood trees. Plants make the city look pretty.

The yard provided tacit knowledge which the environmental curriculum helped extend to practical applications. The high learning potential of natural resources compared with asphalt was obvious to some children:

> You would never say, "let's go outside and learn about a cement yard." There's only one thing to know about a cement yard . . . it's a cement yard, period. I don't think I learnt anything there. It was all open. There was never a moment without noise. You couldn't relax there, someone was always bothering you.
>
> The wilderness area is a great place to think, to work, to make poems, to listen to the birds, or just to rest. It's a great breeding place for insects, especially ones that eat plants. We learnt that different animals need different habitats. There's always something new to find out. Now we're studying wildlife habitats from different parts of the world.

The aesthetic appeal of nature was strong in its effect on feelings and behavior. Here, emotions were stirred, spirits moved:

It's much prettier to look at when you're trying to think. Nature makes kids good with each other. Cement *is* part of your environment, but it's nice to be surrounded by trees and flowers, and watch the fountain.

Kids feel good because there's lots to do, more things to study. People like cool places, they like to hide behind trees and talk around ponds. There's lots of sticks to play with. Sometimes you like to play in a place where there are lots of weeds.

There's more room to play. It's not so crowded. When people are spread out, they have the room they need. They can run a lot more.

Of course the yard had not expanded physically during development, it had simply become better utilized. Activity had indeed "spread out," by being no longer highly concentrated around a few pieces of equipment. Children saw the importance of daily contact with the environment:

I've learnt to live closer to nature every day instead of three times a year on a camping trip. It's like having the countryside right in your neighborhood. I study up and read about plants and animals, and it's nice to go out there and see and feel things and learn with real examples.

The natural resource settings were special because they were alive. They attracted attention by constantly changing. Children were engaged because they could mold nature with their own hands. Something new was learned everytime, never a repetition of past interactions. These evolving relationships, like those with close friends, fostered a caring attitude:

It's the most useful part of the school. I've learned lots of things there. It makes kids feel better. They think, oh, we're special. We've got something to take care of.

I used to rip leaves off branches and didn't think about what would happen. But now I think about it. The nature area gives you something to think about in the future . . . something to come back to and visit after you leave school.

WHAT IF THE YARD WERE REMOVED?

"How would you feel if the Yard was bulldozed and returned to blacktop?" we asked. Replies were dramatic:

"Kids would feel terrible," "really horrible," "awful," "unhappy," "just very sad," children said, confirming their strong emotional attachments.

How would you justify keeping it?" we followed up, hoping the answers would identify specific meanings of the Yard. There was concern about the destruction of natural habitats and the loss of life:

"The fish would die . . . they would lose their freedom. Lots of plants and flowers would die. I bet some birds have nests in the trees and I know there's a snake or two in the swamp."

The loss of play and learning opportunities was viewed with alarm by children who understood well the play value of the physical environment:

"Kids wouldn't be able to play anymore—well, they'd still be able to play kickball, but that's not everything people like to do, its not much at all. Lots of kids would rather look at fish, race boats, and climb trees."

"You couldn't play hide-and-seek anymore. Kids can't play in an empty place. We eat in there. Hide from our friends. Have grass fights. Have fun. You can't do that with cement all around. Even if there's a lot of structures you can still do more if there's natural stuff. We love to use nature. Kickball would take over again."

There were perceptive comments linking aesthetic/sensory qualities to behavior:

> It would just be hot and gray. There wouldn't be any color left. Kids would just sit around doing nothing. People like to sit around and look at things. If there were no little paths, no shady places, we'd all have to sit on the hot cement with all the ground around but nothing on it!

Some children, with remarkable insight, dwelt on the antisocial consequences of removing the Yard:

> We'd fight, we'd get up to mischief and act mean. More fights would give more crimes later. Instead of talking, people would steal stuff from the school to get their revenge.
>
> All the kids who play in the bushes and peek on people and play with guns and stuff would feel really bad. They'd be really upset and restless. Nobody likes a blacked-over yard. Kids wouldn't behave so well with each other. Now, if they have a fight, they can go in the trees and be friends again.

Many dwelt on thoughts about violence, their reactions to the

school authorities and the arguments they would use to save the
Yard from destruction:

> All the kids would turn against the principal and try to get the Yard
> back the way it was. We'd get all our friends to help and we'd say,
> "Please give us back the Yard the way it was because it was so beautiful.
> Everyone enjoyed it."

Political counterattacks were suggested to protect the Yard that
some children saw as defining the identity of the school (and therefore
their self-identity).

> We'd write to the newspapers. We'd go to the school board and
> tell them they should support nature and be nice to animals. Its very
> boring with just blacktop. Children like the forest. They want animals,
> ponds, streams, things growing. We got the blacktop off so children
> could plant trees and bushes and all the things that nature has made
> up.
> We'd say put everything back or we'll strike the school. Kids would
> be bored all the time. They'd act real mad and bad, then be sad 'cos
> all the stuff was taken away. We'd forget what school we were at 'cos
> it would look like everywhere else.
> You should look at Washington as something special, a new thing
> for the world. Other schools need the same influence. To tear down
> the Yard is just to put yourself down. Us kids love the Yard. We do
> special things there. It's the only place like it. If you tear it down
> there'll be a riot. We're gonna hate you for life and it's the truth.
> What right do you have to take it away. We've learned so much
> more than we would have with just cement. It helps kids learn to get
> on with each other, makes them good with each other. We've grown
> attached to it since we came to this school and watched the trees
> grow bigger and all the animals coming around. There's lots of things
> you can learn from the environment. Kids wouldn't have such respect
> for nature if it was all asphalt. Having a dirt area is really good for the
> economy 'cos kids learn lots of extra things there.

POWER AND THE CHILD'S RIGHT TO A DIVERSE
ENVIRONMENT

The above comments illustrate the children's awareness of the value
of a high-quality environment, even its economic value. But at the
same time there is a poignant expression of powerlessness. Children
had no means on their own of creating decent settings or of pro-

tecting them from destruction (a threat that arose many times) even if they imagined otherwise. They were so accepting of their given environment:

"I didn't mind when the Yard was all concrete, I was used to it," one of them said.

Design intervention was essential to raise the possibility of change and to stimulate nonstereotypical thinking about what could be done. By the same token, once the children's imaginations had been unlocked, the design program was dependent on their ideas about what the Yard could become. As it developed, so did the children's awareness of the value of a diversified environment, one that might live with them, informing their later actions in the world as adults and parents (Wong, 1976).

An indoors-only, 3-Rs view of education amounts to little more than literacy/numeracy training—teaching essential skills to those children whose learning styles are well adapted to a narrowly defined, highly structured learning environment.

But not all children fit this mold. Every class has its share of extra-high-spirited personalities, children from broken homes, abused children, those pushed around by society, emotionally neglected since the day they were born, classified as misfits with a "learning disability." But the environment is the handicapping agent, not the child. To take an obvious example, if a child in a wheelchair cannot get into school because there is no ramp, we do not blame the child; we change the environment. The need to accommodate different learning styles is a more subtle version of the same issue of creating sufficiently diverse settings to meet the needs of all types of children.

Not all children learn effectively within the exclusive walls of a classroom. Education is not something that can be confined to specific spaces and times. To be effective, it must be part of children's everyday lives, and accommodate the varied learning styles and abilities of all children. Well-rounded social and emotional development is best supported in diverse settings outside the classroom.

In their early years, all children need to learn how to live in a rapidly changing society where they may have to change careers two or three times in a lifetime. From the beginning, people must acquire the art of lifelong learning. Instead of being stuffed with information at a single point in time, they must learn to recognize the wealth of opportunities available to anyone motivated to go out to discover and use them. To instill this real-world orientation requires more than standardized classroom learning. Every child needs access to a broader learning environment where personal potentials can be stimulated to learn the 3 Rs *and* other aspects of life.

EXTENDING THE LEARNING ENVIRONMENT

Washington School reinforced a "whole child" developmental phi-losophy, with something to offer every individual. Classrooms func-tioned as conventional learning centers, but their activities extended outdoors, where a variety of learning styles could be accommodated, where positive socialization was supported, where members of the multiethnic Washington community could appreciate each other in socially flexible settings, where all manner of interaction could be accommodated.

The Washington educational environment extended beyond the Yard, to the world at large. On field trips that included working farms, ice cream plants, bakeries, gardens, nature reserves, printing works, and San Francisco's Chinatown, connections were made to the region's natural, economic and social environments. Learning experiences from each trip were incorporated into the Yard-related curriculum. Examples included transplanting specimen plants, pasting up and printing the Yard News, producing a Chinese New Year's parade, and setting up a barnyard where children could care for animals. The things children talked about and wrote about in their journals suggest that these extensions into the real world (or incursions of the real world into the classroom) had a powerful educational impact.

MEASURING THE IMPACTS

The academic performance of the Washington children (measured by standard, statewide tests) was highly competitive. To what degree this was due to the excellent teachers and their innovative programs, or to the environmental and community focus of the school we were not sure. We could see how each of these characteristics reinforced each other, but it was not a relationship amenable to conventional research methods.

The one attempt to measure the "impact" of the environmental curriculum by outside, educational evaluators was a miserable failure because a naturalistic, ethnographic methodology was not adopted. Instead, the educational researchers forced the teachers to narrow their learning objectives to "operational" definitions that could be measured by standardized testing procedures. As a result, much of the richness of individual learning experiences, and details of the settings that supported them, went unrecorded. Our understanding did not advance.

However, it was an important learning experience, teaching us not to try to measure qualitative, educational values by standardized methods that in large part excluded personal knowledge. We therefore developed our own people-environment methodology beyond the frame of reference of official evaluators. Reported here are some of the more general findings regarding the impact of diversified settings on children's playing and learning. A forthcoming volume (Moore & Wong, in press) will describe the impact in more detail.

CONCLUSIONS

The evidence presented here suggests that daily access to diverse, outdoor environments allows children to have many long-lasting learning experiences. How important are they for healthy child development? How important are they as an insurance policy against the destruction of our fragile planet? Only you, the reader, can decide.

Many comments indicated the significance of natural resources in children's playing and learning, a finding firmly supported by the results of systematic questionnaire and behavior-mapping surveys made of children's use and attitudes toward the full range of Yard settings (Moore, 1986a). Firsthand experience of the natural environment will prepare children to make informed, responsible judgments about the wise use of our environment as adult voters and taxpayers.

Disregard for natural resources is one of the principal faults of contemporary environmental design for children, the more surprising when one considers the many playgrounds designed by landscape architects. Technically, essential natural elements such as soil, vegetation, and water can be readily incorporated into the design of playing and learning settings on school sites. They further support the child's right to grow and develop in a healthy, safe environment as stated in the *Declaration of the Child's Right to Play* (International Association for the Child's Right to Play, 1977).

Children, parents, teachers and other caretakers have a right to expect childhood settings to support a wide range of developmental needs. Society's attention to this right has been abysmally poor to date. The situation is unlikely to improve until codified in legislation and local bylaws. Even at the level of gross space allocation for children's activity outdoors, the record is not encouraging, even internationally. At last count, only 10 countries had some form of national standard for children's play spaces in the residential environment (Esbensen, 1979).

Certainly in the U.S., the legal route is an important direction to take. Yet in doing so a word of caution is necessary. Even though the legal protection of the child's right to a developmentally appropriate environment is a worthwhile and powerful strategy, we must be careful that it does not destroy the very thing it is designed to protect. Children's play and the settings that support it are fragile phenomena, easily inhibited or destroyed by heavy-handed rules and regulations. Such instruments must be designed and implemented by people who are willing to listen to children, to observe their behavior carefully and to work with them as collaborators in the processes of environmental design, programming and management (Moore, Goltsman, & Iacofano, 1987). Diversity and participation go hand in hand.

As the Japanese landscape architect, Fumiaki Takano, has noted (personal correspondence), settings can be designed *for* children, *with* children, and *by* children. Each model is valid in a particular context. The design of large public playgrounds, used by many different communities, will most likely be designed using the first model (*for* children); even in this case, however, children can act as design consultants. The primary example of the third model (*by* children) is the adventure playground and related examples such as urban farms (Westland & Knight, 1982). It is the second model, designing *with* children, that is the most feasible and worthwhile alternative in most contexts, a model that demands serious attention from educational planners.

I have tried to demonstrate how diversification of the environment, based on this model, increased children's positive relationships with each other, with their school and in their day-to-day playing and learning activity.

The means of executing diversification objectives in different communities will vary just as geography, cultural characteristics, and climates vary. Community participation, however, will always be an important means of achieving successful programs. The extra effort required surely will be worth the results; for embodied in this model are tremendous educational potentials that are essential to the development of genuine ecological relationships between children, and between them and their environment—between people and our planet.

REFERENCES

Esbensen, S. (1979). *An international inventory and comparative study of legislation and guidelines for children's play spaces in the residential environment.* Ottawa: Canada Mortgage and Housing Corp.

Iacofano, S., Goltsman, S., McIntyre, S., & Moreland, G. (1985). Project PLAE: Using Arts and Environment to Promote Integration of All Children. *California Parks & Recreation, 41*(4), 14–17.

International Association for the Child's Right to Play. (1977). *Declaration of the child's right to play.* Birmingham, England: IPA Resources (c/o Nick Balmforth, 54 Dawlish Ave., Weeping Cross, Stafford ST17 OEU, England).

Moore, R.C. (1978a). Meanings and Measures of Child/Environment Quality: Some Findings from the Environmental Yard. In W.E. Rogers & W.H. Ittelson (Eds.), *New Directions in Environmental Design Research.* Washington, DC: Environmental Design Research Association.

Moore, R.C. (1978b). A WEY to Design. *Journal of Architectural Education, 31*(4), 27–30.

Moore, R.C. (1980). Learning from the Yard: Generating relevant urban childhood places. In P.F. Wilkinson (Ed.), *Play in human settlements.* London: Croom Helm.

Moore, R.C. (1986a). The power of nature: Orientations of girls and boys toward biotic and abiotic play settings on a reconstructed schoolyard. *Children's Environments Quarterly, 3*(3), 52–69.

Moore, R.C. (1986b). *Childhood's Domain: Play and Place in Child Development.* London: Croom Helm.

Moore, R.C., Goltsman, S.M., & Iacofano, D.S. (1987). *The play for all guidelines: Planning, design and management of outdoor play settings for all children.* Berkeley, CA: PLAE, Inc. (1824 A Fourth St., Berkeley, CA 94710).

Moore, R.C., & Wong, H.H. (1977). Washington Environmental Yard (Project WEY). In C. Schoenfeld & J. Designer, (Eds.), *Environmental education in action—1: Case studies of selected public school and public action programs.* Columbus, OH: ERIC/SMEAC Center for Science Mathematics, and Environmental Education, Ohio State University.

Moore, R.C., & Wong, H.H. (in press). *Another way of learning: Child development in natural settings.* Berkeley, CA: MIG Communications.

Moore, R.C., & Young, D. (1978). Childhood Outdoors: Toward a social ecology of the landscape. In I. Altman & J. Wohlwill (Eds.), *Children and the environment.* New York: Plenum Press.

Spradley, J.P. (1980). *Participant observation.* New York: Holt, Rinehart, & Winston.

Westland, C., & Knight, J. (1982). *Playing living learning: A worldwide perspective on children's play.* State College, PA: Venture.

Wong, H.H. (1976). Environmental value change via creation of environmental school yard ecosystems. In R. Martlett (Ed.), *Current issues in environmental education—II.* Columbus, OH: ERIC/SMEAC Center for Science Mathematics, and Environmental Education, Ohio State University.

Wong, H.H. (1977). Muses, monitors and millennia: A celebration of child/environment relations and transitional environmental education curricula. In R.H. McCabe (Ed.), *Current issues in environmental education—III.* Columbus, OH: ERIC/SMEAC Center for Science Mathematics, and Environmental Education, Ohio State University.

11
Play in Diverse Social Contexts: Parent and Teacher Roles

ELIZABETH BLUE SWADENER
JAMES E. JOHNSON
The Pennsylvania State University

The significance of play behavior in early childhood, although not well understood, has been discussed in many ways (Rubin, Fein, & Vandenberg, 1983). Play is viewed by some child psychologists as an antidote to stress; playing alleviates tension and helps the child in coping with the various socialization demands and developmental tasks encountered as a natural part of growing up (Elkind, 1981). Other psychologists and educators have emphasized that play is a vehicle for learning new skills and acquiring new concepts (Fink, 1976). Still others have considered play as serving primarily cognitive consolidating functions, as seen, for example, in the child's construction of reality (Piaget, 1962).

Researchers investigating peer relationships and friendship patterns have proposed that some degree of play capability seems necessary for positive social interaction between children during their early years (Hartup, 1976). Peer status and popularity are seen by these researchers as related to self-concept and emotional well-being of young children. Parents and teachers of young children often find this last way of viewing the value of play in early childhood especially attractive.

EDUCATION THAT IS MULTICULTURAL

A critical distinction is drawn between education that is multicultural and multicultural education (Grant, 1978; Sleeter & Grant, 1987).

214

Education that is multicultural is stated in a more active form to convey a pervasiveness of cultural inclusion in all aspects of the educational environment, and in all subject matter and classroom experiences, versus an add-on or "special topics" approach (Swadener, 1985). Education that is multicultural reflects not only a commitment to the representation and fair presentation of cultural issues, but also encompasses the related issues of gender, class, developmental differences, learning styles, and age.

Education that is multicultural is intended to be applicable to all educational environments, and not limited to obviously pluralistic or mainstreamed settings. Recently, this approach has been expanded to emphasize the underlying causes of inequality and oppression and has been described as "education that is multicultural and social reconstructionist" (Sleeter & Grant, 1986; Sleeter & Grant, 1987). This approach addresses the need for social action, and is the least developed in the multicultural literature—particularly the early childhood literature.

In applying the principles of education that is multicultural to early childhood learning environments and play, several issues become evident. The first concerns children's lack of cognitive readiness to deal with cultural content or recognize stereotypes, with the risk of the formation of superficial or inaccurate conceptions. It has also been argued that young children can better understand information about human diversity after they have had a number of concrete experiences dealing with self-awareness, acceptance of individual and family differences, and special needs. However, to assume that early childhood curricula and other socializing agents of young children need not reflect or incorporate important aspects of human diversity is to shirk from the responsibility of finding age-appropriate ways to do so.

Socialization agents are eager for young children to get along with each other as important preparation for functioning in school and in other settings in which the child must show growing independence from the home. Parents and teachers of young children, accordingly, often make deliberate attempts to foster the development of specific play and social skills in children. These efforts frequently are harmonious and successful in accomplishing this shared goal. Unfortunately, many times they are not.

In this chapter we will examine some of what is known about parents' and teachers' roles in influencing play during the preschool years. Secondly, we will discuss selected research findings, issues and problems which deal with the relationship between parents and teachers. We are particularly interested in this mesosystem in connection with play and prosocial behaviors in diversified social contexts involving children who vary in gender, developmental or special needs status, social class, and race. Our position is that a primary responsibility of socialization agents in today's pluralistic society is to prepare children for functioning in an expanding social world. Expanding the content of the study of play means to us the study of play in expanding social contexts. This entails research and practice in what we call comprehensive early childhood education, or education that is multicultural in nature.

The framework of education that is multicultural also builds upon the literature on the informal or hidden curriculum. In this or any examination of home and school influences on children's play and related attitudes and behavior, the importance of informal learning is obvious. For example, Randall (1976) addresses the role of informal learning in laying a base for multiculturalism in elementary school. Randall also asserts the importance of parents and teachers understanding the effects of different types of play and the conditions under which they occur. Kendall (1983) also speaks to the importance of parent involvement in any early childhood program's attempts to reflect pluralism and encourage children's acceptance of diverse peers. As noted by Kendall (ibid., p. 27), "Interpreting the multicultural curriculum to parents is one of the teacher's most important responsibilities."

ROLES AND RELATIONSHIPS

In order to put into perspective our theme of socialization agents cooperating to facilitate intergroup acceptance and positive social interaction of children from diverse backgrounds, let us first review some of the literature on how parents and teachers influence young children's play. We will deal with these influences as they operate separately in their respective microsystems of the home and the school. Secondly, we will address ourselves to this topic as it pertains to the home-school mesosystem.

Microsystem: Roles of Parents and Teachers

The development of play and social skills during the early years has been described in the literature as progressing in levels or states. The rate and end point of this development are influenced by environmental factors (microsystem and mesosystem), as well as biological and psychological factors. Development in this domain, furthermore, is inextricably bound up with the child's development in other domains such as language and social cognition.

Play Levels

Play behavior needs to be described in terms of both its cognitive level and its social level. To assess play development these forms need to be examined together and hierarchically. Rubin and his associates' method of nesting Parten's (1932) social participation play types (solitary, parallel, associative, cooperative) with Smilansky's (1968) cognitive play types (functional, constructive, dramatic, and games with rules) is often used (e.g., Rubin, Maioni, & Hornung, 1977). The need to consider simultaneously the social and cognitive aspects of play has been demonstrated repeatedly. For example, the developmental status of solitary play is indeterminant without an assessment of the cognitive content of the child's activity.

Two and 5-year-olds, respectively, are known to exhibit approximately equal amount of solitary play in classroom or day-care settings. However, older children typically engage in solitary game or constructive play (e.g., making something), while the younger children usually manifest solitary-functional or fantasy play (e.g., simple toy use). The play types are ordered from parallel-functional at the low end of interactive- (associative or cooperative) or solitary-constructive or dramatic, or games-with-rules play at the high end in this nested hierarchical category system.

The above categories are general in nature, refer to a broad array of behaviors, and are difficult to rank order. Much more about the internal developments of each of these play types needs to be learned. Nevertheless, such categories have proven useful in helping practitioners differentiate levels of play in diverse contexts (Spidell, 1986). Their usefulness is attested to by the degree to which the play categories have been shown in research studies to be systematically related to environmental factors and to other variables making progress in different developmental domains. Environmental factors include parental and teacher beliefs and behavior.

Parental Influences

As dominant figures in the child's life since birth, parents' roles in the development of play behavior and skills are particularly critical during the early years. As part of a more all-encompassing influence affecting the child's entire development and personality, specific factors are known to shape the play patterns and dispositions that children acquire, characteristics not easily changed by subsequent experiences, as one sometimes hears in teachers' complaints that by the time they have young children in their charge, peer and plaything preferences are so highly resistant to change that it is next to impossible to alter discriminatory or segregated group dynamics and play practices.

However, far more than unconscious biases and value structures are learned from parents—particularly in the area of gender discrimination and sex-role development. In addition, children are very sensitive to parental influence on their cognitive and social play abilities (Jennings & Connors, 1983). The first and second years of life, for example, are particularly crucial for the development of the ability to participate in infant and toddler game routines or bouts, and to engage in simple episodes of imaginative play. Accommodation to children is necessary at this time in order to compensate for the child's developmental immaturity. For example, children need modeling and support to participate in continued, repetitive turn taking. A playful attitude is acquired as a result, as well as an understanding of what it means to share socially in fantasy or pretense. These acquired qualities bode well for later success in the give-and-take world of the preschool peer group.

Smilansky (1968) interpreted the underdeveloped play of preschool children in her study as due to deficits in their background for which the teacher had to overcome with play-enriched classroom environments. She noted that during the early years children need both *general* and *specific* identification with parents. General identification, or attachment, requires a warm, nurturant, accepting parent, who displays unconditional love for the child. Specific identification, for Smilansky, requires the adult's modeling and encouraging of make-believe play.

Feitelson and Ross (1977) and Singer (1973), among others, agree that young children need to be taught the concept of nonliterality or pretense, and should be encouraged to adopt an "as if" stance toward ostensible reality when appropriate occasions arise. This is indispensable for the emergence and consolidation of playfulness (Lieberman, 1977), or, more specifically, a fantasy-making predisposition (Singer, 1973). Other background factors include provisions for toys, space to play, privacy, and time to be with parents to acquire play skills, as well as time away from parents to practice these skills (Dunn & Wooding, 1977; Singer, 1973). Furthermore, parental play involvement is related to intellectual and emotional development.

Parental participation and encouragement consistently raises young children's level of play. In other words, parent–child play interaction and peer competence are linked.

Parental attitudes and beliefs have been associated with playfulness in children (Bishop & Chace, 1971; Dreyer & Wells, 1966; Kleiber, Barnett, & Wade, 1978). For instance, Kleiber et al. hypothesized that parental permissiveness may be related to playfulness in children as shown in previous research. Using Lieberman's (1977) 12-item scale for measuring playfulness in children and Bishop and Chace's (1971) home inventory as the parent measure, they found that permissiveness in the home was related to playfulness, in general, but playfulness in boys was inversely related to owning sports equipment, receiving training in sports, and having parents who watched sports events. Bishop and Chace (1971), found that responses by mothers but not by fathers to their instrument related positively to potential creativity in children.

Parental influences on the development of sex-role learning in early childhood has been the subject of much research. Several studies have reported gender-related patterns in parent–child play. For example, Landerholm (1981) examined how mothers and fathers engaged their infants in physical contact, social-verbal stimulation, and object use during play. Results showed that both parents had more physical contact with boys than with girls. Mothers, compared with fathers, showed more social or verbal stimulation in their play with children. Finally, parents used significantly more objects when playing with daughters than with sons. MacDonald and Parke (1984) found that fathers engaged in significantly more physical play with children, but that mothers engaged in more object-mediated play, based on an analysis of in-home videotapes. While parents did not differ in directiveness or verbal behavior, both parents talked more to girls.

In sum, parental behaviors and beliefs influence play in young children. Parents prepare their children to play with other children and find peer acceptance. Parents may also facilitate openness and acceptance of others from different backgrounds. Negative parental influences can cause their child to be closed and rejecting of encounters involving others who are different in various ways.

Teacher Influences

The role of the teacher in the play of young children is multidimensional. Various research studies have been done delineating these roles (Collier, 1985; Manning & Sharp, 1977).

Figure 1 displays one way of conceptualizing the different aspects of the teachers' role in play. As can be seen, there are two basic categories, making provisions for children's play and intervening into children's play. The first category consists of four subcategories for time, space, materials, and preparatory experiences (Griffing, 1983). The second category consists of four subcategories labelled parallel playing, co-playing, play tutoring, and spokesperson for reality.

Time refers to assuring that a sufficient portion of the day is set aside in the schedule to allow quality play to evolve, typically a minimum of 30 minutes as a rule of thumb in most preschool or day-care centers. Space refers to making sure that children have an adequate physical area in which to play, both indoors and outdoors, and that the spatial organization is conducive to quality play. Materials refer to the provision of toys and objects used in play, and preparatory experiences refers to appropriate preparation for the enactment of specific themes or the use of selected materials in play episodes.

Parallel playing occurs when the adult is close to the child and plays with the same materials, possibly to comfort or to encourage the child. Co-playing is when the adult joins in play but lets the child control the course of play, again possibly to support the activity. Such approval typically causes play to last longer. Play tutoring occurs when the adult initiates or directs play either with (inside intervention) or without (outside intervention) coplaying. This form of adult involvement has been used in play training studies (Smilansky, 1968). Spokesperson for reality occurs when play is used as a vehicle for teaching, usually interrupting play for the sake of having the child learn or think about something.

Examples of empirical research studies investigating teacher roles in children's play include those concerned with adult intervention (Johnson, 1986; Smilansky, 1968; Smith & Syddall, 1978; Spidell, 1986; Tizard, Philips, & Lewis, 1976) and ones concerned with play provisions and the physical environment (Kinsman & Berk, 1978; Shure, 1963). Positive and significant relationships have been found between the quality of teacher provisions and interventions and level of play and cognitive and socioemotional development in young children.

Research has also demonstrated that teachers can make a difference in how well children get along with peers who differ in gender, ability, class, and race. Teachers can accomplish these aims by using informal learning opportunities which frequently involve intervention in children's play. Moreover, thoughtful selection of dramatic play props or other informal learning materials can discourage stereotyping and support prosocial behavior. Findings of both quantitative short-term empirical studies and qualitative longer-term ethnographic case

Figure 1.   Teacher's Roles and Children's Play

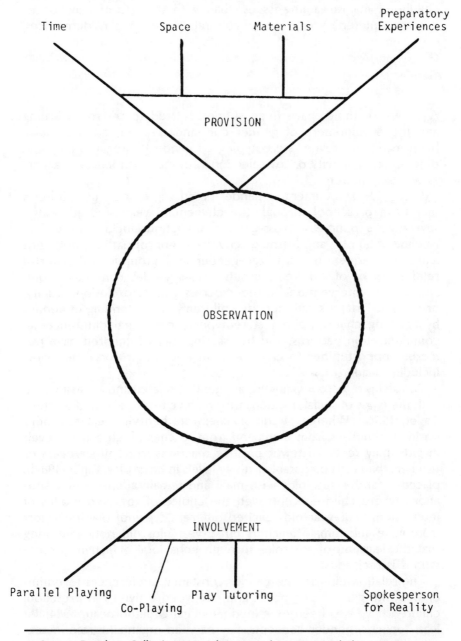

Source: Based on Collier's (1985) Adaptation of Manning and Sharp (1977)

studies have led to this conclusion. More studies in this research literature deal with gender- and race-related issues, as well as early childhood mainstreaming issues, than with the use of play to encourage children's acceptance of cultural diversity or class differences.

Gender

A variety of topics have been studied related to sex-role learning and the development of gender constancy. Various attempts have been made to prevent stereotyping or gender-segregated play and differentiated activity or toy selection with male and female teachers as well as children.

Scott (1984) documented gender-based segregation in children's play from preschool through the elementary years and advocated several ways to increase cross-gender interactions, including the clear labeling of all play and learning activities as appropriate for both girls and boys, frequent use of mixed-gender small group activities, verbal reinforcement of children's positive cross-gender communications, and teacher interventions to reduce cross-gender exclusion, cruelty, or teasing. Teachers can increase children's understanding of gender by teaching children about stereotypes and cultural differences in communication patterns, and by assuring that all children have numerous opportunities to carry out and observe prosocial behaviors including leadership.

Play styles of 2- to 3-year-olds are gender-related and are associated with the types of social reactions they receive from peers and teachers (Fagot, 1984a). Whereas, traditional sex-role behaviors elicited more positive responses from peers and from teachers, high activity levels in girls' play received fewer positive reactions from either peers or teachers than did comparable activity levels in boys' play. Fagot (1984b) placed 2- and 4-year-olds with male and female adults in play situations where children controlled the choice of toys and modes of interaction. Four-year-olds elicited different types of play behaviors from male and female teachers but 2-year-olds did not, suggesting that the learning of sex roles through behavioral or activity expectations is reciprocal.

The relationships among gender constancy, preferences for same- or opposite-gender playmates, and sex-typed activities in preschool children have also been examined (Smetana & Letourneau, 1984). At least for girls, gender concepts may have an organizing role in sex-role development by motivating children to seek social contexts in which to acquire and practice sex-appropriate (or "sex stereotypical") behaviors.

In *Boys and Girls: Superheroes in the Doll Corner,* Paley described in detail the extent of gender stereotyping she has witnessed during 25 years in the classroom. She described the dramatic play of 5-year-olds in contrast to the more "equitable" division of roles of younger children. She commented,

> Kindergarten is a triumph of sexual self-stereotyping. No amount of adult subterfuge or propaganda deflects the five-year-old's passion for segregation by sex. Children of this age think they have invented the differences between boys and girls and, as with any new invention, must prove that it works (Paley, 1984, p. ix).

Busch and Schau (1980) assessed gender knowledge, verbal and behavioral sex typing (in toy play), and occupational stereotyping in native American and Hispanic preschool children. They recommend further research with children from these cultural backgrounds, and emphasize the importance of ongoing participation by parents and teachers in the development of intervention strategies.

Swadener (1986) examined several aspects of the formal and informal curriculum, including gender-related issues, in an ethnographic case study of two mainstreamed, multicultural day-care centers. Weekly observations over the 9-month period of the school year and interviews with teachers and children (ages 3–5) yielded descriptive data on the variety of ways in which each center attempted to prevent gender stereotyping and gender-segregated play and attempted to equalize the treatment of boys and girls. Teachers consistently used nonsexist language, which appeared to minimize sexist language in children's free-play interactions. Teachers actively encouraged leadership, independence, and assertiveness in girls and sensitivity, caregiving, and empathetic behaviors in boys. One center actively worked to maintain a gender-balanced teaching staff.

Weekly activity units and dramatic play themes were devised to decrease further gender stereotyping or exclusion. For example, one center with several more boys than girls in class used dramatic play setups such as "infant nursery," "hospital," and "pet store" to encourage nurturant behaviors in both boys and girls. Several units on community helpers were implemented, in which teachers actively supported girls' rights to assume any professional role, as well as the boys' rights to enact inside household or nontraditional male occupations. Field trips and resource people, especially parents, were also utilized at both centers, many of which emphasized nontraditional careers or activities.

Gender cleavage appeared to be consistently related to the type of activity or setting of the interaction. For example, children at one center chose to sit next to same sex peers at snack 72% of the time and table activity times 65% of the time observed. On the playground, children played with same-gender peers approximately 75% of the time. The least gender-segregated play was observed in various small manipulative activity areas, including art tables, cognitive skills areas (e.g., sorting games) and at the microcomputer in one center. Small groups at this center were gender balanced by teachers' assignment of children to groups, as was the large group seating pattern, assigned by names taped on the carpet.

Age appeared to be associated with the degree of gender segregation in free-play situations. More gender cleavage was observed among the 3-year-olds and young 4-year-olds than among the older 4- and 5-year-old children. The oldest children at both centers included at least two strong cross-gender friendships, consistently observed interacting across all settings and parts of the daily schedule. Consistent with other literature reviewed, the themes of boys' and girls' dramatic play and large motor activities also appeared to contribute to gender segregation (Swadener, 1986). The most frequently observed play themes for boys, for example, consisted of "super heroes" chasing games, followed in frequency by role playing of driving cars, piloting spaceships, and role-playing animals. Girls often carried out family dramatic play themes both inside and outdoors. Although both girls and boys frequented equipment such as the swings and climber, they often did so at different times.

In summary, gender-segregated play has been found in most studies examining the free-play patterns of preschool children. The degree of cross-gender cooperative play appears to be correlated with the nature of the activity (e.g., large motor or dramatic play versus small manipulatives or creative arts), teacher interventions and role modeling, and consistent use of nonsexist language and materials. Provision for *all* children to take on a variety of traditional and nontraditional roles in play, and a gender-balanced teaching staff are also likely contributors to less gender-segregated play.

Mainstreaming: Social Interaction Studies

Social interaction is particularly important to preschool children with handicaps or delays. Play can be a time for learning and for observing models of appropriate behavior. Social interaction with "normally developing" peers also provides opportunities for children with disabilities to use skills and to experience naturally reinforcing events in the environment (Rogers–Warren, Ruggles, Peterson, & Cooper, 1981, p. 57). Social interaction offers opportunities that formalized training cannot provide for the child with a handicap or delay. The role of social interaction in mainstreamed settings is increasingly becoming the subject of early childhood research (e.g., Dunlop, Stoneman, & Cantrell, 1980; Dunn, 1968; Hops, 1981; Johnson & Johnson, 1980; Mercer, 1973; Smith & Greenberg, 1981). As one study on early childhood mainstreaming states:

> Experience with a broad range of peers is not a superficial luxury to be enjoyed by some students and not by others, but rather an absolute necessity for maximal achievement and healthy cognitive and social developing. (Johnson & Johnson, 1980, p. 90)

Indeed, a focus on children's social growth and development has characterized the mainstreaming effort from its inception (Dunlop, Stoneman, & Cantrell, 1980). Research findings over the past several years, however, have been quite mixed in terms of the interaction patterns described. Some earlier findings, for example, found mainstreamed children to be rejected by their nonhandicapped peers, or less well accepted than normally developing children (Gerber, 1977; Goodman, Gottlieb, & Harrison, 1972; Iana, Ayers, Heller, McGettigan, & Walker, 1974).

A recent comprehensive study compared play group behavior of mildly delayed 4-year-old and nonhandicapped 3- and 4-year-old boys (Guralnick & Groom, 1987). The results showed deficits in peer-related social interactions for mildly delayed children. Design features of this study precluded interpreting the results as due to children's reputations, or to the unavailability of responsive peers. Observational measures, playmate preferences in free play situations, and peer sociometric ratings also showed that the children with delays were viewed by peers as less competent and of a lower social status than other peers. The authors of this study do describe, however, "important developmental opportunities" which were available for the delayed children in the mainstreamed playgroups, and argue for placement based on chronological age rather than developmental level (p. 1570).

Other studies, however, have reported quite different findings. For example, Kennedy and Bruininks (1974) found no significant difference in peer status accorded handicapped and nonhandicapped peers. Peterson and Haralick (1977) and Shoggen (1975) also failed to find support for the proposition that children with disabilities are commonly subjected to rejection or isolation.

Dunlop, Stoneman, and Cantrell (1980, p. 132) assert that such discrepancy in findings may be due at least in part to "(a) inattention to variables of potential relevance in the development of social interaction, and (b) the use of sometime simplistic methodology to study complex developmental processes." For example, many studies have employed sociometric measures administered only once or over a very limited time period (Bruininks, Rynders, & Gross, 1974; Bryan, 1974). Studies which have looked more at the development of social skills over time have reported increasing levels of both interaction and positive attitudes toward such interactions, as time in the integrated setting increases (Budoff & Gottlieb, 1976; Hazen & Black, 1984; Kohl & Beckman, 1984).

Greater use of observational methodology in classroom or more controlled settings would improve our understanding of social skills and interaction patterns in mainstreamed settings. Fewer studies have examined specific components of social interaction patterns in mainstreamed settings. Dunlop et al (1980) employed repeated observations and sociometric measures in a mainstreamed classroom. Their data indicated cooperative interaction across ability groups, and increasingly similar patterns of behavior over time. Guralnick and Groom (1987) employed an analogue setting for evaluating the development of social interaction patterns in mainstreamed playgroups. The combined measures of analysis of both social interaction and individual social behavior and peer sociometric ratings provided more thorough documentation of mainstreamed play interactions than many previous studies had afforded.

Positive cross-ability interaction patterns were also observed between handicapped children and their nonhandicapped peers in the case study cited earlier (Swadener, 1986). This study showed increasing cooperation and homogeneity of the two groups of children over the school year. Other studies in the early childhood mainstreaming literature have examined the interrelationships of the types of activities, types of play, and role of the teacher as facilitator of mainstreamed interactions during the various parts of a preschool day (e.g., Brophy & Stone–Zukowski, 1984; Cole, 1986; Gentry, 1983; Kohl & Beckman, 1984; Li, 1983; Swadener, 1986; Villarruel, Dickson, & Martin, 1986). Findings generally suggest the importance of adults in facilitating incipient or transitional stages of play activity.

Cole (1986) examined the teacher's role as mediator of social play between severely and profoundly mentally retarded elementary children and nonhandicapped peers in the context of a structured peer-interaction enhancement program. Treatment consisted of a combination of discussion and role modeling, followed by reduced teacher involvement in the peer interactions. Results demonstrated a positive impact of the intervention on the quality of both handicapped and nonhandicapped children's interactions. Cole discussed the need for more ecologically valid research of naturally occurring relationships between mainstreamed children and their peers, citing limitations of preconceived codes as opposed to more spontaneous, anecdotal evidence of the quality of children's relationships.

Another potential facilitator of cooperative play between handicapped and nonhandicapped peers is the use of a classroom microcomputer. Villarruel et al., (1986) analyzed videotapes of such dyads in dramatic play, block play, at lunch and at a microcomputer and found that computer activities appeared to offer an ideal opportunity for shy and more withdrawn children to talk and participate on a reciprocal basis.

Kohl and Beckman (1984) compared handicapped and nonhandicapped preschoolers' interactions across a variety of classroom activities involving other children and adults. Their analysis revealed similar patterns of behavior between the two groups of children during free-play activities, especially when adults were involved. Apparently, the role of the adult is important in mainstreamed settings to achieve program objectives for group play.

Gentry (1983) found that, almost 50% of the time, interactions involved handicapped and nonhandicapped children when there was a high ratio of handicapped to nonhandicapped children in the classroom. Nonhandicapped children seemed generally accepting of their mainstreamed peers, but some instances of rejection were observed. Handicapped children were more likely to be included with a group of children than to be selected by a nonhandicapped child to play with on a one-to-one basis. When the only choice of a playmate was a handicapped child, the nonhandicapped children engaged in more isolated play, with handicapped children reluctant to initiate contact.

In summary, findings of studies of children's play interactions in mainstreamed settings have varied according to their design and findings in a number of ways. Some studies have shown varying degrees of peer rejection or isolation of handicapped children in mainstreamed settings. More recent studies, however, have shown a variety of ways in which the types of play, type of teacher involvement, and opportunities to interact with mainstreamed peers can have positive effects on cross-ability interactions.

Class-related Factors and Play

Of central importance in the area of class differences in play has been the issue of possible play deficits or underdeveloped skills in imaginative or sociodramatic play in children from low SES groups or from traditional, non-Western cultures. This arena of research and theory in the play literature is one of considerable controversy. The crucial point in this debate revolves around whether there are play deficiencies between groups or if apparent deficits are due to short-comings in research methods.

Technical weaknesses in studies making social-class comparisons include inadequate definition or measurement of the social-class variable, lack of statistical tests, and lack of systematic control of classroom and school variables (McLoyd, 1982). Many studies have based social class on parents' occupation and level of education (e.g., Fein & Stork, 1981; Rubin et al., 1976; Smith & Dodsworth, 1978; Stern et al., 1976; Tizard et al., 1976). Use of nonstandardized measures of social class makes it difficult if not impossible to determine the exact nature of the sample. Moreover, researchers have sometimes confounded race and culture with social class (Rosen, 1974; Smilansky, 1968). Moreover, observations of play often are made exclusively in preschool or day-care settings which reflect predominantly middle-class values, and in programs serving only one SES group or another. Activity centers and thematic play materials found in middle-class settings may be less familiar to low SES children. If young children are not familiar with objects, they tend to explore them initially, and may become inhibited if they suspect their behavior will lead to adverse consequences. This could lead one to underestimate their play skills.

Race-related Factors

McLoyd (1982) suggests examining spontaneous play of young children in a broader context—if not in home and neighborhood settings, then in special playrooms which could be set up near the school, but away from the regular classroom. For example, McLoyd, Morrison, and Toler (1979) found that under such conditions dyads and triads of Black preschoolers exhibited richer sociodramatic play than when observed in the presence of a familiar adult. McLoyd further rec-ommends that coding systems be devised which capture some of the play and communication patterns of low-income, as well as ethnically diverse, children.

Hale (1982) examined the effects of Black culture on child-rearing and play behavior. In her examination of Black child-rearing practices, the importance of family—particularly mothers' influence on the socialization and education of Black children—emerged. Hale recommended that play behavior be used as a source of information about Black children's cognitive style. She advocated that the early childhood curricula stress the relationship between culture and education and recognize unique aspects of Black children's play.

Grant (1984, 1985) utilized ethnographic methods to analyze the differential classroom treatment and interaction patterns of first-grade children and their teachers, in six desegregated classrooms. In "Black Females' 'Place' in Desegregated Classrooms," Grant's analysis showed that teacher's evaluations behaviors toward students, students' orientation toward teachers, and peer interactions, in combination, contributed to the construction of Black females' "place" in these classes. Implications of this study include "hidden costs of desegregation" for Black girls, such as the emphasis on social rather than academic skills, and Black girls most frequently playing the "go-between" or social integrator role for teachers. In a second paper, Grant (1985) described how white girls in the elementary schools in her case study were trained for later "motherwork," or were reinforced for intellectual competence, nurturing roles and deferential behavior. These particular attributes were seen as "central to the stereotypical roles adult white women play" (ibid, p. 1).

Race and gender cleavage is ubiquitous in our mixed-race culture and has generally been found to increase as children grow older. Negative attitudes toward other-race children are present even during early childhood, particularly among children from the majority culture and class. However, early childhood programs which emphasize positive self-concept and racial and gender equality and appreciation in general can have a positive effect on children, as seen in friendship choices on other sociometric measures, as well as measures of racial attitudes of young children (Crooks, 1970; Horton and Finnegan, 1973; Kirn, 1973; Swadener, 1986).

Teacher Beliefs

Teacher's behavior is also mediated by beliefs and attitudes. Teachers, like parents and other providers of play experiences, make decisions that influence what, where, how, when, and with whom young children play. These decisions are not made randomly or haphazardly, or based on temporary feelings or moods, but are in most cases based on basic and stable values and beliefs or a system of beliefs (Spidell, 1985).

A number of empirical studies have been done examining teacher beliefs about play and learning as an important factor in defining the role of the teacher in relation to children's play. Not surprisingly, teachers in early childhood education generally share a common core of beliefs, likely due to similar teacher-training backgrounds and experiences. Many researchers have found that teachers of young children usually have rather strong convictions about the importance of play and other self-directed activities for the development and well-being of young children (Bloch & Wichaidt, 1986; Hess, Price, Dickson, & Conroy, 1981; Winetsky, 1981).

Teacher beliefs concerning sex-typed play, segregated play and related attitudes about gender, race, SES, or special needs status, and beliefs about other issues relevant to play in a broad social context are not so uniform. Research related to teacher beliefs and background in these aspects of human diversity has generally been limited to public school settings and teachers working with older children (e.g., Apple, 1983; Boyle, 1982; Grant & Sleeter, 1985; Metz, 1978). Clearly more research with early childhood teachers regarding attitudes and teaching behavior in the domains of race, class, gender, and mainstreaming is called for.

MESOSYSTEM: RELATIONS OF PARENTS AND TEACHERS

Although the relationship of parents and teachers is important throughout a child's school career, it is never as critical or intense as when the child is of preschool age or first starting formal schooling. The reasons for this are many, including the perceived importance of the formative years for learning, the critical task of dealing for the first time with discontinuities between the home and the school, and the heightened interest shown by parents at this time, an interest in parent involvement in education which typically goes steadily downhill as the child progresses through the school system. The family–school nexus is usually the very first and most critical mesosystem for the developing young child. Potential and actual opportunities and risks abound.

This mesosystem has typically been described by noting the similarities and contrasts between the family and the school in terms of norms and rules for behavior and value and language codes (Getzel, 1974). The school, ideally, rewards children for what they do (achievements) and attempts to treat them equitably, judging children with presumably universal standards. The potential biases of school stand-ards, however, are well documented. The family, in contrast, values children for who they are (ascriptions) and treats them individually, judging them with particularistic standards. Communication at school is public and relatively formal, and topics discussed must be justified. At home, in contrast, language use can be informal and even idio-syncratic, and topics discussed do not have to be justified. In fact, the reverse is true; why a topic is "off limits" requires an explanation.

More recent descriptions of this mesosystem, however, have down-played these differences, noting changes in certain sectors of society in which schools have sought to become more home-like and families have sought to become more school-like, as in the case of parent involvement activities (Epstein, 1986). At the preschool and elementary levels, nevertheless, profound discontinuities exist in the child's ex-periences. This is particularly the case for children who come from ethnic or social-class groups where different value and language orientations are in place. Yet all children have a great deal of adjusting to do, with respect to the school and teacher, and with respect to other children and their families.

As discussed in the previous section of this chapter, the preschool environment and teacher values and priorities may differ radically from those of the home and community context of many non-Anglo children—particularly those from low SES backgrounds. An example of a thorough, longitudinal study of such differences is found in Heath's (1983) *Ways with Words.* This research describes the lack of cultural congruence between Black children and their white teachers in two Southern communities. The focus of analysis was the role of questioning in language and socialization. A significant contribution of this 5-year study was the fact that it went beyond the classroom and into the homes of both white teachers and Black children. Data were collected on communication patterns and their meanings were discussed in terms of their classroom and broader social implications.

This study recommends increased two-way interaction between the school and the community. Heath contends that the success of efforts to improve school–home communication depend on the par-ticipation of *all* parties involved. She also makes the point that it should not be a matter of outside experts telling teachers what to do and to avoid, nor of teachers telling parents how they should talk to and interact with their children. Health calls for a collaborative interaction between teachers and parents in which they discover together what the problems are and how to address these problems. (Heath, 1982).

The Headstart program and related literature address parent involvement, the role of parents as primary teachers of their preschool children, and the role of educators in assisting economically disadvantaged parents in preparing their children for public school. Further, Headstart preschools have long recognized that "despite the lack of advanced education of many mothers, the schools needed their involvement, interest and understanding—involvement in the classroom as volunteers and paid aides, at home as tutors, and at school on governing boards—to maximize the students' success" (Epstein, 1986). In the Headstart model, the purpose of parent involvement was different than in many parent cooperative-type programs, which utilize parents for financial and other functional program support. Headstart has recognized and put into practice connections between schools and parents to try to improve both family and preschool organizations and the education and socialization of the children.

A wide variety of intervention and enhancement programs have built upon the Headstart model of parent involvement, recognizing the critical role that diverse parents play in their children's school success. To cite a recent example, the "Multilingual Preschool Parent Participation Project," of the Sacramento City Unified School District utilized the first language of parents and children, and attempted to acknowledge and include each family's cultural heritage in classroom experiences. As in Headstart, parents were encouraged to serve as resource persons in the classrooms, and were instructed in ways to participate in classroom instruction as well as in home teaching lessons for parents to practice these skills at home (Fox, Lew, Talbert, & Watts, 1986).

Differing Orientations of Teachers and Parents

Parents and teachers often have different beliefs or expectations about the behavior of young children, the purposes of early education, and each others' roles vis-à-vis the child.

Tizard, Mortimore, and Burchell (1981) investigated parent–staff relationships in British nursery schools, using various interviews which included questions pertaining to the purpose of preschool and the respective roles of teachers and parents. Teachers felt that the primary purpose of preschool was to facilitate language and cognitive development; parents reported that, generally speaking, the preschool experiences were valuable for facilitating social development. Teachers supported the view that one of the roles of the parent was to facilitate social development, but also felt that parents should see themselves as more of a teacher at home and should read and play with their children to foster intellectual development.

Teachers viewed self-discovery and play as important for the child's cognitive and language development and saw their own role to be the provider of ample opportunities for this to occur at school. Parents, in turn, criticized this because they felt the teachers were not teaching their children but were rather just letting the play go on. Parents with more education, however, showed more understanding of what the teachers were trying to accomplish.

Hess et al., (1981) investigated differences between mothers and preschool teachers' socialization goals for children. Mothers placed the greatest value on independence and social skills, but felt that teachers emphasized this too much, particularly with play or expressive activities like singing. Mothers indicated that the preschool teachers should place more emphasis on language and school-related skills. Parents were less likely than teachers to recognize the value of play in learning. Parents also seemed to be less permissive than teachers in their interactional strategies.

Winetsky (1978) reported similar results, but also found that the extent to which parents and teachers differed in their views about child development depended on parental socioeconomic status. Anglo–American middle-class parents were similar to teachers in showing a high priority for the child's self-direction. Mothers who were non-Anglo, working-class, or both, favored conformity and complying with the teacher's authority.

Other researchers who have investigated parents' and teachers' attitudes and beliefs about play and schoolwork have reported consistent findings (Bloch & Wichaidt, 1986; Johnson, 1986). Bloch and Wichaidt's study took place in Bangkok, Thailand. Eighty-one parents and 38 teachers in 10 kindergartens completed questionnaires, showing that teachers preferred play activities (e.g., make-believe play) over academically oriented activities (e.g., learning the Thai alphabet) more than parents did. Both parent and teacher attitudes toward play were more favorable the higher the educational level of the respondent.

Johnson (1984) compared preschool teachers and parents in the United States, using questionnaire measures for views on free-play versus academic activities and for different types of play. Parents with and without a college degree were also compared. College-educated parents and teachers, in contrast to less-educated parents, agreed that play is to be preferred over more formal academic activities in preschool settings. Distinctions were also made between play types. Essentially, divergent or imaginative play (e.g., pretending to be a favorite character) was viewed most favorably. Teachers and college-educated parents ranked expressive play next in importance (e.g., dancing and movement expression). Parents without a college degree favored convergent play (e.g., building a specific structure with blocks) and physical play (e.g., balance and coordination activities). These data suggest variation in awareness of mainstream child-rearing ideology pertaining to childhood play and academic emphases.

Other writers have analyzed the reciprocal relationship of parents and teachers of young children (Florio & Shultz 1978, Joffe, 1977; Katz, 1980; Strom, 1975). Strom encourages parents to have more respect for children's play and to spend more time observing their child's play because observation is an "effective form of reinforcement." Joffe (1977) addresses the differences in what Black and white parents want from teachers, and discusses factors associated with the degree of parent participation. She provides case study data on Black parents who were frequent participants in their child's program and discusses implications for teachers.

Other Areas of Divergence

Along with differences in orientation about general education researchers have also shown that parents and teachers often vary in their beliefs and practices about education that is multicultural.

Interviewing parents representing diverse racial, ethnic, linguistic, religious, and income groups, Swadener (1985) collected a set of "parent concerns" for use in pre- and in-service training of preschool teachers, for working with diverse families. Among the concerns expressed by parents were the following: (1) Lack of awareness and respect for cultural customs, for example, the making of paper head-dresses for native American parents was seen as an offensive, inauthentic experience, and the making of Halloween masks was viewed by Hmong parents as inappropriate for school, since in their culture masks represent deceased relatives and are worn only by shamen in religious ceremonies, (2) Communications from school coming home exclusively in English, when one or both parents could speak or read little English, (3) The celebration of Christian holidays in preschool and public school settings, without representation of other major religions, and the related issue of separation of church and state, where public programs were concerned, (4) The exclusion of children from classroom celebrations when prohibited by their religion (e.g., Jehovah's Witness families), and (5) Assumptions made about parents' ability to buy "required" items for their children (e.g., gym shoes, treats for the class, or tickets for field trip events), when parents had low incomes, a concern that was particularly voiced by single parents.

Other frequent concerns included the infrequent inclusion or inaccurate representation of non-Anglo traditions, history, and culture. In fact, two parents interviewed were choosing to leave their predominately white, middle-class community, in favor of moving back to a majority Black or Asian community in a more urban setting for this reason. Another frequently voiced concern came from single parents, primarily mothers, who felt that there was teacher prejudice against their children and themselves, and that lingering stereotypes of implications of a "broken home" persisted with many middle-class teachers.

ENHANCING ACCEPTANCE OF DIVERSITY

Understanding the influences of parents and teachers separately and in unison on children's play is an important prerequisite for building an expanded and more inclusive definition of early childhood education and research. We have proposed that an important goal is to prepare young children to meet the challenges of living in a pluralistic societies. The role of the adult in children's play can be used in a variety of ways to bring this about.

Case Study Highlights

The mainstreamed, multicultural centers in the case study discussed earlier (Swadener, 1986) did a variety of things to encourage children's acceptance of and friendship with their diverse peers. Teachers frequently used "individual differences" activities, open-ended questions in discussions, and both facilitated and encouraged frequent contact and shared activities with mainstreamed peers. Teachers also assigned valued roles to children with handicaps (e.g., teaching children sign language or about their braces). Friendships were seen to grow throughout the school year between mainstreamed and normally developing peers. Factors which appeared to contribute to these friendships included opportunities for children to play together outside of school, shared interests in both outside and in-class activities, and the teachers' active encouragement of children to include mainstreamed peers in their play and other activities.

The classroom support models for mainstreamed children differed at each center. One program utilized a resource teacher, who worked one to one with special needs children, and did virtually all of the classroom activities with the child with the most severely retarded child. At the other center, two team teachers (one certified in special education and the other in preschool and kindergarten) worked together with all the children, supported by therapists, who provided individual and small group therapy and assessments.

Sociometric data included structured interviews with each child, which dealt with playmate and activity preferences, career choices and "peer projections," attitudes about mainstreamed peers, and reactions to activities dealing with various aspects of human diversity. While no mainstreamed children at the first center described above were named as frequent playmates, three were named at the other center (which had a higher percentage of children with disabilities in the classroom and utilized a team-teaching model). At this center, a strikingly consistent response to the question, "What do you like to do most with Jimmy?" (a handicapped peer) was, "Learn sign language *from* him." Although Jimmy had begun the school year with few communication skills, and was considered to be at least 2 years behind his peers developmentally, a combination of factors contributed to his high rate of interactions with normally developing peers, as well as to their valuing of him as a playmate and someone from whom they could learn a new skill—sign language.

Several of Jimmy's peers play with him outside of school, with the teachers encouraging of parents planning such get-togethers, and two children took horseback riding lessons with Jimmy in the spring and summer. Attempts to keep Jimmy in the classroom for more activities with his peers, rather than removing him for various therapies at sometimes inappropriate times, also appeared to contribute to other children's degree of acceptance and inclusion of Jimmy in play. The teachers' role also included modeling enjoyment of their interactions with mainstreamed children, and utilizing a variety of forms of play to encourage children's acceptance of their diverse peers.

SUMMARY

Parents and teachers are important in influencing young children's specific play behavior and general social functioning. Negative adult behaviors as well as the lack of positive ones can foster hesitancy and avoidance tendencies in children and also may serve to make children more reluctant to accept others as partners in social interaction. In contrast, positive developmental consequences can be expected to occur when parents and teachers deliberately seek to promote positive social behavior and to encourage favorable attitudes in their children.

An important tenet raised in this chapter has been that constructive outcomes becomes accentuated through the working together of parents and teachers. The likelihood of achieving mutual goals is enhanced through education that is multicultural. For early childhood educators, this entails recognition of the cognitive limitations of young children and their special vulnerabilities concerning the influence of the informal or hidden curriculum. Care should be taken to encourage authentic and age-appropriate activities dealing with aspects of human diversity.

Selective review of the literature on the antecedents of play development and peer relationships indicated that parents often have the primary predisposing influence on preschoolers' play tendencies and peer-preference proclivities. Teachers were seen as reinforcing, helping shape, or attenuating established patterns of children's social interactions and related attitudes. Researchers have examined, in particular, parental effects on the acquisition and the development of certain play skills and response biases. Sex-typed socialization practices are also prevalent, and often yield predictable results in the area of gender-stereotypical play behavior and attitudes.

Teacher influences on play were reviewed in terms of a multidimensional model which included components for play provisions, observation, and intervention. Teachers' beliefs and practices determine in part how well children get along with peers who differ in gender, ability, class and race.

The family–school connection is a very important first mesosystem influencing the developing child. Both similarities and discontinuities between the home and classroom in behavioral expectations, language use, and values exist. Teachers and parents may radically differ in their priorities for children. The literature reviewed strongly suggests that parents and teachers need to establish close and open networks of communication and must seek ways to cooperate with each other from their diverging orientations.

This chapter also highlighted selected findings from a recent case study of two mainstreamed, multicultural day-care centers, focusing on teacher and parent joint and separate roles. Designing and implementing programs for enhancing the acceptance of diversity were seen to operate on both adult and child levels in this study, and were met with mixed success. Whether or not a "pure" interpretation of education that is multicultural is possible in early childhood settings, the programs studied created milieus in which a number of aspects of human diversity were openly acknowledged and included frequently in the informal or spontaneous curriculum. In other ways, however, stereotypes prevailed—particularly in the arena of gender in free-play situations. Perhaps the most promising patterns were the positive interactions between mainstreamed children and their peers. Influences from both home and school contributed to this favorable outcome.

In conclusion, children's play and social behavior may be said to reflect and to express varied social contexts. Learning how this interacts with what is known about the impact of the physical environment remains unclear. Yet, it is increasingly important to attempt to put together these two strains of influence in order to understand better the antecedents and processes of play and their general significance in development. Parent and community involvement and partnership with teachers of young children are seen as integral to creating early environments which prepare children to participate more fully in pluralistic societies and to appreciate the many aspects of human diversity.

REFERENCES

Apple, M.W. (1983). Curricular form and the logic of social control. In M.W. Apple & L. Weis (Eds.), *Ideology and practice in schooling.* Philadelphia: Temple University Press.

Barnett, L.A., & Kleiber, D.A. (1984). Playfulness and the early play environment. *Genetic Psychological Monographs, 144,* 153–164.

Bishop, D., & Chace, C. (1971). Parental conceptual systems, home play environment and potential creativity in children. *Journal of Experimental Child Psychology, 12,* 318–338.

Bloch, M.N., & Wichaidt, W. (1986). Play and school work in the kindergarten curriculum: Attitudes of parents and teachers in Thailand. *Early Child Development & Care, 24,* 197–218.

Boyle, M. (1982). *Teaching in a desegregated and mainstreamed school: A study of the affirmation of human diversity.* Unpublished doctoral dissertation, University of Wisconsin–Madison.

Brophy, K., & Stone-Zukowski, D. (1984). Social and play behavior of special needs and non-special needs toddlers. *Early Childhood Development and Care, 13*(2), 137–54.

Bruininks, R., Rynders, J.E., & Gross, J.C. (1974). Social acceptance of mildly mentally retarded pupils in resource rooms and regular classes. *American Journal of Mental Deficiency, 78,* 377–383.

Bryan, I. (1974). An observational analysis of classroom behaviors of children with learning disabilities. *Journal of Learning Disabilities, 7,* 26–34.

Budoff, M., & Gottlieb, J. (1976). Special class EMR children mainstreamed:

A study of an aptitude (learning potential) X treatment interaction. *American Journal of Mental Deficiency, 81,* 1–11.

Busch, J.W., & Schau, C.G. (1980). *Multicultural sex-role development in young children: Intervention strategies, final report.* Office of Education, Washington, DC, Women's Educational Equity Act Program.

Cole, D.A. (1986). Facilitating play in children's relationships: Are we having fun yet? *American Educational Research Journal, 23*(2), 201–215.

Collier, R.G. (1985, March). *Preschool teachers and children's play.* Paper presented at the annual meeting of the Association for the Anthropological Study of Play. Washington, DC.

Crooks, R.C. (1970). The effects of an interracial preschool program upon racial preference, knowledge or racial differences, and racial identity. *Journal of Social Issues, 126,* 137–143.

Dreyer, A.S., & Wells, M. (1966). Parental values, parental control, and creativity in young children. *Journal of Marriage & the Family, 28,* 83–88.

Dunlop, K.H., Stoneman, Z., & Cantrell, M.L. (1980). Social interaction of exceptional and other children in a mainstreamed preschool classroom. *Exceptional Children, 47*(2), 132–141.

Dunn, J., & Woodring, C. (1977). Play in the home and its implications for learning. In B. Tizard & D. Harvey (Eds.), *Biology of play.* London: Heinemann.

Dunn, L.M. (1968). Special education for the mildly retarded—Is much of it justifiable? *Exceptional Children, 35,* 371–379.

Elkind, D. (1981). *The hurried child: Growing up too fast too soon.* Reading, MA: Addison-Wesley.

Epstein, J. (1986, April). *School and family connections: Toward an integrated theory of family—school relations for student success in school.* Paper presented at the annual meeting of the American Educational Research Association, San Francisco.

Fagot, B.I. (1984a). Teacher and peer reactions to boys' and girls' play styles. *Sex Roles, 11*(7–8), 691–702.

Fagot, B.I. (1984b). The child's expectations of differences in adult male and female interactions. *Sex Roles, 11*(7–8), 593–600.

Fein, G., & Stork, L. (1981). Socio-dramatic play: Social class effects in interpreted preschool classrooms. *Journal of Applied Developmental Psychology, 2,* 267–279.

Feitelson, D., & Ross, G.S. (1973). The neglected factor—play. *Human Development, 16,* 202–223.

Fink, R.S. (1976). Role of imaginative play in cognitive development. *Psychological Reports, 39,* 895–906.

Florio, S., & Schultz. (1978). Social competence at home and at school. *Theory into Practice, 18*(4), 234–243.

Fox, E., Lew, M., Talbert, J., & Watts, E.C. (1986, April). *Summary of the final evaluation report of the multilingual preschool parent participation project of the Sacramento City Unified School District.* Paper presented at the annual meeting of the American Educational Research Association, San Francisco.

Gentry, B. (1983). Does mainstreaming insure integration. (ERIC Doc. No. AN ED 231108.)

Gerber, P.J. (1977). Awareness of handicapping conditions and sociometric status in an integrated preschool setting. *Mental Retardation, 15,* 24–25.

Getzel, J.W. (1974). Socialization and education: A note on discontinuities. *Teachers College Record, 76,* 218–225.

Goodman, H., Gottlieb, J., & Harrison, R.H. (1972). Social acceptance of EMR's integrated into a non-graded elementary school. *American Journal of Mental Deficiency, 76,* 412–417.

Grant, C.A. (1978, September/October). Education that is multicultural: Isn't that what we really mean? *Journal of Teacher Education,* No. 5.

Grant, C.A., & Sleeter, C.E. (1985). Who determines teacher work: The teacher, the organization, or both? *Teaching & Teacher Education, 1*(3), 209–220.

Grant, L. (1984). Black females' "place" in desegregated classrooms. *Sociology of Education, 57,* 98–111.

Grant, L. (1985, April). *Training for motherwork: Socialization of white females in elementary school.* Paper presented at American Education Research meeting, Chicago.

Griffing, P. (1983). Encouraging dramatic play in early childhood. *Young Children, 38*(4), 13–22.

Guralnick, M.J., & Groom, J.M. (1987). The peer relations of mildly delayed and nonhandicapped preschool children in mainstreamed playgroups. *Child Development, 58,* 1556–1572.

Hale, J.E. (1982). *Black children: Their roots, culture and learning styles.* Provo, UT: Brigham University Press.

Hartup, W.W. (1976). Peer interaction and the behavioral development of the individual child. In E. Schopler & R.J. Reichler (Eds.), *Psychopathology and Child Development.* New York: Plenum.

Hazen, N., & Black, B. (1984). Social acceptance: Strategies children use and how teachers can help children learn them. *Young Children, 39*(6), 26–60.

Heath, S.B. (1982). Questioning at home and at school: A comparative study. In G. Spindler (Ed.), *Doing the ethnography of schooling: Educational anthropology in action.* New York: Holt, Rinehart, & Winston.

Heath, S.B. (1983). *Ways with words: Ethnography of communication: Communities and classrooms.* Cambridge, England: Cambridge University Press.

Hess, R.D., & Price, G.G., Dickson, W.P. & Conroy, M. (1981). Different roles for mothers and teachers: Contrasting styles of child care. In S. Kilmer (Ed.), *Advances in early education and day care, 111,* 1–28.

Hops, H. (1981). *Behavioral assessment of exceptional children's social development.* Aspen Systems.

Horton, R., & Finnegan, R. (1973). *Modes of thought: Essays on thinking in western and non-western society.* London: Faber and Faber.

lana, R.P., Ayers, D., Heller, H.O., McGettigan, J.F., & Walker, V.S. (1974). Sociometric status of retarded children in an integrated program. *Exceptional Children, 40,* 267–271.

Jennings, I.D., & Connors, R.E. (1983). *Children's cognitive development and free play: Relations to maternal behavior.* Washington, DC: March of Dimes Birth Defects Foundation. (ERIC Doc. No. ED 229 162)

Joffe, C.E. (1977). *Friendly intruders: Child care professionals and family life.* Berkeley, CA: University of California Press.

Johnson, J.E. (1984, March). *Attitudes toward play and beliefs about development: An empirical analysis.* Anthropological Association for the Study of Play. Clemson, SC.

Johnson, E.A. (1986, April). *Short-term and delayed effects of adult intervention in kindergarten children's sociodramatic play on social and emotional adjustment.*

Johnson, R., & Johnson, D.W. (1980). *The social integration of handicapped students into the mainstream. In M. Reynolds (Ed.), Social acceptance and peer relationships of the exceptional child in the regular classroom.* Reston, VA: Council for Exceptional Children.

Katz, L.G. (1980). *Mothering and teaching: Some significant distinctions.* Champaign-Urbana: University of Illinois. (ERIC Document Reproduction Service No. 190–204).

Kendall, F.E. (1983). *Diversity in the classroom: A multicultural approach to the education of young children.* New York: Teachers College Press.

Kennedy, P., & Bruininks, R.H. (1974). Social status of hearing impaired children in regular classrooms. *Exceptional Children, 40,* 336–342.

Kinsman, C.A., & Berk, L.E. (1979). Joining the block and housekeeping areas: Changes in play and social behavior. *Young Children, 29*(4), 66–75.

Kirn, K.G. (1973). *Racial identification and preference in young children as a function of race and sex of experimenter and child.* Unpublished doctoral dissertation, University of Florida.

Kleiber, D.A., Barnett, L.A., & Wade, M.E. (1978, October). *Playfulness and the family context.* Miami, FL: SPRE Research Symposium of the National Recreation and Parks Association.

Kleiber, D.A. & Barnett, L.A. (1980). Leisure in childhood. *Young Children, 35*(5), 47–53.

Kohl, F.L., & Beckman, P.J. (1984). A comparison of handicapped and non-handicapped preschoolers' interactions across classroom activities. *Journal for the Division of Early Childhood, 8*(1), 49–56.

Landerholm, E.J. (1981). *Comparison of mothers' and fathers' play with their male and female infants.* Detroit: National Association for the Education of Young Children (ERIC Document Reproduction Service No. ED 225 666).

Lederberg, A.R. (1985). *Stable and unstable friendships: An observational study of hearing and deaf preschoolers.* Unpublished dissertation. Dallas: Texas University.

Lieberman, J.N. (1977). *Playfulness: Its relationship to imagination and creativity.* New York: Academic Press.

Manning, K., & Sharp, A. (1977). *Structuring play in the early years at school.* London: Ward Lock Educational. (figure 1).

MacDonald, K., & Parke, R.D. (1984). Bridging the gap: Parent–child play interaction and peer interaction competence. *Child Development, 54*(3), 626–635.

McLoyd, V. (1982). Social class differences in sociodramatic play: A critical review. *Developmental Review, 2,* 1–30.

McLoyd, V., Morrison, B., & Toler, B. (1979). *The effects of adult presence vs. absence on children's pretend play.* Paper presented at Hampton-Michigan Research Exchange, Hampton Institute, Hampton, VA.

Mercer, J.R. (1973). *Labelling the mentally retarded.* Berkeley, CA: University of California Press.

Metz, M.H. (1978). *Classrooms and corridors.* Berkeley: University of California Press.

Newman, V. & Johnson, J.E. (1981). Fantasy play: Acting out stories. *Offspring, 22,* 25–34.

Paley, V.G. (1984). *Boys and girls: Superheroes in the Doll Corner.* Chicago. University of Chicago Press.

Parten, M.B. (1932). Social participation among preschool children. *Journal of Abnormal and Social Psychology, 27,* 243–269.

Peterson, N.L., & Haralick, J.G. (1977). Integrations of handicapped and non-handicapped preschoolers. An analysis of play behavior and social interaction. *Education & Training of the Mentally Retarded, 12,* 235–245.

Piaget, J. (1972). *Play, dreams, and imitation in childhood.* New York: Norton.

Randall, R.S. (1976). *Informal Learning.* (ERIC Document No. ED 125954)

Rogers–Warren, A.K., Ruggles, T.R., Peterson, N.L., & Cooper, A.Y. (1981). Playing and learning together: Patterns of social interaction in handicapped and nonhandicapped children. *Journal for the Division of Early Childhood.*

Rosen, C.E. (1974). The effects of sociodramatic play on problem-solving behaviors among culturally disadvantaged children. *Child Development, 45,* 920–927.

Rubin, K.H., Fein, G.G., & Vandenberg, B. (1983). Play. In P.H. Mussen (Ed.), *Handbook of child psychology: Vol. 4. Socialization, personality, and social development* (4th ed., pp. 693–774). New York: Wiley.

Rubin, K.H., Maioni, T.L., & Hornung, M. (1976). Free play behavior in middle- and lower-class preschoolers: Parten and Piaget revisited. *Child Development, 47,* 414–419.

Scott, K.P. (1984). *Teaching social interaction skills: Perspectives on cross-sex communication* (ERIC document No. AN ED 252445)

Shoggen, P. (1975). An ecological study of children with physical disabilities in school and at home. In R.I. Weinberg & F.H. Wood (Eds.), *Observation of pupils and teachers in mainstream and special education settings:*

Alternative strategies. Minnesota Leadership Training Institute/Special Education, University of Minnesota.

Shure, M.E. (1963). Psychological ecology of a nursery school. *Child Development, 34,* 979–994.

Singer, J.E. (1973). *The child's world of make-believe.* New York: Academic Press.

Sleeter, C.E., & Grant, C.A. (1986). Educational equity, education that is multicultural and social reconstructionism. *Journal of Educational Equity and Leadership, 61,* 105–118.

Sleeter, C.E., & Grant, C.A. (1987). An analysis of multicultural education in the United States. *Harvard Educational Review, 57*(4), 421–444.

Smetana, J.G., & Letourneau, K.J. (1984). Development of gender constancy and children's sex-typed free play behavior. *Developmental Psychology, 20*(4), 691–696.

Smilansky, S. (1968). *The effects of sociodramatic play on disadvantaged preschool children.* New York: Wiley.

Smith, C., & Greenberg, M. (1981). Step by step integration of handicapped preschool children in a day care center for nonhandicapped children. *Journal for the Division of Early Childhood.*

Smith, P.K., & Dodsworth, C. (1978). Social class differences in the fantasy play of preschool children. *Journal of Genetic Psychology, 133,* 183–190.

Smith, P.K., & Syddall, S. (1978). Play and non-play tutoring in preschool children: Is it play or tutoring which matters? *British Journal of Educational Psychology, 48,* 315–325.

Spidell, R.A. (1986, April). *Teacher intervention and beliefs in preschool children's play.* Paper presented at the annual meeting of the American Educational Research Association, San Francisco.

Spindler, G. (1982). *Doing the ethnography of schooling: Educational anthropology in action.* New York: Holt, Rinehart, & Winston.

Stern, V. (1981). *The symbolic play of lower-class and middle-class children: Mixed messages from the literature.* Washington, D.C.: National Institute of Education.

Stern, V., Bragdon, N., & Gordon, A. (1976). *Cognitive aspects of young children's symbolic play.* Unpublished paper. Bank Street College of Education, New York.

Stevenson, M.B., Leavitt, L.A., Thompson, R.H., & Roach, M.A. (1983, April). *Play in the family: Fathers and mothers with their infants and preschoolers.* Paper presented at the biennial meeting of the Society for Research in Child Development, Detroit.

Strom, R.D. (1975). Parents and teachers as play observers. *Childhood Education, 51*(3), 139–141.

Swadener, E.B. (1985). *Implementation of education that is multicultural in early childhood settings: Teacher training and classroom follow-up.* Final report to University of Wisconsin System Ethnic Studies Coordinating Committee.

Swadener, E.B. (1986). *Implementation of education that is multicultural in* early childhood settings: A case study of two day care programs. Unpublished doctoral dissertation, University of Wisconsin–Madison.

Tizard, B., Philips, J., & Lewis, I. (1976). Play in preschool centres: Effects on play of the child's social class and of the educational orientation of the centre. *Journal of Child Psychology & Psychiatry, 17,* 265–274.

Tizard, B., Mortimore, J., & Burchell, B. (1981). *Involving parents in nursery and infant schools: A resource book for teachers.* London: Grant McIntyre Limited.

Villarruel, F., Dickson, W.P., & Martin, C.A. (1986). *Using a microcomputer to create social interactions among handicapped and nonhandicapped children in a mainstreamed preschool.* Paper presented at the annual meeting of the American Association of Mental Deficiency, Denver.

Winetsky, C.S. (1978). Comparisons of the expectations of parents and teachers for the behavior of preschool children. *Child Development, 49,* 1146–1154.

Woodard, C. (1984). Guidelines for facilitating sociodramatic play. *Childhood Education, 60,* 172–177.

12

Rivalry as a Game of Relationships: The Social Structure Created by the Boys of a Hawaiian Primary School Class*

JOHN J. D'AMATO
Center for Development of Early Education, Honolulu

The dynamics of children's play and other interactions are both keyed and constrained by children's ideas of social structure. These ideas entail certain values, promoting the interactional moves and countermoves associated with those values. But they also influence the construction of situations and interpretation of events in ways that help to control emergent interactional dynamics. Children's social structures thus have the effect both of setting up certain games of relationship and of keeping these games playable.

This chapter is about such games of relationship. In particular, it concerns the peer group structure created by the boys of one cohort of children at Ka Na'i Pono School, a four-classroom, K–3 school operated as an educational laboratory by KEEP, the Kamehameha Early Education Program. Data on the children of Cohort 7 were gathered primarily in their second-grade year, but also during their third-grade year. All but a few of the children were part-Hawaiian in racial ancestry, about three-fourths were from families receiving public assistance, and all were from households which participated in relatively low-income social networks. This chapter is divided into three parts. The first describes general features of the interactional dynamics of the children of Cohort 7; the next describes the social

---

* This chapter is based upon a presentation entitled, "Coping with Rivalry: The Social Organization of Risks of Self in a Class of Hawaiian Second Graders," at the annual meetings of the American Anthropological Association, Washington, D.C., 1985.

structure created by the boys of the class; and the last relates the children's social dynamics to issues of culture, class, and school politics.

HAWAIIAN CHILDREN'S RIVALRY: FRIENDLINESS, COURAGE, AND PLAYFULNESS

The interactional processes of Hawaiian schoolchildren have much in common with ones which have been described for Oglala Sioux (Wax, 1976), Kwakiutl (Wolcott, 1974), urban Black (Goodwin, 1982; Keiser, 1972; Labov, 1972, 1982; McDermott, 1974; Rosenfeld, 1971), and other American minority children (Ellis & Newman, 1972; Schoem, 1982) as well as for certain populations of children in such diverse settings as Micronesia (Colletta, 1980), the West Indies (Abrahams, 1972), Britain (Beynon & Atkinson, 1984; Lacey, 1976), and Japan (Rohlen, 1983). In this chapter, the interactional processes of Hawaiian schoolchildren and cognate social dynamics will be treated as versions of the game of rivalry. As used herein, rivalry refers to a process of peer contention initiated, managed, and evaluated by peers (D'Amato, 1986). Players in this game assume that peers represent an autonomous social stratum, that membership in this stratum is fixed, and that peers are equals, as compared with the members of superordinate and subordinate social strata. Players also assume, however, that differences in prestige within the peer stratum are achievable and that failure to merit inclusion in this stratum is also a possibility. Consequently, players orient their actions to demonstrating worthiness of acceptance by peers and to achieving some advantage over peers. Players exercise care, however, in making claims to worthiness and status. Consistent with the premise that peers form a distinct and fixed social stratum, rivalry does not provide for superiors to act as game judges, referees, and managers and to forbid conflict. Peers themselves are expected to control emergent possibilities of conflict. For this reason, players of the game of rivalry are assertive about rights but avoid being pretentious or combative unless they are in fact willing to provoke conflict (D'Amato, 1986; cf. Boggs, 1985; Brown, 1972; Colletta, 1980; Goodwin, 1982; Keiser, 1972; Labov, 1972; Marcus, 1978; Mitchell-Kernan, 1972). The idea is to show that one is as good as peers but not to assert that one is qualitatively superior to peers.

Among accomplished players of the game, rivalry is characteristically expressed by means of playful sequences of interaction in which peers take turns using actions such as teasing, jokes, and ritual insults to belittle each other in funny and theoretically harmless ways. Such interactions both test and express friendship. In directing acts of belittlement at peers, players threaten to deny peer status to peers. They thus affirm the idea of peer group status as the highest good attainable, suggest the quality of relative superiority, and imply the warning that force will be met with force. In accepting the return of teasing, joking, and similar actions from peers and in the smiles, laughter, and other signs of friendliness that frame the trades, players validate each other's claims to worthiness, express humility, and define their contention as a playful, entertaining, and harmless diversion. They thus create interactional sequences the content and structure of which symbolize the idea that no one is better than anyone else, while also revealing meaningful differences between individuals (D'Amato, 1986; cf. Boggs, 1985; Howard, 1974; Labov, 1972; Mitchell–Kernan, 1972).

Regardless of how tolerant of laughter at self and otherwise adroit peers are at doing group play with the idea of balance or parity, rivalry always may and periodically does escalate beyond playfulness to conflict. This is an especially probable outcome of rivalry among schoolchildren. It takes time for children to learn to do acts of belittlement and claims to merit without provoking peers, to accept and counter such acts without becoming angry, and otherwise to keep an emergent interaction under control and in some semblance of balance. It also takes time for them to grow so large that they are likely to inflict serious injuries in fights and thus for them to arrive at a shared interest in avoiding fighting except as a last resort. Most importantly, school adults' ideas of social order are extremely likely to be at variance with those of schoolchildren who play the game of rivalry and thus to engender conflict among the children (Boggs, 1985; D'Amato, 1986; Labov, 1982; Roberts, 1970; Wax, 1976; Wolcott, 1974).

As is typical for Hawaiian schoolchildren (Gallimore, Boggs, & Jordan 1974), the children of Cohort 7 expressed the values of their own very volatile version of rivalry by means of the terms, "nice" and "tough." "Nice" referred to certain pleasing qualities of person and behavior. "Nice" meant looking nice, smelling nice, and taking certain concrete actions, such as sharing goods with friends, helping when necessary with schoolwork and peer affairs, and welcoming others into activities at recess. Most of all, being nice meant simply expressing an attitude of friendliness through smiles, warm and voluble greetings, touching, and other, often nonverbal, means.

Letters written by the children of Cohort 7 to Toby B., a boy who moved away after second grade, indicate the children's commitment to friendliness as an interactional form and group ideal. All the letters contain warm expressions of affection, often mixed in with the most mundane news. Mapu wrote:

> I want you to come back to KEEP
> I MISS you I hope you come back I love
> you, we have thether [tether] ball at KEEP School,
> we have hard work we do / and x

Mapu then listed all the names of the children in the class. On the back of her letter, she drew a picture of a girl and a boy standing between two trees under smiling clouds, a smiling sun, and the legend, "I LOVE YOU."

Louella, another girl in the class, wrote the following letter:

> How are you I hope you will come back
> and I hope the baby [Toby B.'s new sibling] is well and
> I hope it will be a girl or a boy but
> most of all I miss you and we had
> the Cook Idnd [island] Daces [Dancers] today and
> I hope your mom and dad are happy
> but most of all I reay [really] reay reay
> miss you
>
> Love Louella and my
mom

From these letters, it may seem that Louella and Mapu thought of Toby B. as a boyfriend, but this was not the case. Mapu and Louella were writing to a sweet and sentimental social form designed to make a peer feel welcomed and valued within the peer group. They were able to say things like, "I love you," in such offhand ways because the expression of affection was so customary with them.

The boys' letters were also very affectionate. Pete's was the most remarkable. Though Pete and Toby B. had been enemies, Pete exuded friendship, often sounding personally offended that Toby B. had moved away:

> How are you feeling in Maui?
> are you haveing fun ther?
> when are you comeing to Hawaii?
> I hope you are having fun
> becuse we are haveing real good
> fun here in Hawaii. becuse we
> are going to do grease for

chirsmas   are you going to come
and wach us or are you going to
stay ther in Maui. but still are
you never comeing to Hawaii?
and boy you should see what
kind of moveis ther are in
Hawaii. we can see Xandu [Xanadu] and
grease, Somky and the Bint [Smokey and the Bandit], and
empire strikes back, and that
one call Lady in red, rocky II,
the fog, superman, malaui [Malabu] high,
and boy did you see the moveeises
at Sunset divein   it was cup of
gold and cup of honey at the moveise   it was a funny moveies
the name was candyman   and . . .
you should see Saterday night fever
it is so bad   you no the lady
her going take off her clotes
man it is so bad   you are going
to like see the moveise
at kam [shopping center] the name is   I will
tell you what the name is
but you are going to be sorry
it is foxy girl   we made it for
you but you are not here
and you should not [have] gone to
maui   we are haveing so good
fun that we think you
was with us in KEEP
i hope someday you will
be comeing back to Hawaii
we are doing very good
here in hawaii and you
should see   we have 4 [teachers]
ther names are mrs I mrs
Lee miss L and a nice
Hawaii lady. 1 day I hope
you can [come] back in hawaii and
we are the Bogie [Boogie] Phantoms
they Pete, Kaleo, Mark, and the
boss is Brent.   now can
you come back to Hawaii?

WE NEED YOU
WITH US

        your firend
        Pete

The sheer vitality of Pete's letter reflects Pete's own charisma but is also suggestive of the strength of the children's commitment to idealistic visions of their peer group and peer affairs. In most general terms, niceness represented an ideal of peer solidarity for the children. By telling Toby B. that the class was suffering for Toby B.'s want, Pete expressed this ideal, evoking an image of the peer group as a good and necessary locus of identity. As it did for Pete, so did it give pleasure to all the children to think of their peer group in this way and to give substance to the fantasy through free, selfless, and often shamelessly flattering gestures of affection.

"Toughness" was a very different ideal. Being tough meant being brave; it meant standing up for one's rights when challenged. Children sometimes talked about toughness in terms of an explosive sensitivity to affront especially characteristic of Hawaiians, and all of the children prized this sort of reputation. For example, in talking about how a person feels when another person makes trouble, Mark said, "You come all RED inside, you like BEEF!" Pete said, "Us Hawaiians—if you get us too mad—the kind like punch you out, when we grumble, we no grumble nice." Pete was asked what made a Hawaiian person angry. "Brah, they no can ignore nothing. But if you're nice Hawaiian, that's good for you. If you mean Hawaiian, that's MORE good for you." The need to demonstrate sensitivity to affront had to do with the children's beliefs about acceptance and social order. They worked on the premise that the management of peer relationships was ultimately each child's own responsibility and that good treatment from peers needed to be assured by creating and maintaining a reputation for not backing away from challenges. For example, in talking about why it was hard for a person to walk away from a challenge, Tolbert explained, "Once they make trouble, they asking for trouble." "Yeah?" "I no scared, man." Louella was asked why a person could not walk away from challenges: "It's hard." "Why?" "Like—the other—the other person gonna think they're chicken." Melody explained, "If you no fight, hanh, they gonna make trouble to you. Tease you, make any kind." "What if you told the teacher?" "Then you faggot." Brent was asked why it was hard to ignore problems. "They keep on teasing, tha's why." "Why do they do that?" "Cause they think you no can fight." Perhaps the most succinct expression of the idea that children have to stand up for their rights on their own came from a kindergarten girl. She had just won a fight with a kindergarten boy. She explained, "My Mommy say, 'If can, ignore. If no can, beef 'em.'"

Paradigmatically, the children demonstrated toughness through confrontations. Representing a ritual test of worthiness, confrontations and their outcomes were critical in determining a child's peer standing. The members of Cohort 7 maintained accounts of confrontations as a kind of oral history of their cohort, recalling encounters even from kindergarten days in making and defending judgments of who was tougher than whom. Being tough, however, meant being brave in a variety of senses; it also meant being able to manage pain on one's own, to satisfy needs on one's own, and to demonstrate a kind of smooth competence in accomplishing ordinary things. In these and other ways, toughness referred to an ideal of personal autonomy, to having the capacity to cope with all aspects of the world by oneself. The children called this capacity that of being able to "handle," and they tried to show an ability to handle in everything from the doing of classroom performances to the way in which they managed pain stemming from playground accidents. Most of all, the children showed toughness simply as an attitude, a kind of monitory, "I can handle" air, expressed through clothing, posture, and other means. Capable of being very sweet and affectionate, the children were also extremely proud and courageous and showed this in their actions and bearing.

Though very different, the children's values of solidarity and autonomy formed a necessary complementarity. Showing friendliness is how the children attempted to validate each other's claims and to quiet worries about acceptance and status. Showing toughness is how the children tried to assert their individual rights, to establish and maintain reputations that would discourage others from attempts at dominance and other forms of ill treatment. Together, toughness and niceness amounted to a face-to-face strategy for negotiating the politics of peer-managed processes of peer contention. To do this successfully, children had to be both tough and nice.

Equally necessary in managing peer relationships, toughness and niceness were usually expressed simultaneously by children in their actions. Confrontations represented the interactional paradigm for showing toughness and acts of sharing, helping, and caring that for showing niceness, but these activities are best appreciated as the poles of an interactional continuum. Between the poles of this continuum lay a variety of forms of interaction and self-presentation which expressed both autonomy and solidarity. At the midpoint of the continuum were playful contests of will, skill, wit, and courage. The playfulness and element of contention in these contests expressed solidarity and autonomy equally, and it was here that the children began interaction and tried to keep interaction. Through the contentiousness of the encounters, children asserted their own and checked others' claims to merit and status; through the smiles, laughter, and other tokens of solidarity framing the contests, children tried to keep contention friendly and lively interests in relative status in the background. Thus handled, playful contests were a diverting and pleasurable way for children to make statements of autonomy without also disturbing premises of solidarity and provoking conflict.

The classroom provided the children with many opportunities for playful contention. The children would vie with one another for the seat at the teacher's right at the reading center in order to be the one to pass out the books, for the seat near the tape recorder at the listening center in order to be the one to control the volume and to get the "choice" headset, for the last position or the first position in a line just to be the last or first one out of the room, and so on. Girls especially vied over classroom housekeeping tasks and positions of proximity to the teacher. All of the children would vie for the turn to speak in lessons if any one of them had indicated an interest in performing. The consequence of this was that teachers received multiple responses to questions and other initiatives as children tried to balance the performances of peers with ones of their own (Au, 1981; Boggs, 1985; D'Amato, 1986). The children invented games, too, and vied with one another on this basis. Among others, there were contests to see who could do the highest Kung Fu kicks, the loudest finger snapping, the best job at breaking pencils with one-finger karate chops, and the fastest walking that was not yet counted running by teachers. The children even contended with one another over milk cartons at lunch and snack time. A picture of a president was on each carton, and the children all tried to get the ones with the picture of George Washington. Recess provided the children with many structures of contention. Among these were board games such as Connect-4, one-on-one contests like hopscotch and tetherball, team sports such as kickball and sham battle (a version of dodge ball), chase games such as chase–master, boys–chase–boys, and boys–chase–girls, and role play such as "Baby," "Puppy," "Boy-friend," and play fighting. Lastly, of course, the children vied with one another by means of teasing, joking, and other forms of verbal contention. Sometimes teasing and joking were spinoffs from other activities, and sometimes were enjoyed in their own right as entertaining diversions.

The children could show considerable skill in using playful contention to assert and validate identity claims. This type of interaction, however, always involved the possibility that one child's moves might give offense and provoke conflict. This possibility was enhanced by the processes of school and the children's own mischievousness and fondness for taking gambles. Owing to scarce goods and opportunities at school and to constant evaluation, school was always presenting the children with new frameworks in which to test relative status and inducing new imbalances in their peer relationships. The children themselves often treated their peer relationships like toys and would try to see what it took to get these relationships to do interesting and amusing things. The net effect of all this is that affronts kept emerging from the children's playful contentions, pushing them into confrontation and conflict. Almost daily, there were fights among the children, and always the children's interactions featured lively disputes (Boggs, 1978) and other forms of rough talk. The children's commitment to establishing symmetries of respect in peer relationships did succeed in creating social order, moreover, a form of order in which each child was kept in sight, if not of everyone else, then at least of someone else in the class. But it did so by means of a kind of constant jockeying for advantage and regard in which claims to special distinction were no sooner made than checked.

Much of the children's contention was merely histrionic. They loved the theater of grand disputes and would imbue the most minor of events with the aura of great crimes and treacheries just for the sheer fun of the drama of it all. But their determination to hold each other to states of balance and to defend personal claims was often both stirring and touching for they could display both enormous vulnerability and enormous courage. Once Mark was discovered crying in some bushes; he was hiding so that others would not see him cry. What had happened is that he had been snubbed while waiting to play the "long" version of tetherball. In this version, the winner of a game did not hold the turn to play. Instead, both winner and loser would be replaced by new players. Mark had assumed that he would be playing Noe, but Noe had let Estrella cut in line. This had meant that Noe would be playing Estrella instead and therefore that Noe did not much value Mark as a partner. It was this inferred slight that had made Mark cry and hide in the bushes.

Another playground incident illustrates the children's courage. Yuki was playing hopscotch with another girl. Doreen, by far the largest child in the class, sat on the cement lanai, watching. She had cut her foot on a piece of glass, and the cut had had to be sewn up. Doreen was using crutches because she could not put weight on the foot.

Emerging from the cafeteria, Pete took in the game and then announced, "I the best, you know."

"Not! He cheats!" retorted Yuki. Though not one of the tougher girls, Yuki would not allow Pete to get away with such blatant boasting.

"Shut your Japanee mouth," Pete responded, and he gave her a shove.

Doreen was sitting within arm's reach of Pete. At once, she took a swing at his leg, missed, and then struggled to her feet. She had trouble getting up, and there was some laughter from children who had been denied recess and were sitting close enough to the scene to follow it. Doreen finally got positioned in front of Pete and "made her body big." This involves inflating the lungs so that the chest puffs out, throwing the shoulders forward, and balling the fists so that the muscles of the arms and shoulders bunch. To do this is to issue a challenge and a warning.

Doreen's injury made the situation awkward for her, but angry and determined, she bumped her shoulder into Pete's chest. Pete tried to make light of the situation. Perhaps he could not take Doreen seriously in view of her injury; more likely, he was trying to duck her challenge by mocking it. Smiling, he said, "Like slaps?" as if it were in his power to hit her with impunity.

Refusing to be disregarded, Doreen again banged her shoulder into Pete's chest. Pete's smile faded. He banged back and the two began leaning into each other. The playground supervisor now intervened, separating the two children and making them sit apart to "cool off." Doreen was so unsteady on her feet this day that she might well have lost a fight with Pete, but it simply was not in her to allow him to throw his weight around as he had.

Pete himself was a volatile mixture of sensitivity and combativeness. For example, in the course of a tetherball round robin during a physical education period, Pete won some games but then lost to Tolbert. Tolbert also won some games but then lost to Jake. Theirs was the last game. As the children lined up to return to class, Tolbert and Jake, who were close friends, relished a victory which in a sense they had shared.

"I winners, looks like," said Jake.

"Yeah," agreed Tolbert. "You win me, I win Pete." Tolbert and Jake looked back at Pete to see what effect this inference would have upon him. The effect was immediate. Pete stormed up the line toward Tolbert and Jake, accidentally knocking down Freddie, who cried. Pete lunged at Tolbert, missed, and then when Brent laughed at the miss, Pete tackled him instead, landing on top of both Brent and Kevin, another innocent bystander. "Sorry, 'anh?" Pete said to Kevin as he went after Brent again. The children's teacher, who had begun leading them back to the classroom, halted the line and made Pete sit against the wall to cool off. As the line of children began moving again, Pete yelled at Tolbert, "How come you never challenge

me then? Fucker!" "Come on, come on," he said to Jake, daring
him to fight. When Pete himself returned to the classroom later on,
he slammed the door shut and then surveyed his classmates for some
sign of trouble from them.

So it was for the children. Schooldays for them were always rife
with challenges to identity claims and rich in vignettes of face and
pride. Each day, the children did their best to hold their own against
real or imagined challenges, to preserve the rights, usually generously
conceived, that were the due of people like them, and when all else
had failed, to inflict some pain upon those who had not given them
their due.

Some individuals usually fared better than others in the children's
rivalry, but beyond this, there appeared to be little form to their
relationships. Though logical, their interactions could seem almost
chaotic, blind cycles of playfulness, affront, and conflict. It turned
out, however, that the values underlying the children's interactions
were themselves aspects of a deeper level of social structure. The
children were not only living out the problematical dynamics associated with their values; they had themselves confronted and were
attempting to control these dynamics. What they had done was to
create two social structures, one for the boys, one for the girls.
Though very different from one another in their methods, these
social structures were alike in both enjoining children to participate
in rivalry but also giving them means of controlling rivalry.

Space limitations make it impossible to discuss both the boys' and
girls' social structures. This chapter focuses on the boys' social structure, primarily because the boys provided accounts of their social
structure, and the girls did not. Owing to this, the boys' social
structure may be interpreted with more confidence. An interpretation
of the girls' social structure may be found elsewhere (D'Amato, 1986).

THE BOYS' SOCIAL STRUCTURE

The Boys' Side, the Girls' Side, and the Two Gangs

The problem faced by the children of Cohort 7 was essentially this:
How is an individual to display capacities required to win peer
acceptance and regard without simultaneously offending peers and
provoking conflict? The boys' basic strategy for solving this problem
was to divide themselves into the tough and the not tough, to divide
the tough into two rival groups, and to use these divisions as a kind
of situational stagecraft, setting up interaction so that the not tough

could avoid the tough and enemies could avoid one another. The boys themselves, however, did not talk about the significance of their social structure in quite this way.

The first information about the boys' social structure came after lunch one day during spring of the children's second-grade year. Tolbert was lying on a cot in the sickroom with an icepack pressed to a large goose egg on his forehead. Asked what had happened, he replied, greatly excited, "Mr. D'Amato! Mr. D'Amato! you know what? The *gaaangs* was fighting!" At once, he was asked questions about what the gangs were and who was in them.

According to Tolbert, the children of the class were divided into a boys' side (or team) and a girls' side (or team). All of the girls were on the girl's side, but not all of the boys were on the boys' side. Some boys did not like to fight and played with girls or by themselves at recess instead of joining the play fighting and other doings of the gangs. As Tolbert phrased it, the boys on the girls' side were "too shrimpy" to be in the gangs. He defined "shrimpy" as small, but there was more to it than that. He included Toby B. as a gang member, and Toby B. was one of the smallest boys of the class. When this was pointed out, Tolbert agreed that Toby B. was small but added that he was very brave. "He cry and still yet he fight." Rather than just size, it was courage or toughness that distinguished boys on the boys' side from ones on the girls' side.

According to Tolbert, only seven boys were in the gangs. Pete, Kaleo, and Brent made up one gang, Jake, Tolbert, Toby B., and Jamie, the other. The five boys who were disparaged for being on the girls' side were Freddie, Mark, Steve, Toby Loo, and Kevin. Tolbert said that Jake and Pete were the leaders of the two gangs since they were the strongest and bravest boys. In explaining the functions of Jake and Pete as leaders, Tolbert said, "If-if-if I fight Pete, hanh, then Jake help me." The reverse situation was described symmetrically but worded rather differently. If Brent "challenge me," Tolbert said, then "Pete make trouble to me. He always make trouble." Being the leader of a gang, then, meant being the dominant boy in the gang and standing up for other boys, if necessary, against the larger members of the opposite gang. Tolbert also threw some light on other relationships in the two gangs. Tolbert said that he himself was a leader and that if somebody fought with Jamie, he would help Jamie. Asked why he would help, Tolbert said that Jamie was his cousin. Asked how he was related to Jamie, Tolbert said that he was not really related to Jamie, that Jamie was his best friend. Tolbert said that Jake and Toby B. were cousins in the same way, that all of the boys in Jake's gang, in fact, were cousins. In talking about the people in Pete's gang, who represented a second set of cousins, Tolbert said that Kaleo was not a leader because he was not strong enough. Tolbert's opinion of Brent was especially low. Brent, one of the largest boys, was also not a leader because "he so shrimpy. Even he eat plenty vegetable and he shrimpy."

Over the next two days, Tolbert's account was checked out with a few girls, most boys, and all gang members. In all major respects, Tolbert's account was supported, but there was some disagreement over important details. There was agreement about who was in the gangs and who was not; most of the other gang members used notions such as the girls' side and the boys' side in distinguishing those who were from those who were not, and for none of the boys were these and similar terms unfamiliar. There was agreement about who was in which gang and also an underlying understanding of what it meant to be in the gangs and of what it took to get into them. Mark sometimes played with the boys from Jake's gang. In explaining why he had not joined Jake's gang, Mark said, "They only make trouble to me. I no like fight." A last point on which there was agreement was that Jake was the leader of the one gang. There was disagreement, however, about the leader's identity in the other gang. Most boys called it Pete's gang, but some called it Kaleo's. Nevertheless, the extent of agreement among the boys about the gangs and other features of organization was impressive.

Data on heights and weights tended to support the depiction of the gangs as fighting groups. One would expect something of a physical balance between the gangs and the gang members to be the larger boys. This was generally so. Five of the six or seven largest boys were gang members; two of the three largest, Jake and Pete, were gang leaders. There was also a rough physical balance between the gangs.

Data on the boys' recess activity and playmate choices supported

Table 1. The Boys' Model of Social Organization

Boys on the boys' side:		Boys on the girls' side
Pete's gang	Jake's gang	
Pete	Jake	Steve
Kaleo	Tolbert	Mark
Brent	Toby B.	Toby Loo
	Jamie	Kevin
		Freddie

Table 2.   Heights and Weights of the Second Grade Boys

Boys	Peer Status	Height (in.)	Weight (lb.)	Rank Order
Jake	Jake's gang	54.0	71.5	1
Brent	Pete's gang	52.0	72.3	2
Pete	Pete's gang	50.5	68.0	3
Tolbert	Jake's gang	51.0	55.8	4
Freddie	Girl's side	49.0	59.0	5
Kaleo	Pete's gang	48.5	56.0	6
Steve	Girl's side	49.5	51.5	7
Mark	Girl's side	48.0	50.5	8
Jamie	Jake's gang	48.3	47.8	9
Toby B.	Jake's gang	47.5	47.0	10
Toby Loo	Girl's side	48.0	45.5	11
Kevin	Girl's side	44.5	43.8	12

the reality of the gangs as groups. The relationship between gang affiliation and recess choices was not perfect but generally strong.

There were three main areas on the playground: the upper playground, containing the jungle gym and most of the playground equipment; the lower playground, containing the tetherball posts and the sandbox; and a side area, which the children used as a field for team sports. The upper playground was the turf of Jake's gang. As a rule, Jake, Toby B., and other boys would gather on the jungle gym or in a grassy area nearby. There, they would do pretend fighting or play chase games. While games of boys-chase-girls and chasemaster, which usually included girls, might attract boys from Pete's gang, boys-chase-boys games and the play fighting done on the upper playground involved only the boys of Jake's gang. The boys in Jake's gang did not always keep to the upper playground. Tolbert was fond of tetherball and of flirting with the girls who played tetherball. Consequently, he often spent much or all of recess on the lower playground. But most members of Jake's gang and Jake himself were usually found near the jungle gym.

The lower playground and side area were the turf of Pete's gang. With the exception of Tolbert, the male athletes of the class were the boys in Pete's gang. Pete, Kaleo, and Brent usually played tetherball at recess and were also the prime movers in games of sham battle and other team sports. Jake, Tolbert, and other boys in Jake's gang often joined Pete and his gang in team sports. Unless the second grade was playing the third grade, the gang opposition would show up in the fact that boys in opposing gangs tended to play on opposing teams. For their part, Pete, Kaleo, and Brent usually stayed away from the upper playground and particularly from the jungle gym.

The other boys fit in where they could. Except for tetherball, all the boys' activities were closed ones: A child had to have permission or receive an invitation to join. Steve was usually let in on the doings at the jungle gym, and Freddie was also tolerated there. Kevin divided his time between staying in the classroom and playing in both upper and lower playground areas. Mark and Toby Loo, however, tended to stick with tetherball. One did not need to negotiate entry rituals to play but merely to stand in line and wait one's turn. Toby Loo and Mark tended to maintain low profiles at recess.

Table 3 shows what the boys did during 20 recesses spanning the last 3 months of the school year. The data cover about an eighth of the children's recesses during second grade. The data are mostly useful in showing a difference in location between boys in Jake's gang and boys in Pete's and thus the influence of the two-gang structure upon the boys' social choices. About two-thirds of Brent's activities, through three-fourths of Kaleo's, to well over three-fourths of Pete's took place on the lower or side playground. On the other hand, over two-thirds of Jamie's activities, through over three-fourths of Toby B.'s, to well over three-fourths of Jake's took place on the upper playground. Owing to Tolbert's preference for tetherball, he spent about half his time on the lower playground. His pattern of play is similar to that of other boys in Jake's gang, however, in the number of times he chose to do pretend fighting and to play on the jungle gym and other equipment.

Similar patterns turned up on field trips and in seating for movies and other events. The boys of a gang tended to stay together, and boys on the girls' side again fit in where they could.

The Bump on Tolbert's Head

In view of the supporting data, it was attractive to accept the boys' talk and think of the gangs as structures which had emerged from their conflicts in classic, zero-sum game fashion. But it was clear from the beginning that the boys' gangs could not be the fighting units that the boys made them out to be. During the 20 recesses for which activity data were collected, the boys of the boys' side were involved in nine fights involving blows or wrestling. Of these fights, only two were between boys from different gangs. All but two of the rest involved boys of the same gang. In the following year, data on recess fights were again collected with much the same results. It was actually cousins with whom gang members were fighting, not enemies. Group confrontations of one gang versus the other, furthermore, were exceedingly rare. No more than three group confrontations occurred

Table 3. Activities of the Second-grade Boys over a Span of 20 Recesses

	Total Days Present	Days on Playground	Lower Area					Side Area			Upper Area		Total Activities	
			Tether-ball	Board Games	Hop-scotch	Sandbox	House (w/girls)	Team Sports	Chasemaster & Boys Chase Girls	Girls Chase	Play Fighting	Play on Playground Equipment*	Lower and Side Areas (Pete's turf)	Upper Area (Jake's turf)
Pete's gang														
Pete	20	17	12	3	2	2		3	2	1	1	1	22	4
Kaleo	18	15	9	2		2	1	3	3		1	1	17	5
Brent	20	17	11	1	1	1		2	3	2	2	5	16	10
Jake's gang														
Jake	19	16	3			1		2	5	4	4	14	6	23
Tolbert	20	19	12			1	1	2	4	3	3	7	16	14
Jamie	19	16	3		1	1	1	1	3	1	1	11	7	15
Toby B.	18	15	4			1		2	5	2	2	12	7	19
Boys on the girls' side														
Toby Loo	20	18	14		1				1	1	1	2	15	4
Mark	20	18	14		1	2		2	2	1	1	3	19	6
Steve	19	18	2			1	1		2		2	14	4	16
Kevin	20	14	6			1	1		2	1	1	6	8	9
Freddie	18	14	6		1	1	1		3	2	3	8	8	13

*Play on jungle gym, slides, and monkey bars.

during the children's second- and third-grade years. Even fights between certain rivals from the two gangs were very rare. Despite all the talk about Pete standing up for boys in his gang and Jake for ones in his, these two boys had only two fights during the two-year period of observation. Jake and Kaleo—the other boy mentioned as leader of the opposite gang—did not have a single fight. On a number of occasions, Jake and Pete or Jake and Kaleo exchanged angry words, and the leaders of the gangs might stand up for followers before situations heated up. Jake would do so for Tolbert in Tolbert's scrapes with Brent, and Pete for Brent in his encounters with Tolbert. Indeed, Tolbert and Brent maintained something of a game in which the one would tease or bait the other for the sake of getting him involved in a confrontation with Jake or Pete. When serious trouble was at hand, however, Jake, Pete, and Kaleo seemed to exhibit a remarkable talent for staying away from each other, and followers had to fend for themselves. The boys' gang versus gang ideology, in short, matched up poorly with the facts of their conflicts. That ideology neither organized fighting in terms of the gang opposition nor inhibited fighting within the gangs. If anything, the reverse was the case.

The very situation in which the gangs came to light shows the danger of taking the boys' talk about the gangs at face value. As Tolbert lay on the cot after lunch with the icepack pressed to his head, there was no more urgent topic for him than the gangs. His memories of fights which Jake, Toby B., Jamie, and he had had with Pete, Kaleo, and Brent were all that he wanted to talk about, and he did not particularly care to be interrupted by my requests for information about general features of the boys' relationships. Listening to Tolbert, it occurred to me to ask which boy in the rival gang had been responsible for the bump on his head. Tolbert replied that Toby B., a boy in his own gang, had caused the bump, not Pete, or Kaleo, or Brent. "Was it an accident?" I suggested helpfully. "He trew 'em," replied Tolbert matter of factly, this thing that Toby B. had thrown having been a wooden slipper. By now seriously confused, I protested that I had been given to understand that the gangs had been fighting and that that was how Tolbert had gotten his bump. No, Tolbert explained, it was not at lunchtime that the gangs had been fighting but at recess, 2 hours earlier. Here was Tolbert, perhaps 10 minutes away from having been thumped soundly in the head with a wooden slipper by Toby B., a boy in his own gang, volunteering not one word about that incident, but talking instead with obvious relish about the recess fight—which, it turned out, involved but three boys—and many much, much older affrays. In a last defense of my own understanding of reasonable links between events and talk, I expressed surprise that it was Toby B. who had inflicted Tolbert's injury. "I thought you guys were supposed to be cousins," I said. "Tha's different," Tolbert shrugged. "We was playing." As used here by Tolbert and, in fact, as a rule, the boys' gang versus gang ideology made much less sense as a description of group dynamics than it did as a rhetoric of self-presentation. Gang-versus-gang confrontations were grand and heroic concepts, extremely effective in projecting toughness and camouflaging less than flattering circumstances such as knocks on the head received in play. Taken together with the fact that boys from opposite gangs tended to avoid one another, the boys' gang versus gang ideology looked like a way for the boys to have their cake and eat it, too. It both validated claims to tough identities and protected boys from needing to do much to put the claims to the test.

On the other hand, there was a strong connection between the boys' fighting and the gangs, but one much more complex than that suggested by the boys' talk. The two-gang structure kept the idea of fighting and the social importance of establishing and protecting a reputation for being a fighter always before the boys. As the boys were well aware, a boy's standing depended largely upon his demonstrating a willingness to perceive and to oppose peers' assertions of superiority or dominance. Certain claims to dominance and superiority, however, were inherent in the gangs. Within each gang, differences in dominance had emerged which were obvious, stable, and accepted by everyone. Yet if asserted conspicuously, these differences in dominance were supposed to be and, indeed, would be rejected by boys. The opposition between the gangs, similarly, amounted to a standing claim to superiority and thus to a standing challenge to which the boys would again be responsive if it surfaced clearly. The boys' two-gang structure, in short, was something of a trap of machismo. It required boys to fight against challenges but also built certain challenges into their relationships. Boys on the boys' side did not have to look for fights; the two-gang structure ensured that fights would eventually find them.

Viewed comprehensively, the boys' social structure makes most sense as a system which both required boys to live up to the value of being tough and enabled them to live with that value. On the one hand, the boys' social structure promoted conflict by turning the value of being tough into a criterion for group membership and status. The distinction between the boys' side and the girls' side established the general requirement that boys engage in peer contention and fight to be socially successful; and the dominance hierarchies of the gangs and the gang-versus-gang opposition established enduring structural circumstances out of which challenges and conflict were certain to emerge. On the other hand, the boys' social structure created the possibility of different types of fights: fights between boys from different gangs; fights between boys of the same gang; and fights between the tough and the not tough. Of these, only fights between enemies were regarded as serious fights. Furthermore, the idea of being enemies entitled boys from different gangs to avoid each other and therefore to minimize the likelihood of serious fights. The boys of the gangs talked as though they operated in terms of a rule of confrontation, but in fact the idea of belonging to rival gangs provided them with an unassailable rationale for behaving in terms of a rule of avoidance. It only made sense to play with friends and to avoid enemies. In sum, the boys' social structure promoted conflict by establishing toughness as a hallmark of identity, by requiring boys to be sensitive to suggestions of dominance or superiority, and by creating the very real possibility of serious fights between enemies. At the same time, however, the commonsense actions and choices associated with the gang-versus-gang structure tended to assure that serious fights would be minimized. The boys' social structure was indeed a trap of machismo but one carefully placed.

Where fighting was most likely—that is to say, within the gangs— the trap of machismo was also lightly cocked for the idea of possessing a common enemy gave boys means of limiting and resolving conflict among themselves. Within the little domain of a gang, a boy could make claims to fighting prowess and the like without running much risk of offending his audience and generating counterclaims. Such claims were usually made relative to people in the opposite gang. Similarly, one boy's expertise—in tetherball, for example—did not necessarily jeopardize the claims of other gang members. Since the boys of a gang were allies, the accomplishments of one boy might be taken to support the group identity shared by all. The idea of the gang also enabled boys to control the possibility of conflict emerging from play. "Everybody knew" that the boys of a gang were cousins who by definition accepted each other's claims to worthiness. Consequently, the spills and other mishaps which boys caused each other in play might be ignored or dismissed instead of being made reasons for fighting. A boy might even allow a friend to slug him on the arm or back to make amends for some unintentional injury. When the boys of a gang did fight, they did not and were not expected to go all the way, for these were fights between friends. Furthermore, they resolved such fights with acts of reconciliation. In part, reconciliation followed simply from the weight of routine for the boys faced the same situations and people every day. There was nothing to do after a fight with a friend but to resolve the situation or turn the friend into an enemy. In part, however, reconciliation followed from the boys' sentiments. The boys of a gang called themselves cousins, and by the end of 3 years of playing and fighting together, they were. Despite the anger they could show in the heat of the moment, they were troubled after fights with friends. Fights between boys from opposite gangs, by contrast, were not followed by reconciliation. They were followed instead by avoidance, which served in its own way to revalidate tough identities. That boys avoided each other, meant that they took each other seriously as rivals.

The different aspects of the two-gang structure made for two distinct cycles of interaction among boys of the boys' side. Within the gangs, boys would engage in playful contention which eventually would blossom into conflict, usually because boys had tripped over some feature of gang dominance hierarchies. Afterwards, there would be a brief period of avoidance, then reconciliation, and finally a renewal of playful contention. For boys from different gangs, avoidance was the rule. This would be broken eventually by playful contention to which the boys would have found their way through happenstance, fondness for taking risks, or momentary and misplaced optimism about relationships. Playful contention would lead to conflict, and conflict to avoidance, punctuated, eventually, by new rounds of playful contention and conflict.

A Book and a Pair of Socks

At any one time, it was almost certain that boys on the boys' side would just be living through or getting over some conflict. An exercise in collecting sociometric data illustrates the point. Children were each asked to name three individuals with whom they liked to play at recess and three with whom they did not. It was assumed that gang members' responses would reflect the gang structure, but this was only partly so. Table 4 displays the gang members' responses. A "+" indicates a positive response, a "−," a negative response (e.g., Tolbert liked to play with Jake and did not like to play with Pete). Toby B. and Jake gave four positive responses; all are shown.

As can be seen, most responses from Jake, Tolbert, and Toby B. in the one gang and Kaleo and Brent in the other were consistent with the two gang structure. Those of Jamie, however, were the reverse of expectations, and Pete's seemed to have been made completely outside the two-gang structure. He named none of the

Table 4. Responses of Gang Members to the Instructions, "Name 3 children that you like to play with at recess," and "Name 3 children that you do not like to play with at recess"

Respondents		Jake's Gang				Pete's Gang			Other Second-grade Boys					Second-grade Girls				Third-grade Boys	
		Jake	Tolbert	Toby B	Jamie	Pete	Kaleo	Brent	Toby Loo	Mark	Kevin	Steve	Freddie	Noe	Norino	Laura	Yuki	JT	Chico
Jake's gang	Jake	▨	+	+	+								−		+			−	−
	Tolbert	+	▨	+		−	−		+				−						
	Toby B.	+	+	▨		−	−	−		+				+					
	Jamie	−	−		▨	+	+	+								−			
Pete's gang	Pete					▨		−						+	−		−	+	+
	Kaleo		−	−	−	+	▨	+			+								
	Brent	−	−		+	+	+	▨					−						

boys in his own gang as people he liked to play with, and none in the opposite gang as ones he did not like to play with. On the day before the sociometric exercise, the children were observed at recess and for the rest of the day. Two confrontations occurring during this time seem related to the boys' "inconsistent" sociometric responses. At the least, these confrontations demonstrate the dynamics which were continually at work within and between gangs.

The first of the confrontations involved Jamie. His supporter in this confrontation was Brent. His antagonists were Jake, Toby B., and Freddie. What happened was this: Jamie, brilliant in his tactics for subverting adult rules, had brought a book to school in the morning. Normally, the teachers confiscated possessions brought to school by the children since such things often stirred up envy or found their way into the hands of the larger children. But Jamie's book was *The Book of Mormon,* and his teachers had been reluctant to take it even for the duration of the schoolday. The book had also raised some false hopes. One teacher confided that she thought Jamie might be turning over a new leaf. Jamie's book and angelic demeanor on this day, however, were merely a ploy to enable him to smuggle something else by the adults. Within his book, the unreconstructed

Jamie had hidden a page of photographs which he had taken from a men's magazine.

At school that morning, Jamie had shown the book and its contents to a number of people but not to Jake. It is not clear why he had not. He may have been avoiding the loss of the pictures to Jake. On the other hand, he may have been toying with Jake's rights as gang leader and seeing what Jake would do in response to being left out. Boys like Jamie, who stood relatively low in the boys' dominance hierarchy, often did this sort of thing for they had little to lose and much to gain.

At recess, Jamie appeared on the playground somewhat late, book in hand. Freddie, Toby B., and Jake had been on the jungle gym for some time. When Jamie continued to avoid Jake, going to the swings instead of the jungle gym, Jake dispatched Freddie and Toby B. to fetch Jamie. Jake later said that he had only wanted to borrow Jamie's book. A struggle ensued, Freddie holding Jamie while Toby B. tried to wrest the book away, and then Brent entered the fray on Jamie's side. All recess long, Brent had been making sorties on the boys at the jungle gym, running up to tease Jake about Jamie's book—which Brent himself had seen—and then darting away again. Jake next arrived on the scene, but then the playground supervisor broke up the confrontation and confiscated Jamie's book, the apparent cause of the squabbling.

Jake, Toby B., and Freddie returned to the jungle gym. From a position at the base of the playground, Jamie now taunted those boys with scathing insults. There was real anger in Jamie's voice. Owing to birth defects, Jamie was missing a hand and a foot. He could not run, play, and fight as well as the rest of the children. Jamie had made his mark in the class with coups of personality such as his *Book of Mormon* gambit, and he was enraged at his cousins for the shoddiness of their behavior and the fact that it had cost him his book. Perhaps feeling bad about the situation, the boys at the jungle gym did not respond to Jamie's taunts and insults.

The bad feelings generated by this encounter were eventually resolved. When the "inconsistencies" in Jamie's sociometric responses were discovered, he was queried again about his gang affiliation. Ever mischievous, Jamie smiled and announced that he belonged to Pete's gang. He then called out to Toby B. "Yeah, Tobe?" he said, "I stay in Pete's gang," and he and Toby B. laughed at this fine joke. No reconciliation between Jamie and the other boys was observed to occur on the day of the confrontation over the book, however, and it may have been this confrontation that was responsible for Jamie's sociometric responses on the following morning. On the other hand, so quickly did events develop that it may have been something else entirely or merely Jamie's mischievousness again. In any case, the encounter between Jamie and the other boys illustrates the sort of conflict that continually flared up within the gangs. In the course of boys' work to create recognition or to protect social position, affronts would be given or received and friends would suddenly find themselves in the middle of some new confrontation. Usually brief, such confrontations would serve nonetheless to make a strong case for a boy's courage and right to decent treatment from peers.

The second confrontation involved Pete. It seems directly related to Pete's sociometric responses and shows the more intense but controlled character of confrontations between boys from different gangs. Pete's supporters in this encounter were Chico and J. T., the two third graders named by Pete as children with whom he liked to play. Pete's antagonists were Tolbert, Jake, Toby B., and Brent. This encounter started in the classroom just before lunch. Pete had rolled up his pants to show off his disco socks. These were flashy, knee-length affairs, featuring shiny, metallic threads. Thus displayed, Pete's socks were a boast that practically begged for a putdown. Tolbert obliged. As Pete strutted by on his way to a gathering for song rehearsal at the front of the room, Tolbert said, "Hoo! Chicken legs!"

Brent laughed at Tolbert's putdown, and thus encouraged, Tolbert also giggled. "Wait," Pete said with malevolence to Brent, and then he began to march on Tolbert, eventually backing him up against the classroom wall. Holding Tolbert in a loose headlock, Pete made a feint at Tolbert's eyes with his fingers. Tolbert, still counting himself ahead, continued to smile. But then Jamie laughed at Tolbert's situation, and Tolbert grew angry. The teacher caught sight of the boys, however, and summoned them to the gathering. Pete released Tolbert.

Had the interaction instigated by Pete's socks not crossed the gang opposition, the situation might have been resolved without scuffling, at least, without major conflict. Kaleo, for example, was quite skilled at checking Pete's flamboyance without simultaneously provoking him. But in taunting Pete in public, Tolbert had in effect dared Pete to act on the standing challenge between the gangs. A fight was now almost a foregone conclusion.

Lunch was nearly at hand, and the boys waited until the short recess after lunch to bring the situation to climax. As was customary after lunch, Jake, Tolbert, and Toby B. gathered on the jungle gym on the upper playground; they were joined by Mark and Steve and ultimately by Brent. Jamie was called back to the classroom to finish some work.

Pete stayed on the lower playground, waiting for the third graders to finish lunch. Pete needed allies. Kaleo, his best friend, was absent, and Brent had become one of his antagonists. That left the third graders as possible supporters. In the cafeteria in the morning, Pete had played Connect-4, a board game, with two of the third graders, J. T. and Chico, and it was these two boys Pete now enlisted as allies. As soon as J. T. and Chico emerged from the cafeteria, Pete joined them, and soon the three boys moved into the upper playground. They sat on the slides, a short distance from the boys on the jungle gym.

This occupation of the slides was provocative since it represented an incursion into Jake's territory. Jake, Tolbert, Toby B., and Brent rose to the challenge by beginning a game of chasemaster. Laughing, poking each other, and throwing a little play fighting into their game of tag, too, the boys spilled over into the territory Pete had claimed by the slides. They were flirting with the possibility of fighting Pete as if rolling dice to see which one of them would end up doing it. Soon, Pete said something to Brent, Brent mocked Pete, and Pete took off after him. Brent led Pete a merry chase, down the hill, through the sandbox, and around the school building. In a gay, celebratory mood, the other boys raced after Brent and Pete, but broke off the chase at the sandbox, all of them leaping into it and landing in a pile. There they stayed, wrestling, laughing, and getting out to take a flying leap back in again, reveling in the chaos of the moment and their release from habitual playground positions and postures. By this time, Jamie had arrived outside, and he joined Jake, Tolbert, and Toby B. in the sandbox. Having made one complete circuit of the school building, Brent came hurtling by again with Pete in hot but still distant pursuit. Someone laughed about Pete's inability to catch up with Brent. Perhaps it was Jamie. In any case, Pete responded by taking on the boys in the sandbox. He shoved Jamie, making him fall, and then advanced on Toby B. Tolbert intervened by placing himself between Pete and Toby B. but got shoved backwards for his trouble. At about this time, the playground supervisor arrived. Tolbert picked himself up, Pete went for Tolbert again, but J. T. now stepped between the two boys. He was facing Tolbert instead of restraining Pete, however, so that it was ambiguous as to whether he were stopping the fight or taking Pete's side. He could well have been doing both. The playground supervisor read the situation the first way, although Tolbert seemed to interpret it the second way as he quickly put the supervisor between himself and the much larger J. T. The supervisor took Pete and Tolbert away to cool off, and the drama broke. The two third graders drifted away. Jake helped Jamie find his slipper in the sandbox, and then he and the remaining members of his gang went back to the jungle gym. There they relived the fight and boasted about what they would have done to Pete had he had no third-grade allies. The rest of the day passed without event. The boys steered clear of one another, Pete of the boys in Jake's gang, those boys of him, and Brent of everyone.

Like the confrontation which began with Jamie's book, the sandbox fight is illustrative of the dilemma faced by the boys of the boys' side. A boy had to be assertive of his identity, but in doing so, he was always likely to generate counterperformances. Eventually, some event would put too great a public strain on emotions, identities, and relationships, and boys from opposite gangs would find themselves locked into the buildup to a fight. As shown equally clearly by the sandbox fight, however, the boys' social structure did not require them to engage in all-out battles with enemies. Rarely, if ever, did fights across the gang opposition take the form of melees, and never was such fighting without elements of calculation. The grand spectacle of these conflicts, however, went a long way to suggest things that were not there and to hide things that were. Thus, the sandbox fight was not really a gang-versus-gang fight but could pass for one; and while it appeared that no one in the sandbox on that day was operating on anything other than the surge of fighting spirit, it is obvious that Pete and Jake were. Through tacit negotiations, these two boys managed not to fight even though they were as close to one another and thus presumably to fighting as Pete and anyone else. Fights across the gang opposition soon led back to avoidance but had continuing symbolic and entertainment value. They became part of the oral history of the class, of the tradition proving that boys did engage in the grand and serious business of gang-versus-gang rivalry. To participate in this tradition, boys did not have to do the sorts of things they liked to imagine themselves doing. They were required only to make a good showing, to live through the sort of brief and inconclusive shoving match that unfolded between Pete and Tolbert. But then again, they had to do no less than this.

The Dolphin Story

While gang-related conflicts continually percolated through the boys' relationships, the two-gang structure was also continuously at work preventing conflict and supporting play. This was apparent in rival gang members' self-conscious avoidance of one another and conflictual situations. Having left the playground for the cafeteria one day, for example, Pete explained, "If I stay outside, I only gonna fight."

Boys even used the option of avoidance in the middle of gambling with the possibility of fighting. Pete and Jake did this regularly. A few days after the sociometric exercise, for example, Jake was playing tetherball against Brent. Pete was waiting in line. Owing to an innocent mistake, Pete prematurely declared Jake the loser. When Jake finally did lose, a dispute, ostensibly over tetherball rules, developed between him and Pete. On Pete's second turn, the dispute grew heated.

"Shut up!" he snapped.

"Why, cause you don't know how to talk?" Jake demanded.

"Nooo," said Pete, uncertain of where to take his own response.

"Go scotch tape 'em!" said Jake. He was trying to ridicule Pete by revealing that Pete was not willing to try to make him shut up.

"Yeah, well go get the scotch tape, I gonna tape 'em!" said Pete.

"Yeah, go glue 'em shut!" Jake continued, heightening the ridicule. "Glue 'em shut!"

"Yeah, go bring the glue!" retorted Pete.

"Eh, you! You like glue 'em, not me!" As he spoke, Jake turned to head to the jungle gym. He had shown what he wanted to, at least to his own satisfaction.

"You!" called Pete in a parting shot, reminding everyone that he was ready to fight any time Jake was. If neither boy actually won this confrontation, neither lost it. They had flown their flags, and the availability of separate gang territories had enabled them to break off their encounter at an opportune moment without loss of face to either. "Everybody knew" that Pete and Jake were not afraid of each other and would fight if necessary; at least, no one except perhaps Doreen would ever openly suggest otherwise.

The positive implications of the two-gang structure were especially evident within the gangs for the trust that came from being cousins supported and helped return boys to play. This was often apparent in the relationship between Kaleo and Pete, so explosive was the one and interactionally astute the other.

Kaleo was the master politician among the boys. It turned out that it was he who was the real leader of the Pete–Kaleo–Brent gang. Brent indicated this at the beginning of third grade. I asked whether he were still in Pete's gang. Indignantly, he replied, "Mines!" I discovered that he was saying that he was the new leader of the gang and that the boys of that gang rotated the leadership position.

"First grade, Kaleo. Second grade, Pete. Now me," Brent explained. "How did you guys decide that?" I asked him. "Kaleo said," he replied.

Though remarkably skilled at defining contexts in ways that made room for everyone, Kaleo's patience was often tried by Pete. One day, for example, the second grade was playing the third grade in kickball. He and Pete were the key players on the second-grade side, but that team began to lose badly. Pete turned on his teammates, accusing them of gross incompetence. Finally, he retired to the swings and from that position, showered more abuse upon them.

Toward the end of recess, the kickball game broke down, and Kaleo went to confront Pete by the cafeteria door. Soon the boys were making their bodies big and bumping chests. The playground supervisor intervened, but Kaleo was extremely reluctant to sit down and cool off. Kaleo was part-Black, and according to Kaleo, one of Pete's insults from the swings had been, "Get 'em out you black asses!" The children often did not intend the racist connotations of terms like "black asses," and Pete may not have been aware of the special applicability of this insult to Kaleo. In any case, it had angered Kaleo deeply. Despite the supervisor's requests that the boys sit down, Kaleo blocked Pete's path to the cooling off wall for a time, refusing to relax from his fighting pose.

During the last minutes of recess, Kaleo and Pete sat far apart along the wall at the base of the playground. They did not look at each other. In the classroom about 10 minutes later, the children gathered on the rug for a large group activity. Kaleo sat down. Pete sat down next to him. Nothing passed between them, but Pete sat in such a way that one of his feet touched one of Kaleo's. Both boys were barefoot. Leaning forward from time to time so that his head was just above Kaleo's lap, Pete began to talk to Kaleo, to look into his face, and to smile at him. It was not possible to hear what he was saying, but it was not really necessary to. By talking to Kaleo, probably about anything but the kickball game, Pete was trying to say he was sorry. Kaleo did not back away from the contact that Pete was making with him along the shoulder, side, and leg, and eventually he responded to Pete. It was typical for children to resolve problems in this way. By resuming customary activities, children who had caused offense would try to let their actions speak for feelings of remorse. The reciprocation of these actions indicated forgiveness.

Perhaps the most important role played by the idea of being cousins was simply the relief it gave boys from worries about acceptance and hence the possibilities of play it opened up for them. Another interaction between Pete and Kaleo illustrates the play with self, relationships, and fantasy available within the relatively safe context of interaction between cousins. Pete and Kaleo were working together in the classroom. Pete was writing a story. Kaleo was helping with the story and also serving as the audience. The story was about a dolphin:

> Long ago there was a boy named Pete. he had a mom and a sister. one hot day Pete went on his boat. when he was fishing he saw a dolphin. he caught the dolphin. when he got home he said mom come quick. mom came very fast. Pete named him Kaleo. Kaleo and Pete had good fun in the sea.
>
> by Pete and inc!!!!

Kaleo was pleased with the sentiment of the story but hooted at being cast as a dolphin. To tease Pete, he produced a drawing showing a shark about to bite off a swimmer's leg. As did so many things, this touched off a dispute, grandly and harmlessly histrionic, which finally attracted a tired warning from the boys' teacher. Amused by the note of exasperation that had been in her voice, the two boys shared a smile over the fun it was to be contentious and mischievous boys. If schooldays were full of challenge and conflict for the boys, so too were they full of moments like this. It was these moments that kept friends coming back to each other and made the boys' social structure worth the effort that they had put into creating it. Ultimately, the gangs were much more about friendship than fighting. It was less the case that the boys of the gangs had banded together in order to fight off enemies than that they had used the idea of enemies as a pretext for creating and sustaining friendship.

The Boys of the Girls' Side

The five boys said to be on the girls' side were not a group or even a category. They shared a situation, but their experiences within this situation varied greatly.

The boys not in the gangs tried to make the same presentations of self as the boys who were, but the other children knew that these boys were less likely to fight in response to challenges than to expose fear, suffering, or ineffectual rage. This knowledge could make these boys targets for abuse. On the other hand, not having a reputation for being tough could also excuse these boys from having to engage in the more intense forms of rivalry.

For three of the boys, being lightly regarded as fighters had little significance owing to personal relationships, size, or other qualities.

Kevin, the smallest boy in the class, had a friendship with Kaleo and Pete which protected him from abuse. Kevin was a likable sort, had few pretensions to being tough, and was much less mature in many ways than the other children. His classmates seemed to regard him affectionately as a harmless and much younger sibling. Toby Loo was also relatively small. His strongest relationship was with Tolbert for Toby Loo was also an avid tetherball player. Toby Loo attracted more putdowns than Kevin because he made himself more visible, but he was usually not harassed. Boys like Pete and Jake might reject his friendship, shaking off his arm if he laid it on their shoulders, but they did not go further than this unless Toby Loo invited it. The fact that the larger boys did not grant Toby Loo much significance stung him at times, but it also provided him with some protection. For example, on one occasion Toby Loo hit the tetherball as hard as he could to unwind it from the pole. Pete was not attending the situation, and the tetherball struck him in the head. The tetherball was very hard, and it was perfectly clear that it must have hurt Pete. But he did not betray pain or anger at Toby Loo. It was as though his own status would not allow him to admit that Toby Loo might have hurt him.

Steve was also not especially troubled by not being in the gangs, mostly for the reason that he enjoyed a remarkable relationship with Doreen. Doreen was taken lightly by no one. Steve, however, would stroke and braid her hair in class and could also kid and tease her without fearing for his safety. No other boy and few girls dared to take such liberties with Doreen. In reciprocating Steve's friendship, Doreen would not allow other children to bully him, retaliating swiftly whenever someone took Steve's pencil or paper in the classroom. Steve almost always sought to play with Jake and the other boys at the jungle gym. Indeed, he was a de facto member of Jake's gang. Occasionally, these boys treated Steve roughly, but they rarely went so far as to make him cry. Steve, for his part, did not strain his rights to participate in their doings. He watched as often as he played and stayed away when there was trouble.

For Mark and Freddie, the remaining two boys, things could be very difficult. Both boys were big enough to be in the gangs. That they were not, sometimes made them targets of scorn and bullying. Mark tried to keep a low profile at recess and usually succeeded in passing the time pleasurably at tetherball. He also had some friends in Jake's gang and was liked by Kaleo, too. Sooner or later, however, he would get involved in some sequence of harassment. This affected Mark for he was also very proud. Freddie's experiences were much more difficult. Freddie tried to assert himself as did the tough boys.

Consequently, he frequently attracted scorn, rebukes, and physical abuse, to which he typically responded with tears of rage. Once, after a particularly difficult recess, the children found Freddie lying on the pavement in the parking lot. He explained that he was waiting for a car to come and run over him. While Kevin, Toby Loo, Steve, and Mark found ways of using the status of not being tough to their advantage and created personal networks of their own, only Freddie could find no way of fitting into the boys' peer group. Perhaps a Freddie role was as necessary to the boys' relationships as their other distinctions. Still, the children maintained a connection between themselves and Freddie. Even as Kaleo and other boys and girls laughed at Freddie as he lay on the ground that day in the parking lot, they helped him up and shepherded him back to the playground.

Table 5 shows how the boys on the girls' side responded to the request that they name three persons whom they liked to play with at recess and three with whom they did not like to play. As can be seen, it was the boys in the gangs who held the attention of these boys and not other boys on the girls' side. Correlatively, the boys on the girls' side drew fewer mentions on average than the boys in the gangs. The boys in the gangs averaged 3.1 positive mentions and 2.7 negative mentions from boys in the class. On average, the boys on the girls' side drew 1.2 positive mentions from boys and 0.8 negative mentions. They did not have sufficient standing to gain much consideration as either friends or enemies.

Boys who were not regarded tough could improve their standing, however, by passing the same test of worthiness that gang members had passed. Mark did this at the start of third grade. Toby B. had transferred out, and this left the gangs unbalanced. It was Mark who took Toby B.'s place in Jake's gang. He did so by standing up to Tolbert and Brent. In a sociometric exercise that year, Mark was now one of the boys mentioned most often in both positive and negative ways.

CULTURE, CLASS, AND SCHOOL POLITICS

This chapter began with some general remarks about rivalry and the problematical aspects of rivalry. It then tried to show how the peer group structure created by the boys of Cohort 7 both celebrated rivalry and represented a collective effort at coping with the problematical aspects of rivalry. Not yet considered is a fundamental question, that of why the children of this class, boys as well as girls,

Table 5. Responses of boys on the girls' side to the instructions, "Name 3 children that you like to play with at recess," and "Name 3 children that you do not like to play with at recess"

Respondents	Boys in Gangs							Second-grade Girls									Boys on Girls' Side		
	Jake	Tolbert	Toby B	Jamie	Pete	Kaleo	Brent	Noe	Norino	Trina	Estrella	Melody	Claradine	Louella	Yuki	April	Steve	Kevin	Freddie
Steve							+		+		−	−		+	−				
Kevin*		+	−	+													+	−	
Toby Loo*						+	−	+		+									
Mark	+	+	+	−	−	−													
Freddie		−							+					−			−	+	+

*Made fewer than 3 negative responses.

should have been engaging in peer-managed processes of peer contention in the first place.

One way of addressing this sort of question is to relate children's behavior at school to their socialization at home and to explain socialization, in turn, in terms of either class or cultural variables. Both class and cultural explanations are relevant in the case of Hawaiian schoolchildren.

In explaining school failure among certain minority children, Ogbu (1982a, 1982b, 1985) argues for a connection between the face-to-face practices of minority children and the possibilities of social mobility available to members of their groups. Ogbu's position is weak in its interpretation of peer relationships among children of oppressed minorities (cf. Goodwin, 1982; Keiser, 1972; Labov, 1972). For example, there is little room in Ogbu's account for the generosity which Hawaiian children can show in peer relationships (Ogbu, 1982b; 1985). But the idea of a connection between the dynamics of face-to-face interaction and relative access to social mobility is a seminal one. It clarifies both cultural and class effects upon schoolchildren's relationships as well as the influence of schools themselves.

A problem faced by all people in all societies is that of discovering how to live lives of worth. For members of industrialized societies, forms of rivalry seem to provide one answer to this question; forms of competition provide another.

As discussed elsewhere (D'Amato, 1986), competition is also a process of peer contention, but it is one initiated, managed, and evaluated by superiors or by peers with reference to the standards of superiors. This game entails the idea of a negotiable hierarchy. Players in this game do not regard peer status as fixed and unalterable but instead contend with one another on the premise that those who succeed in peer contention will rise in social hierarchies. Rather than trying to show that they are as good as peers and conversely that peers are not better than they, competitors try to show that they are better than peers and conversely that peers are not as good as they. The object in this game is to influence the evaluation of superiors so as to rise in social hierarchies to the benefit of oneself and society.

In industrialized societies, rivalry seems to arise as an answer to the question of how to live a life of worth among people who do not have or do not believe they have access to most avenues of social mobility. These people include the members of caste-like minorities but also people of lower socioeconomic status generally (Wilcox, 1982). For them, the idea of a negotiable hierarchy is an illusion. Their opportunities for doing performances which win recognition and approval lie in frameworks such as religion, the arts, revitalization movements, entertainment media, family life, but above all, in peers. For people in these sociostructural circumstances, contention with peers—necessarily initiated, managed, and judged by peers—becomes a primary means of locating value in self and society.

Competition, on the other hand, is the logical, but in its own way, expensive option for people who believe and have reason to believe in the possibility of mobility. To compete, is in many ways to suppress the self. Whether played by Hawaiians (D'Amato, 1986; Howard, 1974), American Blacks (Brown, 1972), or Japanese (Rohlen, 1983), the game of rivalry produces charismatic presentations of self, ones suited to the here and now project of winning recognition on the basis of a spontaneous capacity to attract and to divert. Competition seems to produce more cautious and less spontaneous presentations of self, ones attuned to the often critical influence of present evaluations on the future.

To be sure, processes of peer contention, whether managed by superiors or peers themselves, are not everywhere the same. But in industrialized societies, there do appear to be consistent relationships among social class, beliefs in possibilities of mobility, and processes of peer contention. Rohlen (1983), for example, shows that at superior

Japanese high schools, students are responsive to teacher initiatives and concerned with gaining positive teacher evaluations of performances in lessons. At inferior schools, however, students are absorbed in peer-managed processes of interaction and are unresponsive to teacher attempts to initiate competitive instructional contests among them. As Ogbu (1982a) would predict, in the superior schools, students tend to come from middle- and upper-middle-class families and have a chance of going on to top universities, which, of course, will have effects throughout their lives. At the inferior schools, however, students tend to come from relatively low-income families. They know that they will not be going on to universities. Consequently, high school has few structural implications (D'Amato, in press) in their lives.

Relatively restricted access to means of legitimate mobility has doubtlessly affected the forms of interaction practiced in Hawaiian social networks and taught to children. But it is not only in industrialized societies that one finds forms of rivalry or for that matter ones of competition. As was the case for much of Polynesia, traditional Hawaiian society was stratified in terms of hereditary classes. Mobility between classes was limited. The system of stratification was mirrored within social strata through strong notions of authority between generations. The main opportunity for mobility available to commoners, and in some ways for the elite as well, was thus a kind of collective march by generation through successive genealogical statuses. Both the stratified character of Hawaiian society and this type of genealogical mobility were reflected in the Hawaiian kinship system. As is well known, the primary distinctions of this system were ones of age and sex. The same term, for example, covered mother's brothers, father's brothers, and male parent, and this logic applied as well to mother's sisters, father's sisters, and female parent. Similarly, kin terms were extended to cover male siblings and male cousins, female siblings and female cousins, male children and nephews, female children and nieces, and so on. As Fox (1967) notes, the terms of this kinship system drew symbolic lines between generational strata, treating each as an autonomous context of interaction, and within each, rivalry seems to have been the interactional norm (Marcus, 1978). To be sure, modern Hawaiians have not remained somehow unaffected by the industrialized society that has engulfed them. But cultures are historical facts. Throughout the past 100 years of especially rapid change, Hawaiians have maintained large and active Hawaiian friendship and kinship networks (D'Amato, 1986). If it is implausible to suppose that Hawaiians have not been affected by social change, so is it implausible to suppose that Hawaiians have not interpreted and adapted to change in terms of Polynesian themes of social structure, interaction, and self-presentation. It is these themes, too, that are at least partly responsible for Hawaiian children's rivalrous peer dynamics.

Whether originating in facts of class culture, ethnic culture, or, most reasonably, both, home life themes of social structure were quite apparent in the peer group structures of Cohort 7. Hawaiian children, like urban Black children from poor families (Stack, 1975), receive caretaking from a variety of mostly female kin members. In consequence, many Hawaiian children are raised partly and sometimes wholly in the company of cousins, and most have known cousins as intimates. Hawaiian children are expected not to fight cousins, but they tend to be left to their own devices in situations of conflict (D'Amato, 1986). Consequently, it is with cousins that Hawaiian children tend first to learn the dynamics of conflict, conflict resolution, and friendship in peer-managed processes of contention. Doubtless, it is these experiences that form the precedent for Hawaiian children's widespread use of "cousin" to mean "friend." "Gang," similarly, has a special meaning in Hawaiian kinship and friendship networks. It refers to those peers—kin or friends—who play active roles in the networks of Hawaiian households. To say "my gang," is to mean "my friends." With the terms, "cousin" and "gang," the boys of Cohort 7 were using the evocative language of their home lives to transform strangers into intimates and to place interaction with strangers within the frames of familiar processes and comfortable structures.

Relating schoolchildren's peer interactions to home life considerations, however, is only one method of approaching the issue. School itself provides another type of account of the dynamics of schoolchildren's peer relationships. Accepting the constraints of school and participating in its processes requires children to make a gift of power to teachers (D'Amato, in press). As suggested by the work of Ogbu (1982a) and demonstrated empirically by that of Lacey (1976) and Schoem (1982), the children of a class will not make this gift of power, regardless of the values practiced by them in their home lives, if they do not value the particular education being offered at their schools or do not believe in the likelihood of their group's succeeding in this education. Rather than building their peer relationships at least partly around teachers' concerns and teachers' evaluations of their relative standing, the children will organize their relationships in terms of peer standards and peer judgments. School itself, in other words, has the capacity to instruct children in the ways of rivalry. For Hawaiian children, school has few credible structural implications. They are therefore able to confront the politics of school directly. Reflexively, this intensifies the children's peer rivalry (D'Amato, in press).

In sum, there are at least three ways of accounting for the rivalry of the children of Cohort 7, and each provides a relevant perspective on the phenomenon. But however one accounts for the children's rivalry, the most important fact of that rivalry is that it was based upon values, ideals, and a coherent philosophy of relationships. The children did not contend for the sake of contending, but contended, and also controlled their contention, in the service of positive personal and social goals. It was this that made it possible for the staff of Ka Na'i Pono School to develop classroom processes that appealed to the children and were in fact accepted by them. As shown at Ka Na'i Pono School, it is possible for structures like gangs and ones like reading groups to coexist. In contrast to the cases reported by Labov (1982) and McDermott (1974), there was not an inverse relationship between peer status and academic status among the boys of Cohort 7. The leaders among the boys tended to be members of reading groups toward the top of the academic hierarchy. By the end of third grade, both Kaleo and Jake were members of the top group. The other boys were scattered throughout the five reading groups of the class, the tough and the not tough found equally in the lower, middle, and higher groups. Moreover, as a group, the children of this class met national norm levels on standardized tests of reading achievement (Klein, 1981). At least with these children, rivalry was not necessarily an impediment to academic success. It certainly was no impediment to play or to friendship.

REFERENCES

Abrahams, R.D. (1972). Joking: The training of the man of words in talking broad. In T. Kochman (Ed.), *Rappin' and stylin' out: Communication in urban black America*. Chicago: University of Illinois Press.

Au, K. (1981). Participation structures in a reading lesson with Hawaiian children: Analysis of a culturally appropriate instructional event. *Anthropology & Education Quarterly, 11*(2), 91–115.

Beynon, J., & Atkinson, P. (1984). Pupils as data gatherers: Mucking and sussing. In S. Delamont (Ed.), *Readings on interaction in the classroom*. London: Methuen.

Boggs, S. (1978). The development of verbal disputing in part-Hawaiian children. *Language in Society, 7*, 325–344.

Boggs, S. (1985). *Speaking, relating, and learning: A study of Hawaiian children at home and at school*. Norwood, NJ: Ablex.

Brown, H.R. (1972). Street talk. In T. Kochman (Ed.), *Rappin' and stylin' out:*

Communication in urban black America. Chicago: University of Illinois Press.

Colletta, N. (1980). *American schools for the natives of Ponape. A study of Education and culture change in Micronesia.* Honolulu: East–West Center.

D'Amato, J. (1986). *We cool, tha's why: A study of personhood and place in a class of Hawaiian second graders.* Doctoral dissertation, University of Hawaii.

D'Amato, J. (in press). A peer group theory concerning resistance and compliance in minority classrooms. *Elementary School Journal.*

Ellis, H.G., & Newman, S.M. (1972). The greaser is a "bad ass"; the gowster is a "muthah": An analysis of two urban youth roles. In T. Kochman (Ed.), *Rappin' and stylin' out: Communication in urban black America.* Chicago: University of Illinois Press.

Fox, R. (1967). *Kinship and marriage.* Harmondsworth, England: Penguin.

Gallimore, R., Boggs, J., & Jordan, C. (1974). *Culture, behavior, and education: A study of Hawaiian–Americans.* Beverly Hills, CA: Sage.

Goodwin, M.H. (1982). Processes of dispute management among urban black children. *American Ethnologist, 9*(1), 76–96.

Howard, A. (1974). *Ain't no big thing.* Honolulu: University of Hawaii Press.

Keiser, R.L. (1972). Roles and ideologies. In T. Kochman (Ed.), *Rappin' and stylin' out: Communication in urban black America.* Chicago: University of Illinois Press.

Klein, T. (1981). Results of the reading program. *Educational Perspectives, 20*(1), 8–10.

Labov, W. (1972). Rules for ritual insults. In T. Kochman (Ed.), *Rappin' and stylin' out: Communication in urban black America.* Chicago: University of Illinois Press.

Labov, W. (1982). Competing value systems in the inner-city schools. In P. Gilmore & A.A. Glatthorn (Eds.), *Children in and out of school: Ethnography and education.* Washington, DC: Center for Applied Linguistics.

Lacey, C. (1976). Intragroup competitive pressures and the selection of social strategies. In C.J. Calhoun & F.A. Ianni (Eds.), *The anthropological study of education.* Chicago: Aldine.

Marcus, G.E. (1978). Status rivalry in a Polynesian steady-state society. *Ethos, 6*(4), 242–269.

McDermott, R. (1974). Achieving school failure: An anthropological approach to illiteracy and social stratification. In G. Spindler (Ed.), *Education and cultural process.* New York: Holt, Rinehart, & Winston.

Mitchell–Kernan, C. (1972). Signifying, loud-talking and marking. In T. Kochman (Ed.), *Rappin' and stylin' out: Communication in urban black America.* Chicago: University of Illinois Press.

Ogbu, J. (1982a). Cultural discontinuities and schooling. *Anthropology & Education Quarterly, 13*(4), 290–307.

Ogbu, J. (1982b). Equalization of educational opportunity and racial/ethnic inequality. In P.G. Altbach, R.F. Arnove, & G.P. Kelly (Eds.), *Comparative education.* New York: Macmillan.

Ogbu, J. (1985, December). *Variability in minority school performance: A problem in search of an explanation.* Paper presented at the annual meeting of the American Anthropological Association, Washington, DC.

Roberts, J.I. (1970). *Scene of the battle: Group behavior in urban classrooms.* Garden City, NY: Doubleday.

Rohlen, T.P. (1983). *Japan's high schools.* Berkeley: University of California Press.

Rosenfeld, G. (1971). *"Shut those thick lips!" A study of slum school failure.* New York: Holt, Rinehart, & Winston.

Schoem, D. (1982). Explaining Jewish student failure. *Anthropology & Education Quarterly, 13*(4), 308–322.

Stack, C. (1975). Who raises Black children: Transactions of child givers and child receivers. In T.R. Williams (Ed.), *Socialization and communication in primary groups.* Chicago: Aldine.

Wax, R.H. (1976). Oglala Sioux dropouts and their problems with educators. In J.I. Roberts & S.K. Akinsanya (Eds.), *Schooling in the cultural context.* New York: McKay.

Wilcox, K. (1982). Ethnography as a methodology and its applications to the study of schooling: A review. In G. Spindler (Ed.), *Doing the ethnography of schooling.* New York: Holt, Rinehart, & Winston.

Wolcott, H.F. (1974). The teacher as enemy. In G. Spindler (Ed.), *Education and cultural process.* New York: Holt, Rinehart, & Winston.

13

Cultural Continuities and Discontinuities: Impact on Social and Pretend Play

DIANA T. SLAUGHTER
Northwestern University

JOSEPH DOMBROWSKI
Illinois State Psychiatric Institute

There have been many definitions of culture and many applied to understanding children's play. Since America is a pluralistic nation, professionals who study individual development have a special need to be aware of the role of culture in children's play. In a recently published volume entitled *Play and Culture,* Schwartzman (1980, p. 7) comments:

> Studies of play and studies of culture have evolved, for the most part, as separate fields of inquiry. Fortunately, this situation is changing as more and more researchers have come to realize that both subjects stand to gain from the pursuit of integrated investigations that assume play and culture mutually influence one another.

Suffice it to say that one implied goal in studying children's play can be the defining of culture, that is, the definition of the culture comes out of the study, as part of our understanding of the play itself.

Ethnographic researchers, according to Schwartzman (1976), have typically assumed at least one of four attitudes toward play. First, they frequently perceive play as anticipatory socialization behavior; second, play is viewed as a repertoire or collection of game activities; third, play is perceived as an externalization of conflicts engendered by child-rearing patterns in the culture; and fourth, play may be perceived as inconsequential to the main thrust of the ethnographic research report. Schwartzman (1976, p. 317) emphasizes that much ethnographic work on the "texts" of children's play is needed:

> Anthropologists should contribute to these studies by producing "ethnographies of children's play" which are both textual and contextual in orientation. Currently there are few . . . and because of this almost all theorizing about play has been done on the basis of studies of Western children. . . .

Schwartzman's point could easily be extended to include socially and ethnically different children within Western societies. Ethnographies of the texts of these children's play are also sparse. Among these children, unlike among non-Western children, there has been some attention to studies of the developmental processes involved in play. However, because much ethnographic and contextual information is unavailable to assist in interpreting and theorizing about obtained data, the play of these children, particularly if their families are of lower socioeconomic backgrounds, is often unfairly perceived to be deviant or deficient, in comparison with the play of mainstream Western children (McLoyd, 1982).

The primary purpose of this chapter is to analyze critically recently available culture and personality studies of children's play behavior which (a) focus on developmental processes, and (b) adopt a subcultural or cross-cultural paradigm. Particular attention is given to the role of culture in children's pretend play and social play. Psychological contents and processes involved in these forms of play help to regulate the self in social interaction. We will generally use the reviews published by Schwartzman (1976, 1978) as cutoff points for the studies reviewed.

THE CONCEPT OF CULTURE

Historically, the idea of culture as intimately a part of the play itself, as opposed to strictly external to play, has been proposed in several forms by several scholars over the past 50 or more years (Schwartzman, 1978). Freud (1961) suggested that the internal psychological environment projected itself out from the individual and so shaped culture. According to Schwartzman (1978), Margaret Mead (1928) was among the first scholars to argue that the motivation for a child's behavior extended beyond the influence of physiology and psychology, and that this behavior was very malleable and shaped greatly by the child's culture. The concept of cultural relativism emphasizes the effect of the environment on the person, a concept first extensively popularized in American scholarship by the research and writings of Mead.

Kardiner (1939) and Linton (1945) synthesized the psychological ideas of Freud and the anthropological ideas of Mead into a "psychocultural" theory. Kardiner saw the individual as being shaped from the outside by what he identified as the "primary institutions" of economy and of child-rearing practices; in turn the culture itself is shaped through projective systems expressed by individuals in response to the collectively experienced impact of the primary institutions. Thus, projective systems (e.g., rituals, taboos) are "secondary institutions" designed to relieve internal tensions created by the primary institutions acting on individuals. In this synthesis is the foundation for a continuing school of personality and cultural research termed the "configurationist school." The model may be described as primary institutions affecting individuals, who in turn form secondary institutions. With minor adumbrations the model serves as the original linkage between inside and outside forces working on the individual and culture.

In the 1950s, Whiting and Child (1953) identified two levels within the primary institutions described by Kardiner, the "maintenance systems" as distinct from the "child-rearing systems." These maintenance systems were essentially social structural and economic (Whiting, 1963, used this expanded schema in the ambitious *Six Cultures* project). In summary, they envisaged their scheme as follows: Child behaviors and cultural products are formed from individual personality processes, which are formed in large part by child-rearing practices, and in turn are influenced by overall societal maintenance structures (see B. Whiting, 1963, p. 5).

Perhaps the first to draw the causal relationships into a reciprocal series of feedback systems was Centner (1963), who made extensive descriptive reports on the play of African children in the Belgian Congo at the time of its independence in the late 1950s and the early 1960s. Her depiction, as illustrated by Schwartzman, is essentially like that of Whiting and Child, with the addition that all factors (i.e., culture, personality, and play) reciprocally feed back with each other. In addition, play behaviors and cultural products feed back onto the culture. This idea is significantly different from the configurationist idea in that it (a) introduces the feed back between each factor and (b) depicts the entire system as a closed loop, suggesting that there is a type of dynamic balance within the system. Centner also labeled "play" as a major category equivalent to Kardiner's secondary institutions, and Whiting and Child's child behaviors and cultural products.

Roberts and Sutton-Smith (1962) have elaborated the play portion in their "conflict-enculturation hypothesis" of play. They also emphasized the reciprocal nature among culture, play, and individual, and that play is both generative and expressive of the personality and the culture. They were able then to relate the types of play and games to the nature of the culture. For example, games of strategy, chance, and physical skill correspond, respectively, to cultural training for obedience, responsibility, and achievement.

In her review, Schwartzman (1978) emphasized the need to relate the play itself to its value and place in the culture in order to derive the *meaning* of the play, and warned about the short-sightedness of artifically separating either the "text" or the "context" of the play from each other.

Definitions of culture, as applied to the study of play, have typically either been historical-descriptive, or functional. The functional approach, which reaches its most idiographic form in the culture and personality studies, stresses cultural integration. The study of forces tending toward cultural integration partly includes research into how societies perpetuate themselves through child rearing and socialization of their young. Play as spontaneous, but also learned, behavior is thought to be critically important to the transmission of culture and to have an important role in the modification of culture (Sutton-Smith, 1974). However, the definition of culture should be expanded to include a focus on intergenerational transmission of behavior in both culturally continuous and discontinuous contexts. Children's play, as spontaneous, but learned, behavior should be studied in both types of contexts.

Recent studies include a focus on what we would characterize as either continuous or discontinuous cultural contexts. Studies which stress cultural continuity are of two types: (a) studies which stress links between the child's family and its current broad ecological context that span at least four decades (i.e., at least two generations), and in which considerable assimilation to an identified dominant, usually national, culture has occurred, and (b) studies which stress similar links or ties, but in which despite assimilation, an identifiable, distinct culture is maintained. Basically, only one type of study stresses cultural discontinuity. However, studies of this type fall into two subgroups: (c1) studies in which links or ties between the child's family and its current broad ecological context span no more than two decades (i.e., at most one generation), and in which assimilation is occurring; and (c2) studies in which links between the child's family and its context are similar to those in (c1), but in which diverse sociocultural groups are contrasted. In this chapter, each type of study will be analyzed and critiqued, following a preliminary discussion of the cultural role of social and pretend play in children's development.

THE CULTURAL ROLE OF CHILDREN'S SOCIAL AND PRETEND PLAY

There are many types of play, and almost as many taxonomies designed to classify the types of play. Generally, the taxonomies indicate that older children engage in more sociable forms of play, and that they seem to prefer social play activities over solitary ones. Parten (1933), for example, conducted an observational study of peer interaction in the preschool period with children ages 2 to 5. She observed older children during free play to engage in more cooperative play than younger children. While engaging in cooperative play, both sexes seem to prefer same-sex play groups. In contrast to the more sedate, orderly, female-dominated play groups, male-dominated play groups reveal more rough-and-tumble, assertive interactions. Cooperative play is characterized by two or more children sharing a common, if not identical, activity. They may discuss their activity, borrow or loan toys, and they have a commonly shared goal. Among participating children, there may be a division of roles. Usually, only 4- or 5-year-olds engage in truly cooperative play as, prior to these ages, children can typically play with only one playmate at a time.

Some of the identified play activities of children have an "as-if," fantasy, or make-believe quality. According to Fein (1981a), it is useful to distinguish between two types of pretend play: symbolic and sociodramatic. Both types of play refer to activities with an "as-if" quality, but they appear at different points in development. Fein (1981a, p. 308) states:

> Symbolic play (is) . . . solitary play in which the child represents one thing as if it were another with no attempt to develop or coordinate pretend activities with a partner, and sociodramatic play (is) . . . pretense that is shared or coordinated with a partner . . . there are empirical grounds for believing children shift from solitary to social pretense, and that this shift marks a developmental accomplishment of considerable importance.

Among Western children, symbolic play follows sensorimotor play and appears around 12 months. The capacity for collaborative play develops around 30 months; however, it is not until age 3 and above that sociodramatic forms of play are evident. As an important form of childhood expression, among contemporary Western children pretend play begins to wane around age 6, when they begin to focus more on games with rules (Fein, 1981b).

According to Fein (1981b), the long-term functions and consequences of pretend play have not been conclusively addressed. Some believe that pretense is the basis for all imaginative thought, while others (e.g., Sutton–Smith, 1979) stress its potential importance to collective symbolic activities. Short-term benefits have been easier to document empirically. There is evidence that the provision of opportunities for spontaneous object play as well as pretense training enhances both divergent and convergent thinking skills (Fein, 1981b, p. 1110). Play or story enactment, but not increased opportunities for sociodramatic play, appear to reduce children's egocentrism and enhance their person perspective-taking skills. Though results are equivocal, language skills, and other adaptive ego functions may be enhanced.

Fein (1981b, p. 1111) concludes:

Three observations seem warranted: (a) theoretical considerations are guiding research, but (b) these are taking the form of mini-theories addressed to particular aspects of pretense, rather than "grand" theories purporting to account for the entire phenomenon, and (c) these theories are drawing basic concepts from other areas (e.g., language, perspective taking, cognition, or personality). . . .

From our perspective, however, such trends are somewhat disappointing because sociocultural factors in social and pretend play are thereby neglected by psychologically oriented theorists and researchers. In our view, it is precisely the absence of consideration of such factors that contributes most to the absence of "grand theories" of pretense which would provide an integrative, coherent perspective on this apparently very important developmental phenomenon. Further, it is the absence of such theoretical formulations which contributes to bias in our observations of social and pretend play of non-Western children, and frequently, of children of socially and culturally nonnormative backgrounds within Western cultures. The recent debate between McLoyd (1982, 1983) and colleagues (Smith, 1983; Sutton–Smith, 1983) is an excellent case in point.

Essentially implying that the predisposition toward pretense may well be universal, McLoyd (1982) argued that a careful examination of the methods used in existing studies of socioeconomic influences on pretend play do not support a view of average social-class differences in individual capacities for pretense favoring middle-class populations. Like Fein (1981b), McLoyd concluded that situational factors contributing to actual assessment procedures may contribute most to obtained significant levels and trends toward SES differences in dramatic play. Critics (Smith, 1983; Sutton–Smith, 1983) of McLoyd's review argued that she had essentially trivialized the really important issues: Namely, that socioeconomic differences do exist in children's life-styles and circumstances within American and other Western cultures, and that these differences, whether they can be "empirically" proven or not, do have enormous consequences for children's psychological growth and development.

Two different perspectives on how social class impacts psychological development were offered by the critics. According to Sutton–Smith (1983, p. 3), persistent SES differences in play:

> are of a kind which parallels those that have appeared in the research . . . with the lower-class children, in general, being more physical (less symbolic) and more authoritarian (less egalitarian) in their play . . . these differences have arisen from the more hierarchical and manual character of lower class life. . . . Conversely, according to Smith [1983, p. 8]: . . . while levels of pretend and sociodramatic play have important correlates, their unique importance for any particular area of competence development remains questionable. In earlier phases of human evolution, I have argued that pretend and fantasy may have facilitated spontaneous play which was more complex in cognitive and social domains . . . however, contemporary education and training programs can provide adult-guided or structured activities which are equally useful . . . while pretend and sociodramatic play is clearly enjoyable, its developmental significance is that of providing one way in which certain experiences can be gained—an option rather than an imperative. Differences in such forms of play would then be just that—differences, but not necessarily deficits. . . .

In a reply which argued for more intraindividual, rather than group-oriented, comparative work, McLoyd (1983, pp. 15–16) responded to her critics:

> Understanding the internal logic of the social or cultural milieu within which pretend play functions is far more important theoretically, than knowing whether certain groups engage in more or less pretend play . . . the comparative framework too often forecloses and retards serious study of more complex issues such as the relationship between

certain social and cognitive behaviors and the larger cultural and social ecology. . . .

However, McLoyd stops short of providing her own theoretical perspective on this crucial issue.

We agree with Smith (1983) that the phenomenon of pretend play is somewhat analogous to the human appendix—at one time in human evolution pretend play may well have had a unique function in intra-organismic development, serving to promote cognitive and social complexity. We believe the impetus to pretense, like the impetus to engage in social play, is essentially biologically based, and, unless actively constrained by a culture, it will be expressed by individual members. Over time, pretense has served to perpetuate the human species and, as such, the predisposition to engage in such behavior is now genetically encoded. However, human cultures have also evolved over time, and many have generated options to support the basic biological impetus, as Smith suggests. Further, at this point in human history it should not be difficult to consider that people can imagine and enter into social relationships which are, from a strictly biological perspective, dysfunctional. That is, social groups do exist which do not actively support or encourage childhood pretense.

In addition, sometimes the content of the pretense is unlikely to lead to the kind of adult persons that humans would deem socially desirable. As one example of this latter point, we offer the following description of the pretend play of the two sons of Hoess, commandant of Auschwitz concentration camp during World War II (Friedrich, 1981, p. 45):

> Hoess's children, to whom the servile prisoners brought presents, understood their father and the world he ruled. A French prisoner named Charlotte Delbo caught a glimpse of that understanding. . . . She saw (the) two boys, aged about 11 and seven, both blond and blue-eyed. The older one had a sword in his belt and he screwed an imaginary monocle into his eye as he ordered the younger one, who represented all the prisoners in the camp, to march faster and faster.
>
> Soon the prisoners to whom these orders are addressed can no longer follow. They stumble on the ground, lose their footing. Their commandant is pale with rage. With his switch, he strikes, strikes, strikes. He screams. . . . The little boy staggers, spins around, and falls flat on the grass. The commandant looks at the prisoner whom he has knocked to the ground with contempt, saliva on his lips. And his fury subsides. He feels only disgust. He kicks him—a fake kick, he is barefoot and he's just playing. But the little boy knows the game. The kick turns him over like a limp bag. He lies there, mouth open, eyes glazed over.

Then the big boy, with a sign of the stick to the invisible prisoners that surround him, commands *Zum Krematorium,* and moves on. Stiff, satisfied, and disgusted. . . .

The preceding excerpt suggests that the relationship between culture and children's social and pretend play should never be unduly romanticized. It is possible that under certain conditions, particularly since there is little evidence that pretend play can serve cathartic functions relative to aggressive behavior (Fein, 1981b), no pretense would in fact be best. However, even severe societal constraints on pretense need not result in restrictions in individual, social, and cognitive complexity; individual outcomes depend upon what other options are provided or offered by the culture for personal growth and development, and the extent to which these other options are genuine opportunities to impact other psychological processes traditionally linked to social and pretend play.

In summary, children's social and pretend play appear to be biologically based, sustained as an evolutionary contribution to human psychological growth and development. Cultural factors regulate the amount and type of expression of these play forms.

SOCIAL AND PRETEND PLAY IN CULTURALLY CONTINUOUS CONTEXTS

All of the recent (i.e., published since 1978) cross-cultural studies reported here were done in the child's native land.[1] The children participate in continuous cultures in which their families have resided for at least two generations. On occasion, children in other cultures are contrasted to children in American culture. In both instances, the assumptions of the authors include an assumption of a continuous cultural context. In addition to a focus on social and/or pretend play, some studies also considered other types of play.[2]

---

[1] Schwartzman's (1980) edited volume includes several empirical studies of the play of American (White) children which also emphasize their cultural context (e.g., papers by Klonsky, Beran, and Mechling). As the papers are more readily available, they are generally not discussed in the present review.

[2] Udwin and Shmukler (1981) define *imaginary* (pretend) play as the introduction of time, space, or character not immediately in the perceptual environment into play. Other types of play include: *functional* (e.g., exploratory, gross motor, rough and tumble play); *constructive* (e.g., making use of objects to build something); and *artistic* (e.g., music, art).

Bloch (1984a) reported on the breadth of Senegalese children's play, the areas they use, the timing of play during the day, and the interactions of children with adults and each other. Her descriptive report emphasizes the children's ability and desire to prepare the toys that they needed from the simplest of scraps. Children find time in the day to play; to pursue play actively (i.e., fabricating the necessary play props); and to play in ways generally universal (i.e., relative to the psychological processes and behaviors evoked).

In another paper (Bloch, 1984b), and in her chapter in this volume, Bloch reported her records of the particulars of the amount and types of play throughout the day. She found that for infants through age 6, girls engaged in gross motor, rough-and-tumble, constructive, or music and arts play as much as boys. Boys were found to decrease their amount of imaginary/pretense play at ages 5 to 6. Overall, functional play was more common in younger children.

Bloch indirectly compared the Senegalese to American children by doing telephone "observations," controlling for age and time of year, but not SES. She found children in both cultures spent similar amounts of time in all activities, including pretense play. However, Americans engaged in all types of play more and Senegalese were in their (Moslem) school a bit more. The striking difference was in the preponderant amount of time that American children spent in gross motor play and watching television in comparison with the Senegalese.

Udwin and Shmukler (1981) observed free play during regular unstructured segments in nursery schools in Israel and South Africa, specifically examining the pretend play in lower and middle socio-economic status children in both nations. The Israelis were comprised of middle socioeconomic status children of West European origin and lower socioeconomic status children of immigrants of Middle Eastern and North African origin; the South Africans were Whites from homes with Western European values. No differences in amounts of pretend play were found between the cross-national groups within the lower social classes. The only difference in amount was within the middle socioeconomic classes: These South Africans spent less time in pretend play in comparison with Israelis. The authors argue that the lower amounts of pretend play are caused by less than adequate parenting, rather than general environmental deprivation, that is, by parents who are unable to provide their children with means of integration, with psychological space, and with instruction and adult models on which to fashion pretend play. In both nations, the amounts of pretend play of the middle-class children exceeded that of the lower-class children.

The free play of preschoolers in kindergarten settings was the subject of two studies. Al–Shatti and Johnson (1982) compared 4- to 5-year-old boys and girls in Kuwait and America. They found no statistically significant differences for gender or culture in the types of play, nor for the degree of sociability observed during play (Parten's categories). Generally, given the narrated descriptions of play, it seemed that the Kuwaiti children were actually more social in their play. Intracultural differences between boys and girls showed some familiar results: Kuwaiti girls showed more sociodramatic play than Kuwaiti boys. However, the American girls in the study showed less sociodramatic play than American boys. In addition, the American girls had more functional than sociodramatic play. Indeed, the American girls had more functional play than did the American boys! Kuwaiti girls again fit the more common picture of having less functional play than the Kuwaiti boys and, among themselves, displayed more sociodramatic than functional play.

Yawkey and Alverez–Dominques (1984) compared free play in 5-year-olds in American and Puerto Rican kindergartens. Their typology of play was somewhat different than usual, being either simple/functional, fantasy, or reality-oriented in a gradient suggesting a developmental play hierarchy. They found that Hispanic girls used more reality-oriented play than Anglo girls and Hispanic boys showed greater amounts of simple/functional play than Anglo boys. However, Anglo boys showed more fantasy play than Hispanic boys. Within the American culture the girls showed significantly more simple/functional play than the boys, and boys and girls both played more at functional and fantasy than reality-oriented levels. In contrast, within the Hispanic culture in Puerto Rico the girls played more at the reality level than the functional level, while the boys did the opposite.

Bower, Ilgaz–Carden, and Noori (1982) observed children in structured play areas in preschool settings in Turkey and in Iran, expecting to confirm a relationship between physical skills and previous opportunities to explore and experience the environment. They found no socioeconomic differences in the use of vertical and horizontal space among Turkish children. However, socioeconomic status differences, favoring middle status children, were obtained for the Iranian children. Among Iranian children a relationship existed between the number of toys in the home and the number of toys and the amount of space used in the trials. School differences were used to explain why they did not find a similar relationship among Turkish children. The Turkish preschool strongly emphasized free play. This emphasis may have accounted for the absence of SES differences as well as the overall greater use of space by the Turkish children.

The youngest age group studied was of infants, 12 and 18 months of age. Hrncir, Speller, and West (1983) studied the effect of motivation on intelligence testing from a cross-cultural perspective. The authors postulated that performance on the Bayley Mental Scales would correlate with the level of spontaneous play mastery rather than the level of mastery elicited through encouragement by verbal suggestion and modeling (termed the "executive" capacity). With a sample of American and Bermudan children the authors found spontaneous play mastery to be significantly positively related, and executive capacity to be negatively related, to Bayley MDI at 12 and 18 months. In short, their hypothesis was verified. More germane to this review, they also reported some relative means for undifferentiated, transitional, and pretend play at those ages in the two cultures. The Bermudan infants at 12 months are reported as tending toward "more sophisticated play," a status already achieved by American infants. However, measures across the two cultural groups were not always as comparable as they might have been. It could be, for example, that Bermudan infants, as compared with American infants, spent less time overall in the study actively playing.

Taken together, the findings of the studies, particularly the Al-Shatti and Johnson (1984) and the Yawkey and Alverez–Dominques (1984) studies, illustrate the considerable importance attached to careful sampling techniques and descriptions in this type of research. However, few of the more recent papers offered enough narrative description. For example, an earlier study by Roy (1973) covers aspects of play not covered in many of these more contemporary studies. In describing the play of children in urban as well as rural settings in India, where she lived for a long time, Roy focused not only on the types of play, but how the children play (i.e., their mood), the breadth of play, its content, and cultural meaning. Her account presented a surprisingly rich and vivid picture of the childhood world that is frequently missing in the more parsimonious reports of empirical studies. Perspectives like that of Roy would be, in our view, very valuable to giving contextual meaning to the play of children.

SOCIAL AND PRETEND PLAY IN CULTURALLY DISCONTINUOUS CONTEXTS

Few studies of the play of immigrant, refugee, or migrant children have been conducted. These children develop in what we would describe as culturally discontinuous contexts. In particular, they are likely to be living with parents who have resided in their current cultural-ecological setting for less than one generation.[3] Discussion follows of recent studies conducted from such a perspective.

Christman (1979) looked at the levels of sociodramatic play in 3- and 4-year-old Mexican–American migrant children. The amount of sociodramatic play was found to be "very low," with boys scoring less than girls at age 3, but not age 4. Overall, a higher level of sociodramatic play was found with 4-year-olds compared with 3-year-olds. The significance of the level of play is not specified, either in relation to Mexican culture and development, or in relation to American culture and development. There was no discussion of the children themselves, either as to any adjustment conflicts, or special strengths and resiliencies. Further, the setting of the study may be an important factor in the findings with these 3- and 4-year-olds. It was vaguely described as a "structured play setting" within a "center" that was "outside the regular classroom" (Christman, 1979, p. 107).

In another paper, Robinson (1978) describes the play of Vietnamese refugee children. She observed 9- to 12-year-old children in four San Francisco schools. Robinson found differences between the play of Vietnamese boys and girls similar to those found in other cultures: Namely, that boys' play is more "aggressive and competitive" and girls' play is more "passive and accommodating." Though good examples of the children's play are given in this narrative report, there is no reference to the play of Vietnamese children in Vietnam. Differences described between the Vietnamese girls and boys and their American peers were simply attributed to the former group's limited familiarity with American culture, the resultant individual trepidations and avoidant coping patterns. For example, Robinson (1978, p. 14) found that the Vietnamese children ". . . engaged in play forms that strengthen social relations and clarify social rules, rather than participating in play that breaks down the social structure they are trying to build . . ." She immediately attributed the results to "a lack of understanding of the rules well enough to break them," on the children's part, thus neglecting to consider that the style could be culturally characteristic of the Vietnamese.

Both the Christman (1979) and Robinson (1978) studies focus on the play of children whose families are currently living and working

---

[3] Internationally adopted children are not considered in this chapter. Many such children know no cultural-ecological context other than that provided by adoptee families. For such children, genuine dual cultural consciousness is typically an adolescent phenomenon.

apart from the cultural-ecological setting in which the parents were reared. The play of such children could be expected to mirror aspects of the "old culture," aspects of the "new culture," currently being accommodated, as well as the children's personal adaptive responses to their family's transitional status. However, because the authors do not discuss any earlier ethnographic descriptions of either Mexican or Vietnamese children at play, it is impossible to distinguish those play behaviors which are likely to have been enduring and inter-generationally transmitted, from those more immediately personally and/or situationally determined. Repeated, more systematic obser-vations of the play of the same children in the same ecological setting (e.g., an urban ethnic neighborhood) but different contexts (e.g., at home versus at school) could have addressed this problem. Further, because the focus of these studies was descriptive, rather than hy-pothesis testing and comparative, few conclusions could be drawn as to the *cultural meaning* of the social and pretend play of the children in these studies.

Two studies, one by Young (1985) and the other by Child (1983), compare and contrast the play of children from several cultures. In each instance, the families of many of the children have shared a common culture for no more than one generation. Therefore, the children are being reared in different, discontinuous cultural contexts, though they currently share a common cultural-ecological setting.

In the Young study, Canadian culture provides the common cul-tural-ecological setting. In addition, all children attend the same public elementary school, and therefore, one immediate, important aspect of their overall social ecology is shared. However, children in the study had parents of dissimilar and varied cultural-familial back-grounds: South Asian, West Indian, Southeast Asian, Portuguese/ Italian, and Anglo–Canadian. Young contends that the differential cultural capital or value placed upon skills and personal attributes associated with the cultural-familial backgrounds of the children de-termined the level of skill children were permitted to demonstrate in games associated with competitive sports and athletic programs in the upper school grades. As soccer was an activity highly valued by school physical education faculty, during recess and free play children would voluntarily initiate the game. The soccer game sym-bolized an important activity in the school's social ecology from whose participation members derived social status.

In this instance, the non-Anglo–Canadian children, coming from cultures in which soccer play is more of a long-standing tradition, were considerably more skilled. These children would form exclusive teams that were highly structured, solely with members who were clearly skilled at the game. Spontaneous play and joking occurred among teammates, but rarely between this group and other teams. In contrast, the teams of less skillful players tended to be composed of Anglo–Canadians. Their games were far less likely to be highly structured or focused solely at all times by all members on soccer per se. Regulations about team membership, as well as the rules of participation in the game, were highly variable and fluid.

Young (1985, p. 136) concludes:

> Regardless of the extent to which competition was played down by the staff . . . successful involvement in most playground activities called for not simply participating but rather some public display of skill. Participation without the appropriate level of skill was likely to lead to peer criticism, informal exclusion, and negative status allocation . . . [the] dilemma . . . that all children should share equally in the resources allocated to play—is confronted with the requirements of ability that have a culturally specific dimension . . . the staff risks promoting, in the name of fairness and equality, a system that is culturally discriminatory and which forces students [from those cultural backgrounds, in this instance, Canadian backgrounds] into activities in which they have only limited opportunities for success. . . .

Young did not consider how status was allocated within the school as a whole, such that the intense soccer participation could be an adaptive strategy used by the non-Anglo–Canadians, nor did he consider the contribution of innate physical attributes toward team clustering. The study does demonstrate that, given the presupposition that social status is a scarce commodity, there will be winners and losers in school-related games conferring status as a prize. Further, even the informal texts of children's play in the school playground will be partly structured around the requirements for being skillful in the more formal games. Finally, and most important, the study points to the importance of parental (and teacher) culture to peer social play as a potential determinant of individual mastery or success within subsequently encountered social systems.

Child (1983) studied the play of preschoolers from an East Asian cultural-ecological region whose families were currently living in England. Her study was deliberately designed to include a sociocultural perspective. In addition to English children of middle- and working-class backgrounds, the study included children of the resident, largely lower-income Asian minority groups: Sikh, Muslim, and Hindu. The three identified subcultural (ethnic) groups, all from the Indian subcontinent, are distinctly different religious and linguistic communities. Child also regarded the English middle and lower classes (home ownership distinguished the two groups in this study) as having distinct, identifiable cultures. The researcher conducted repeated, focused observations of children's play behaviors in three different "play buses," which traveled to no fewer than five "inner city" sites each week. Observations were made of the types (e.g., tactile; artistic; imaginative (pretend); physical; constructive), as well as of the modes (e.g., scope or attention span of child; passivity/activity; playfulness; sociability) of play.

Child found that Asian children engaged in less pretend play, whether with persons or objects, in comparison with English children (SES and ethnic group comparisons are not reported); Asian children, especially Muslims and Sikhs, were also significantly less likely to be engaged in play (passivity), to be less often actively engaged, and to be less playful in comparison with English children. No characteristic type of play varied directly with the age (children ranged from ages 2 to 5 in the study) or sex of the Asian children. As their ages increased, English children were more likely to engage in pretend play than other forms of play. Finally, English children, particularly middle-class English children, most often initiated talk, whether to play supervisors, other children, or to themselves. Only lower-class English children received more talk from play supervisors than middle-class English children. With the exception of Muslim children, who were second only to the middle-class English children in having conversations among themselves, Asian children were more likely to play alone, and did little talking.

Much of the interpretive framework used in this study focuses upon cultural-ecological differences between English and Asian families and communities. Asian children are described as being reared in cultures in which respect and deference for adults is strongly emphasized; the important contribution of religious beliefs and values to the way children from Asian cultures approach the world is also stressed. However, the author assumes that the "play bus" is an equivalent stimulus for all the children, and that all groups of children have equivalent access to the play supervisors. There is no discussion of how the behavior of the Asian children could, in fact, be an adaptive response to the differential behaviors of the play supervisors toward Asian, as contrasted to English, children. Because each type of play is indexed by only one "indicator," there is the added problem of confounding preferred activity with the presumed underlying psychological process. Before concluding that *Asian* children do not engage as often in pretend play, as do English children, for example, it would be important to study the children in their culturally indigenous environments, using a broader array of possible indicators of pretense that are also clearly culturally relevant.

Ariel and Sever (1980) report a study in which the pretend play of rural (indigenous) and urban Arabic children was compared and contrasted to that of Israeli Kibbutzim children. Narrated observation protocols of the 5- to 6-year-old children in each group were scored for (a) contents of make-believe play, (b) color, and (c) dynamity. *Both* groups of Arabic children differed markedly from the Israeli children in regard to the incidence, contents, color, and dynamity associated with pretend play. Arabic children in this sample, particularly the rural group, hardly "play" (low "color" relative to both social interaction and make-believe play) and formulate few metarules about the mode of play (low "dynamity").

Ariel and Sever (1980) argued that, if compared with urban children, rural children would be most disadvantaged with respect to peer group contacts, as well as ties between families of children found to play together. Noting that cooperative pretend play requires that children have prior working relationships, the authors predicted, and were not surprised to find, that rural Arabic children engaged in the least amount of cooperative pretend play. In addition, commenting on the similarities between the rural and urban Arabic groups, the authors (Ariel & Sever, 1980, p. 173) note:

> What is crucial is not the physical aspects of the environment, but the culturally prescribed patterns of verbal and non-verbal interaction among the child's "significant others". . . . Both [Arabic groups] are characterized by the relative absence of verbal interchange between adults and children. Verbal exchange is unidirectional and authoritative: from the adult to the child. The culture does not allow the child to argue with an adult, express views or relate things. The verbal feedback the child receives is narrow and limited . . . adults and children in the kibbutz engage in many lively two-sided conversations throughout the day, centering around a great variety of topics. . . .

The authors conclude by emphasizing that:

> the content, structure, and development of individual and social play are not universal, but culture-bound . . . the expressive language of make-believe play is closely culture-bound in both structure and contents . . . an enriched environment and formal education alone do not seem to make the play of children of a "traditional" society significantly more dynamic and colorful and richer in themes. . . . (Ariel & Sever, 1980, pp. 174–175)

In short, whether children use pretend play as a vehicle for personal and cultural expression is itself culturally determined, as are the resultant opportunities for the commingling and integration of selected psychological processes.

SOCIAL AND PRETEND PLAY IN CONTINUOUS CULTURAL CONTEXTS: SOME SUBCULTURAL ISSUES

In every society, there are cultural groups who have shared interdependent relations with the dominant culture since its existence. In comparison with the dominant cultural group(s), such groups have less power and influence, but they share many values and beliefs. However, they also maintain, for many and varied reasons, a somewhat independent existence. Because of this quasi-independent status, such groups frequently confront psychological issues in relation to the dominant culture similar to those faced by resident members of two autonomous cultures.

In the United States, many Asian–Americans (e.g., Chinese and Japanese–Americans as well as Pacific Islanders), American Indians, as well as selected Hispanic–American groups (e.g., Mexican–Americans, Puerto Rican–Americans, Cuban–Americans), and African–Americans (e.g., historically Black Americans, West Indians, descendants of former African nationals) constitute relatively unassimilated members of continuous cultures. Substantial numbers of entire families of these groups have resided in America for two or more generations.

The specific reasons for the more limited assimilation of these groups are as diverse as the groups. Although many members of each group would resist our designation as a "subculture," we believe they would agree that each of these groups collectively commands fewer economic and social resources within the American cultural-ecological context, in comparison with those groups more actively perceived to be identified with the White American majority population. They would also agree that, given historically distinctive language patterns, geographical locations, cultural-familial traditions, and cultural products, these groups have a measure of cultural autonomy. Designation as a "subculture" implies additionally that the groups share many values, beliefs, rituals, and normative behaviors in common with the dominant majority culture, and that families socialize their children accordingly. As Boykin and Toms (1985) have stated in discussion of Black culture and Black children, it seems most parsimonious to argue that the children of such cultures are socialized in at least three contexts which are often commingled and overlapping: (a) in the context of the dominant American culture; (b) in the context of the ethnic culture; and (c) in the context of minority status within a majority culture.

When considering American cultural minorities, research literature has focused almost exclusively on Black and Hispanic–Americans. Since 1978, several empirical studies have been published which specifically address the cultural patterns of these groups in discussions of the children's play behaviors (e.g., Lefever, 1981; McLoyd, 1980; Montare & Boone, 1980; Nevius, 1982; and Nevius, Filgo, Soldier, & Simmons–Rains, 1983).

Nevius (1982) investigated the hypothesis that the age, SES, sex, and ethnicity (Black, Mexican–American, Anglo) of 5- and 6-year-old children would impact their social participation (Parten's [1933] categories) during free play. Ethnicity contributed most to social participation but, due to the small sample sizes ($N = 58$), its effects were not examined independent of the other variables. In subsequent analyses of the same data, Nevius et al. (1983) found that a stronger relationship existed between free-choice activities (e.g., gross motor activity, fine motor activity, dramatic play, sand and water play), and Parten's social participation categories, than any of the earlier sociocultural or demographic variables. The authors argue that type of play, rather than sociocultural factors per se, determines social relations in the multicultural preschool.

Unfortunately, however, in this study only 7.5% of the play activity was categorized as dramatic play, 50% of which was classified as Associative. This suggests that, relative to the other types of play, the overall incidences of both social and pretend play were too low in this sample of observed behavior to assess the effects of specific ethnic cultures on these types of child play.

McLoyd (1980) studied pretend play within dyadic social interactions of 36 Black, low-income preschool children, ages 3.5 and 5 years. The purposes of the study were to determine (a) whether these Black, lower-income children engaged in significant amounts of pretend play under appropriate situational contexts, and (b) the types of reality transformations made during the play by the children. Same-age and mixed-age dyads were observed and videotaped during a 20-minute free-play session. All dyads were same-sex dyads. Only verbalized utterances were scored for transformations, so as to be as parsimonious as possible in designating evidence of pretense.

About two-fifths of the children's utterances represented transformations, data roughly paralleled in studies of White, middle-class children. Two basic transformations, objects modes and ideational, were identified during the children's pretend play. There were four types of object mode transformations and four types of ideational transformations, for a total of eight observed transformations. There were no significant effects on the types of transformations by dyadic age, but there were effects by dyadic sex. Girls made significantly more transformations than boys, and the transformations, when related to personal events and characters, were less "fantastic," and more consistent with anticipatory socialization roles.

Two published studies (Lefever, 1981; Montare & Boone, 1980) with different aims, and very different methods, focus on aspects of social play and aggression in Black children. Lefever argues that playing the "dozens," a form of ritualized language play dependent upon cooperative peer behaviors, is an important anticipatory training ground for learning individual self-protection within Black, especially lower-income, communities. The author states that: "The usual participants in the game are adolescent Black males, but . . . Black females also play, and at least one study has shown that the game is played by White high school boys" (Lefever, 1981, p. 73). According to Lefever (1981, p. 76):

> By playing the game, young Black men learn how to face up to an antagonistic society and to deal with conflicts both with the larger White society and within their own family and peer groups . . . the dozens evolved as a way to develop self-control and to handle one's temper. . . .

Lefever does not consider, however, placing this type of play within the context of the extensively rich oral cultural traditions (McLoyd, 1983; Sutton–Smith, 1983) so generally characteristic of African cultural-ecologies.

Montare and Boone (1980) report a study of three different cultural groups of lower income early adolescent males: Black, Puerto Rican, and White American, ages 9 to 13. The purpose of the study was to examine the effects of family structure (paternal presence or absence) on aggressive behavior emitted during constructive play in a 15-minute videotaped session by the boys. Participants were observed in a room consisting only of members of their respective cultural group; each group was divided into two equal teams and instructed that the two groups had 15 minutes to build a cube with pieces of a puzzle. The team completing the task in the shortest amount of time would receive a reward. Measures of both physical and verbal aggression were obtained during the experimental portion of the taping.

The authors found that Puerto Ricans had significantly more aggressive responses than either whites or Blacks. In addition, the effects of the presence or absence of the father on the incidence of aggressive responses were greatest for Whites, considerably less for Blacks, and almost negligible for Puerto Ricans. Assuming that the task had equivalent cultural meaning to all groups, the authors argue that the results reflect differential combinations of majority-minority status within the broader ecological communities in which these youth's families function. Puerto Ricans, as national and local minorities, overcompensate relative to "macho" behavior, for such status. Low-income Whites, as local minorities only, are pressed into action only if fathers are not present in the home. Finally, Blacks were national, but not local, minorities in the communities from which these samples were drawn. This factor, in addition to maternal identification, would account for lower aggression scores, particularly among Black, father-absent boys.

Montare and Boone do not consider an equally viable, but less deficit-oriented, more culturally consonant hypothesis: that the degree to which one's paternal deprivation is atypical relative to one's peer group is the degree to which family structure will be predictive of peer interaction. This is a tenable, *post hoc* alternative hypothesis. During the study, national estimates of the percentages of father absence in Puerto Rican, Black, and White families were, respectively, 48, 40, and 31. In short, average rates of aggression differ according to the percentages of father absence in the total communities involved; differences in the behaviors of boys from father-present and -absent homes are accentuated as the relative uniqueness of the "father-absent" status increases.

In conclusion, our literature search revealed only one study of the social and pretend play of some of the newer emergent cultural minorities (e.g., Vietnamese, Laotian, Cambodian). The paucity of studies in this area suggests that much research is needed into the play behaviors of American minority (and majority) children from the perspective of their cultural identities.

In the case of Black and Hispanic–American children, studies of their social and pretend play behaviors do exist, but most do not emphasize cultural context and, as a result, biased interpretations of the behaviors of these culturally different children are generated because the children's behaviors are routinely compared with those of majority culture children. Since the latter group is perceived to be normative, culturally different children are inappropriately considered to be deficient. In this review, we included the most culturally sensitive of such studies but, as noted, even these studies were problematical.

Generally, the play of American cultural minority children tends to be studied only from the perspective of the interests of researchers identified solely with the American majority culture. There are few studies of the type indicated by Boykin and Toms (1985) in which the focus would be upon the minority child's adaptation to one or more "cultures" within the same ecological setting. As another example of research which is decidedly not present in contemporary literature, Wilkerson's (1974) review of literature indicating the value of toys to stereotypical racial socialization of all children in American culture has apparently generated no follow-up studies, even if only to refute her assertions as to the role of social and pretend play in perpetuating American racism.

SUMMARY AND CONCLUSION

The purpose of this chapter has been to review critically culture and personality studies published since 1978 on children's social and pretend play behavior. The selected empirical studies had to focus on developmental processes and adopt a research paradigm which emphasized cultural, whether cross-cultural, cross-national, or subcultural, contexts.

In our literature searches, we found many cross-cultural studies, and many psychologically oriented studies of children's play, but when we required an overlap between the two areas, remarkably few empirical researches emerged. Aside from 15 to 20 such studies published in an edited volume by Schwartzman (1980) on *Play and Culture,* about 18 other studies were in the available research literature, 16 of which are reviewed in this chapter. We found all but 2 of the 18 made explicit reference to social and/or pretend play among children. These 2, a study of adult attitudes toward children's play in Thailand by Bloch and Wichaidit (1986), and a study of humor in Black, Mexican- and Anglo-American preschool children by McGhee and Kach (1981), were not reviewed.

Because two comprehensive literature reviews (Schwartzman, 1976, 1978) stressing the relationship between play and culture had been produced, we limited our search to the time period following the second of these reviews. However, with few exceptions, these studies did not seem to have been conducted in the tradition of inquiry suggested by Schwartzman. Instead, the research literature appears to have an almost shotgun approach to scientific investigation in the area of studies of cultural influences on children's play behavior. To impose some conceptual order, we decided to (a) focus on a type of play behavior for which there has been the most theoretical discussion relative to cultural influences, namely pretend play, and (b) discuss the existing researches from the perspective of the assumed models of culture and personality revealed by the choice of sample populations, research problems, and research designs in the investigations.

Understanding Context: The Concept of Cultural Ecology

In this chapter we offer a perspective on culture which emphasizes both cultural integration (continuity) and change (discontinuity). Building upon the psychocultural perspective on culture and personality, we have additionally argued that studies of play and culture should focus not simply on the integration of personality and culture, but also upon how change in one parameter impacts change in the other. The developing child's impetus for social and pretend play is, we believe, biologically based and evolutionarily adaptive, but cultural transmission regulates the expression (i.e., the amount, content, breadth or range, mood, meaning) of this play. Further, over time it is probable that the play itself reciprocally impacts culture.

We have contended that the child's family is the essential mediating link between the transmission of culture and emergent patterns of play. We believe it is empirically possible to identify the number of generations in which a child's family has essentially lived in a similar cultural-ecological context. Some families have lived for two or more generations (i.e., through the grandparent generation), while others have so lived for one or fewer. We have designated the former as *culturally continuous contexts* for participating children in these families, and designated the latter *culturally discontinuous contexts* for the children.

Children and families in discontinuous cultural contexts are not yet enmeshed or embedded in the values, beliefs, sanctions, normative behaviors, and so forth, of their newly adoptive cultures, either structurally (institutionally) or personally. In these cultural contexts, children learn their culture as traditionally transmitted by their family, but (a) they also learn of alternative forms of conduct and expression, reflective of the immediate cultural ecology, and (b) there are values, basic mores and norms that the children must learn that adults personally significant to them cannot teach.

Discontinuous cultural contexts provide a different set of choices from those available to children embedded in what we have chosen to designate as continuous cultures. In the latter situations, the family has resided for two or more generations in a highly similar cultural-ecological context. Though these cultures will undoubtedly have changed, the children are tutored, supervised, and regularly exposed to personally significant adults who are also highly familiar with all the essential values, basic mores and norms of the culture.

Many families experience continuous cultures whose family members, collectively, for whatever reasons, have not been fully embedded or enmeshed in, either institutionally or personally. The developing children experience aspects of the family's traditional culture, but must also depend upon extrafamilial persons to acquaint them with many significant aspects of the dominant culture within which they and their families reside. Further, members of both the child's traditional, but minority, culture and the dominant culture teach the child about the cultural meaning of its minority status.

Our review included studies whose primary sample populations could be categorized into one of the above three types of cultural-ecological contexts: (a) continuous, assimilated; (b) discontinuous, unassimilated; or (c) continuous, unassimilated.

Critical Issues in Studies of Culture and Pretend Play

The studies reviewed have been discussed by the cultural model used in the research. In conclusion, general issues facing researchers in this area will be addressed.

Generally, most reports do not go into enough depth about cultural context. There is little focus on how children learn to play from adults and peers, their modes of play, or the role of culturally prescribed options in their play behaviors. Frequently gender differences are found, but given the absence of adequate contextual information, they are not explained well. Importantly, SES and race can be included in studies, not reviewed here, that do not necessarily treat either of these variables as cultural dimensions (see, e.g., McLoyd, 1982, for a review of the impact of SES on children's pretend play). Conversely, for example, Child (1983) informs the reader that the intent is to treat SES as a "cultural" variable, and Lefever (1981) has an obvious interest in establishing links between the Black experience of racial stratification in America, and the primary function of "playing the dozens" in Black adolescent communities.

Recent studies often attempt to control for SES within cultural-ecological context. Studies also consider immediate situational effects (e.g., school values or activities supported by classroom type) before moving to interpretive analyses based upon the cultural-familial characteristics of the populations addressed. This seems to be a good interpretive strategy, particularly since few studies directly report data on interactions between children and family members.

Comparative studies always exacerbate the problem of equivalence of stimuli, in this instance, the equivalence of cultural meaning. Most studies made little or no effort to determine either participants' or other community persons' perspectives on respondents' play behaviors. Studies such as those conducted by Bloch and Wichaidit (1986) on adult attitudes toward children's play, as well as of children's attitudes toward play such as those of Beran (1980) were rare. Several studies, for example, report that children in traditional cultures or in lower socioeconomic groups within more modern cultures, engage in less social and pretend play, in comparison with other children. However, by rearranging the situational context in which Black, lower-income children were studied, McLoyd (1980) found she was able to generate substantial amounts of pretense in these 3.5- and 5-year-olds, amounts equivalent to what had been obtained with middle-income populations. Her study demonstrates the necessity of obtaining respondent perceptions even from culturally diverse populations within one culture, such as American culture. It also demonstrates the necessity for repeated, systematic observations of children in different settings within the same cultural-ecological context.

In addition to the problem of equivalence of cultural meaning, there are educational and ethical issues which frequently arise in these researches that investigators do not adequately address. For example, how little pretense is "too" little? There is a tendency in the literature to attribute only positive benefits to pretense (see, e.g., Fein, 1981a, 1981b) forgetting, or at least setting aside for the moment, its biologically based roots in human evolution. Children can and have pretended about characters and events, thus reinforcing their understanding and mastery of the cultural and personal issues involved, that from a worldwide perspective are not socially desirable. We hope the review contributes to dispelling some of the "romanticism" currently associated with valuation of pretense in Western-dominated cultures.

Despite the many changes in cultures and families today, most studies stress play in continuous cultural contexts. We definitely need to understand more about the play of children from the perspective of changing cultures and families. How much of children's play reflects traditional cultural inputs, how much newer inputs, how much an effort at adaptive mastery of both? One barrier to pursuit of such studies has been the problem of how to conceptualize cultural context in such situations. We hope this review has helped to attenuate that problem. Given the increasing cultural diversity in preschool- and school-age populations, it is especially important that scientific information on these populations, now extremely sparse, become available.

By way of standard setting, we can envision the *ideal* study integrating cultural considerations into studies of social and pretend play behavior. Such a study would assume that the internalized culture may itself sanction certain individual expressions. Therefore, because culture may impact behavioral competence *and* performance differently, the research must necessarily consider the perspectives of study participants. Further, individuals may deliberately use aspects of their cultures adaptively, as coping mechanisms, in interpersonal transactions. Therefore, rich, descriptive narrations would accompany careful sampling of the types, range, and content of the play engaged in by similar-aged children representative of all subcultures, and both sexes, in the culture. The study design would include repeated observations of individual play behaviors in diverse settings within the culture. Interpretation of obtained data would minimally consider: (a) the relevant adaptive behavioral traits from the respondents' culture(s) as mediated by family relations; (b) the potential use of such traits in immediate, compensatory behavioral styles in extrafamilial settings; and (c) the *interaction* between cultural and situational contexts such that: (1) sanctioned individual behaviors may actually be identifiable cultural attributes; and (2) stereotyping of a given culture may occasion diverse, sometimes unwanted, interpersonal interactions.

Finally, much of what is studied in the area of culture and play, as well as how it is studied, appears dictated primarily by researchers with the power and authority to define a viable cultural ecological context. In addition to ignoring the impact of culture change, the researchers have chosen not to address two culturally related issues of intense concern to ethnic minority communities worldwide: (a) the simultaneous accommodation and adaptation of children to multiple cultural referential sources, and (b) the early socialization of children of dominant majority cultures into attitudes of superior privilege. Play, as a universal phenomenon, is obviously implicated in both.

REFERENCES

Al-Shatti, A., & Johnson, J. (1984). *Free play behaviors of middle class Kuwaitis and American children.* Paper presented at the annual meeting of the American Educational Research Association, New Orleans.

Ariel, S., & Sever, I. (1980). Play in the desert and play in the town: On play activities of Bedouin Arab children. In H. Schwartzman (Ed.), *Play and culture.* (pp. 164–174). West Point, NY: Leisure Press.

Beran, J. (1980). Attitudes of Iowa children toward their play. In H. Schwartzman (Ed.), *Play and culture* (pp. 187–197). West Point, NY: Leisure Press.

Bloch, M. (1984a, May/June). Play materials. *Childhood Education, 345–348.*

Bloch, M. (1984b). *A study of young Senegalese children's social play with adults and children.* Paper presented at the annual meeting of the American Education Research Association, New Orleans.

Bloch, M., & Wichaidit, W. (1986). Play and school work in the kindergarten curriculum: Attitudes of parents and teachers in Thailand. *Early Child Development & Care, 24,* 197–218.

Bower, E., Ilgaz–Carden, A., & Noori, K. (1982). Measurement of play structures: Cross-cultural considerations. *Journal of Cross-Cultural Psychology, 13*(3), 315–329.

Boykin, A., & Toms, F. (1985). Black child socialization: A conceptual framework. In H. McAdoo & J. McAdoo (Eds.), *Black children: Social, educational, and parental environments* (pp. 33–54). Beverly Hills, CA: Sage.

Centner, T. (1963). *L'enfant africain et ses jeux dans le cadre de la vie traditionnelle au katanga.* Elisabethville, Belgium: CEPSI.

Child, E. (1983). Play and culture: A study of English and Asian children. *Leisure Studies, 2,* 169–186.

Christman, M. (1979). A look at sociodramatic play among Mexican–American children. *Childhood Education,* 106–110.

Fein, G. (1981a). Pretend play: New perspectives. In E. Mavis Hetherington & R. Parke (Eds.), *Contemporary readings in child psychology* (2nd ed., pp. 308–312). New York: McGraw-Hill.

Fein, G. (1981b). Pretend play in childhood: An integrative review. *Child Development, 52,* 1095–1118.

Freud, S. (1961). *The future of an illusion.* (J. Strachey, Trans.). New York: Norton. (Original work published 1927).

Friedrich, O. (1981, September). The Kingdom of Auschwitz. *Atlantic Monthly,* pp. 30–60.

Hrncir, E., Speller, G., & West, M. (1983). *What are we testing? A cross-cultural comparison of infant competence.* (ERIC Document, Reproduction Service No. Ed. 230 309)

Kardiner, A. (1939). *The individual and his society.* New York: Columbia University Press.

Lefever, H. (1981). "Playing the dozens": A mechanism for social control. *Phylon, 42*(1), 73–85.

Linton, R. (1945). *The cultural background of personality.* New York: Appleton–Century–Crofts.

McGhee, P., & Kach, J. (1981). The development of humor in Black, Mexican–American and White preschool children. *Journal of Research & Development in Education, 14*(3).

McLoyd, V. (1980). Verbally expressed modes of transformation in the fantasy play of Black preschool children. *Child Development, 51,* 1133–1139.

McLoyd, V. (1982). Social class differences in sociodramatic play: A critical review. *Developmental Review, 2,* 1–30.

McLoyd, V. (1983). Class, culture, and pretend play: A reply to Sutton–Smith and Smith. *Developmental Review, 3,* 11–17.

Mead, M. (1928). *Coming of age in Samoa.* New York: Morrow.

Mechling, J. (1980). Sacred and profane in the Boy Scouts of America. In H. Schwartzman (Ed.). *Play and culture,* (pp. 206–212). West Point, NY: Leisure Press.

Montare, A., & Boone, S. (1980). Aggression and paternal absence: Racial-ethnic differences among inner-city boys. *Journal of Genetic Psychology, 137,* 223–232.

Nevius, J. (1982). Social participation and culture in play groups of young children. *Journal of Social Psychology, 116,* 291–292.

Nevius, J., Filgo, D., Soldier, L., & Simmons–Rains, B. (1983). Relation of social participation to activity in young children's free choice play. *Educational & Psychological Research, 3*(2), 95–102.

Parten, M. (1933). Social play among preschool children. *Journal of Abnormal & Social Psychology, 28,* 136–147.

Roberts, J., & Sutton–Smith, B. (1962). Child training and game involvement. *Ethnology, 2,* 166–185.

Robinson, C. (1978). *The uses of order and disorder in play: An analysis of Vietnamese refugee children's play.* (ERIC Document Reproduction Service No. ED 153 944)

Roy, B. (1973, November). Play spans the ages, *Childhood Education,* 83–89.

Schwartzman, H. (1976). The anthropological study of children's play. *Annual Review Anthropology, 5,* 289–328.

Schwartzman, H. (1978). *Transformations: The anthropology of children's play.* New York: Plenum.

Schwartzman, H. (Ed.). (1980). *Play and culture.* West Point, NY: Leisure Press.

Smith, P. (1983). Differences or deficits? The significance of pretend and sociodramatic play. *Developmental Review, 3,* 6–10.

Sutton–Smith, B. (1974). Toward an anthropology of play. *Association of Anthropology Study of Play Newsletter, 1,* 8–15.

Sutton–Smith, B. (Ed.). (1979). *Play and learning.* New York: Gardner.

Sutton–Smith, B. (1983). Commentary on social class differences in sociodramatic play in historical context: A reply to McLoyd. *Developmental Review, 3,* 1–5.

Udwim, O., & Shmukler, D. (1981). The influence of sociocultural, economic and home background factors on children's ability to engage in imaginative play, *Developmental Psychology, 17*(1), 66–72.

Whiting, B. (Ed.). (1963). *Six cultures: Studies of child rearing.* New York: Wiley.

Whiting, J., & Child, I. (1953). *Child training and personality: A cross-cultural study.* New Haven, CT: Yale University Press.

Wilkerson, D. (1974). Radical socialization through children's toys: a socio-historical examination. *Journal of Black Studies, 5*(1), 96–109.

Yawkey, T., & Alverez-Dominques, J. (1984). *Comparisons of free play behaviors of Hispanic and Anglo middle-class SES five-year olds.* Paper presented at the annual meeting of the American Educational Research Association, New Orleans.

Young, J. (1985). The cultural significance of (male) children's playground activities. *Alberta Journal of Educational Research, 31*(2), 125–138.

Author Index

Subject Index